West's Law School
Advisory Board

AN INTRODUCTION TO THE

ANGLO–AMERICAN LEGAL SYSTEM

READINGS AND CASES

Fourth Edition

By

Edgar Bodenheimer
1908-1991
Late Professor of Law Emeritus
University of California, Davis

John B. Oakley
Professor of Law
University of California, Davis

Jean C. Love
Martha-Ellen Tye Distinguished Professor of Law
University of Iowa

AMERICAN CASEBOOK SERIES®

THOMSON
WEST

Mat #40196144

American Casebook Series and West Group are trademarks registered in the U.S. Patent and Trademark Office.

COPYRIGHT © 1980, 1988 WEST PUBLISHING CO.
COPYRIGHT © 2001 WEST GROUP
© 2004 West, a Thomson business
      610 Opperman Drive
      P.O. Box 64526
      St. Paul, MN 55164–0526
      1–800–328–9352

Printed in the United States of America

ISBN 0–314–15087–0

 TEXT IS PRINTED ON 10% POST CONSUMER RECYCLED PAPER

Preface to the First Edition

This volume has grown out of earlier unpublished materials which the senior author has tested in the classroom with several variations. The work originated with materials assembled by Professor Bodenheimer in 1967 for a year-long course in the legal process and its historical foundations. In 1976 and 1977, Professors Bodenheimer and Love edited and substantially revised these materials to fit the needs of the intensive, 15-hour course called Introduction to the Anglo-American Legal System that is offered to beginning students at the University of California at Davis. In 1979 and 1980, Professors Bodenheimer and Oakley made further extensive revisions, casting the materials into the form in which they are now published. While our intent has been primarily to provide teaching materials for Introduction to Law courses such as that at Davis, we have also attempted to put these materials into a form that will be useful as a reference work for potential and beginning law students, as well as a primer for educated lay persons who seek to increase their understanding of the role and structure of law in modern Anglo-American society.

The preparation of the materials was guided by the conviction that students entering law school need to become acquainted with some basic distinctions and classifications which form part of the conceptual apparatus of the law. Furthermore, a legal system like Anglo-American law, which has historical roots in many important areas, cannot be understood without some knowledge of English legal history, including the rudiments of the forms of action at common law and the reasons for the rise of the rival system of equity. Of equal significance is the need to expose the beginning student to the methodological tools used by American courts in dealing with judicial precedents and statutory enactments. This work follows the customary method of using illustrative cases as well as theoretical discussions in describing the operation of *stare decisis*, the difficult art of determining the *ratio decidendi* of a case, the relative roles of logic and policy in the legal process, and the intricacies of statutory interpretation.

We wish to thank the authors and publishers who have graciously consented to our use of their copyrighted works. We are deeply indebted to Chancellor James Meyer, Vice-Chancellor Leon Mayhew, and Dean of Law Richard C. Wydick of the University of California at Davis for the financial support which made the production of the manuscript possible. We also wish to express our gratitude to Carole

Hinkle for the painstaking manner in which she prepared the final copy of the manuscript.

EDGAR BODENHEIMER
JOHN B. OAKLEY
JEAN C. LOVE

Davis, California
July, 1980

Preface to the Fourth Edition

A comment on the first edition of this book contained the observation that students, although receiving a great deal of information, were asked to do little in the way of active problem-solving.[1] The authors took up that challenge in the second and third editions, published in 1988 and 2001, in which we substantially increased the number of principal cases and associated questions and comments. This edition continues that trend.

We are delighted to carry forward the most distinctive feature of the third edition: reprinting as an appendix the full text of "The Case of the Speluncean Explorers." This famous article by the late Professor Lon L. Fuller, written in the style of a fictional case and first published in 1949 in the Harvard Law Review, is ideally suited to engage students in a problem-oriented approach to learning about law and the legal system. We are grateful to the Harvard Law Review Association and the estate of Professor Fuller for their permission to reprint "The Case of the Speluncean Explorers."

The sequence and basic scope of the six chapters remain unchanged. The citations to additional reading at the conclusion of each chapter have been revised, expanded, and brought up to date. We have retained most of the original text, with appropriate revision to reflect new developments, while adding edited reports of many new cases. Among the areas receiving expanded coverage through illustrative cases are the separation of powers, the right to jury trial, the expanding scope of liability for loss of consortium, and statutory construction. The new cases emphasize recent decisions of the United States Supreme Court, but also include an eclectic group of decisions by state appellate courts. Instructors who wish to introduce students to the case method of legal analysis will find they have ample resources to do so; instructors who wish to emphasize textual description of the key features of the Anglo-American legal system will find all the necessary materials still at hand, and may pretermit the illustrative cases as they see fit.

We have numbered all footnotes consecutively within each chapter. The footnotes are our editorial statements except as otherwise indicated. We have added an attribution in brackets to all footnotes that have been carried over from material quoted or reprinted in the main text. A new format for citations is designed to make sources easily accessible to readers of all backgrounds. We have added the initials of all authors. Titles of books are italicized. Titles of articles appear within quotation marks. The full names of periodicals are printed without abbreviation. We acknowledge with thanks the excellent research and editorial assistance provided to us by Bill Fritz, who was our primary research assistant; by Melanie

---

1. L.E. Gerwin and P.M. Shupack, "Karl Llewellyn's Legal Method Course: Elements of Law and Its Teaching Materials," 33 Journal of Legal Education 64, 77–78 (1983).

Stutzman, who prepared the final draft of the manuscript; and by Robin Drey, Ann Peper, Michelle Roddy, and Josh Weidemann, the research assistants who helped us to proof the manuscript.

The present authors remain much impoverished by the death in 1991 of our senior colleague and mentor, Edgar Bodenheimer.[2] Edgar continues to exert an enduring influence over the text of this book, and over the thinking of its present authors. We have also been influenced by two current colleagues and dear friends, Patrick Bauer and Patricia Cain, whose contributions to this work are invaluable, and greatly appreciated.

JOHN B. OAKLEY
JEAN C. LOVE

Davis, California
Iowa City, Iowa
September 2003

---

2. For a sense of our shared loss, see J.B. Oakley, "Remarks in Honor of Edgar Bodenheimer," 26 U.C. Davis Law Review 503 (1993).

Summary of Contents

Page

PREFACE TO THE FIRST EDITION --- iii
PREFACE TO THE FOURTH EDITION --- v
TABLE OF CASES -- xiii

INTRODUCTION: The Nature and Functions of Law -------------- 1
A. Prefatory Comments--- 1
B. Definitions of Law --- 1

CHAPTER I. Law and the Process of Classification ------------------- 5
A. The Meaning and Importance of Classification ------------------ 5
B. Some Basic Distinctions and Classifications of the Law ------------ 8

CHAPTER II. Common Law, Equity, and the Development of the
Anglo–American Court System ------------------------------- 26
A. The Common Law Courts and the Writ System --------------------- 26
B. The Forms of Action at Common Law ------------------------------- 35
C. Equitable Jurisdiction and the Court of Chancery ------------------ 46
D. Establishment of the Common Law in the United States --------- 51
E. The Merger of Law and Equity------------------------------------- 56
F. Modern English and American Courts------------------------------- 58

CHAPTER III. Statutes, Case Law, and Judicial Precedent --------- 79
A. Overview--- 79
B. The Doctrine of *Stare Decisis* ------------------------------------- 81
C. Statutory Law and Case Law ------------------------------------- 86
D. The Problem of Retroactivity --- 105

CHAPTER IV. The *Ratio Decidendi* of a Case------------------------ 119
A. Overview--- 119
B. The Evolution of Products Liability at Common Law in New
York--- 124

CHAPTER V. Logic and Policy in Legal Reasoning-------------------- 141
A. Theoretical Perspectives-- 141
B. Logic and Policy in Judicial Opinions ----------------------------- 150

CHAPTER VI. Fundamentals of Statutory Interpretation ----------- 166
A. Overview--- 166

Page

B. Basic Approaches to Statutory Interpretation ------------------------- 169
C. Intrinsic Aids: Linguistic Canons of Statutory Construction ------ 179
D. Legislative History and Other Extrinsic Aids------------------------ 184
E. Contemporary Approaches to Statutory Interpretation in the
    United States--- 189
F. Substantive Canons of Statutory Construction: Criminal Law --- 204
G. Substantive Canons of Statutory Construction: Civil Law -------- 213
H. Reasoning From Statutes by Analogy ----------------------------------- 226

APPENDIX --- 230
INDEX --- 253

Table of Contents

Page

PREFACE TO THE FIRST EDITION _____ iii
PREFACE TO THE FOURTH EDITION _____ v
TABLE OF CASES _____ xiii

INTRODUCTION: The Nature and Functions of Law _____ 1
A. Prefatory Comments _____ 1
B. Definitions of Law _____ 1

CHAPTER I. Law and the Process of Classification _____ 5
A. The Meaning and Importance of Classification _____ 5
B. Some Basic Distinctions and Classifications of the Law _____ 8
   1. International Law and Municipal Law _____ 8
   2. Civil Law and Common Law _____ 9
   3. Public Law and Private Law _____ 11
   4. Substantive Law and Adjective Law _____ 12
   5. Legislation, Case Law, and Customary Law _____ 12
   6. Separation of the Legislative, Executive, and Judicial Powers _____ 14
     Notes and Questions _____ 17
     Note by the Editors: Background to the Constitutional Controversy Over the Period of Limitation Applicable to Private Civil Suits Under § 10 of the Securities Exchange Act of 1934 _____ 17
     Plaut v. Spendthrift Farm, Inc. _____ 19
     Notes and Questions _____ 24
Further References _____ 24

CHAPTER II. Common Law, Equity, and the Development of the Anglo–American Court System _____ 26
A. The Common Law Courts and the Writ System _____ 26
   1. Common Law Courts _____ 26
     A.W. Scott & R.B. Kent, Cases and Other Materials on Civil Procedure _____ 26
   2. Modes of Trial _____ 30
   3. The Writ System _____ 31
     W.P. Blackstone, Commentaries on the Laws of England ___ 31
     Examples of Early Writs _____ 32
     R. Pound & T. Plucknett, Readings on the History and System of the Common Law _____ 32
     Statute Westminster II _____ 34

Page

A. The Common Law Courts and the Writ System—Continued
   Notes and Questions--- 35
B. The Forms of Action at Common Law ------------------------------- 35
   1. Introduction-- 35
   2. A Summary of the Chief Forms of Action at Common Law --- 37
      (a) Replevin --- 37
      (b) Detinue -- 37
      (c) Debt --- 38
      (d) Covenant --- 38
      (e) Trespass --- 38
      (f) Trespass on the Case----------------------------------- 39
      (g) Trover-- 40
      (h) Special Assumpsit-------------------------------------- 40
      (i) General Assumpsit-------------------------------------- 41
      (j) Real Actions and Ejectment --------------------------- 42
          Problems--- 43
   3. Illustrative Cases -- 44
      Guy v. Livesey--- 44
      Notes and Questions--- 44
      Higgins v. Butcher --- 45
      Notes and Questions--- 45
C. Equitable Jurisdiction and the Court of Chancery----------------- 46
   1. Equity and Justice -- 46
      Aristotle, The Nicomachean Ethics--------------------------- 46
      St. Germain, The Doctor and the Student-------------------- 47
   2. The Court of Chancery and the Development of Equity-------- 48
D. Establishment of the Common Law in the United States ---------- 51
   W.F. Walsh, A History of Anglo–American Law ------------------- 51
E. The Merger of Law and Equity----------------------------------- 56
F. Modern English and American Courts----------------------------- 58
   1. Modern English Courts--- 58
      (a) Jurisdiction -- 58
          A.W. Scott & R.B. Kent, Cases and Other Materials on Civil
          Procedure-- 58
      (b) Diagrams of Court Structure --------------------------- 59
          W. Fryer & H. Orentlicher, Cases and Materials on Legal
          Method and Legal System------------------------------- 59
   2. Modern American Courts-- 60
      (a) Note on the Dual System of State and Federal Courts---- 60
      (b) State Court Systems----------------------------------- 62
      (c) The Federal Court System ----------------------------- 65
          i. Basic Structure ------------------------------------ 65
          ii. Basic Jurisdiction-------------------------------- 67
          iii. Jurisdictional Diagrams ------------------------- 69
      (d) The Constitutional Right to Jury Trial of Civil Actions
          in Federal Courts------------------------------------- 71
          An Introduction to the Case Method of Legal Instruction -------- 71
          Rogers v. Loether------------------------------------- 71
          Curtis v. Loether------------------------------------- 74
Further References-- 78

Page

CHAPTER III. Statutes, Case Law, and Judicial Precedent 79
A. Overview... 79
B. The Doctrine of *Stare Decisis* 81
   E. Bodenheimer, *Jurisprudence: The Philosophy and Method of the Law* 82
C. Statutory Law and Case Law.. 86
   Baldwin v. State.. 86
   Whitney v. Fisher 89
   Notes and Questions.. 92
   Nicholson v. Hugh Chatham Memorial Hospital, Inc. 92
   Notes and Questions.. 98
   Cox v. Haworth 99
   Harris v. Sherman 102
   Notes and Questions.. 105
D. The Problem of Retroactivity.. 105
   The *Graves* Case 106
   The *Sunburst* Case 108
   The *Linkletter* Case 110
   Developments Since *Linkletter* 114
   Notes and Questions.. 116
Further References... 117

CHAPTER IV. *The Ratio Decidendi* of a Case..................... 119
A. Overview... 119
   E. Bodenheimer, *Jurisprudence: The Philosophy and Method of the Law* 119
   Note by the Editors: Reasonable Application of the *Ratio Decidendi* 122
   Problems 123
B. The Evolution of Products Liability at Common Law in New York.. 124
   Winterbottom v. Wright 124
   Thomas and Wife v. Winchester.. 126
   Loop v. Litchfield 129
   Devlin v. Smith.. 130
   Statler v. George A. Ray Mfg. Co..................................... 132
   MacPherson v. Buick Motor Co... 134
Further References... 139

CHAPTER V. Logic and Policy in Legal Reasoning............. 141
A. Theoretical Perspectives.. 141
   P.E. Treusch, "The Syllogism," in J. Hall, *Readings in Jurisprudence* 141
   O.W. Holmes, *The Common Law* 143
   L.G. Boonin, "Concerning the Relation of Logic to Law"..... 144
   Note by the Editors: Types of Legal Reasoning.................. 148
   Problems 149
B. Logic and Policy in Judicial Opinions 150
   Borer v. American Airlines, Inc....................................... 150
   Hay v. Medical Center Hospital of Vermont 153
   Questions.. 159
   Note by the Editors: Duty of Care Owed by Landowners...... 159
   Hynes v. New York Central R.R. Co................................. 159
   Hynes v. New York Central R.R. Co................................. 162
Further References... 165

CHAPTER VI. Fundamentals of Statutory Interpretation 166
A. Overview... 166
   H.L.A. Hart, *The Concept of Law* 166
   Note by the Editors: The Hart/Dworkin Debate.................. 168
   Problems 168

		Page
B.	Basic Approaches to Statutory Interpretation	169
	1. Historical Introduction	169
	2. Description of Three Basic Approaches	170
	(a) The Literal Rule	170
	(b) The Golden Rule	170
	(c) The Purposive Approach	170
	Note by the Editors: The Case of the Speluncean Explorers	171
	United States v. Kirby	171
	Holy Trinity Church v. United States	171
	Caminetti v. United States	173
	United States v. American Trucking Ass'ns	175
C.	Intrinsic Aids: Linguistic Canons of Statutory Construction	179
	1. Expressio Unius Est Exclusio Alterius	179
	2. Noscitur a Sociis	181
	3. Ejusdem Generis	182
	Note by the Editors: Thrust and Parry	183
	Note by the Editors: The Survival of the Canons	183
D.	Legislative History and Other Extrinsic Aids	184
	M. Radin, "Statutory Interpretation"	184
	J.M. Landis, "A Note on Statutory Interpretation"	185
	Schwegmann Bros. v. Calvert Distillers Corp.	186
	R. Posner, "Economics, Politics, and the Reading of Statutes and the Constitution"	187
	Pepper v. Hart	188
E.	Contemporary Approaches to Statutory Interpretation in the United States	189
	West Virginia University Hospitals, Inc. v. Casey	189
	Note by the Editors: The United States Supreme Court's Use of Legislative History	201
	Note by the Editors: The Role of Justice Breyer on the United States Supreme Court	202
	Note by the Editors: The State Courts' Use of Legislative History	202
F.	Substantive Canons of Statutory Construction: Criminal Law	204
	McBoyle v. United States	204
	Moskal v. United States	206
G.	Substantive Canons of Statutory Construction: Civil Law	213
	Van Beeck v. Sabine Towing Co.	214
	Mobil Oil Corp. v. Higginbotham	216
	Clymer v. Webster	219
	Hill v. City of Germantown	224
H.	Reasoning From Statutes by Analogy	226
	R. Pound, "Common Law and Legislation"	226
	Note by the Editors: Analogical Use of Statutes	227
Further References		227
APPENDIX		230
	The Case of the Speluncean Explorers	230
INDEX		253

Table of Cases

The principal cases are in bold type. Cases cited or discussed in the text are roman type. References are to pages. Cases cited in principal cases and within other quoted materials are not included.

Abner A. Wolf, Inc. v. Walch, 385 Mich. 253, 188 N.W.2d 544 (Mich.1971), 58

Admiralty Commissioners v. S.S. Amerika, [1917] A.C. 38, p. 215

Alden v. Maine, 527 U.S. 706, 119 S.Ct. 2240, 144 L.Ed.2d 636 (1999), 61

Alpers, United States v., 338 U.S. 680, 70 S.Ct. 352, 94 L.Ed. 457 (1950), 182

American Trucking Ass'ns, United States v., 310 U.S. 534, 60 S.Ct. 1059, 84 L.Ed. 1345 (1940), **175**

Arizonans for Official English v. Arizona, 520 U.S. 43, 117 S.Ct. 1055, 137 L.Ed.2d 170 (1997), 62

Atlas Roofing Co., Inc. v. Occupational Safety and Health Review Com'n, 430 U.S. 442, 97 S.Ct. 1261, 51 L.Ed.2d 464 (1977), 58

Babbitt v. Sweet Home Chapter of Communities for a Great Oregon, 515 U.S. 687, 115 S.Ct. 2407, 132 L.Ed.2d 597 (1995), 182

Baker v. State, 170 Vt. 194, 744 A.2d 864 (Vt.1999), 105

Baldwin v. State, 125 Vt. 317, 215 A.2d 492 (Vt.1965), **86,** 90, 92

Board of Trustees of University of Alabama v. Garrett, 531 U.S. 356, 121 S.Ct. 955, 148 L.Ed.2d 866 (2001), 61

Boerne, City of v. Flores, 521 U.S. 507, 117 S.Ct. 2157, 138 L.Ed.2d 624 (1997), 24

Borer v. American Airlines, Inc., 138 Cal.Rptr. 302, 563 P.2d 858 (Cal.1977), **150**

Bowers v. Hardwick, 478 U.S. 186, 106 S.Ct. 2841, 92 L.Ed.2d 140 (1986), 117

Caminetti v. United States, 242 U.S. 470, 37 S.Ct. 192, 61 L.Ed. 442 (1917), **173**

Carolene Products Co., United States v., 304 U.S. 144, 58 S.Ct. 778, 82 L.Ed. 1234 (1938), 7

Church of the Holy Trinity, United States v., 36 F. 303 (C.C.S.D.N.Y.1888), 172

City of (see name of city)

C & K Engineering Contractors v. Amber Steel Co., 151 Cal.Rptr. 323, 587 P.2d 1136 (Cal.1978), 58

Clymer v. Webster, 156 Vt. 614, 596 A.2d 905 (Vt.1991), **219**

Cox v. Haworth, 304 N.C. 571, 284 S.E.2d 322 (N.C.1981), **99,** 105

Curtis v. Loether, 415 U.S. 189, 94 S.Ct. 1005, 39 L.Ed.2d 260 (1974), 57, **74**

Devlin v. Smith, 89 N.Y. 470, 11 Abb. N. Cas. 322 (N.Y.1882), **130,** 135, 137

Doney v. Northern Pac. Ry. Co., 60 Mont. 209, 199 P. 432 (Mont.1921), 108, 109, 110

Fox Film Corp. v. Doyal, 286 U.S. 123, 52 S.Ct. 546, 76 L.Ed. 1010 (1932), 107

Gideon v. Wainwright, 372 U.S. 335, 83 S.Ct. 792, 9 L.Ed.2d 799 (1963), 116

Goulet v. Asseler, 22 N.Y. 225 (N.Y.1860), 36

Graves, People ex rel. Rice v., 242 A.D. 128, 273 N.Y.S. 582 (N.Y.A.D. 3 Dept.1934), 106, 107, 108, 109, 110

Great Northern Ry. Co. v. Sunburst Oil & Refining Co., 287 U.S. 358, 53 S.Ct. 145, 77 L.Ed. 360 (1932), 109

Gutierrez v. Ada, 528 U.S. 250, 120 S.Ct. 740, 145 L.Ed.2d 747 (2000), 181

Guy v. Livesey, 79 Eng.Rep. 428 (Court of King's Bench, 1619), **44,** 45, 149

Harper v. Virginia Dept. of Taxation, 509 U.S. 86, 113 S.Ct. 2510, 125 L.Ed.2d 74 (1993), 115

Harris v. Sherman, 167 Vt. 613, 708 A.2d 1348 (Vt.1998), **102,** 105, 148

Harter, State ex rel. School Dist. of Sedalia v., 188 Mo. 516, 87 S.W. 941 (Mo.1905), 182

Hay v. Medical Center Hosp. of Vermont, 145 Vt. 533, 496 A.2d 939 (Vt. 1985), **153**

Hiatt v. Yergin, 152 Ind.App. 497, 284 N.E.2d 834 (Ind.App. 2 Dist.1972), 58

Higgins v. Butcher, 80 Eng.Rep. 61 (Court of King's Bench, 1606), **45,** 215

Hill v. City of Germantown, 31 S.W.3d 234 (Tenn.2000), **224**

Holy Trinity Church v. United States, 143 U.S. 457, 12 S.Ct. 511, 36 L.Ed. 226 (1892), **171,** 173, 174, 181

Hynes v. New York Cent. R. Co., 231 N.Y. 229, 131 N.E. 898 (N.Y.1921), 149, **162**

Hynes v. New York Cent. R. Co., 188 A.D. 178, 176 N.Y.S. 795 (N.Y.A.D. 2 Dept.1919), 149, **159**

Jarecki v. G. D. Searle & Co., 367 U.S. 303, 81 S.Ct. 1579, 6 L.Ed.2d 859 (1961), 181

J. I. Case Co. v. Borak, 377 U.S. 426, 84 S.Ct. 1555, 12 L.Ed.2d 423 (1964), 18

Kimel v. Florida Bd. of Regents, 528 U.S. 62, 120 S.Ct. 631, 145 L.Ed.2d 522 (2000), 61

Kirby, United States v., 74 U.S. 482, 19 L.Ed. 278 (1868), **171**

Knapp v. Wing, 72 Vt. 334, 47 A. 1075 (Vt.1900), 87

Lampf, Pleva, Lipkind, Prupis & Petigrow v. Gilbertson, 501 U.S. 350, 111 S.Ct. 2773, 115 L.Ed.2d 321 (1991), 18, 19

Lawrence v. Texas, ___ U.S. ___, 123 S.Ct. 2472, 156 L.Ed.2d 508 (2003), 117

Linkletter v. Walker, 381 U.S. 618, 85 S.Ct. 1731, 14 L.Ed.2d 601 (1965), 111, 114

Long v. Rockwood, 277 U.S. 142, 48 S.Ct. 463, 72 L.Ed. 824 (1928), 107

Loop v. Litchfield, 42 N.Y. 351 (N.Y. 1870), **129,** 132, 135

MacPherson v. Buick Motor Co., 217 N.Y. 382, 111 N.E. 1050 (N.Y.1916), **134**

Mapp v. Ohio, 367 U.S. 643, 81 S.Ct. 1684, 6 L.Ed.2d 1081 (1961), 111

McBoyle v. United States, 283 U.S. 25, 51 S.Ct. 340, 75 L.Ed. 816 (1931), **204**

Mobil Oil Corp. v. Higginbotham, 436 U.S. 618, 98 S.Ct. 2010, 56 L.Ed.2d 581 (1978), **216**

Montana Horse Products Co. v. Great Northern Ry. Co., 91 Mont. 194, 7 P.2d 919 (Mont.1932), 108

Montgomery v. Stephan, 359 Mich. 33, 101 N.W.2d 227 (Mich.1960), 98

Morrison, United States v., 529 U.S. 598, 120 S.Ct. 1740, 146 L.Ed.2d 658 (2000), 61

Moskal v. United States, 498 U.S. 103, 111 S.Ct. 461, 112 L.Ed.2d 449 (1990), **206**

Muskopf v. Corning Hospital Dist., 55 Cal.2d 211, 11 Cal.Rptr. 89, 359 P.2d 457 (Cal.1961), 150

Nevada Dept. of Human Resources v. Hibbs, 538 U.S. 721, 123 S.Ct. 1972, 155 L.Ed.2d 953 (2003), 61

New England Sav. Bank v. Lopez, 227 Conn. 270, 630 A.2d 1010 (Conn.1993), 227

Nicholson v. Hugh Chatham Memorial Hospital, Inc., 300 N.C. 295, 266 S.E.2d 818 (N.C.1980), **92**

Nieberg v. Cohen, 88 Vt. 281, 92 A. 214 (Vt.1914), 88

Peak v. United States, 353 U.S. 43, 77 S.Ct. 613, 1 L.Ed.2d 631 (1957), 3

People v. _____ (see opposing party)

People ex rel. v. _____ (see opposing party and relator)

Pepper v. Hart, [1993] 1 All E.R. 42 (House of Lords, 1992), 171, **188**

Philpott v. Superior Court in and for Los Angeles County, 1 Cal.2d 512, 36 P.2d 635 (Cal.1934), 36

Plaut v. Spendthrift Farm, Inc., 514 U.S. 211, 115 S.Ct. 1447, 131 L.Ed.2d 328 (1995), 17, **19**

Prentis v. Atlantic Coast Line Co., 211 U.S. 210, 29 S.Ct. 67, 53 L.Ed. 150 (1908), 15

Rice, People ex rel. v. Graves, 242 A.D. 128, 273 N.Y.S. 582 (N.Y.A.D. 3 Dept.1934), 106, 107, 108, 109, 110

River Wear Commissioners v. Adamson, [1876–77] 2 App.Cas. 742 (HL 1877), 170

Rogers v. Loether, 312 F.Supp. 1008 (E.D.Wis.1970), **71**

Ross v. Bernhard, 396 U.S. 531, 90 S.Ct. 733, 24 L.Ed.2d 729 (1970), 58

School Dist. of Sedalia, State ex rel. v. Harter, 188 Mo. 516, 87 S.W. 941 (Mo.1905), 182

Schooner Peggy, United States v., 5 U.S. 103, 2 L.Ed. 49 (1801), 21, 22, 106, 113, 114

Schwegmann Bros. v. Calvert Distillers Corp., 341 U.S. 384, 71 S.Ct. 745, 95 L.Ed. 1035 (1951), **186**

Southern Pac. Transportation Co. v. Superior Court, 58 Cal.App.3d 433, 129 Cal. Rptr. 912 (Cal.App. 1 Dist.1976), 57

State ex rel. v. _____ (see opposing party and relator)

Statler v. George A. Ray Mfg. Co., 195 N.Y. 478, 88 N.E. 1063 (N.Y.1909), **132,** 135, 139

Sunburst Oil & Refining Co. v. Great Northern Ry. Co., 91 Mont. 216, 7 P.2d 927 (Mont.1932), 108, 109, 110, 112

Teague v. Lane, 489 U.S. 288, 109 S.Ct. 1060, 103 L.Ed.2d 334 (1989), 115, 116, 117

Tennessee Valley Authority v. Hill, 437 U.S. 153, 98 S.Ct. 2279, 57 L.Ed.2d 117 (1978), 180

Thomas v. Washington Gas Light Co., 448 U.S. 261, 100 S.Ct. 2647, 65 L.Ed.2d 757 (1980), 82

Thomas v. Winchester, 6 N.Y. 397 (N.Y. 1852), **126,** 129, 130, 131, 132, 133, 134, 135, 136, 139

Tilley v. Hudson River R. Co., 24 N.Y. 471, 23 How. Pr. 363 (N.Y.1862), 222

Torgesen v. Schultz, 192 N.Y. 156, 84 N.E. 956 (N.Y.1908), 133

Townsley v. Ozaukee County, 60 Wis. 251, 18 N.W. 840 (Wis.1884), 180

Triggs, People v., 106 Cal.Rptr. 408, 506 P.2d 232 (Cal.1973), 122

United States v. _____ (see opposing party)

Vacher & Sons, Ltd. v. London Society of Compositors, [1913] A.C. 107 (H.L. 1913), 170

Van Beeck v. Sabine Towing Co., 300 U.S. 342, 57 S.Ct. 452, 81 L.Ed. 685 (1937), **214**

West Virginia University Hospitals, Inc. v. Casey, 499 U.S. 83, 111 S.Ct. 1138, 113 L.Ed.2d 68 (1991), **189**

Whitney v. Fisher, 138 Vt. 468, 417 A.2d 934 (Vt.1980), **89,** 92, 105, 149

Williams v. Taylor, 529 U.S. 362, 120 S.Ct. 1495, 146 L.Ed.2d 389 (2000), 115

Williams v. Taylor, 529 U.S. 420, 120 S.Ct. 1479, 146 L.Ed.2d 435 (2000), 116

Wiltberger, United States v., 18 U.S. 76, 5 L.Ed. 37 (1820), 204

Winterbottom v. Wright, 1842 WL 5519 (Unknown Court 1842), **124,** 137, 139

Woodhouse v. Woodhouse, 99 Vt. 91, 130 A. 758 (Vt.1925), 87, 90

*

AN INTRODUCTION TO THE

ANGLO–AMERICAN LEGAL SYSTEM

READINGS AND CASES

Fourth Edition

*

Introduction

THE NATURE AND FUNCTIONS OF LAW

A. PREFATORY COMMENTS

It is not possible to gain an insight into the nature of any institution of human life without an inquiry into the purposes or functions which the particular institution is designed to accomplish. Nobody can intelligently discuss problems of government and arrive at a considered judgment with respect to the policies which should be promoted by public officials or agencies without first forming an opinion as to the general aims and ends for which governments are established. This is equally true for the institution of law, at least in the secular, political sense with which we are concerned. We treat law as a particular kind of governmental institution. From this perspective, we assert that no official within the institution of law—no judge, attorney or other person with official duties in the administration of law—can adequately discharge his or her duties unless familiar with the general purposes which the law is supposed to perform for society.

There exists in the law a separate discipline designed to investigate the nature of law, its guiding ideas and social goals, and the general character of the methods and techniques employed for the effectuation of its ends. This discipline is known as "Jurisprudence." This subject, in most of its ramifications, is dealt with in a separate course in many law schools. The subject cannot in its full scope be taught to students who have not as yet acquired a background in the positive rules, sources, and methodology of the law. And yet beginning students who have decided to launch upon a legal career ought to engage at least in some initial and preliminary reflection upon the meaning of the institution to the service of which they intend to devote their lives and best energies.

B. DEFINITIONS OF LAW

Such reflection, unfortunately, is rendered difficult by the fact that there is no general agreement among jurists and other legal thinkers as to what the goals and purposes of legal regulation are or ought to be.

1

There does exist a large measure of consensus as to the minimum objectives which the institution of law is designed to serve. But when we turn from the minimum and most elementary goals of legal control to the broader ends and ideals for the attainment of which the law can be used, we shall encounter a perplexing multitude and variety of viewpoints. Let us set out a number of classic definitions of law which may be considered representative and which have influenced the course of legal development, together with an eclectic sample of modern opinion:

Classic Definitions

Cicero (106–43 B.C.)—"Law is the highest reason, implanted in nature, which commands what ought to be done and forbids the opposite." (*De Legibus*, Bk. I (51 B.C.)).

St. Thomas Aquinas (1226–1274)—"Law is an ordinance of reason for the common good, made by him who has care of the community, and promulgated." (*Summa Theologica*, Part II, First Part, Qu. 90, Art. 4 (1265–1273)).

Hobbes (1588–1679)—"Civil Law is to every Subject, those Rules, which the Commonwealth hath commanded him, by Word, Writing, or other sufficient Sign of the Will, to make use of for the Distinction of Right and Wrong; that is to say, of what is contrary, and what is not contrary to the Rule." (*Leviathan*, Ch. XXVI (1651)).

Locke (1632–1704)—"The end of law is not to abolish or restrain, but to preserve and enlarge freedom." (*Two Treatises on Civil Government*, Bk. II, Ch. VI (1689)).

Austin (1790–1859)—"Every positive law ... is set by a sovereign person, or a sovereign body of persons, to a member or members of the independent political society wherein that person or body is sovereign or supreme. Or (changing the expression) it is set by a monarch or sovereign member to a person or persons in a state of subjection to its author." (*The Province of Jurisprudence Determined*, Lecture VI (1832)).

Jhering (1818–1892)—"Law is the sum of the conditions of social life in the widest sense of the term, as secured by the power of the State through the means of external compulsion." (*Law as a Means to an End*, Ch. VIII (1877–1883)).

Carter (1827–1903)—"Law is not a command or body of commands, but consists of rules springing from the social standard of justice or from the habits and customs from which that standard has itself been derived." ("The Ideal and the Actual," 24 American Law Review 752 (1890)).

Recaséns–Siches (1903–1977)—"Law was not born into human life by reason of the desire to render tribute or homage to the idea of justice, but to fulfill an inescapable urgency for security and certainty in social life. The question of why and wherefore men make law is not answered in the structure of the idea of justice, nor in the suite of outstanding values which accompany it as presupposed by it, but in a subordinate value—security—corresponding to a human need." ("Human Life, Society and Law," Ch. VI, in *Latin–American Legal Philosophy* (1939)).

The definitions of law set forth above are heterogeneous but not necessarily contradictory. Each of them accentuates an element or ingredient in social control through law which may be considered indispensable or at least desirable for the effective operation of a sound legal system. As you re-read the above definitions, ask yourself what each author perceives to be the role of law in human affairs.

Modern Opinion

Fred Rodell, Professor of Law, Yale University—"The Law is the killy-loo bird of the sciences. The killy-loo, of course, was the bird that insisted on flying backward because it didn't care where it was going but was mightily interested in where it had been." (*Woe Unto You, Lawyers!* 23 (1939)).

William O. Douglas, Associate Justice, U.S. Supreme Court—"Common sense often makes good law." (Peak v. United States, 353 U.S. 43, 46 (1957)).

Dwight D. Eisenhower, 34th President of the United States—"The clearest way to show what the rule of law means to us in everyday life is to recall what has happened when there is no rule of law." (Address on first observance of Law Day, May 5, 1958).

Reverend Martin Luther King, Jr.—"It may be true that the law cannot make a man love me, but it can keep him from lynching me, and I think that's pretty important." (*Wall Street Journal*, November 13, 1962).

Roscoe Pound, Dean Emeritus, Harvard Law School—"Law is experience developed by reason and applied continually to further experience." (*Christian Science Monitor*, April 24, 1963).

Archibald Cox, Professor of Law, Harvard University—"[T]hrough the centuries, men of law have been persistently concerned with the resolution of disputes ... in ways that enable society to achieve its goals with a minimum of force and maximum of reason." (*The New York Times*, May 24, 1974).

Robert H. Bork, Judge, U.S. Court of Appeals, District of Columbia Circuit—"[Law is] vulnerable to the winds of intellectual or moral fashion, which it then validates as the commands of our most basic concept." (*The New York Times*, January 4, 1985).

Ronald M. Dworkin, Professor of Jurisprudence, Oxford University and Professor of Law, New York University—"Moral principle is the foundation of law." (*The Christian Science Monitor*, May 20, 1986).

Which of these views about law do you find most attractive? Most accurate? Is there necessarily some tension between what the law is, and what it should be? Do lawyers have any special responsibility to seek to resolve or reduce this tension? Are lawyers likely to be well equipped to make valid moral judgments about which laws are good and which are evil? Is the risk of mistake or failure or lack of expertise a valid excuse for lawyers to be indifferent to the moral virtue of the laws they exploit and enforce?

We hope that your thoughts on these important questions will be informed by the balance of our book, and that from time to time you will revisit this initial inquiry into fundamental questions about the nature and functions of law, the evaluation of particular laws and legal systems, and the responsibilities of lawyers.

Chapter I

LAW AND THE PROCESS
OF CLASSIFICATION

A. THE MEANING AND IMPORTANCE
OF CLASSIFICATION

One of the main objectives of the law is to bring a measure of order into the chaotic world of reality, to regulate the relations between people, and to adjust their conflicting interests. Such ordering of human affairs cannot, as a matter of basic social policy, be done on an individual basis, i.e., by determining for each citizen what his individual rights and duties should be. It must be done on a *generalized* basis, by dividing the citizens into certain legally significant groups or categories and fixing the rights, duties, and privileges of each of these groups. A major function of a legal system is thus to *classify* things and phenomena found in the external world, i.e., to group and segregate them into classes, and to explain the distinctions and relationships between the classes.

Classification means, figuratively speaking, that one takes objects which are equal or quite similar in their appearance, characteristics, and qualities, puts them into a bottle, and marks the bottle with a label. For instance, we put stones consisting of a compound called beryl and being of a yellowish-green color into a bottle and label it "emerald." We fill a bottle with stones consisting of corundum and characterized by a transparent blue color and give it the tag "sapphire." We then compare the two types of stone *as a class* (not individually) and note their characteristics and distinctions.

The law constantly combines individual persons in generalized abstractions, such as creditor and debtor, vendor and purchaser, citizen and alien, landlord and tenant, owner and possessor, bailor and bailee, employer and employee. Sometimes it is very hard to determine in an individual case whether or not a certain person does or does not fall within some classification which carries with it specific legal rights or duties, or to which some other legal consequence attaches. There are cases, for example, in which it is difficult to decide whether a certain person who pays for the services of others has hired "employees" or entered into contracts for personal services by "independent contractors." A host of legal consequences from tax law to tort law turn on this classification.

The law is filled with such problems of debatable classification. Precise and orderly thought is an essential virtue for a lawyer, because such thought assists in unraveling the complexities of a given set of circumstances and evaluating their legal consequences in light of the applicable legal classifications. Rigorous thought about the terms and justifications of legal classifications cannot eliminate ambiguity from the law, but it can do much to reduce it.

Besides its importance as a basic element of legal reasoning, classification is an aspect of law of special significance for two related reasons. First, American law is derived from governments subject to written constitutions, which impose upon the law itself classifications of permissible and impermissible legal rules. Second, one of the most important constitutional criteria for the validity of a rule of law is that it apply to people equally. This raises a paradox of sorts—how can classifications, whose whole purpose is to treat people and things differently, be reconciled with the constitutional mandate of human equality under the law?

In the United States, judges have the ultimate power to determine whether legal rules are valid under the constitutions of the federal government and the various states. At its most basic level, constitutional law prescribes the existence and limitations of the power of particular institutions of government to impose legal consequences on particular classifications of things and phenomena. Thus, all constitutional law may be seen as a problem of the classification of governmental power. For example, does the Constitution classify the licensing of automobile drivers as a function of state governments, or of the federal government? This will determine which government has the power to license drivers. But even the appropriate government's power is not absolute. For instance, an automobile driver licensing law which requires licensees to execute loyalty oaths might be classified as an unreasonable infringement of free speech, and unconstitutional for that reason alone, even though the law was enacted by the government with the general authority to regulate driver licensing.

A special problem of American constitutional law is the right to "the equal protection of the laws." The American legal system is in large part premised upon a profound (though not yet wholly fulfilled) commitment to treating all people as equal in the eyes of the law. How can American law both classify people for purposes of treating them differently, as landlords are treated differently than tenants, while still purporting to afford them "equal protection"? The answer is that equality does not preclude classification; the legal equality of people under the law does not mean that all classifications of people into groups accorded different legal treatment are unconstitutional, nor does it mean that only identically situated identical twins (if there were any) would have any claim to equal legal treatment. Concern for equality under law is basically concern for the justification of legal classifications in terms of the objectives that they are intended to accomplish.

All people have certain similarities and certain differences, all are members of the human race and yet all are unique individuals. The law treats people differently to a greater or lesser extent according to how classifications of their similarities and differences are manipulated. The constitutional norm of equality under the law does not prohibit classifications which treat people differently, but it does demand that such classifications be justified by some goal other than the unequal treatment itself, and that the classifications serve that goal in some direct or even essential way. This problem of the "nexus" between legal classifications and the purposes they serve is one of the most intractable of American constitutional law. The basic principle is that classifications serving a reasonable purpose are permitted, while unreasonable discrimination is outlawed.

Suppose, for example, that the legislature wants to promote traffic safety. It decides to accomplish this by limiting the number of vehicles on public highways. Can the legislature accordingly prohibit anyone from operating a vehicle on the public highways except adult males? except adults with perfect vision uncorrected by lenses? except adults who have never been convicted of a serious crime? except adults who have never been cited for a traffic violation? Each of these statutory classifications of who may drive on the public highways would reduce the number of cars being driven, and to that extent would probably promote traffic safety. Yet you will probably want to object that some or all of these classifications are somehow "unfair"; your perceptions of unfairness will reflect your individual reaction to the importance of the goal of traffic safety and the degree to which each classification serves that goal, as weighed against the value of treating people as equals despite such differing characteristics as gender, acuity of vision, or arrest and conviction records—characteristics which vary in the degree to which they are within the control of an individual, and which also vary in their relevance to whether a given individual is or is not likely to be a safe driver. Much of American constitutional law confronts courts and lawyers with similar problems of whether a particular legal classification is in some fundamental sense unfair, and of the extent to which considerations of fairness ought to play a role in determining whether a legal classification is valid under the "equal protection clause" or any other clause of the Constitution.[1]

---

1. In a famous footnote to an equal-protection case decided at the dawn of the modern constitutional era, the Supreme Court suggested that the Court's usual presumption of the reasonableness of legislative classifications should be qualified when classifications burden specific constitutional rights, or disparately affect "discrete and insular minorities" likely to suffer prejudice from the unchecked operation of the political process. United States v. Carolene Products Co., 304 U.S. 144, 153 n.4 (1938). The "more searching judicial inquiry" that the *Carolene Products* Court suggested might be appropriate in some circumstances has since become a well-established feature of American constitutional law. See J.H. Ely, *Democracy and Distrust* 14–33, 73–77 (1980). Most legislative classifications are upheld if there is any "rational relationship" between the classification and some

B. SOME BASIC DISTINCTIONS AND CLASSIFICATIONS OF THE LAW

Among the myriad classifications of a highly developed legal system, most are of a technical character, just as distinctions between particular species of beetles or pine trees turn upon the technical minutiae of biological classification. At this point in your study of legal classification, you will be introduced solely to some very broad and basic terms and classifications which do not pertain to specific legal topics, but to law, legal science, or legal systems in general.

1. INTERNATIONAL LAW AND MUNICIPAL LAW

The chief difference between these two branches of the law is that international law deals with the external (foreign) affairs of nations, while municipal law regulates their internal affairs. International law is concerned with usages, customs, rules, and contractual arrangements which nation-states have consented to observe in their dealings with each other. The law contained in treaties and other agreements between nations, the law found in the decisions of international courts, and the law developed by the United Nations are examples of legal source materials pertaining to the field of international law.

One of the problems of the study of international law is that nations consider themselves "sovereign," that is, subject to no higher authority. How can sovereign nations be bound by rules of international law, then, if there is no way to enforce those rules except by one sovereign nation declaring war on another? Some theorists contend for this reason that "international law" is not law at all, because it is for the most part observed by consent rather than enforced by higher authority. (Some enforcement powers are lodged in the U.N. Security Council, but weakened by the veto prerogative vested in five nations.) Other theorists point out that certain rules of international law are so universally observed, even by unwilling nations, that it is the concept of sovereignty, rather than the concept of international law, which needs reexamination.

In any event, international law is clearly distinguishable from municipal law, which is the domestic law of a state or nation. Municipal law regulates primarily the relations between individuals, as well as the relations between individuals and their government. International law regulates primarily the relations between states, although international

legitimate goal of economic or social policy. But courts exercise "strict scrutiny" of classifications that impinge on "fundamental interests" protected by the Constitution independently of equal-protection principles, or that employ "suspect classifications" adversely impacting particular groups likely to be viewed with prejudice by the larger polity. Such strict scrutiny almost always leads to the determination that a challenged classification is unconstitutional. Modern constitutional debate has thus come to focus principally on just what counts as "fundamental interests" and "suspect classifications." There is, for example, much current legal controversy over the proper constitutional analysis of interests and classifications relating to human sexuality, sexual preferences, and reproductive rights.

agreements may establish rights and responsibilities on the part of individuals. The federal law of the United States, the law of the state of California, the law of Mexico and of France are examples of systems of municipal law. In countries with a federal structure, municipal law is of a multiple character. In the United States, for example, there are the laws made by Congress, the laws of the fifty states, and the laws of cities and counties, among others.

One problem of which you should be aware is that the states of the American union are sometimes referred to as "sovereign" states. The sovereignty of these states is, however, of considerably smaller scope than the sovereignty of nations. The United States Constitution carves out large areas of regulation in which federal power is paramount over state power. Constitutionally-authorized federal laws and treaties take precedence over inconsistent state laws. It is doubtful, under these circumstances, whether the term "state sovereignty" conveys any clearly discernible meaning.

2. CIVIL LAW AND COMMON LAW

Most of the municipal legal systems of the world may be said to belong to one of two large groups of legal orders which are distinguished from each other by their historical origins and also by certain structural characteristics. These two groups are the "civil law" and the "common law."[2]

The civil law system grew out of ancient Roman law, which reached its highest development in the Roman Empire during the first two centuries A.D. The civil law may be described as a modern adaptation of Roman law, but it is important to note that many changes were made over the course of time in all of the modern civil law systems which set them apart from ancient Roman law to a substantial extent.

The civil law system is today in effect in Continental Europe (although the Roman law influence has always been weaker in the Scandinavian countries than in the rest of Continental Europe), in Latin America, in Japan, and (with some admixture of common law) in the Union of South Africa.

Civil law ingredients of varying degrees of strength can be found in the laws of the Islamic world. Currently the Russian judicial system is based on European civil law systems. Recent reforms in Russia (and other former Soviet entities) include experimenting with jury trials and making the judiciary more independent from other governmental control. Further westernization of the Russian legal system is likely, but the nature of the reforms is uncertain.[3]

2. When we speak of the "common law" as distinguished from the "civil law," we are using the term "common law" in a broad sense, which includes "equity" (see *infra* Ch. II.C).

3. See S.P. Boylan, "The Status of Judicial Reform in Russia," 13 American University International Law Review 1327, 1330–31, 1343 (1998).

The law of the People's Republic of China, after the Chinese Revolution of 1949, followed the Soviet model in many important respects. After the Sino–Soviet split and the Cultural Revolution, the influence of Soviet law diminished. Furthermore, during the 1960's and 1970's the role of law as such was downgraded. Law was believed to be a reactionary institution that could ultimately be dispensed with in a socialist society.

A change in the attitude towards law began in the 1980's. China has enacted codes of civil law, criminal law, and criminal procedure. Respect for law is encouraged by the government, although mediation—pursuant to a tradition going back to Confucius—is preferred to litigation as a mode of conflict resolution. One reason for the new approach to law has been the recent increase in trade with foreign nations, including the United States. Such trade requires rules and orderly procedures for resolving contractual and other disagreements. Although China has incorporated some elements of western law, this does not necessarily mean that western notions of freedom, equality, reciprocity, and legal rights are sure to follow. "History has shown us that China put its own spin on Buddhism, Marxism, and even Christianity. Capitalism, liberalism, and democracy may prove no more inviolate."[4]

The state of Louisiana, which was acquired in 1803 from the French, is in part a civil law jurisdiction. Its comprehensive civil code, which covers the fields of contracts, torts, property, family law and inheritance, may be traced back to the Napoleonic Code of 1804. But Louisiana has also had a strong influx of the common law, especially in the areas of procedure and evidence. Other New World jurisdictions which form a blend of the civil law and common law are Puerto Rico and the Canadian province of Quebec.

The common law is a system which had its roots in medieval England. It was shaped in the courts of the English king and applied on a nationwide basis, on the assumption that it represented the common customs and convictions of all Englishmen. Its counterpart in medieval times was the custom of the manor (feudal estate), as distinguished from the custom of the realm.

The common law was adopted by the American states during and after the War of Independence, and after the attainment of independence it became the foundation of the laws of the several states. Other common law jurisdictions are England, Scotland (with a strong civil law admixture), Ireland, Canada (with the partial exception of Quebec), Australia, and New Zealand. India may be called a common law jurisdiction in a limited sense, inasmuch as the influence of Hindu customary law is also substantial.

Few generalizations can be made with respect to the legal systems of the black African countries. Elements of the civil law, common law, and

---

4. R. LaKritz, "Taming a 5,000 Year–Old Dragon: Toward a Theory of Legal De- velopment in Post–Mao China," 11 Emory International Law Review 237, 266 (1997).

tribal customary law can be found in varying proportions, and modern codifications are in progress in many of these states.

Although substantial differences exist between legal systems within the civil law group and also (to a lesser extent) between legal systems in the common law group, there are some characteristics which civil law systems share when compared with their common law counterparts. The starting point of legal reasoning in civil law countries is almost always a statute or code provision. Judicial precedents, at least in theory, play a secondary role; their authority is considered to be no greater than that of legal writers. However, in actual practice prior decisions are widely followed by the courts. In the common law orbit, legal arguments often center around the interpretation and applicability of earlier judicial decisions, especially those rendered by the highest court of the jurisdiction in question; but statutes and administrative regulations are gaining an ever-increasing importance.

Certain differences also exist in the structure of legal procedure in the two rival systems. The judges in civil law jurisdictions take a very active part in the interrogation of witnesses and conduct of the proceedings, and the role of counsel is correspondingly diminished. Under the system of the common law, the initiative in a court trial is exercised primarily by the attorneys for the parties, while the judge plays a less active role. Civil law systems, because of the dominant position of the judge, are often referred to as "inquisitorial," in juxtaposition to the "adversarial" model of the common law, in which the attorneys for the parties bear primary responsibility for shaping the content and course of litigation. As with differences in legal reasoning, these differences in the role of the judge between civil law and common law systems are tending to narrow over time. In constitutional and administrative litigation especially, modern American judges play an increasingly active role in the definition of issues and the development of facts at trial.

3. PUBLIC LAW AND PRIVATE LAW

The municipal law of a state or country is frequently subdivided into public and private law, although there is some disagreement as to where the dividing line should be drawn. Private law, generally speaking, is concerned with disputes among private citizens or private organizations. These disputes may arise out of a contract, out of a wrongful act (tort), out of a business transaction, or they may involve family relations or ownership of property. The basic private law subjects are Contracts, Torts and Property. After taking courses in the fundamentals of these subjects, you will be ready to study some of the other important private law subjects which are special applications of contract, tort and property law principles, such as Commercial Law, Trusts and Estates, Corporations, Securities Law and Labor Law.

Public law, in its most general sense, involves relations between private citizens or organizations and the government. The protection of civil liberties, the protection of the citizen against arbitrary acts of executive or administrative organs, the validity of legislation, and governmental regulation of trade and commerce are subjects which belong to the field of public law. Important public law courses are Constitutional Law, Administrative Law, Taxation, and Trade Regulation.

The field of procedure should also be classified as a public law subject, because it deals with the rules followed by public organs—the courts—in conducting their business. The course in Civil Procedure introduces you to the operation of courts and court systems; related courses are Evidence, Conflict of Laws, and Federal Jurisdiction. Criminal Law is also a public law subject, because it is concerned with public sanctions—sanctions imposed by the state in the form of imprisonment, fines, etc.—upon offenders against the public order. Criminal Procedure covers the operation of courts in the enforcement of the criminal law.

4. SUBSTANTIVE LAW AND ADJECTIVE LAW (Procedural)

A classification which cuts across the division of the law into public law and private law is that which differentiates between substantive and adjective law. Substantive law creates, defines, and delimits rights, duties, and obligations. Adjective law prescribes the forms of procedure by which substantive rights or obligations are enforced by the courts or other public agencies. Adjective law is simply another term for procedural law.

Substantive law tells me *what* rights I have if X violates his contract with me (Can I get damages? Do I have the right to cancel the contract?), or if Y negligently drives his car into mine (May I recover for mental shock? May I recover if I, too, have been negligent?).

The adjective law informs me as to *how* I have to go about enforcing my rights. Where should I file my complaint? What should be the content of the complaint? Do I have the right to a jury trial? What kind of evidence offered in support of my claim will be accepted by the court? If the decision goes against me, do I have a right to a new trial, or may I file an appeal? How can I enforce a judgment or decree in my favor?

5. LEGISLATION, CASE LAW, AND CUSTOMARY LAW

The term "legislation" is today applied for the most part to the deliberate creation of legal norms or precepts by an organ of government which is set up for this purpose and which gives articulate, authoritative expression to such legal precepts in a formalized legal document.[5] This formalized legal document is often a statute or code. The legislative acts of Congress and of the several state legislatures are known as "statutes." A code, as distinguished from a statute, contains a systematic compilation of related enactments (as, for example, the Penal Code of the State of California, which specifies most crimes under California law and the procedure for prosecuting them).

---

5. Some legislation, as for example in California, is created by the popular "initiative" process.

There also exists today a large body of law promulgated by the executive and administrative agencies of government in the exercise of a limited legislative authority. This type of law is usually published in the form of executive orders or administrative regulations. Such law is similar in character to statutory law.

Case law originates in the decisions of courts or other tribunals having power to decide particular controversies. In the course of determining such controversies, the tribunal often will find that no legislative law dispositive of the dispute in question is in existence, or that the available legislative law is ambiguous in its application to the problem at hand. In such a case, the court must articulate and apply a legal norm or principle which will decide the dispute between the parties. Many of the rules and principles of the common law (including equity) originated in this fashion. One of the most difficult problems for legal historians, political scientists and philosophers of law is to determine what has been, and what ought to be, the source for judicially created rules of decision. When no legislative law clearly applies, are judges bound in any way in their fashioning of case law? Must the judge reach the decision which best accords with custom, or precedent (that is, case law formulated by prior judges in more or less analogous cases), or justice (and if so, what if the judge's view of justice is different from that of society as a whole)?

While clear answers to these questions are hard to find, and even harder to defend, there does exist in the American legal system a substantial degree of consensus on the important differences between legislation and case law. A rule of legislative law is cast in an authoritative textual form and, unless the statute is unconstitutional, judges are bound by the statute as interpreted by them. A judge is not considered free to revise a statute, ignore it, or supplant it with a rule which seems to the judge to be better reasoned. Much greater flexibility falls to the judge under the various views of the judicial role in dealing with case law. While subordinate courts must adhere to case law promulgated by courts of higher jurisdiction, courts of parallel jurisdiction are generally free to follow separate paths in the formulation of case law. Moreover, a court is not bound to follow its own precedents, and may elect to refuse to follow a case law rule which it promulgated earlier (generally when the court was composed of a different set of judges). Thus, courts take much greater liberties with case law than they are permitted to take with legislative law.

In one sense, legislation and case law come together when vague or ambiguous legislation must be interpreted by a court. Various courts of parallel jurisdiction may confront the same statutory language in different cases, and come to inconsistent results. This frequently happens in cases involving vague clauses of the Constitution. The Supreme Court of Oregon, for example, might decide that capital punishment is unconstitutional under the Eighth Amendment to the Constitution; this would not be binding on the Supreme Court of Arizona's consideration of the same question. The United States Supreme Court is the court of supreme jurisdiction in the construction of the federal Constitution, however, so once the United States Supreme Court decides the status of capital punishment under the federal Constitution, that result is binding on all other courts in the country. (But nothing is simple in our federal system—all the states have their own constitutions, whose construction is the ultimate responsibility of each of their highest courts. Thus, even after the United States Supreme Court has upheld the death penalty under the federal Constitution, the supreme court of a state with a cruel-and-unusual-punishment clause in its own constitution might still rule that the death penalty is forbidden in that state by the state constitution, even though it is permitted by the federal Constitution. On all questions of state law—whether involving state statutes, the case law of state courts, or the state constitution—the highest court of the relevant state has the last word, just as the Supreme Court of the United States has the last word on all matters of federal law.)

Another type of law, in the opinion of some, is customary law. Unlike legislation and case law, customary law is not set by an organ of government but develops through actual and continuous practice in the community, accompanied by the conviction that the mode of behavior evinced by the practice is legally obligatory. To some extent, international law may be said to be the most important modern form of customary law. Other examples of customary law are generally found in primitive legal systems, including the feudal antecedents of the Anglo–American legal system: unwritten rules of inheritance of property and testamentary disposition (i.e., by will); rules concerning the tenure and cultivation of land; impediments to marriage recognized in a tribal community but not formalized in a legal enactment; and commercial usages of traders and shippers.

In modern American society, the principal importance of customary practice is not as a body of law which is obligatory of its own force, but rather as a source of case law. American courts have shown a marked propensity for converting vocational or business customs, such as accustomed ways of behavior in the medical profession, the commercial usages of bankers, or conventional methods of operating a mine, into legally obligatory standards of behavior by incorporating custom into case law when no other standard of behavior has been set by statute. It is important to note, however, that courts have not abandoned the traditional flexibility of case law even when incorporating customary standards of behavior into case law; many courts have refused to give legal effect to a custom found to be "unreasonable" from the perspective of public policy, social justice, or the interests of outsiders not fairly charged with knowledge of the custom.

6. SEPARATION OF THE LEGISLATIVE, EXECUTIVE, AND JUDICIAL POWERS

Article III, Section 1 of the Constitution of California provides: "The powers of the Government of the State of California shall be divided into three separate departments—the Legislative, Executive, and Judicial; and no person charged with the exercise of powers properly belonging to one of these departments shall exercise any functions appertaining to either of the others, except as in this Constitution expressly directed or permitted." Most state constitutions have similar provisions, and the separation-of-powers principle also underlies the fabric of the federal Constitution.

Such constitutional divisions of governmental powers into legislative, executive, and judicial powers make it necessary to define or at least to circumscribe the meaning of these basic concepts of our public law. This task is not an easy one, because there exist borderline or twilight zones in which these concepts overlap or shade into one another. It is possible, however, to define at least the hard core of these notions.

The most characteristic feature of legislative activity in the American legal system was well explained by Oliver Wendell Holmes, Jr., writing for the United States Supreme Court in Prentis v. Atlantic Coast Line Co., 211 U.S. 210 (1908). Legislation, said Justice Holmes, "looks to the future and changes existing conditions by making a new rule to be applied thereafter to all or some part of those subject to its power." *Id.* at 226. Legislation is, essentially, the making of new law by means of a formalized pronouncement of a law-making body. The law enacted by a legislative organ consists typically of general rules, principles, or other normative pronouncements which permit, command, or disallow a certain course of conduct. Legislation normally deals with classes of persons and an indefinite number of situations. A disposition or command that is addressed to one or a few named persons or a single concrete situation is not a legislative act in the genuine sense of the term.

Congress does, however, have power to enact "Private Laws", which are published in the official collection of federal statutes known as Statutes at Large. Typical examples of private laws are the following: (1) enactments excepting named individuals from immigration or naturalization requirements established by general laws; (2) enactments granting certain individuals compensation not authorized by the Federal Tort Claims Act; (3) waivers of claims that the Federal Government has against particular persons under a general law. Private acts are of an essentially executive character, since they deal with one individual situation. When a bill for such a law is introduced by a senator or congressperson, there is rarely any discussion on the floor of Congress; there may be a limited discussion in a subcommittee. Such legislation is sanctioned by long usage which can be traced back to the powers of the English Parliament. Most state constitutions prohibit such granting of privileges or immunities to specific persons.[6]

An executive or administrative act may be defined as an exercise of governmental power in a concrete situation to accomplish some public purpose. If the President of the United States sends a note to a foreign

---

6. See, for example, California Constitution, Art. I, Sec. 7(b): "A citizen or class of citizens may not be granted privileges or immunities not granted on the same terms to all citizens." For a discussion of private bills, see Note, "Private Bills in Congress," 79 Harvard Law Review 1684 (1966).

government protesting against an inimical act directed against the United States, he acts in an executive capacity. If the Department of the Interior authorizes the construction of a new six-lane highway, it proceeds in an administrative fashion.

Executive or administrative power is in its essence the power to act according to discretion for the public advantage. Under a purely executive type of government, the public officials of the state would have unlimited discretion to act for the sake of what they conceive to be the public good. Under a "government of laws," such as ours, executive and administrative discretion is limited by a large and intricate network of legal rules and regulations. Under our system of government, executive and administrative power must be exercised according to law.

Judicial power is employed for the purpose of settling controversies between private individuals or groups, between private persons and the government, or between different units of government. In the words of Justice Holmes, "judicial inquiry investigates, declares, and enforces liabilities as they stand on present or past facts and under laws supposed already to exist." *Id.*

A judicial act is distinguished from a legislative act by the fact that the latter determines the rights of individuals generally and in the abstract, while adjudication is in most cases the concrete application of a legal rule to a dispute between the parties before a court. Judicial action is, on the other hand, distinguished from executive action in that the latter is not, or at least not necessarily or typically, undertaken for the purpose of settling a dispute.

The separation-of-powers principle has not been fully and completely realized in our constitutional structure, federal and state. The general principle has been qualified by a number of exceptions. Thus, the right conferred upon the President of the United States and the Governors of the several states to veto legislation gives to the executive branch of the government a share in the processes of legislation. Furthermore, the President may make treaties (which often lay down norms of law) with the consent of the Senate. The Senate, which is essentially a legislative body, exercises executive functions by participating in the appointment of many federal officials. Congressional power to pass private laws has already been mentioned. Judicial powers have been vested in many federal and state administrative agencies, and such agencies also frequently issue rules and regulations which are legislative in character. The Senate acts as a judicial body when it tries impeachments of public officers. Courts have promulgated codes of pleading and procedure, which are manifestly legislative in character, and often fashion case law which governs future cases just as clearly as would explicit acts of legislation. Courts also engage in executive functions when they supervise the administration of estates in bankruptcy, appoint guardians, and make decisions in uncontested probate cases. Some of these departures from the principle of the separation of governmental powers have been sanctioned directly by constitutional mandate; others have developed in governmental practice and might be viewed as a form of customary law.

Notes and Questions

(1) One author has taken the position that "any power, whatever its nature, necessarily takes its character from the department to which it is assigned by the constitution or the legislature." Whatever proceeds from a court of justice, he maintains, is judicial, and whatever power or duty is imposed upon the executive department is executive, and therefore free from interference by the other branches of the government. For example, the power to try contested elections, when vested in the courts, is judicial; when it is assumed by the legislature, it is legislative and may not be controlled by the courts.[7]

What objections may be raised against this theory?

(2) Suppose Congress confers the Congressional Medal of Honor upon a distinguished war hero. Is this a legislative or executive act?

(3) President Clinton appointed Ruth Bader Ginsburg to the United States Supreme Court. The Senate concurred in the appointment. How should these actions be characterized?

(4) Some years ago, the Supreme Court of Wisconsin issued a decree requiring every lawyer practicing law in Wisconsin to become a member of the state bar association. Was this action judicial, legislative, or executive?

(5) President Carter negotiated, and the Senate ratified, a treaty with Panama relinquishing U.S. sovereignty over the Panama Canal. Were these actions legislative or executive?

NOTE BY THE EDITORS: BACKGROUND TO THE CONSTITUTIONAL CONTROVERSY OVER THE PERIOD OF LIMITATION APPLICABLE TO PRIVATE CIVIL SUITS UNDER § 10 OF THE SECURITIES EXCHANGE ACT OF 1934

To illustrate the separation-of-powers principle, we are including a case, Plaut v. Spendthrift Farm, Inc., 514 U.S. 211 (1995), at the end of this chapter. The issue in *Plaut* is "whether § 27A(b) of the Securities Exchange Act of 1934, to the extent that it requires federal courts to reopen final judgments in private civil actions under § 10(b) of the Act, contravenes the Constitution's separation of powers...." *Id.* at 213.

The Securities Exchange Act of 1934 was enacted in the midst of a great economic depression triggered by the stock market crash of 1929. That crash had followed a period of reckless speculation and market manipulation that drove stock prices to unrealistic heights. When prices collapsed, millions of Americans were ruined by the loss of their investments. This in turn led to a

---

7. W. Bondy, *The Separation of Governmental Powers; in History, in Theory, and*   *in the Constitutions* (1896, republished in 1967), pp. 80–81.

catastrophic contraction of the economy, and millions more were ruined by the loss of their jobs.

Franklin D. Roosevelt was elected President in 1932 on a platform of a giving Americans a "New Deal" through active regulation and management of the national economy by the federal government. The Securities Exchange Act was one of several New Deal statutes designed to promote fair and honest dealing on the New York Stock Exchange and other financial markets where the stocks (instruments of investment) and bonds (instruments of debt) of major American corporations are traded. Its principal strategy was to create a regulatory agency, the Securities and Exchange Commission (SEC), vested with broad powers to define the rules that would govern the process of fair dealing.

Section 10(b) of the 1934 Act prohibits the use of "any manipulative or deceptive device"—defined by the SEC in Rule 10b–5 to include a much broader range of sharp dealing than would be actionable as fraud under traditional principles of the common law—"in connection with the purchase or sale of any security." It is a federal crime wilfully to violate the Act or the SEC's rules and regulations thereunder, although criminal prosecutions are rare. The SEC itself can and often does bring civil actions against violators for fines and injunctive relief. But the most active means of enforcement of § 10b and the SEC's Rule 10b–5 has long been private civil actions for damages brought by investors who seek compensation for harm suffered as a result of the defendant's violation of § 10b and Rule 10b–5.

Although the 1934 Act did not expressly create such a private right to sue for damages, it has long been held to have done so by implication. Basically, courts construing the 1934 Act in its early years took the view that Congress wanted the Act to be effective, that private suits for damages were a far more effective device for enforcing the Act than reliance on the SEC's limited staff and resources, and that Congress must therefore have created by implication what it had not created expressly: a private right of action for damages. J.I. Case Co. v. Borak, 377 U.S. 426 (1964). As is often the case with private rights of action created by federal law—even those created expressly, rather than by implication—Congress did not enact an accompanying statute of limitations. For many years, the federal courts "borrowed" the statute of limitations applied by state courts in similar types of suits and applied them in § 10(b) actions, but this had the drawbacks of being unpredictable and inconsistent. Essentially, the same suit might be timely if brought in one state, but untimely if brought in another state, even though the basis for the suit was not state law at all, but a federal statute of nationwide applicability.

The Supreme Court sought to cure these problems when it decided, in Lampf, Pleva, Lipkind, Prupis & Petigrow v. Gilbertson, 501 U.S. 350 (1991), that a uniform federal limitation period should be applied to all § 10(b) suits. Instead of borrowing a state statute of limitations, the Supreme Court decided to borrow a federal statute of limitations. But the period of limitations that the Supreme Court judicially created for such suits was rather short—within one year of the date of discovery of the violation of the Act, but no more than three years from the date the violation occurred. This meant that someone who violated the Act and succeeded in concealing the violation for more than three years was given immunity from any private civil liability under § 10(b) to those harmed by the violation. Furthermore, the Court made its ruling retroactive, meaning that cases which had been brought under a longer state statute of limitations were now subject to dismissal if they did not satisfy the shorter federal statute of limitations.

Lampf was a popular decision with the kinds of persons and firms typically named as defendants in § 10(b) suits—stock brokers, brokerage firms, corporate officers and accountants, and issuers of securities. It was a very unpopular decision with those plaintiffs whose cases were now subject to dismissal. And the general sentiment was that it undercut the very point of the 1934 Act—to promote a financial culture of full disclosure and fair dealing, with stern disincentives against cutting corners. *Lampf* was decided on June 20, 1991. Within six months, Congress had passed (on November 27) and the first President Bush had signed (on December 19) a statute amending the Securities Exchange Act to add new § 27A.[8] Subsection (a) applied only to § 10(b) civil actions that had been commenced before *Lampf* was decided, and were still pending in federal court. As to these pending actions, the amendment retroactively restored the old regime of looking to local law to determine the applicable period of limitations. Subsection (b) went further, however. It sought to permit the reopening of § 10(b) suits that were pending on June 20, 1991, but were thereafter dismissed as untimely on the authority of *Lampf*.

One such dismissed suit had been brought by Ed Plaut and others who had purchased shares of stock in an unsuccessful breeder of thoroughbred horses, the aptly named Spendthrift Farm, Inc. Mr. Plaut and the other plaintiffs filed a motion on February 11, 1992, seeking to reopen their suit as authorized by new § 27A(b) of the amended Securities Exchange Act. The plaintiffs satisfied all of the requirements set forth in § 27A(b).

PLAUT v. SPENDTHRIFT FARM, INC.

Supreme Court of United States, 1995.
514 U.S. 211, 115 S.Ct. 1447, 131 L.Ed.2d 328.

JUSTICE SCALIA delivered the opinion of the Court.

The question presented in this case is whether § 27A(b) of the Securities Exchange Act of 1934, to the extent that it requires federal *issue*

---

8. Section 27A reads as follows:

Sec. 27A. (a) EFFECT ON PENDING CAUSES OF ACTION. The limitation period for any private civil action implied under § 10(b) of this Act that was commenced on or before June 19, 1991, shall be the limitation period provided by the laws applicable in the jurisdiction, including principles of retroactivity, as such laws existed on June 19, 1991.

(b) EFFECT ON DISMISSED CAUSES OF ACTION. Any private civil action implied under § 10(b) of this Act that was commenced on or before June 19, 1991—

(1) which was dismissed as time barred subsequent to June 19, 1991, and

(2) which would have been timely filed under the limitation period provided by the laws applicable in the jurisdiction, including principles of retroactivity, as such laws existed on June 19, 1991, shall be reinstated on motion by the plaintiff not later than 60 days after the date of the enactment of this section.

issue courts to reopen final judgments in private civil actions under § 10(b) of the Act, contravenes the Constitution's separation of powers. . . .

. . . .

. . . [Petitioners] filed a motion to reinstate [their § 10(b)] action previously dismissed with prejudice. The District Court found that the conditions set out in §§ 27A(b)(1) and (2) were met, so that petitioners' motion was required to be granted by the terms of the statute. It nonetheless denied the motion, agreeing with respondents that § 27A(b) is unconstitutional. . . . 789 F.Supp. 231 (1992). The United States Court of Appeals for the Sixth Circuit affirmed. 1 F.3d 1487 (1993). We granted certiorari. 511 U.S. 1141 (1994).[9]

. . . .

. . . Article III[10] establishes a "judicial department" with the "province and duty . . . to say what the law is" in particular cases and controversies. Marbury v. Madison, 1 Cranch [5 U.S.] 137, 177 (1803). The record of history shows that the Framers crafted this charter of the judicial department with an expressed understanding that it gives the Federal Judiciary the power, not merely to rule on cases, but to decide them, subject to review only by superior courts in the Article III hierarchy—with an understanding, in short, that "a judgment conclusively resolves the case" because "a 'judicial Power' is one to render dispositive judgments." Easterbrook, Presidential Review, 40 Case W. Res. L. Rev. 905, 926 (1990). By retroactively commanding the federal courts to reopen final judgments, Congress has violated this fundamental principle.

The Framers of our Constitution lived among the ruins of a system of intermingled legislative and judicial powers, which had been prevalent in the colonies long before the Revolution, and which after the Revolution had produced factional strife and partisan oppression. In the 17th and 18th centuries colonial assemblies and legislatures functioned as courts of equity of last resort, hearing original actions or providing appellate review of judicial judgments. G. Wood, The Creation of the American Republic 1776–1787, pp. 154–155 (1969). Often, however, they chose to correct the judicial process through special bills or other enacted legislation. It was common for such legislation not to prescribe a resolution of the dispute, but rather simply to set aside the judgment and order a new trial or appeal. M. Clarke, Parliamentary Privilege in the American Colonies 49–51 (1943). . . .

. . . .

9. Last Term this Court affirmed, by an equally divided vote, a judgment of the United States Court of Appeals for the Fifth Circuit that held § 27A(b) constitutional. Morgan Stanley & Co. v. Pacific Mut. Life Ins. Co., 511 U.S. 658 (1994) (per curiam). That ruling of course lacks precedential weight. Trans World Airlines, Inc. v. Hardison, 432 U.S. 63, 73, n.8 (1977). [Footnote by the Court.]

10. Article III, § 1 states that "the judicial Power of the United States shall be vested in one Supreme Court, and in such inferior Courts as Congress may . . . establish."

This sense of a sharp necessity to separate the legislative from the judicial power, prompted by the crescendo of legislative interference with private judgments of the courts, triumphed among the Framers of the new Federal Constitution. . . .

. . . The essential balance created by this allocation of authority was a simple one. The Legislature would be possessed of power to "prescrib[e] the rules by which the duties and rights of every citizen are to be regulated," but the power of "[t]he interpretation of the laws" would be "the proper and peculiar province of the courts." The Federalist No. 78, pp. 523, 525. . . . The Judiciary would be, "from the nature of its functions, . . . the [department] least dangerous to the political rights of the constitution," not because its acts were subject to legislative correction, but because the binding effect of its acts was limited to particular cases and controversies. . . .

. . . . .

Section 27A(b) effects a clear violation of the separation-of-powers principle we have just discussed. It is, of course, retroactive legislation, that is, legislation that prescribes what the law was at an earlier time, when the act whose effect is controlled by the legislation occurred—in this case, the filing of the initial Rule 10b–5 action in the District Court. When retroactive legislation requires its own application in a case already finally adjudicated, it does no more and no less than "reverse a determination once made, in a particular case." The Federalist No. 81, at 545. . . .

It is true, as petitioners contend, that Congress can always revise the judgments of Article III courts in one sense: When a new law makes clear that it is retroactive, an appellate court must apply that law in reviewing judgments still on appeal that were rendered before the law was enacted, and must alter the outcome accordingly. See United States v. Schooner Peggy, 1 Cranch [5 U.S.] 103 (1801) [(courts are obligated to apply law in force at time of their decision, including time of appellate judgment)] . . . . Since that is so, petitioners argue, federal courts must apply the "new" law created by § 27A(b) in finally adjudicated cases as well; for the line that separates lower court judgments that are pending on appeal (or may still be appealed), from lower-court judgments that are final, is determined by statute, *see, e.g.,* 28 U.S.C. § 2107(a) (30–day time limit for appeal to federal court of appeals), and so cannot possibly be a constitutional line. But a distinction between judgments from which all appeals have been forgone or completed, and judgments that remain on appeal (or subject to being appealed), is implicit in what Article III creates: not a batch of unconnected courts, but a judicial department composed of "inferior Courts" and "one supreme Court." Within that hierarchy, the decision of an inferior court is not (unless the time for appeal has expired) the final word of the department as a whole. It is the obligation of the last court in the hierarchy that rules on the case to give effect to Congress's latest enactment, even when that has the effect of overturning the judgment of an inferior court, since each court, at every level, must "decide according to existing laws." *Schooner Peggy, supra,* 1 Cranch, at 109. Having achieved finality, however, a judicial decision becomes the last word of the judicial department with regard to a particular case or controversy, and Congress may not declare by retroactive legislation that the law applicable to that very case was something other than what the courts said it was....

To be sure, § 27A(b) reopens (or directs the reopening of) final judgments in a whole class of cases rather than in a particular suit. We do not see how that makes any difference. The separation-of-powers violation here, if there is any, consists of depriving judicial judgments of the conclusive effect that they had when they were announced, not of acting in a manner—viz., with particular rather than general effect— that is unusual (though, we must note, not impossible) for a legislature. To be sure, a general statute such as this one may reduce the perception that legislative interference with judicial judgments was prompted by individual favoritism; but it is legislative interference with judicial judgments nonetheless. Not favoritism, nor even corruption, but power is the object of the separation-of-powers prohibition. The prohibition is violated when an individual final judgment is legislatively rescinded for even the very best of reasons, such as the legislature's genuine conviction (supported by all the law professors in the land) that the judgment was wrong; and it is violated 40 times over when 40 final judgments are legislatively dissolved.

It is irrelevant as well that the final judgments reopened by § 27A(b) rested on the bar of a statute of limitations. The rules of finality, both statutory and judge-made, treat a dismissal on statute-of-limitations grounds the same way they treat a dismissal for failure to state a claim, for failure to prove substantive liability, or for failure to prosecute: as a judgment on the merits. *See, e.g.,* Fed.Rule Civ.Proc. 41(b); United States v. Oppenheimer, 242 U.S. 85, 87–88 (1916). Petitioners suggest, directly or by implication, two reasons why a merits judgment based on this particular ground may be uniquely subject to congressional nullification. First, there is the fact that the length and indeed even the very existence of a statute of limitations upon a federal cause of action is entirely subject to congressional control. But virtually all of the reasons why a final judgment on the merit is rendered on a federal claim are subject to congressional control. Congress can eliminate, for example, a particular element of a cause of action that plaintiffs have found it difficult to establish; or an evidentiary rule that has often excluded essential testimony; or a rule of offsetting wrong (such as contributory negligence) that has often prevented recovery. To distinguish statutes of limitations on the ground that they are mere creatures of Congress is to distinguish them not at all. The second supposedly distinguishing characteristic of a statute of limitations is that it can be extended, without violating the Due Process Clause, after the cause of action arose and even after the statute itself has expired. *See, e.g.,* Chase Securities Corp. v. Donaldson, 325 U.S. 304 (1945). But that also does not set statutes of limitations apart. To mention only one other broad category of judgment-producing legal rule: Rules of pleading and proof can similarly be altered after the cause of action arises, Landgraf v. USI Film Products, *supra,* 511 U.S., at 275, and n.29, and even, if the statute clearly so requires, after they have been applied in a case but before final judgment has been entered. Petitioners' principle would therefore lead to the conclusion that final judgments rendered on the basis of a stringent (or, alternatively, liberal) rule of pleading or proof may be set aside for retrial under a new liberal (or, alternatively, stringent) rule of pleading or proof. This alone provides massive scope for undoing final judgments and would substantially subvert the doctrine of separation of powers.

. . . .

Petitioners also rely on a miscellany of decisions upholding legislation that altered rights fixed by final judgment of non-Article III courts . . . or that altered the prospective effect of injunctions entered by Article III courts, [Pennsylvania v.] Wheeling & Belmont Bridge Co., 18 How. [59 U.S. 421, 431–32 (1855)]. These cases distinguish themselves; nothing in our holding today calls them into question. . . .

. . . .

. . . The nub of [the] infringement [of the separation-of-powers principle] consists *not* of the Legislature's acting in a particularized and hence (according to the concurrence) nonlegislative fashion;[11] but rather of the Legislature's nullifying prior, authoritative judicial action. . . .

. . . [T]he doctrine of separation of powers is a *structural safeguard* rather than a remedy to be applied only when specific harm, or risk of specific harm, can be identified. In its major features (of which the conclusiveness of judicial judgments is assuredly one) it is a prophylactic device, establishing high walls and clear distinctions because low walls and vague distinctions will not be judicially defensible in the heat of interbranch conflict. . . . Separation of powers, a distinctively American political doctrine, profits from the advice authored by a distinctively American poet: Good fences make good neighbors.

We know of no previous instance in which Congress has enacted retroactive legislation requiring an Article III court to set aside a final judgment, and for good reason. The Constitution's separation of legislative and judicial powers denies it the authority to do so. Section 27A(b) is unconstitutional to the extent that it requires federal courts to reopen final judgments entered before its enactment. The judgment of the Court of Appeals is affirmed.

Justice Breyer, concurring in the judgment.

I agree with the majority that § 27A(b) of the Securities Exchange Act of 1934, 15 U.S.C. § 78aa–1 (1988 ed., Supp. V) (hereinafter § 27A(b)) is unconstitutional. In my view, the separation of powers

---

11. The premise that there is something wrong with particularized legislative action is of course questionable. While legislatures usually act through laws of general applicability, that is by no means their only legiti- mate mode of action. Private bills in Congress are still common, and were even more so in the days before establishment of the Claims Court. . . . [Footnote by the Court.]

inherent in our Constitution means that at least sometimes Congress lacks the power under Article I to reopen an otherwise closed court judgment. And the statutory provision here at issue, § 27A(b), violates a basic "separation-of-powers" principle—one intended to protect individual liberty. Three features of this law—its exclusively retroactive effect, its application to a limited number of individuals, and its reopening of closed judgments—taken together, show that Congress here impermissibly tried to apply, as well as make, the law. Hence, § 27A(b) falls outside the scope of Article I. But, it is far less clear, and unnecessary for the purposes of this case to decide, that separation of powers "is violated" whenever an "individual final judgment is legislatively rescinded" or that it is "violated 40 times over when 40 final judgments are legislatively dissolved." . . .

. . . .

JUSTICE STEVENS, with whom JUSTICE GINSBURG joins, dissenting. [The dissenters cited many instances where legislation had restored to parties rights lost under prior final judgments. While the retroactivity of such laws was sometimes problematic, it had not previously been thought that there were additional separation-of-powers concerns. Furthermore, the dissenters argued that the separation of powers is not absolute, that there has always been some sharing of powers among the branches of government, and that the majority's view was unduly rigid in light of the difficulties that might arise in the government of a complex society.]

Notes and Questions

Do you agree with the majority opinion that the separation of powers doctrine is violated *whenever* Congress disturbs a final judgment? Does it make a difference whether the legislation is applied to some specific set of litigants or to the general population? Why? Should Congress be allowed to make exceptions for special circumstances? What sorts of special circumstances would warrant disturbing a final judgment? Should Congress have greater leeway in retroactively revising statutory or judge-made law than in attempting to undercut an interpretation of the Constitution?[12]

Further References

Ackerman, B., "The New Separation of Powers," 113 Harvard Law Review 633 (2000).

Baudenbacher, C., "Some Remarks on the Method of Civil Law," 34 Texas International Law Journal 333 (1999).

Bell, J., "Comparing Precedent," 82 Cornell Law Review 1243 (1997).

---

12. In City of Boerne v. Flores, 521 U.S. 507 (1997), the Court held that Congress lacks the power under the "enforcement clause" of section 5 of the Fourteenth Amendment to extend the religious liberty guaranteed against state action by the First and Fourteenth Amendments beyond that recognized by a previous judgment of the Court.

Chayes, A., "The Role of the Judge in Public Law Litigation," 89 Harvard Law Review 1281 (1976).

Dainow, J., "The Civil Law and the Common Law," 15 American Journal of Comparative Law 419 (1967).

Dennis, J.L., "Interpretation and Application of the Civil Code and the Evaluation of Judicial Precedent," 54 Louisiana Law Review 1 (1993).

Farnsworth, E.A., *An Introduction to the Legal System of the United States* (3d ed. 1996).

Friesen, J.L., "When Common Law Courts Interpret Civil Codes," 15 Wisconsin International Law Journal 1 (1996).

Henkin, L., *Foreign Affairs and the United States Constitution* (2d ed. 1996).

Jolowicz, H.F., "The Civil Law in Louisiana," 29 Tulane Law Review 491 (1955).

Kurland, P.B., "The Rise and Fall of the 'Doctrine' of Separation of Powers," 85 Michigan Law Review 592 (1986).

MacCormick, D.N., and Summers, R.S., ed., *Interpreting Precedents: A Comparative Study* (1997).

Merryman, J.H., *The Civil Law Tradition: An Introduction to the Legal Systems of Western Europe and Latin America* (2d ed. 1985).

Nourse, V., "Toward a 'Due Foundation' for the Separation of Powers: The Federalist Papers as Political Narrative," 74 Texas Law Review 447 (1996).

Paust, J.J., "Judicial Power to Determine the Status and Rights of Persons Detained Without Trial," 44 Harvard International Law Journal 503 (2003).

Stein, P., "The Development of Law in Classical and Early Medieval Europe: Interpretation and Legal Reasoning in Roman Law," 70 Chicago–Kent Law Review 1539 (1995).

Vanderbilt, A.T., *The Doctrine of the Separation of Powers and its Present-day Significance* (1953).

Zweigert, K., and Kötz, H., *An Introduction to Comparative Law* (3d ed. 1998).

Chapter II

COMMON LAW, EQUITY, AND THE DEVELOPMENT OF THE ANGLO– AMERICAN COURT SYSTEM

A. THE COMMON LAW COURTS AND THE WRIT SYSTEM

1. COMMON LAW COURTS

We learned in Chapter I that the common law is a system which had its roots in medieval England, was shaped in the courts of the English king, and was applied throughout the English realm. Its development as a distinct body of national law began during the reign of Henry II (1154–1189), who was successful in expanding the jurisdiction of the royal courts. Before his time, the bulk of the law was local customary law, which was administered in local or regional courts and in the private manorial courts of the feudal lords. Afterwards, three royal courts emerged. One of them, the Court of Exchequer, continued to exercise the jurisdiction of the earliest king's court over matters pertaining to the king's property and revenue. The other two competed with the local, regional and manorial courts: the Court of King's Bench asserted jurisdiction over criminal cases and civil actions involving a breach of the peace, while the Court of Common Pleas heard all other civil disputes. The following excerpt details the development of these three courts and describes the competition that ultimately arose between them for jurisdiction over civil actions.

A.W. SCOTT & R.B. KENT, CASES AND OTHER MATERIALS ON CIVIL PROCEDURE

pp. 26–32 (1967).[1]

A. THE EARLIER ENGLISH COURTS

In England there have always been local courts, which are inferior courts of limited jurisdiction. It is unnecessary to enumerate them. They

---

1. Reprinted by permission of the authors and publishers, Little, Brown & Co. (footnotes omitted). Copyright © 1967 by Austin W. Scott and Robert B. Kent.

included county courts, courts-baron, hundred courts, and others. Blackstone gives an account of them in the fourth chapter of his third book.

Of much greater importance are the royal courts, the superior courts of justice. The courts which prior to 1875 had come to have jurisdiction over actions at law were three in number, the Common Pleas, the King's Bench, and the Exchequer. In addition, there was the Court of Chancery, which had jurisdiction over suits in equity.

Common Pleas. The Court of Common Pleas, or Common Bench as it was sometimes called, was early established as a permanent court, with jurisdiction to determine controversies between the King's subjects. In Magna Carta (1215) it was provided that this court should not follow the King from place to place but should be held in some fixed place, and this place was established in Westminster Hall. The court had jurisdiction to hear and determine civil controversies. It was composed in Blackstone's day of four judges, the Chief Justice of the court and three puisne (pronounced *puny*) justices. It had jurisdiction of actions originally brought in the court and actions removed to the court from some of the local courts. It had jurisdiction over "common pleas," that is, controversies between individuals, as distinguished from "pleas of the crown," that is, criminal proceedings. Its jurisdiction over private controversies, however, was not exclusive, since, as we shall see, the Court of King's Bench had jurisdiction over some private controversies, and gradually assumed jurisdiction over other private controversies, as did also the Court of Exchequer. The Court of Common Pleas, however, always had exclusive jurisdiction of certain actions to recover land, known as real actions, until those actions were finally abolished in the nineteenth century.

King's Bench. The Court of King's Bench was established probably in the early part of the thirteenth century. It had jurisdiction over criminal cases. It also had jurisdiction over civil actions involving a breach of the peace. It had jurisdiction also over other actions brought against a person in the custody of the King's marshal of the Marshalsea Prison. It did not, however, have jurisdiction in the case of other civil actions, as, for example, an action of debt. By the use of a fiction it acquired such jurisdiction. If a plaintiff desired to sue a defendant for debt in the King's Bench he might first sue him for trespass, have him arrested and committed to the Marshalsea, and thereafter the court could entertain an action of debt against him. The proceeding would be begun, not by an original writ but by what was known as a "bill of Middlesex," a process directing the sheriff to arrest the defendant to answer a charge of trespass and also (ac etiam) of debt. The charge of trespass was a sufficient ground for arresting the defendant and committing him to the custody of the marshal, and the Court of King's Bench thus acquired jurisdiction to determine the question of the indebtedness of the prisoner. Since the court was anxious to extend its jurisdiction, it came to be held that it was not necessary that the defendant should be actually arrested; it was held that an allegation by the plaintiff that the defendant had been arrested was sufficient and the defendant would not be permitted to deny the allegation. Thus, the Court of King's Bench acquired concurrent jurisdiction over all kinds of civil controversies except real actions [(actions to recover the possession of real property)]. Later it came to be held that a proceeding in the court could be begun by an original writ as well as by a bill of Middlesex. The court was composed of four judges, the Chief Justice of England and three puisne justices.

Exchequer. The Court of Exchequer originally had jurisdiction over controversies affecting the King's property and his revenue. By an ingenious device the jurisdiction of this court was enlarged. If a plaintiff wished to bring an ordinary personal action against the defendant in the Court of Exchequer, he would allege that he, the plaintiff, was indebted to the King, and that the defendant had refused to discharge a liability to the plaintiff, whereby he is the less able (quo minus) to pay the King. The writ by which the proceeding was begun was known as a "writ of Quominus." Thus, the question of the royal revenues being involved, the Court had jurisdiction over the private controversy. This court, like other courts, was only too ready to extend its jurisdiction, and therefore it became unnecessary for the plaintiff to prove his allegation of his indebtedness to the King. It might seem to be a dangerous thing for a plaintiff to admit such an indebtedness if it did not in fact exist, but the King never appears to have taken advantage of the admission. Indeed, it came to be recognized that the allegation was purely fictitious and that its purpose was merely to confer jurisdiction upon the court over the private controversy. The court was composed of a Chief Baron of the Exchequer and three puisne barons.

Thus gradually it came about that the three superior courts of common law had concurrent jurisdiction over actions between subject and subject, except those actions relating to land which were known as real actions, as to which the Court of Common Pleas retained its exclusive jurisdiction until they were finally abolished. In ordinary personal actions, whether they involved tort or contract, the plaintiff might select any of the three courts as the tribunal to determine the litigation. From the point of view of logic and practical convenience it would seem better to have had a single tribunal, but the development of legal institutions is not governed altogether by logic or convenience. It is curious, also, to see how the whole matter was developed through the use of fictions; but fictions have played a great part in the development of the law, both on the procedural and on the substantive side. The notion that fictions are foolish at best and dishonest at worst is a comparatively modern and sophisticated notion and is by no means undebatable. It is fairly arguable that the employment of fictions has been an admirable device when properly used to improve the juridical system.

Exchequer Chamber. The judgment of one of these three courts did not necessarily end a case. It was possible by a writ of error to carry the case to a higher court. To do this it was necessary for the losing party to obtain from the Court of Chancery a writ of error. The party who lost in the court below became the "plaintiff in error," and the party who won in the court below became the "defendant in error." Originally the court of error from the Common Pleas was the Court of King's Bench, the court of error from the King's Bench was the House of Lords, and the court of error from the Court of Exchequer was the Court of Exchequer Chamber, composed at first of the Chancellor and the Treasurer, and later of the Chancellor alone, with the judges of the King's Bench and Common Pleas sitting as assessors. In the reign of Queen Elizabeth (1585) it was provided that a case could be carried from the Court of King's Bench to another Court of Exchequer Chamber, composed of the judges of the Common Pleas and Exchequer. Ultimately, in 1830, it was provided that from each of the three courts of original jurisdiction a case could be carried to a new Court of Exchequer Chamber, and the two older courts of that name were abolished. That court thus came to be composed of the judges of the three superior courts, but when a case was carried up from one of the courts the judges of the other two courts alone sat. From the Court of Exchequer Chamber the case could be carried to the House of Lords. Thus, there came to be an intermediate appellate court and a court of final appeal.

House of Lords. The House of Lords was the final appellate tribunal. Originally the theory seems to have been that Parliament, as the highest court of England, had power to correct errors in the judgments of any lower court, and that the Commons as well as the Lords were entitled to participate in the decision of cases in error. In practice, however, the appellate jurisdiction of Parliament came to be exercised by the Lords alone in the later Middle Ages. But for centuries appeals were dealt with by the House of Lords in the same manner as any other matters coming before the House. As late as 1783, judgments of the Common Pleas and King's Bench were reversed by a bare majority in a House composed almost entirely of bishops and lay peers. But it was finally established in 1844 that, as a convention of the English constitution, only the members of the House learned in the law are entitled to take part in the hearing of appeals. Accordingly the House of Lords, for judicial business, consisted of the Lord Chancellor, ex-Lord Chancellors, and other peers who held or had held high judicial office as chose to attend. In 1876 the House was increased by the creation of salaried peers for life, called Lords of Appeal in Ordinary, to assist the hereditary peers learned in the law.

The Nisi Prius system. The history of the development of the judicial system in England is the history of a contest between the King and the local authorities. Before the Norman Conquest there was a division of authority between the local tribunals on the one hand and the King and his council of advisers which was called the Witan on the other. After the Norman Conquest it became the purpose of the Kings to extend the limits of the royal justice and to limit the power of the local authorities. The purpose of the Kings was to establish a strong centralized government, and to carry out this purpose it was necessary to have strong central courts. If justice was to be administered by the royal courts, however, it was impracticable to compel suitors and witnesses to resort to the King's capital in order to obtain justice. England was much too large for that, particularly before the days of easy communication. How could the King have his centralized court and yet bring justice to every man's door? The problem was solved by the creation of courts which sat at the King's capital, at the same time sending the judges of those courts and others bearing the royal commission at intervals on circuit throughout the realm.

It is of great importance that the student should understand the method by which in England the administration of justice by the royal courts was brought to every man's door. Each of the three superior courts of common law, the King's Bench, the Common Pleas, and the Exchequer, sat as a court at Westminster. The year was divided into four terms, the Hilary Term, the Easter Term, the Trinity Term, and the Michaelmas Term. Each of these terms lasted for only a few weeks. During these terms each of the courts sat on the bench, in banc. Before the court thus sitting were brought for its determination all questions arising in the course of an action, except such as arose at the trial. Thus, the full bench sitting at Westminster in term time determined questions as to the legal sufficiency of the pleadings, such as those which arose on a demurrer. The full bench of the court would also determine questions arising after the trial. It was the full bench which gave judgment on the verdict. It was to the full bench that the party against whom a verdict was given might apply for a new trial. The party against whom the verdict had been given might also make a motion before the full court in arrest of judgment, on the ground that the pleadings of the opposite party were insufficient in law, or he might move for judgment notwithstanding the verdict.

As we have seen, each of the three superior courts of common law sat at Westminster only during four comparatively brief periods during the year. Between these terms of court there were periods of vacation. It was during the vacations that the trials of issues of fact arising in these courts were held. Except in a few cases where the trial was held before the full bench at Westminster in term time, the trials would be held before one or two judges in the various towns in England. For the purpose of conducting the trials, the judges of the superior courts and others commissioned by the King for the purpose would go on circuit. It was the function of the judges on circuit to try the issues of fact raised by the proceedings taken at Westminster.

2. MODES OF TRIAL

One reason for the growing popularity of the royal courts was the fact that they used trial by jury in an ever-increasing number of cases. By contrast, the chief modes of trial used in the early period of English law were wager of law (compurgation), battle, and the ordeal. Wager of law will be described later, in section B.2(e) of this chapter. Battle was a combat or duel between the plaintiff and the defendant, in which the defeated party lost the case. The ordeal (used primarily in criminal cases in the early Middle Ages) was an appeal to the Deity to show by a sign or miracle who was guilty and who was innocent. The accused had to perform a task imposed upon him by the judges. If he performed it to their satisfaction, it was assumed that God was on his side, and that he was innocent. In the ordeal by fire, for example, the accused had to carry a piece of hot iron in his hand for a number of steps, or he was required to pick a stone out of boiling water. After the wound was inflicted, a priest bound up the injured hand or arm. If it healed cleanly after three days, the person in question was deemed innocent. If there was a blister as large as half a walnut or more, he was convicted.

In the course of time, these older modes of trial were supplanted by trial by jury. But it should be noted that the function of the jury during the formative period of the common law differed from that of the jury in our time. Today, the jurors hear the evidence in a trial, listen to the witnesses, look at the documents, and then decide questions of fact on the basis of the evidence. They are supposed to be impartial people who come into court with an open mind. Personal knowledge of the case is grounds for disqualification. The jurors in medieval England, on the other hand, were primarily witnesses who were called in order to tell what they knew about a case. They were a body of neighbors summoned by the king's officials (not only by judges) to give answers to questions under oath. Hence, in its origins, the jury system was less a bulwark of popular liberties than an exercise of the royal prerogative. It was a device used by a strong king to collect information from anyone he pleased in his kingdom.

Henry II introduced jury trial into civil litigation, especially to determine questions of ownership and possession of land. The jurors were usually neighbors of the litigants who were well acquainted with the facts underlying the controversy. If they lacked the requisite knowledge, they were sometimes sent back to the local community to obtain additional information. Unlike the earliest jurors, they were used not only as witnesses but also as judges of the facts who decided whether the plaintiff or the defendant had the better right.

3. THE WRIT SYSTEM

When a litigant wanted a royal court to take jurisdiction of a case, he asked the king (or more precisely, the king's chancellor) to issue a writ. The chancellor was an ecclesiastic. He kept the king's great seal and supervised a staff of clerks who prepared all the documents that were issued in the name of the king. The following excerpts describe and illustrate the common law writ system.

W.P. BLACKSTONE, COMMENTARIES ON THE LAWS OF ENGLAND
Ed. by W.D. Lewis, Book 3, pp. 272–273 (1765).

First, then of the original, or original writ: which is the beginning or foundation of the suit. When a person hath received an injury, and thinks it worth his while to demand a satisfaction for it, he is to consider with himself, or take advice, what redress the law has given for that injury, and thereupon is to make application or suit to the crown, the fountain of all justice, for that particular specific remedy which he is determined or advised to pursue.... To this end he is to sue out, or purchase by paying the stated fees, an original, or original writ, from the court of chancery, which is the *officina justitiae,* the shop or mint of justice, wherein all the king's writs are framed. It is a mandatory letter from the king, in parchment, sealed with his great seal, and directed to the sheriff of the county wherein the injury is committed, or supposed so to be, requiring him to command the wrong-doer or party accused either to do justice to the complainant or else to appear in court and answer the accusation against him. Whatever the sheriff does in pursuance of this writ, he must return or certify to the court of common pleas, together with the writ itself; which is the foundation of the jurisdiction of that court, being the king's warrant for the judges to proceed to the determination of the cause. For it was a maxim introduced by the Normans, that there should be no proceedings in common pleas before the king's justices without his original writ; because they held it unfit that those justices, being only the substitutes of the crown, should take cognizance of anything but what was thus expressly referred to their judgment.

EXAMPLES OF EARLY WRITS

R. POUND & T. PLUCKNETT, READINGS ON THE HISTORY AND SYSTEM OF THE COMMON LAW

pp. 62–63 (1927).

(1) William King of England to the Abbot of Peterborough, Greeting: I command and require you that you permit the Abbot of St. Edmund to receive sufficient stone for his church, as he has had hitherto, and that you cause him no more hindrance in drawing stone to the water, as you have heretofore done. Witness the Bishop of Durham (c. 1070–1080 A.D.).

(2) Henry, King of England, to Nigel of Oilly and William Sheriff of Oxford, Greeting: I command you that you do full right to the Abbot of Abingdon concerning his sluice which the men of Stanton broke, and so that I hear no more complaint thereof for defect of right, and this under penalty of ten pounds. Witness Ralph the Chancellor, at Westminster (c. 1105–1107 A.D.).

(3) Henry King of England to Jordan de Sackville, Greeting: I command you to do full right to Abbot Faritius and the church of Abingdon concerning the land which you took from them, which Ralph of Cainesham gave to the church in alms; and unless you do this without delay, I command that Walter Giffard do it, and if he shall not have done it, that Hugh of Bocheland do it, that I may hear no complaint thereof

for defect of right. Witness, Goisfrid of Magnavill, at Woodstock (c. 1108 A.D.).

(4) The King to the Sheriff, Health. Command A that, without delay, he render to B one hyde of land, in such a vill, of which the said B complains that the aforesaid A hath deforced him; and unless he does so, summon him by good summoners, that he be there, before me or my Justices ... to show wherefore he has failed; and have there the summoners and this writ (c. 1187–1189 A.D.).

Note that these writs were, either wholly or in part, executive orders issued by the King. They were not, or at least not in the first place, devices for instituting litigation. The first writ is simply an order commanding a certain person to do a certain act and refrain from doing another act. The second writ moves a little closer to the use of judicial rather than executive power by setting a fine in case of non-compliance with the King's command. The third writ shows that the King, instead of decreeing a penalty, could simply order that the act be done by a third person. This delegation of power to enforce the law was a precursor of injunctive relief. The fourth writ initiates litigation before royal judges, but only as an alternative to compliance with the King's command to A, transmitted by the sheriff, to give up a piece of land.

At the end of the twelfth century, a new form of writ made its appearance. It did not begin with a demand for restitution, but simply contained an order to the sheriff, combined with a brief statement of the essential facts, that he should summon the defendant to come before the royal court and show why he had done a particular act. This later form of writ tended to become the prevailing form used to institute proceedings in the royal courts.

Such writs had to be obtained from the King's Chancery. They were called "original writs" to distinguish them from writs issued by a court of law during a judicial proceeding.[2]

In its beginning, the original writ was a special license from the King to litigate in the King's court some controversy which would otherwise be litigated in a local or manorial court. It was evidence of an exceptional privilege, a mark of royal favor. Such a writ, since it contained a special permission for one case only, was executive in nature.

But writs soon ceased to be mere favors. They became transformed into writs *de cursu,* routine writs issued as a matter of course. Royal justice was placed at the disposal of anyone who could bring his case within a formula found in one of the existing writs.

---

2. Blackstone, in the excerpts set forth above, states that the original writs were issued by the "court of chancery." The judicial "court" of this name did not come into existence until 1474, i.e., several centuries after the practice of issuing original writs had begun. Blackstone means by the "court of chancery" to refer to the offices of the clerks of the King's Chancellor. The chancery clerks issued original writs not in a judicial capacity but in the form of a "mandatory letter from the King," as Blackstone puts it.

Writs *de cursu* were entered into a Register of Writs kept in the Chancery. If a person found himself aggrieved by the action of another, his lawyer went to the Chancery and examined the Register. If he found a writ fitting the facts of his case, he asked that it be issued to him upon payment of a fee. If none fitted his case, he was without a remedy unless the Chancellor was willing to make a new writ for him.

Whether or not the Chancellor was willing to extend the scope of royal jurisdiction by granting new writs in novel situations depended very much upon whether or not the king whom he served was a strong or a weak king. The feudal lords of England viewed the writ-making power of the Crown with grave suspicion. Every new writ tended to enlarge the jurisdiction of the royal courts at the expense of the private courts of the lords. Hence, the lords had an interest in keeping down the number of writs by which litigation could be instituted in the courts of the king.

Henry II was a strong king able to stand his ground against the pressures of the feudal aristocracy. Under his reign, many new writs were issued, and the common law grew by leaps and bounds. After his death, however, the Crown suffered a number of setbacks and defeats in its attempt to build up a royal justice for the entire country. Under Henry III, a weak king, the King's Council (the predecessor of Parliament) enacted the Provisions of Oxford in 1258, which laid it down that the Chancellor should seal no writs except the existing ones without the sanction of the King and his Council. This enactment secured the control of the King's Council, consisting mostly of feudal dignitaries, over the issuance of new writs and crippled the writ-making power of the Chancery.

In 1285, under the rule of a strong king, Edward I, a part of the writ-making power was restored to the Chancery by virtue of the Statute Westminster II, set forth below. The Chancery was authorized to issue writs in cases similar to those covered by a pre-existing writ. True innovations in writ-making, however, were reserved to Parliament.

STATUTE WESTMINSTER II
13 Edw. I, c. 24 (1285).

Whenever henceforth it shall happen in the Chancery that in one case a writ is found and in a like case falling under the same law and requiring a like remedy no writ is found, then the clerks of the Chancery shall agree in making the writ, or they may adjourn the plaintiffs until the next parliament, and let them write the cases in which they cannot agree and refer them to the next parliament, and let the writ be made with the consent of the wise men of the law; and from henceforth, let it not happen that the court any longer fail complainants seeking justice.

Notes and Questions

(1) F.W. Maitland, a distinguished English legal historian, has stated that "the granting of a newly worded writ was no judicial act." 2 *Collected Papers* 123 (1911). Consider that under the Statute of Westminster II the clerks of the Chancery were authorized to present writs similar to existing writs to Parliament for approval. You may also have noted that entirely new writs, according to the Provisions of Oxford, required the sanction of the King and his Council (the predecessor of Parliament). At an earlier time, the Chancellor issued original writs as a representative of the King, who at that time possessed legislative, executive, and judicial powers. Could it be argued that the evolution of the common law forms of actions occurred by a procedure akin to legislation?

(2) Can you see some good reason why, according to the historical record, hardly any legal system has left the making of new law entirely to its judges?

B.   THE FORMS OF ACTION AT COMMON LAW

1.   INTRODUCTION

The "forms of action" at common law were part and parcel of the writ system. There were many different writs, and each writ embodied one particular form of action. If the name of a writ is likened to the title of a song, the related form of action functioned as the writ's words and music. The forms of action seem arcane in retrospect due to the subtle differences between the tunes and the unique procedural dance that became associated with each. As writs proliferated and came to serve somewhat overlapping purposes, it became easy for unwary counsel to call the wrong tune for a particular occasion, or to make a procedural misstep that halted the litigation in its tracks.

Blackstone points out in the excerpt set forth in Section A that the writs were returned by the sheriff to the Court of Common Pleas, which was the chief court of civil jurisdiction. But when the other two courts of the common law also acquired some measure of civil jurisdiction, the system of original writs was extended to them. Each writ stated briefly the substance of the plaintiff's claim. For each writ there was a particular mode of pleading and a particular type of judgment. The plaintiff's choice of a writ was irrevocable. In the words of F.W. Maitland, "he must play the rules of the game he has chosen." The plaintiff had to identify his action as one in trespass or trover. If he chose an inappropriate writ, he lost the case and had to start all over again by purchasing a different kind of writ.

The forms of action were abolished in England and the United States in the second half of the nineteenth century. Section 307 of the California Code of Civil Procedure provides: "There is in this state but one form of civil action for the enforcement or protection of private rights and the redress or prevention of private wrongs." Identical or similar provisions are found in the codes of virtually all states. The wording of the provision seems to suggest that the multitude of actions at the common law (and, for that matter, in equity) has given way to the creation of one unitary form of action.

If this is a correct description of the present state of the law, that is, if the forms of action actually have been abolished completely, why should it be necessary to engage in any further study of them? The answer to this question is hinted at in the following statement by the English legal historian, Maitland: "The forms of action we have buried, but they rule us from their graves." What did Maitland mean by this statement?

He meant that the statutes declaring that henceforth there shall be one form of action only refer to form rather than substance. Today, in order to obtain relief in trespass or trover, it is no longer necessary for the plaintiff to label his action correctly, to obtain a writ describing the essential elements of the action, and to go through a special system of pleading appropriate to the form of action chosen. If the plaintiff's attorney makes a mistake in describing the action as one of detinue, while in fact it is one of trespass, he may prevail in the suit in spite of the mislabeling. But he will prevail only if the substance of his contentions establishes a good case in trespass. As the California Supreme Court pointed out in Philpott v. Superior Court, 1 Cal.2d 512, 515, 36 P.2d 635, 636–637 (1934), the legislature's abolishing the *forms* of action did not mean to destroy the essential characteristics of the common law actions, that is, of the rights people had to legal relief from the common law courts of England. In a similar vein, the New York Court of Appeals in Goulet v. Asseler, 22 N.Y. 225, 228, 78 Am. Dec. 186 (1860) made the following observations: "Although the Code has abolished all distinctions between the mere forms of action, ... yet actions vary in their nature, and there are intrinsic differences between them which no law can abolish.... The mere formal differences between such actions are abolished. The substantial differences remain as before...." The statements made by these two courts are representative of the position taken by courts throughout the United States.

The truth is that the whole substance of the common law was shaped and molded by the forms of action. Their abolition did not, as such, create any new rights or remedies. Hence, as a general rule, a common law action can be maintained only in those cases where some kind of action was available under the old system. Only in a limited number of situations has the modern law provided new remedies or enlarged the scope of old ones. In light of these facts, it may be said that the forms of action at common law constitute the genetic material out of which most of the modern law has evolved. Only by digging among the fossils of the forms of action can one gain a full understanding of the strange bends and fractures in the skeleton of the common law today.

The survey of the most important forms of action at common law which follows is quite concise and general. The beginning student will learn more about common law actions in his or her courses in Torts, Contracts, and Property.

2. A SUMMARY OF THE CHIEF FORMS OF ACTION AT COMMON LAW

(a) Replevin

This action had its roots in the ancient remedy of distress, and for several hundred years it was used for no other purpose than to restore to the owner chattels that had been wrongfully distrained. Distress was used in medieval England by feudal lords to enforce the feudal services owed to them by their tenants. If the tenant defaulted in his services, or if he failed to pay his rent when due, the lord could seize his cattle or other personal goods without a court order and keep them until the tenant performed.

The purpose of replevin was to restore to the tenant chattels that had been unlawfully distrained. If the tenant wished to challenge the seizure, he would obtain a writ of replevin which would direct the sheriff to locate the chattels and redeliver them to the plaintiff before the action was tried. The plaintiff was required, however, to give bond or security for the return of the chattels if the decision should be for the defendant. This unusual procedure had its reason in the fact that the goods distrained by the landlord usually consisted of cattle or agricultural tools which were indispensable to the husbandry of the tenant, that is, his ability to run his farm and feed his family.

In the course of time, the action was extended to cover all cases of unlawful taking of chattels. If the chattel itself could not be recovered, its value could be obtained. It also became possible for the defendant, upon giving a counter-bond, to keep possession of the chattel during the litigation.

(b) Detinue

Originally, this action was limited to cases of bailment. Where a person had delivered goods to another to keep them for him, and the bailee refused to return the goods at the termination of the bailment, the bailor could bring detinue. The action was gradually extended to any case of unlawful detention of a chattel, no matter how the defendant had obtained possession. As a result of this development, detinue became an alternative to replevin in those cases in which the defendant had taken a chattel unlawfully from the plaintiff and later refused to return it to the plaintiff.

The judgment in detinue was that the plaintiff recover the chattel or its value, at the option of the defendant. Thus, the defendant in detinue could not be forced to give up the chattel itself, if he refused to surrender it. Damages could be recovered for the injury suffered by plaintiff because of the unlawful withholding.

(c) Debt

Debt was an action for the recovery of a specific sum of money. The amount to be recovered had to be fixed and certain, that is, the exact amount of the debt had to be stated in the complaint.

The action split off into four varieties: (1) Debt on a Record was brought to recover money due on a judgment of a domestic court of record. A court of record is one whose acts and proceedings are recorded, and which has the power to fine or imprison for contempt. (2) Debt on a Statute lay where the plaintiff was seeking to recover a definite sum due from the defendant as a penalty or forfeiture under a statute. The action could not be used when the statute provided for unliquidated (i.e., undetermined) damages rather than a fixed sum. (3) Debt on a Specialty could be used where the defendant had promised in a document under seal to pay a sum certain. (4) Debt on a Simple Contract was available to enforce a defendant's unsealed promise to pay a sum of money, provided that the *quid pro quo* (consideration) promised by the plaintiff (such as goods or services) had already been received by the defendant. The action could also be used to recover on an obligation imposed upon the defendant by law, other than statute or record, to pay a liquidated sum, as, for example, on a foreign judgment, or on a judgment of a domestic court not of record, or for money received and kept by defendant under such circumstances that the law imposed a duty on him to pay it over to the plaintiff.

For many centuries, the requirement that the amount sued upon must be a sum certain was rigidly interpreted by the courts. As Ames points out, "if [plaintiff] demanded a debt of 20 pounds and proved a debt of 19 pounds, he failed as effectually as if he had declared in detinue for the recovery of a horse and could prove only the detention of a cow." In the course of the nineteenth century, the requirement was gradually relaxed in England as well as in the United States.

(d) Covenant

The province of covenant was the recovery of damages due for the breach of a sealed contract, whether the damages were liquidated or unliquidated. When the damages were liquidated upon breach of a sealed instrument, debt and covenant were concurrent remedies. When the damages were unliquidated, covenant was the only common law remedy. (Later, special assumpsit developed as a remedy for the recovery of unliquidated damages for breach of an unsealed contract.)

(e) Trespass

The term "trespass" is a translation of the Latin word *transgressio,* and it denotes an act which transcends, or passes beyond, the bounds of legal right and invades the rights of another person. The action of trespass is in its nature a tort, or an action *"ex delicto,"* arising from an act made wrongful by law, as opposed to an action on a contract, or *"ex contractu,"* arising from an act made wrongful only by agreement.

The writ of trespass came into use in the thirteenth century. The writ averred that defendant's act had been committed *vi et armis et contra pacem Domini Regis*—with force and arms and against the peace of the Lord King. The requirement of a forcible act was the cause of the rule that a plaintiff, in order to prevail in trespass, had to show a direct and immediate injury. An indirect injury was not actionable in trespass.

There were three major subdivisions of the action of trespass. Trespass to the person lay when the defendant had committed an act of battery, assault, or false imprisonment against the plaintiff. Trespass *de bonis asportatis* involved the carrying away, destruction, or damaging by the defendant of a chattel in plaintiff's possession, or to the possession of which the plaintiff was immediately entitled. Trespass *quare clausum fregit* allowed recovery for an unlawful intrusion upon plaintiff's land. Relief in trespass was limited to damages.

Trial in trespass was by jury, which made the action very popular. In some of the other common law actions, such as debt and detinue, the defendant could wage his law, that is, swear that he was innocent of the charge and win the case by having twelve oath-helpers (compurgators) confirm the truthfulness of his oath. This mode of trial was obviously very unsatisfactory from the point of view of the plaintiff, but it was not abolished in England until 1833.

(f) Trespass on the Case

It has been pointed out that trespass could be maintained only for harms to persons or property that were directly and immediately caused by a forcible act of the defendant (although insistence on the use of force decreased as time went on). Trespass could not be maintained for indirect or consequential injuries. If the defendant threw a log at the plaintiff traveling on the highway, trespass would lie. If he wrongfully left a log on the highway and the plaintiff stumbled over it, the defendant was not responsible in trespass.

In the course of time—probably by virtue of the authorization to grant "similar writs" contained in the Statute of Westminster II—a form of action developed which was designed to give redress for indirect and consequential injuries to the person, goods, or land of the plaintiff. This action was called "trespass on the case," or simply "case." It lay for various kinds of negligent acts, for the commission of a nuisance, for malicious prosecution, fraud and deceit, libel and slander. It also became the remedy for injuries to non-possessory interests in property, such as easements. Trial in trespass on the case was by jury.

One difference between trespass and case—which has survived into the modern common law of torts—was that nominal damages were deemed proper in simple trespass, so that the action could be used for the sole purpose of vindicating a right. Actual, material damages had to be proved in trespass on the case.

(g) Trover

Trover began its career as a subdivision of trespass on the case, but it gradually developed into an independent action. Originally it lay only where the plaintiff had lost a chattel and the defendant had found it and converted it to his own use. Subsequently, the scope of the action was enlarged so as to cover any act constituting a conversion, that is, unlawful appropriation of plaintiff's chattel by the defendant.

Trover became more or less concurrent with detinue, but it was more popular than detinue because the plaintiff in trover had a right to a jury trial. Moreover, by suing in trover the plaintiff rather than the defendant could exercise the option of leaving the defendant in possession and recovering the full value of the chattel at the time of the defendant's conversion (essentially a forced judicial sale to the defendant) as well as additional damages, if any, caused by defendant's wrongful taking.[3]

(h) Special Assumpsit

The action of assumpsit was originally a subdivision of trespass on the case. It split off from case and became a separate action about 1500. It assumed two distinct forms, "special assumpsit" and "general assumpsit." Trial for both forms of assumpsit was by jury.

Special assumpsit lay against persons engaged in a particular calling who had undertaken (assumpsit) to do certain work for the plaintiff and had performed it so unskillfully as to cause a loss to the plaintiff. The earliest cases of assumpsit were suits against surgeons who had undertaken to cure the plaintiff but had treated him inexpertly; against contractors who had agreed to build well but built unskillfully so that the house collapsed; and against barbers who had undertaken to shave the plaintiff with a clean razor but had used a dirty one which caused an infection.

In these cases, the plaintiff sought to recover damages for a physical injury to his person or property attributable to the active misconduct of the defendant. The breach of promise by the defendant was merely incidental. The action thus sounded in tort rather than contract. (This situation is consistent with the finding of legal anthropologists that tort actions have been a regular feature of legal orders from their early beginnings, while contracts play a subordinate role in the legal systems of pre-commercial civilizations.)

While special assumpsit originally required a misfeasance on the part of the defendant, it was later extended to cases of mere nonfeasance. Thus, when the defendant agreed to build a house for the plaintiff and failed to live up to his promise, he would be held liable in damages.

---

3. In most jurisdictions the right to sue for conversion is the modern equivalent of trover. In a modern conversion action the plaintiff ordinarily is entitled to the full value of the chattel at the time of the conversion plus prejudgment interest, in which case the owner relinquishes title and in effect forces the judicial sale of the chattel to the defendant.

Special assumpsit would also lie for a breach of contract to sell goods, for failure to pay the purchase price for goods, and for failure to pay compensation for the performance of services. This development, which coincided with the rise of a commercial class in England, turned special assumpsit into the most important action for breach of contract. The plaintiff in assumpsit could not, however, enforce compliance with the terms of the contract, such as performance of the promise to build a house; he could only claim damages for nonperformance or faulty performance. Furthermore, special assumpsit was restricted to the breach of unsealed promises.

(i) General Assumpsit

General assumpsit originated in the seventeenth century and became an action for the enforcement of promises implied in fact and promises implied in law, as distinguished from express promises. A promise implied in fact arose out of a transaction which had not been reduced to the form of a distinct bargain. Examples were services rendered by a tailor or innkeeper or common carrier without any specific agreement as to the amount of compensation. For many centuries, there was no action by which a reasonable compensation could be recovered. When general assumpsit became available in these types of cases, it appeared in two varieties: (a) *quantum meruit* ("as much as he deserved"), an action by which reasonable compensation for services could be recovered if the services were rendered under circumstances in which a remuneration was to be normally expected; (2) *quantum valebant* ("as much as they are worth"), an action by which, in the absence of a specific agreement to the price, the reasonable value of goods sold to the defendant could be recovered.

Having taken the step of implying promises in fact and enforcing them, the courts went one step further. They also implied promises "in law." For example, if the defendant, by mistake, received a payment intended for the plaintiff, he was held responsible to the plaintiff under an implied promise to pay over the money erroneously received. Here the promise was purely fictitious, since there was no agreement between the parties, and the courts used the term "quasi-contract" for the purpose of classifying the promise. General assumpsit in this area developed into an action for the recovery of money or other property in situations where the defendant was deemed unjustly enriched at the expense of the plaintiff.

General assumpsit was also allowed as an alternative to the action of debt, for the purpose of collecting a simple contract debt resulting from an unsealed contract. The reason was that trial by jury was the exclusive mode of trial in general assumpsit, while the defendant could wage his law in an action of debt. This variety of the action was called *indebitatus assumpsit*. If a contract had been fully executed by the plaintiff and nothing remained to be done but the payment of the price for goods or services by the defendant, the plaintiff could declare either in special assumpsit on the express contract or in general assumpsit on an implied (fictitious) promise to pay.

(j) Real Actions and Ejectment

At the early common law, a person who claimed a freehold interest in land, such as an estate in fee simple (full ownership and disposition) or an estate for life, could bring one of the real actions (writ of right, assize of novel disseizin, writ of entry) in order to vindicate his right and title against an intruder. These actions, which fell into disuse at a relatively early period of time, were called "real actions" because the plaintiff, if successful, recovered the "res" or thing itself for which suit was brought rather than damages. A lessee for years was not considered to have a freehold interest in land, and therefore he could not use the real actions if he was ousted from the land during the term.

In the thirteenth century, certain writs were invented to enable a lessee for years to recover the possession of land. These writs developed out of the writ for trespass on the case and eventually became merged in the action of ejectment.

The action of ejectment could be maintained to recover a leasehold interest, but not to recover a freehold interest. But this limitation—inasmuch as ejectment soon proved to be an expeditious and popular action triable by jury—was circumvented by the invention of certain fictions. The history of ejectment is in fact the history of fictions used for the purpose of making the action available to *any* holder of land—whether freeholder or leaseholder—who had been ousted from the possession of land. The courts of King's Bench and Exchequer were particularly eager to wink at the use of sham devices to circumvent the limitations of ejectment, since the real actions were the monopoly of the Court of Common Pleas and the other two courts were anxious to expand their jurisdiction at the expense of Common Pleas. However, the latter court, too, used the fictions, its judges feeling perhaps that an open and above-board extension of the action was not within the judicial function.

In order to make the action available to a freeholder it was necessary for the freeholder to create a lease for years. Hence, when A claimed a freehold interest in land in the possession of B, A first had to execute a lease to X. X then went on the land and made himself comfortable on it until he was ejected. If he was not ejected, the courts said that if he was "spied" by the occupant, this should be deemed a disturbance of his peaceful possession equivalent to an ouster. After X had been ejected (or "spied"), X maintained an action against B. If he recovered possession of the land, he handed it over to A, the real party in interest.

After a while, the courts developed yet another fiction. A proceeded as before, that is, he delivered a lease to X, who then went on the land. Then A immediately procured a second friend, Y, who also went upon the land and ousted X. This second friend was called the "casual ejector." X would then sue Y for recovery of possession. Of course, it would be unfair to allow recovery without notice to the actual occupant, B, so the courts refused to give judgment unless B was given an opportunity to defend his possession.

The action of ejectment continued in this condition for several centuries. Then, between 1650 and 1660, Chief Justice Rolle of the Common Pleas hit upon an ingenious idea. Why was it necessary to insist that X and Y be men of flesh and blood? Why couldn't they be converted into figments of the imagination? This idea was adopted. The two friends of the person ousted became fictitious persons called John Doe and Richard Roe, or John Goodtitle and Richard Shamtitle. The action was purported to be brought by Doe, who was alleged to be a tenant of the real party in interest, A. It was brought against Roe, who was alleged to have ousted Doe. Attached to the declaration was a letter by Roe to B, the person in possession, notifying B that he could come in and defend the action, inasmuch as Roe had no intention of doing so. The courts would permit B to defend the action only if he entered into the so-called "consent rule," that is, if he admitted the fictitious lease, entry, and ouster in writing. The declaration was then changed making him the real defendant. This sham procedure was used in England and the United States until the latter half of the nineteenth century.

Problems

In the following cases, A sued B at a time when the common law forms of action were still in effect. What action or actions could be maintained by A?

(1) B used a steamroller for repairs on a highway. After working hours, he parked it at the side of the highway, but part of it protruded into the driving lane. In the dark of a foggy night, A drove his automobile into the steamroller and was severely injured.

(2) B entered A's land without A's permission and appropriated some timber stacked up on the land. A made a demand for the return of the timber, but B refused to comply with the demand.

(3) A and B made a contract not under seal by which A was to sell and deliver a horse to B for a price of $100. A delivered the horse and B accepted delivery, but B refused to pay for it.

(4) A entered into a written contract under seal with B, whereby B promised to install a steam boiler in the basement of A's house for a stated compensation. B failed to install the steam boiler.

(5) A loaned an expensive watch to B for a few days. B dropped the watch and damaged it. He returned the watch, but refused to pay for the repair.

(6) A owns Blackacre. B ousts A under a claim of title and takes possession of Blackacre.

(7) A purchases an apartment building from B. C, one of the tenants, mistakenly sends a current rent payment of $500 to B, the

former owner. B refuses to return the money to C or to turn it over to A, and C, lacking other funds, is in breach of the lease.

3. ILLUSTRATIVE CASES

The following case demonstrates the common law writ of trespass to the person.

GUY v. LIVESEY

Court of King's Bench, 1619.
79 Eng. Rep. 428.

Trespass of assault and battery; for that the defendant did assault, beat, and wound the plaintiff; *necnon* for that he assaulted and beat the wife of the plaintiff, *per quod consortium uxoris suoe* for three days *amisit*. The defendant pleaded not guilty; and it was found against him in both, and damages assessed to eighty pounds (it being in truth a great battery to the husband); and the damages given, for that the plaintiff's wife went with the defendant and lived with him in a suspicious manner. And it was now moved in arrest of judgment, that the husband ought not to join the battery of his wife with the battery which was done to himself; and he cannot have an action for the battery of his wife, but ought to join his wife with him in the action; for the damage done to the wife, she ought to have (if she survive her husband); and so the defendant may be twice punished for one and the same battery, if the plaintiff here should recover; for this recovery of the husband shall not bar her of bringing her action, if she survive him. Wherefore if the husband will bring the action, he ought to have joined his wife with him.

But all the Court held, that the action was well brought; for the action is not brought in respect of the harm done to the wife, but it is brought for the particular loss of the husband, for that he lost the company of his wife, which is only a damage and loss to himself, for which he shall have this action, as the master shall have for the loss of his servant's service. And a precedent was shewn in 28 Eliz. in this Court, where one Cholmley brought an action for the battery of his wife, *per quod negotia sua infecta remanserunt*; and had judgment to recover. And another precedent was cited to be in the Exchequer in *Doyley's case*, that such an action was adjudged good.—Wherefore it was adjudged here that the plaintiff should recover.

(handwritten margin notes: "and also" / "whereby the husband lost the consortium of his wife for three days" / "because her affairs remain undone")

Notes and Questions

(1) In the 1600's, English courts took the position that, when a man and a woman married, they became one, and "the one" was "the husband." The wife could recover damages in a tort action only if her husband were willing to file a claim on her behalf. In *Guy v. Livesey*, the husband sued for his own personal injuries as a direct tort victim, but he did not file a claim to recover damages on behalf of his wife as a direct tort victim. The court, of course, was careful to note that, if the wife

were to outlive her husband, she could sue the defendant in her own name as a direct tort victim at a later point in time. Today, both wives and husbands having standing to sue as direct tort victims.

(2) The husband in *Guy* also sued *"per quod consortium uxoris suoe,"* meaning literally that he sued as an indirect tort victim for the loss of consortium of his wife. Under English common law, husbands (but not wives) were allowed to recover for loss of consortium, which encompassed the loss of services, emotional support, and sexual relations that a wife had provided to her husband prior to the time of the tort. Today, by contrast, either spouse can recover for loss of the other's consortium.

(3) In *Guy*, was the husband suing for the indirectly inflicted "loss of consortium" that was caused when the defendant assaulted and beat his wife, or for the directly-inflicted "alienation of affections" that was caused when the defendant took her away to live with him for three days "in a suspicious manner," or both?

(4) Contrast *Guy* with the following case.

HIGGINS v. BUTCHER

Court of King's Bench, 1606.
80 Eng. Rep. 61.

The plaintiff declar'd that the defendant assaulted and beat, . . . his wife such a day, of which she died such a day following; to his damage, ... And it was moved by Foster Serjeant, that the declaration was not good; because it was brought by the plaintiff for beating his wife: and that being a personal tort to the wife, is now dead with the wife: and if the wife had been alive, he could not without his wife have this action; for damages shall be given to the wife for the tort offer'd to the body of his wife. *Quod fuit concessum*: and by Tanfield Justice, if a man beats the servant of J. S. so that he dies of that battery, the master shall not have an action against the other for the battery and loss of the service, because the servant dying of the extremity of the battery, it is now become an offence to the Crown, being converted into felony, and that drowns the particular offence, and private wrong offer'd to the master before, and his action is thereby lost: *quod* Fenner and Yelverton *concesserunt.*

which was granted

Justices Fenner + Yelverton concure

Notes and Questions

(1) In *Higgins* the husband was suing for the death of his wife, and he was not allowed to recover. Insofar as he was suing on behalf of his wife's estate in the form of a survival action, he was barred by the ancient common law rule that a personal cause of action in tort did not survive the death of the possessor. This rule was known as "the rule of abatement." Insofar as he was suing in his own behalf for the loss of his wife's services, sex, society and companionship, he was barred by another ancient common law rule called "the felony-merger doctrine." Accord-

ing to this doctrine, the common law did not allow a civil recovery for an act that constituted both a tort and a felony. Rather, the civil wrong was drowned in the felony. When the felon was convicted, the punishment was death to the felon and forfeiture of the felon's property to the Crown. Thus, after the criminal punishment had been imposed, nothing remained of either the felon or the felon's property on which to base a civil action. Since all homicides were felonious, the common law did not recognize a suit for wrongful death.

(2) Under modern law, the old English rules described in Note 1 have been replaced by legislation known as "survival statutes" and "wrongful death statutes." The former give a cause of action to the representative of the estate of a deceased for the harm suffered by the deceased between the time of the tort and the time of the death. The latter give a cause of action to the members of the deceased's immediate family for their post-death loss of financial support, loss of services, and loss of society and companionship.

C.   EQUITABLE JURISDICTION AND THE COURT OF CHANCERY

1.   EQUITY AND JUSTICE

The system of equity originated in the late Middle Ages as a rival of the common law. The chief agency responsible for its development was the Court of Chancery. The first two excerpts expound the notion of equity, as interpreted by Aristotle and a famous English barrister of the sixteenth century. The note which follows deals with the development, functions, and jurisdiction of the Court of Chancery.

ARISTOTLE, THE NICOMACHEAN ETHICS

Trans. by H. Rackham (Everyman's Library ed., 1947), pp. 313–317.

We have next to speak of Equity and the equitable, and of their relation to Justice and to what is just respectively. For upon examination it appears that Justice and Equity are neither absolutely identical nor generically different. Sometimes, it is true, we praise equity and the equitable man, so much so that we even apply the word equitable as a term of approval to other things besides what is just, and use it as the equivalent of "good," denoting by "more equitable" merely that a thing is better. Yet at other times, when we think the matter out, it seems strange that the equitable should be praiseworthy if it is something other than the just. . . .

These then are the considerations, more or less, from which the difficulty as to the equitable arises. Yet they are all in a manner correct, and not really inconsistent. For equity, while superior to one sort of justice, is itself just: it is not superior to justice as being generically different from it. Justice and equity are therefore the same thing, and both are good, though equity is the better.

The source of the difficulty is that equity, though just, is not legal justice, but a rectification of legal justice. The reason for this is that law is always a general statement, yet there are cases which it is not possible to cover in a general statement. In matters therefore where, while it is necessary to speak in general terms, it is not possible to do so correctly, the law takes into consideration the majority of cases, although it is not unaware of the error this involves. And this does not make it a wrong law; for the error is not in the law nor in the lawgiver, but in the nature of the case: the material of conduct is essentially irregular. When therefore the law lays down a general rule, and thereafter a case arises which is an exception to the rule, it is then right, where the lawgiver's pronouncement because of its absoluteness is defective and erroneous, to rectify the defect by deciding as the lawgiver would himself decide if he were present on the occasion, and would have enacted if he had been cognizant of the case in question. Hence, while the equitable is just, and is superior to one sort of justice, it is not superior to absolute justice, but only to the error due to its absolute statement. This is the essential nature of the equitable: it is a rectification of law where law is defective because of its generality. In fact this is the reason why things are not all determined by law: it is because there are some cases for which it is impossible to lay down a law, so that a special ordinance becomes necessary.

ST. GERMAIN, THE DOCTOR AND THE STUDENT
pp. 45–46 (1532).

[St. Germain agrees with Aristotle that equity is an exception from the law in cases where the law is deficient because of its generality. He continues:]

. . . Wherefore it appeareth, that if any law were made by man without any such exception expressed or implied, it were manifestly unreasonable, and were not to be suffered: for such cases might come, that he that would observe the law should break both the law of God and the law of reason. As if a man make a vow that he will never eat white-meat, and after it happeneth him to come there where he can get no other meat: in this case it behoveth him to break his avow, for the particular case is excepted secretly from his general avow by his equity or *epieikeia,* as it is said before. Also if a law were made in a city, that no man under pain of death should open the gates of the city before the sun-rising; yet if the citizens before that hour flying from their enemies, come to the gates of the city, and one for saving of the citizens openeth the gates before the hour appointed by the law, he offendeth not the law, for that case is excepted from the said general law by equity, as is said before. And so it appeareth that equity rather followeth the intent of the law, than the words of the law. And I suppose that there be in like wise some like equities grounded on the general rules of the law of the realm.

Stud. Yea verily; whereof one is this. There is a general prohibition in the laws of England, that it shall not be lawful to any man to enter into the freehold of another without authority of the owner or the law: but yet it is excepted from the said prohibition by the law of reason, that if a man drive beasts by the highway, and the beasts happen to escape into the corn of his neighbor, and he, to bring out his beasts, that they should do no hurt, goeth into the ground, and setteth out his beasts, there he shall justify that entry into the ground by the law. Also notwithstanding the statute of Edw. 3, made the 14th year of his reign, whereby it is ordained, that no man, upon pain of imprisonment, should give any alms to any valiant beggar, that is well able to labour; yet if a man meet with a valiant beggar in so cold a weather, and so light apparel, that if he have no clothes, he shall not be able to come to any town for succour, but is likely rather to die by the way, and he therefore giveth him apparel to save his life, he shall be excused by the said statute, by such an exception of the law by reason as I have spoken of.

2. THE COURT OF CHANCERY AND THE DEVELOPMENT OF EQUITY[4]

The common law, in its early period, had exhibited considerable flexibility. There was a great deal of equity in it. Under Henry II, many new writs were granted, and the Register of Writs expanded rapidly. Then, as shown in Section A, the development of the common law was to a large extent arrested by the passage of the Provisions of Oxford. The Statute of Westminster II restored a part of the writ-making power of the Chancery, but the clerks of the Chancery did not make expansive use of the powers granted to them. There were many situations in which the plaintiff could get no relief, or where the relief which was afforded was clearly inadequate. To give an example: The plaintiff bought a house from the defendant and asked for a conveyance. The defendant refused to convey. The plaintiff was determined to get that particular house, but all the common law courts would give him was damages. What the plaintiff needed was a judicial decree that would order the defendant to perform the terms of the contract and that would be enforceable by contempt sanctions.

It was this condition of relative sterility and inflexibility which caused the rise of equity jurisprudence. Litigation at common law was also very expensive, and a poor litigant could hardly afford it. What could be done by an impecunious litigant or one who felt that the highly technical rules of the common law prevented him from getting relief?

The common law courts were the chief instruments of the king in dispensing justice. But their jurisdiction was not exclusive. The king, in delegating to the common law courts his power to do justice, reserved to himself the power to do justice extralegally, by executive fiat. Thus the king himself, as a member of his council, could hear and determine a

---

4. The text of this section is based on G.R.Y. Radcliffe and G. Cross, *The English Legal System* (6th ed. 1977), Ch. VIII, with additional information drawn from A.K.R. Kiralfy, *The English Legal System* (8th ed. 1990), and T. Hanger, "The Modern Status of the Rules Permitting a Judge to Punish Direct Contempt Summarily," 28 William & Mary Law Review 553 (1987).

case. Many people took advantage of this residual power of the king. If they felt they deserved relief, and if the common law courts were unable or unwilling to grant it, they might present a petition to the king and his council and ask for a remedy, not as a matter of right, but of grace ("For the love of God and by way of Charity," as the customary invocation read.).

Many of these petitions were dismissed as frivolous on the ground that there was an adequate remedy at the common law. But a certain number of them were entertained, and such petitions, if they alleged a defect or inadequacy in the common law, were referred to the Chancellor, who was a member of the council. At first, the Chancellor, in hearing these petitions and rendering decisions on them, acted only as a delegate of the council. But even before the close of the fourteenth century, we find petitioners addressing the Chancellor directly, and beginning with the fifteenth century, the decree was made in his name. Thus equitable remedies, like the legal remedies they supplemented, came over time to be bureaucratized. Equitable relief always retained, however, the flexible, relatively non-technical nature which was its original *raison d'être.*

At first, the jurisdiction of the Chancellor was very vaguely defined. The Chancellors of the early period were almost invariably bishops or other high ecclesiastical dignitaries. They intervened in order to correct the harshness of the common law on grounds of conscience and morality. Furthermore, they were concerned much more with the facts of the individual case than with laying down any general principles which their successors might follow. Nevertheless, there were certain types of cases, three of which are described below, in which it came to be recognized that the Chancellor would grant relief.

First, the Chancellor recognized and protected the so-called "uses." If the legal estate in any property was held by A "to the use" of B, the Chancellor would give effect to the "equitable" rights of B, while fully recognizing that the legal title to the property was in A. This enforcement of uses as equitable rights gave rise, in the course of time, to a whole new body of law known as the law of trusts.

Second, the Chancellor often gave relief in cases where a contract or other legal transaction had come into existence through fraud, mistake, or duress. The common law granted very limited redress in such cases and was unable to order the cancellation of fraudulent instruments.

Third, the Chancellor generally took a far broader view of contracts than the common law courts did in the Middle Ages. He was ready to enforce an obligation that had been created by the mere fact of mutual agreement. The common law courts, by contrast, demanded either that the obligation be created in a document under seal, or that there be performance by one party to the contract. (These were the limitations of the two types of action designed to enforce contracts at the early common law—the actions of covenant and debt.) Even when the common law courts interfered in contract matters, they would only grant damages. The Court of Chancery, on the other hand, would sometimes enforce the contract directly by issuing a decree of specific performance, which compelled the defendant to perform the defendant's obligation pursuant to the terms of the contract. Such decrees were issued when the legal remedy of damages was inadequate. In some cases, the plaintiff would request both a decree of specific performance and compensatory damages for the losses that the plaintiff had sustained prior to the time of the trial. When the Court of Chancery awarded such "incidental" legal relief, it was said to be exercising its "equitable clean-up jurisdiction." Another equitable remedy created by the Chancery was the injunction, which prohibited the defendant from engaging in future tortious misconduct that threatened to injure the plaintiff.

Equitable remedies were subject to enforcement by charging the defendant with contempt of court for failing to comply with the court's order. Civil contempt sanctions (indefinite fines or jail terms) were imposed to coerce future compliance with equitable decrees, and criminal contempt sanctions (fixed fines or jail terms) were imposed to punish past violations of equitable decrees.

The procedure which the Chancellor used in exercising his jurisdiction was very different from the procedure of the common law courts. The common law judge was like a referee at a fight. He saw to it that the rules were observed and awarded points to the parties, but he could not develop new rules of procedure as the fight developed before him. The Chancellor, on the other hand, had complete discretion in procedural matters. He intervened in the proceeding whenever he deemed it desirable. He summoned the defendant before him by the writ of subpoena and subjected him personally to an examination. The object of this examination was defined in ecclesiastical language. It was "to ascertain the condition of the defendant's conscience and to purge it by an appropriate prescription, if necessary." In doing this, the Chancellor had full power to subject the defendant to an oath, which forced him to disclose the secrets of his case. There was no jury in equity proceedings.

The Chancellor did not always hear a case personally. He often delegated authority to an official known as the Master of the Rolls. The losing party had the right, however, to apply to the Chancellor for a rehearing.

In time, the Chancellor extended his jurisdiction into more and more fields in which the common law claimed a monopoly, and strained relations ensued between the common law courts and the Chancery. In the sixteenth century, the common lawyers' jealousy of the Chancery had grown to considerable proportions. This feeling of animosity was accentuated by the conduct of Chancellor Wolsey, who made it a practice to issue injunctions prohibiting parties from suing in the common law courts on the ground, for example, that the defendant had an equitable defense which the common law court would not recognize, and who also sometimes prevented parties from enforcing a judgment which they had obtained from a common law court on the ground that it was inequitable.

The common law courts struck back. On several occasions they issued writs of habeas corpus ordering the release of prisoners who had been held in contempt and imprisoned by the Chancellor for disobeying injunctions. Finally, in 1616, Chief Justice Coke of the King's Bench caused a defendant in a common law action who had dared to apply to Lord Chancellor Ellesmere for an injunction against the enforcement of a judgment allegedly obtained by gross fraud and imposition to be indicted criminally. This action brought matters to a head, and the conflict was submitted to the Crown for a decision. King James I decided in favor of the Chancery and dismissed Lord Coke from office.

Following the period of the Commonwealth and the restoration of the monarchy in the seventeenth century, relations between the common law courts and the Court of Chancery improved. One important reason for this betterment in their mutual relations was a change in the character of equity. As we have seen, equity started out as a discretionary jurisdiction based on the moral ideas of the individual chancellors who exercised it. John Selden, who lived in the early seventeenth century, objected to the system of equity then administered by the Chancellor as a "roguish thing," because it varied with each Chancellor's type of conscience. The equity of the later seventeenth and of the eighteenth century, on the other hand, was discretionary only in theory. In practice, it developed into a system of formulated rules, and precedents were followed by the Chancellor as they were by the common law judges. In its new form, equity was not so much a correction of, or departure from, the common law, but a body of rules supplementing it. It should be noted, however, that many of the rules of equity were formulated in a more flexible and elastic manner than most of the rules of the common law. This left a margin of discretion in the judges in equity which enabled them—to a larger degree than was possible at the common law—to adapt the rule to the facts of the individual case.

The change in the general character of equity was accompanied by a change in the type of person administering it. The practice of appointing ecclesiastics as Chancellor ended with Wolsey, who died in 1530. With few exceptions, all Chancellors after him were secular officials. They were, however, not necessarily lawyers. Some of the early secular chancellors were statesmen or politicians. Only after 1675 did it become a practice to appoint only lawyers to the post of Chancellor.

D. ESTABLISHMENT OF THE COMMON LAW IN THE UNITED STATES

W.F. WALSH, A HISTORY OF ANGLO–AMERICAN LAW
pp. 85–96 (2d ed. 1932).[5]

§ **45. English common law in the American colonies.**—The task of tracing in detail the development of American law has never been

---

5. Footnotes have been omitted except as indicated. Reprinted by permission of the publisher, Bobbs–Merrill Co. Copyright © 1932 by William F. Walsh.

attempted. Nevertheless, the outlines of this development in colonial times have been sketched based on sufficient original evidences to give a very fair representation of the ways in which laws were established and enforced prior to the Revolution. In Massachusetts in 1636 a resolution of the general court after entreating the governing officers "to make a draft of laws agreeable to the word of God," directed the magistrates to hear and determine all causes "according to the laws now established, and where there is no law, then as near the law of God as they can." ... The subsidiary law, in the absence of local statute, was the law of God. The magistrates administered a rude justice dependent on their interpretation of the divine law, based largely on their discretion in cases not expressly covered by enacted laws.... There was no reception of the common law in these enactments. It was ignored.

In the actual practice of this early law in the courts, the common law was not followed or applied.... The terms of the common law were used, as were common-law forms of action, but very loosely and informally, with wide variations. Common-law forms of deeds and contracts were followed, but the authority of the English common law was always denied except as the rule had been adopted by colonial statute.

The magistrates and judges during the early period were not trained lawyers. The first judge who was a professional lawyer was made chief justice in 1712. From that time until the Revolution, the common law was drawn on more extensively, but its binding authority was not recognized except as it was specifically adopted by statute or decision in specific instances. John Adams said: "Our ancestors were entitled to the common law of England when they emigrated; that is to say to so much of it as they pleased to adopt and no more. They were not bound or obliged to submit to it unless they chose."

In the early Connecticut and New Haven colonies we have very much the same colonial law as in Massachusetts, with nothing like reception or adoption of the common law....

. . . .

In New York the reception of the common law was more complete than in the other colonies. The royal governors accustomed the people to the use of the common law. But prior to 1700 there were probably very few trained lawyers and judges, and though law actions ostensibly were conducted according to the English law, it was necessarily a kind of layman's law in fact, departing in many ways from common-law rules.... In 1700 a trained lawyer became chief justice, and he undertook to establish definitely the rules and practice of the common law in New York. A court of Chancery was established prior to 1727. In Governor Tyron's report, 1774, he said: "The common law of England is the fundamental law of the province, and it is a received doctrine that all the statutes enacted before the province had a legislature are binding upon the colony."

. . . .

In Maryland we find the earliest recognition in the colonies of the common law as a subsidiary system. The first laws of 1642 provided for the trial of civil causes according to the law and usage of the province, and in cases where they failed, then according to equity and good conscience, "not neglecting (so far as the judge shall be informed thereof and shall find no inconvenience in the application to this province) the rules by which right and justice useth and ought to be determined in England," indicating that the common law might be looked to for guidance and illustration rather than as positive law. In 1662 it was enacted that where the laws of the province had no provision, justice should be administered according to the laws and statutes of England— "All courts shall judge of the right pleading and the inconsistency of the said laws with the good of the province according to the best of their judgment." ... In Virginia and the Carolinas, we find the enactment of codes of law based on the common law and made necessary by the absence of lawyers and law books, the establishment of layman courts and administration necessarily involving a rude kind of natural justice worked out in the discretion of the judges in cases not expressly covered by the statutes....

It seems clear, therefore, that in colonies which formally adopted the common law—Maryland, Virginia, the Carolinas—as in colonies which ignored it as a subsidiary law, substituting the divine law, or reason and equity, the law actually administered was a popular law without lawyers or trained judges, differing radically from the contemporary common law of England, and that in some of the colonies, notably in New York, considerable development in this law had taken place during a period just preceding the Revolution, and that the groundwork had been laid for the actual reception of the common law of England as part of our legal system, which in fact took place through developments in the law in the different states after the Revolution.

. . . .

§ 46. Special characteristics of colonial law.—From the standpoint of the legal historian, a very interesting characteristic of this early colonial law is its popular informal character, with courts of laymen generally consisting of several persons administering customary law according to the general sense of reason and justice of the community as expressed in the sense of reason and justice of the magistrates or judges who decided the cases. The special needs of a newly-settled country with a homogeneous population in each colony equal in most respects socially and economically, without lawyers or English law books, demanded this type of court, which resembled the popular courts of the earlier time in England rather than the developed contemporary common-law courts. But more important than this are the special characteristics of American law by which it is distinguished from the common law of England, which had their origin and historical explanation in the colonial period. The most prominent characteristic of this kind is the strong tendency to codification. In nearly every colony most of the law under which the people lived was expressed in codes more or less elaborate and complete, the codes of Pennsylvania ... foreshadowing in many ways the New York Code of Civil Procedure which has been copied in a large majority of the other states. Though in several of the colonies the English common law was formally adopted as the fundamental subsidiary law subject to local statutes and modifications to meet special local conditions as determined by the courts, as a practical matter, it was quite impossible to give it effect without lawyers trained in it or English law books from which it might be acquired. This practical reason was, no doubt, the immediate occasion for the enactment of codes as complete as possible in these colonies. In New England and New Jersey where the common law was not so adopted, codes of law were even more necessary, as the law outside of the statutes was left to the discretion of the judges and magistrates in their interpretation of reason and justice. The American tendency to codification, therefore, rests on this well-established historical foundation.

.   .   .   .

§ 47. Relation of English common law to law in the United States.—Judge Story said in a leading case: "The common law of England is not to be taken in all respects to be that of America. Our ancestors brought with them its general principles, and claimed it as their birthright; but they brought with them and adopted only that portion which was applicable to their condition."

Kent said:—"The common law, so far as it is applicable to our situation and government, has been recognized and adopted, as one entire system, by the constitutions of Massachusetts, New York, New Jersey and Maryland. It has been assumed by the courts of justice, or declared by statute, with the like modifications, as the law of the land in every state. It was imported by our colonial ancestors, as far as it was applicable, and was sanctioned by royal charters and colonial statutes. It was also the established doctrine, that English statutes, passed before the emigration of our ancestors, and applicable to our situation, and in amendment of the law, constitute a part of the common law of this country."

There can be no doubt that the New England colonies and New Jersey did not adopt the common law except as they expressly adopted parts of it in their statutes and their customary law as decided by their courts. New York actually applied the English law more fully than any other colony, and developed courts trained in common-law principles at an earlier date and more completely than did any other colony, and the leadership of New York in the development of American law in the last century was aided to a considerable degree by that early development. Maryland and the southern colonies formally adopted the common law, but it seems clear that its actual application by courts trained in that law had not progressed very far until a comparatively short time prior to the Revolution. It is clear, of course, that such law as the colonists were acquainted with was English law, that they brought with them and used the language and general principles and the forms of action of that law, but in most of the colonies the binding effect of English law was not recognized. They adopted similar law, but with extensive changes and modifications to meet their special needs. This law, even when it coincided with English law, bound them because they had enacted it or established it by their own decisions, not because it had been decided by English courts. Nevertheless, the common law as a general system of legal principles was adopted by the states after the Revolution and in most of the new states thereafter, as stated by Kent.[6] What is this common law? It seems clear that no rule of the English law became law in the United States until the question of whether it was "applicable to our situation and government," as stated by Kent, or "applicable to their condition," as stated by Story, had first been determined either by legislation or decision. Whether any specific part of that law was so applicable or not had to be determined by the law-making power of each state, whether legislative or judicial. By constitutional provision or by statute, we have, at least, adopted the common-law system as distinguished from any other, such as the civil law. We have established a common law in each state, agreeing on most points but varying in different ways on many others, each with its own system of courts, practice, and procedure.

In determining the rule to be applied in any case in which the law has not been settled either by statute or former decisions, it is the duty of the court to apply the common-law rule, but in determining what that rule is, the court is not limited to English decisions prior to American independence. It is free to consider English decisions of a later date, and decisions on the same question in other American states. From all of these decisions the court decides what principle of law applies to the case and how the application should be made. As between conflicting decisions in England and in different states, the court decides what rule shall be applied, based on sound reason and policy. The court is simply exercising the judicial function of declaring the law, a function as old as the common law and of its essence from the beginning. The change from the early colonial law is in the development of the courts, from laymen doing justice of a rude, popular sort, with scant knowledge of legal

6. New York Const. Kent–Radcliff Rev. 1802, I, 15: "And this convention doth . . . ordain, determine and declare, that such parts of the common law of England, and of the statutes of England and Great Britain, and of the acts of the legislature of the colony of New York, as together did form the law of the said colony" on April 19, 1775, "shall be and continue the law of this state."

Declaration of Rights, Continental Congress, 1774:

"5. That the respective colonies are entitled to the common law of England, and more especially to the great and inestimable privilege of being tried by their peers of the vicinage, according to the course of that law.

"6. That they are entitled to the benefit of such of the English statutes as existed at the time of their colonization; and which they have, by experience, respectively found to be applicable to their several local and other circumstances."

principles, to judges who are professional lawyers trained in the common-law system of jurisprudence. The decisions of the courts of any state establish the law of that state, and those decisions establish rules often differing from the English law, ancient or modern, or from decisions in other states arrived at after a like process. In this way is developed a common law of each state, based on the principles of the English common law, but varying from it in many cases, and varying as between the different states. There can be no doubt, therefore, that the "reception" of the common law after the Revolution was a continuation, fundamentally, of what had taken place in the colonial period. In both periods the English common law was adopted only in detail, as each rule was made the law by statute or by decisions.

E. THE MERGER OF LAW AND EQUITY

The development of equity outside of the common law resulted in many inconveniences and had many confusing aspects. There were two systems of law with different rules. There were two sets of courts. The systems of pleading and procedure were entirely different. Cases could not be transferred from a common law court to the Court of Chancery, and vice versa. A party seeking relief in the wrong court had to start all over again. Equitable defenses could not be set up in actions at law. In many cases, a controversy would be decided entirely differently, depending on whether it was settled in a court of law or equity.

Because of these shortcomings of the dual system of courts (to which reasons of economy might be added), the demand for reform became strong both in England and the United States. The same 19th century wave of reform that led to the putative abolition of the forms of action also resulted in English and American trial courts generally receiving a unified jurisdiction over all civil actions, regardless of whether the relief sought was formerly within the exclusive competence of courts of common law or equity. A single mode of pleading and procedure in civil cases was instituted; in the United States this was called "Code pleading," and was pioneered by New York's adoption of David Dudley Field's innovative Code of Civil Procedure in 1848. The large majority of the states, including the State of California, followed the example of New York.

The question remains, however: How complete is the merger? Does the abolition of the separate courts of law and equity and the concurrent administration of these two branches of the law mean that there is no longer a distinction between law and equity? The answer to this question is that the procedural merger of law and equity has not done away with the distinction between the substantive rules of "law" (meaning the rules applied by the common law courts prior to the merger of law and equity) and "equity" (meaning the equitable remedies formerly applied by the Chancery and other courts of equity). The substantive rules of the two systems remain, to a large extent, intact. The respective types of relief given under each system also remain unaffected by the fusion. We speak of legal and equitable estates, of legal and equitable ownership.

The common law action for damages is basically different from the equitable action for specific performance. And we still have to familiarize ourselves with the complex rules under which courts of equity granted injunctions. Furthermore, the facts that must be pleaded and proved in order to obtain equitable relief are largely the same as before the merger, including proof that the remedy at law (meaning the common law) is inadequate.

In one important respect, there remains a general disparity in the procedure for trying those civil cases that raise "equitable" as opposed to "legal" issues. Generally, disputed facts in equitable cases are decided by the trial judge rather than a jury. This reflects the fact that the federal Constitution and most state constitutions guarantee the right to jury trial in civil cases only when a common law remedy is sought.[7] When equitable relief is sought, there is no right to a jury trial. Legislatures have been reluctant to provide for jury trials, except as constitutionally required, because they are a cumbersome and expensive means of resolving disputes. Thus, the use of jury trials in equitable cases has generally been left to the discretion of the trial court, which may in extraordinary circumstances empanel a jury to decide questions of fact on an advisory basis. If the case raises a mixture of legal and equitable issues, as when a plaintiff sues for breach of contract and prays for both specific performance and compensatory damages for losses incurred prior to the time of the trial, a party is generally entitled to a jury trial on the legal issues only.

The continuing significance of the distinction between law and equity is emphasized by cases in which the legislature has created a new statutory remedy, and the courts are asked to determine whether a person claiming relief under the statute is entitled to a jury trial. The general rule in such instances is that, when the statutory remedy "cannot be classified by looking to its counterpart in English practice, the nature of the remedy must be examined to determine if it more clearly resembles a traditional legal, or a traditional equitable, remedy." Southern Pacific Transportation Co. v. Superior Court, 58 Cal.App.3d 433, 436, 129 Cal.Rptr. 912, 914 (1976). Thus, the Supreme Court of the United States held that the Seventh Amendment right to jury trial applied to an action for damages for housing discrimination created by the Civil Rights Act of 1968, because "the relief sought here—actual and punitive damages—is the traditional form of relief offered in the courts of law." Curtis v. Loether, 415 U.S. 189, 196 (1974).

Often this mode of analysis leads to inconclusive results, and the final determination whether the remedy gives rise to a right to jury trial

[7] The federal Constitution guarantees the right to jury trial both in criminal cases (the Sixth Amendment) and in civil cases (the Seventh Amendment). Although the Sixth Amendment right to jury trial in criminal cases applies to trials in state as well as federal courts, the Seventh Amendment right to jury trial in civil cases applies only to trials in federal courts. Thus, the question whether the parties to a state civil case have a right to jury trial depends solely on whether the state constitution or a state statute provides such a right.

turns on the solicitude of particular courts for jury trials as a matter of social policy. In general, the federal courts have been more receptive to claims of a right to jury trial than have the state courts. *Compare* Ross v. Bernhard, 396 U.S. 531 (1970), *with* C & K Engineering Contractors v. Amber Steel Co., 23 Cal.3d 1, 151 Cal.Rptr. 323, 587 P.2d 1136 (1978); Abner A. Wolf, Inc. v. Walch, 385 Mich. 253, 188 N.W.2d 544 (1971); Hiatt v. Yergin, 152 Ind.App. 497, 284 N.E.2d 834 (1972). When a statute creates a cause of action to be adjudicated by an administrative tribunal rather than a conventional court, however, even the federal courts have not insisted on jury trials. See Atlas Roofing Co., Inc. v. Occupational Safety and Health Review Comm., 430 U.S. 442 (1977).

F. MODERN ENGLISH AND AMERICAN COURTS

1. MODERN ENGLISH COURTS

(a) Jurisdiction

A.W. SCOTT & R.B. KENT, CASES AND OTHER MATERIALS ON CIVIL PROCEDURE

pp. 33–34 (1967).[8]

The judicial system of England was completely reorganized in 1875. Shortly before that time the conclusion had come to be generally accepted that the system of separate courts was unnecessarily cumbersome and that the court organization should be simplified by merging the courts into a single court, with a trial branch and an appellate branch. This complete merger was not, however, effected. By the Judicature Act, 1873, 36 & 37 Vict., c. 66, which went into effect in 1875, and by subsequent acts amending it, a new system of court organization was established. The local courts were not wholly abolished, and the county courts were retained. Moreover, the House of Lords continued to be the highest court of appeal. The three superior courts of law, the Court of Common Pleas, the Court of King's Bench, the Court of Exchequer, and the Court of Chancery and the High Court of Admiralty and the Court of Probate, together with the Court of Exchequer Chamber, were merged into a single court called the Supreme Court of Judicature. That court was divided into a lower branch, called the High Court of Justice, and an upper branch, called the Court of Appeal. The High Court of Justice is now divided into three divisions, namely the King's Bench Division, the Chancery Division, and the Probate, Divorce and Admiralty Division. For a time there was also a Common Pleas Division and an Exchequer Division. These were abolished in 1880.

The Court of Appeal in practice consists of the Master of the Rolls and eight Lords Justices of Appeal. It ordinarily sits in two divisions of three judges each, and has general appellate jurisdiction. In the House of

---

8. Reprinted by permission of the authors and publishers, Little, Brown & Co. Copyright © 1967 by Austin W. Scott and Robert B. Kent.

Lords appeals are now heard by at least three, and quite usually five, of the members who are eligible for such duty. Those who are eligible comprise the Lord Chancellor, the Lords of Appeal in Ordinary, and peers who have held high judicial office. The highest court of appeal for the dominions and colonies is the Judicial Committee of the Privy Council. Such appeals have been eliminated with respect to Canada and most other dominions.

(b) Diagrams of Court Structure

W. FRYER & H. ORENTLICHER, CASES AND MATERIALS ON LEGAL METHOD AND LEGAL SYSTEM

p.   680 (1967).[9]

(1) Organization of English Courts in 1873

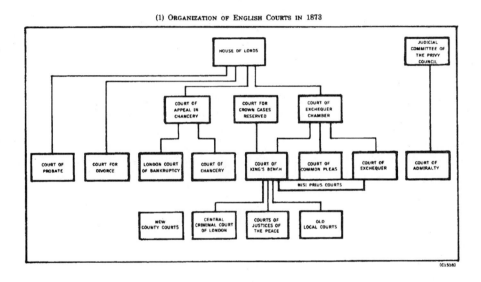

9. Copyright © West Publishing Co., 1967.

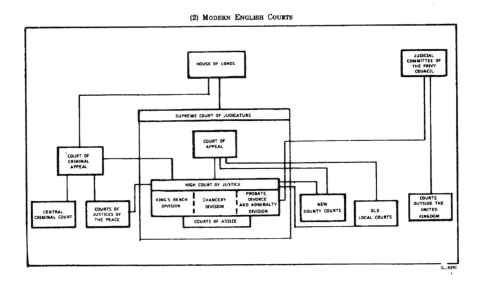

(2) MODERN ENGLISH COURTS

2. MODERN AMERICAN COURTS

(a) Note on the Dual System of State and Federal Courts

By definition, the "federal" system of government entails two levels of authority to make and administer law. In the United States, the competence to regulate most aspects of the day-to-day lives of citizens and the basic institutions of daily life remains with state governments, and most civil and criminal cases are accordingly heard in state courts and decided by rules of law created according to state constitutional processes. By their ratification of the federal Constitution, however, the original 13 states, which had emancipated themselves from British rule in the Revolutionary War, relinquished part of their sovereignty and subordinated themselves to the constitutional authority of a national government composed of a federal union of states. The federal government was endowed with the power to regulate matters thought likely to create friction among the states if left to state regulation.

Just as the concept of "separation of powers" (see Chapter I.B.6., *supra*) has led to continuing debate about the proper scope and interrelationship of the legislative, executive, and judicial powers distributed among the branches of the national government and of the governments of each of the states, so too has the concept of "federalism" led to continuing debate about the proper scope and interrelationship of those powers granted by the Constitution to the "federal" government (i.e., the national government) and those powers reserved by the Constitution to the states. Indeed, "federalism" and "separation of powers" are closely connected concepts, both fundamental to American constitutionalism. "Separation of powers" may be conceived to deal with the allocation of governmental power *horizontally*, within any given government, and "federalism" to deal with the allocation of governmental power *vertically*, between the national tier of government and the partially subordinate but also partially independent tier of the government of the fifty states. No one disputes that the Framers of the Constitution created a federal system of government, integrating the national and state levels of government, as part of the same system of checks and balances that argued for the separation of powers among the branches of the national government: a somewhat jealous relationship between the state and national levels of government would prevent either from wielding too much power.

Just what powers may be exercised by each level has remained recurrently controversial—just, one suspects, as the Framers intended. By and large, the trend of history over the past two centuries has been one of increasing concentration of power in the federal government, although in many instances Congress has chosen to allow the states to continue to regulate in their various ways conduct that Congress could by statute bring under nationwide, federal control. In particular, the federal government's powers with respect to the regulation of commerce and the conduct of foreign affairs have been expansively interpreted in response to the pressures of the industrial revolution, the Civil War, the two World Wars, and the atomic age. With this federal law-making has grown an extensive system of federal courts.[10]

10. The balance of power between the two levels of government continues to be a source of great political debate. *See generally* D. Cariello, "Federalism for the New Millennium: Accounting for the Values of Federalism," 26 Fordham Urban Law Journal 1493 (1999). In a number of recent cases, a bare majority of the Supreme Court has struck down Acts of Congress that it deemed to have intruded too far into the residual sovereignty of the states as preserved by the Constitution. *See, e.g.*, Board of Trustees of the University of Alabama v. Garrett, 531 U.S. 356 (2001) (holding that Congress lacked power to subject states to suits for violation of the Americans with Disabilities Act); Kimel v. Florida Board of Regents, 528 U.S. 62 (2000) (holding that Congress lacked power to subject states to suits for violation of the Age Discrimination in Employment Act); United States v. Morrison, 529 U.S. 598 (2000) (holding that Congress lacked power to enact a portion of the Violence Against Women Act); Alden v. Maine, 527 U.S. 706 (1999) (holding that Congress lacked power to subject states to suits by individual state employees for unpaid wages concededly owed to them under the federal Fair Labor Standards Act). The majority in these and other recent cases limiting the power of the federal government, sometimes referred to as the "federalism five," consists of Chief Justice Rehnquist and (in order of seniority) Justices O'Connor, Scalia, Kennedy, and Thomas. The four dissenters are Justices Stevens, Souter, Ginsburg, and Breyer. This schism between the "conservative" wing of the Court, solicitous of "states' rights," and the "liberal" wing, which takes a more expansive view of federal power, extends to the question of just what individual rights—rights to freedom of speech and religion, to privacy and sexual autonomy, to freedom from discrimination and arbitrary treatment and from police or prosecutorial misconduct, to name just a few—are protected by the federal Constitution. Although here the allegiances of particular Justices are less predictable, in general the Court's conservative Justices are less willing than their liberal counterparts to assert national power in order to protect individuals from state infringements of their liberty. For a critique of these decisions by a distinguished scholar who is both a Senior Judge of the United States Court of Appeals for the Ninth Circuit and Professor of Law Emeritus at the University of California at Berkeley, see J. Noonan, *Narrowing the Nation's Power: The Supreme Court Sides with the States* (2002). After Judge Noonan's book was published, the Court reversed course by upholding the power of Congress to subject states to suits for violation of the Family and Medical Leave Act. See Nevada Dep't of Human Resources v. Hibbs, 538 U.S. 721, 123 S.Ct. 1972 (2003).

The dual system of state and federal courts in the United States would not be so confusing if each system of courts were concerned only with its own system of law. However, each system of courts is constantly confronted with questions which arise under the law created by the other system of government.

Federal law is the supreme law of the land, and state court cases constantly raise issues of federal law. Indeed, some federal laws create rights and duties which are expressly left for their enforcement to cases that plaintiffs may choose to bring either in federal or state courts, and state courts have no privilege under the Constitution to refuse to entertain such suits on federal rights. More frequently, federal issues of a collateral or defensive nature arise in the course of state litigation, as when a defendant in a state criminal prosecution claims that the state police proceeded against him or her in some way which was in violation of the federal Constitution. State courts are obliged to decide all these issues of federal law in good faith, as they think a federal court would under the guiding precedent of the United States Supreme Court. If a federal issue is erroneously decided by a state court, the aggrieved party must pursue the issue to the highest state court in which review can be had before seeking further review from the United States Supreme Court.

The federal "diversity" jurisdiction presents a converse case of interaction between one system of courts and another system of law. Some cases governed solely by state law may nevertheless be brought in federal court because the parties to the cases are citizens of different states, or are aliens. In these cases, it is the federal courts that must attempt, in good faith, to decide how state courts would rule on disputed issues of state law. This decisional process is complicated by the fact that federal courts sitting in diversity cases are dealing with the separate legal systems of 50 different states, and there is no provision for review of their decisions by the supreme courts of those states.[11]

We are going to describe the basic structure of the state courts first, and then we will discuss the structure of the federal courts as well as the basics of federal jurisdiction and federal review of state court decisions. A diagram of the federal court system appears at the end of the chapter.

(b) State Court Systems[12]

Each state has a hierarchy of courts with at least three layers. On the bottom are those dealing with petty cases where small monetary

---

11. This problem has been partially mitigated by the "certification" statutes enacted in most (but not all) states. These statutes allow a federal court (in some states only a federal appellate court) to refer or "certify" a question of state law arising in a pending federal case to the court of last resort of the state whose law is in controversy. The Supreme Court has strongly encouraged the lower federal courts to take advantage of an available certification statute in order to resolve doubt about the meaning of an ambiguous state law before proceeding to determine the constitutionality of that law. See Arizonans for Official English v. Arizona, 520 U.S. 43, 75–79 (1997).

12. Adapted from S. Mermin, *Law and The Legal System* 58–60 (2d ed. 1982), with

amounts or minor criminal penalties are involved. In a nonurban area, the judge of such a court is likely to be called a justice of the peace, and the position might be only a part-time one. In the cities, he or she is likely to be called a magistrate or a judge and might be attached to a specialized court with a name like police court, traffic court, or small claims court. These petty or "inferior" courts are generally not "courts of record"; they make no detailed record of the proceedings beyond the identification of parties, lawyers, and disposition of the case. The procedure may be rather informal. The losing party may appeal to the next level of court, but it is not an appeal in the usual sense, since it typically involves a completely new trial rather than appellate review of the record made in the lower court.

The next level of court is known as a "trial court of general jurisdiction," authorized to hear civil and criminal cases generally. Unlike the petty court, it is a court of record; its procedure is quite formal; it is not confined to, and indeed is usually prevented from entertaining, the petty sort of case. It is often called a "district" court or "circuit" court, though in some places it has such other names as "superior court" or "court of common pleas." (New York State creates a special confusion by establishing a "supreme court" that is *not* a court of last resort. The highest state court in New York is called the Court of Appeals. The New York Supreme Court operates as the state trial court of general jurisdiction, and the Appellate Division of the New York Supreme Court is that state's intermediate appellate court.) Besides the trial court of general jurisdiction—or, in some states, within this court as departments or divisions thereof—there are specialized courts like those handling probate matters, or divorce and other domestic relations issues, or juvenile problems.

The trial court of general jurisdiction exercises *some* appellate jurisdiction when it takes an "appeal" from a petty court, usually by conducting a completely new trial as if the case had never been brought before the petty court. (This is called a "trial *de novo.*") To a limited extent, the trial court of general jurisdiction also exercises the more usual form of appellate jurisdiction. For instance, it may be authorized to review *administrative agency* decisions on the record made before the administrative agency, as distinguished from holding a trial *de novo.* In such a case the agency's fact-findings, while not conclusive, will be upheld by the court in the absence of arbitrariness.

Uppermost in the hierarchy are the appellate courts. In a dwindling number of states there is only one appellate court, and that is the highest court of the state.[13] It hears appeals from the judgments of the

permission of the author. Copyright © 1982 by S. Mermin.

13. The number of states without an intermediate appellate court declined from 23 in 1978 to 10 in 2000, but has remained fixed at 10 since 2000. *See, e.g.,* the website of the West Virginia court system, <http://www.state.wv.us/wvsca/ wvsystem.htm#supreme> ("The Supreme Court of Appeals is West Virginia's highest court and the court of last resort. West Virginia is one of only 10 states with a

trial courts of general jurisdiction, and either affirms or reverses, or occasionally modifies, the judgment. There are some cases in which a litigant seeks to control the trial court's action not by waiting to take an appeal from its judgment, but by seeking directly in the highest court an "extraordinary writ" directing the lower court to do something (e.g., grant a change in the venue or place of trial, or justify its order holding someone in allegedly illegal custody) or refrain from doing something (e.g., from continuing to exercise jurisdiction in a case).

In 40 states there are intermediate appellate courts.[14] Their role varies in the different states. A state may provide that the appeal from a trial court goes to this intermediate court, and that a further appeal is then permissible, after unfavorable judgment, to the highest court. The state may say that in some other classes of cases (deemed more serious) the losing party in the trial court can skip the intermediate court and appeal directly to the highest court. In still other cases, the appeal from the trial court may be allowed only to the intermediate court, and an additional appeal to the highest court is either not allowed or allowed only for special reasons, or is left to the discretion of the highest court to allow. This limited-review type of provision is being increasingly suggested as a means of coping with the overburdened dockets of the states' highest courts.

DISTRIBUTION OF INTERMEDIATE STATE APPELLATE COURTS IN 2003[15]

States With Intermediate Appellate Courts (40)		States Without Intermediate Appellate Courts (10)
Alabama	Minnesota	Delaware
Alaska	Mississippi	Maine
Arizona	Missouri	Montana
Arkansas	Nebraska	Nevada
California	New Jersey	New Hampshire
Colorado	New Mexico	Rhode Island
Connecticut	New York	South Dakota
Florida	North Carolina	Vermont
Georgia	North Dakota	West Virginia
Hawaii	Ohio	Wyoming
Idaho	Oklahoma	
Illinois	Oregon	
Indiana	Pennsylvania	

single appellate court.") (visited Aug. 24, 2003).

14. The latest states to establish intermediate appellate courts on a permanent basis were Mississippi, Nebraska, and Utah. North Dakota's intermediate appellate court was established in 1987 on a temporary basis to relieve the backlog of the state's supreme court, and was supposed to cease functioning on January 1, 1990. Five extensions have been enacted, the latest setting January 1, 2008, as its date of termination. N.D. Cent. Code § 27–02.1–01.

15. This list was compiled from Bureau of National Affairs, Inc., *BNA's Directory of*

State and Federal Courts, Judges and Clerks 2000 Edition (1995–1999), and J.B. Oakley, "Memorandum on Divisional Organization of the United States Court of Appeals for the Ninth Circuit," Tables A–B, in Commission on Structural Alternatives for the Federal Courts of Appeals, *Working Papers* 145, 162–164 (1999), reprinted in J.B. Oakley, "Comparative Analysis of Alternative Plans for the Divisional Organization of the Ninth Circuit," Appendix B, 34 U.C. Davis Law Review 483, 513, 534–535 (2001).

States With Intermediate Appellate Courts (40)		States Without Intermediate Appellate Courts (10)
Iowa	South Carolina	
Kansas	Tennessee	
Kentucky	Texas	
Louisiana	Utah	
Maryland	Virginia	
Massachusetts	Washington	
Michigan	Wisconsin	

(c) The Federal Court System

i. Basic Structure[16]

There are three layers in the federal court hierarchy: the trial courts of general jurisdiction known as the district courts, the 13 courts of appeals, and the Supreme Court. There are also a few specialized trial courts (such as the Claims Court, the Tax Court and the Court of International Trade) and appellate courts (such as the Court of Military Appeals and the Temporary Emergency Court of Appeals which deals with certain economic and energy-related cases).

About half of the states have one federal district court each. In the others, the greater volume of business has necessitated creation of additional districts within the state. Thus in California there are the eastern, northern, central and southern districts, headquartered in Sacramento, San Francisco, Los Angeles and San Diego, respectively. Periodically, Congress adds new judgeships to existing districts in populous areas. The Central District of California currently has 27 judges; the Eastern District of California has 6. Some districts, such as the Eastern District of Oklahoma, still have only one judge each; the largest district, the Southern District of New York (in Manhattan), has 28 judges.

A federal district court case is heard by a single judge (with a jury, where one has been rightfully demanded). Until 1976, special three–judge panels were required in district court cases considering the constitutionality of statutes; such panels are now limited to certain rare types of cases. In addition, in cases of special significance, all the judges of a particular district may choose to sit together on a case. This is called hearing a case "en banc."

The 13 courts of appeals are assigned to 11 numbered "circuits" or areas into which the country is divided, plus a separate circuit for the District of Columbia and a special appellate court called the "Federal Circuit."[17] (The term "circuit" dates from the early days of the federal judicial system, when circuit judges literally "rode circuit," traveling throughout the area of the court and holding sessions at the major towns and cities therein.) One of the busiest is the Second Circuit, which

16. Adapted from S. Mermin, *Law and The Legal System* 166–69 (2d ed. 1982), with permission of the author. Copyright © 1982 by S. Mermin.

17. The Federal Circuit has jurisdiction based on subject matter, rather than geography. In brief, its jurisdiction consists of appeals in federal district court cases involving either patents or contract claims against the federal government, all appeals from the Claims Court and the Court of International Trade, and appeals in a few other special categories of cases.

includes the state of New York (as well as Connecticut and Vermont) and therefore handles much important commercial litigation. The District of Columbia Circuit handles more litigation involving government agencies than do the others. The District of Columbia Circuit covers the smallest area; the Ninth Circuit, the largest (Alaska, Arizona, California, Guam, Hawaii, Idaho, Montana, Nevada, the Northern Marianas, Oregon, Washington).[18] Another large area is covered by the Fifth Circuit, which embraces Louisiana, Mississippi, Texas and the Canal Zone. It is not surprising that these two massive circuits, the Fifth and Ninth, are the busiest of all, necessitating 17 and 28 judges respectively. Judges in the other circuits range from 6 for the First Circuit (Maine, Massachusetts, New Hampshire, Puerto Rico, Rhode Island) to 16 for the Sixth Circuit (Kentucky, Michigan, Ohio, Tennessee).

The courts of appeals normally sit in panels of three judges—sometimes including (when the spot cannot be filled by a regular circuit judge) a district judge from within the circuit or a district or circuit judge from another circuit. Frequently these assigned judges who fill out the ranks of courts of appeals panels are "senior" circuit or district judges, that is, semi-retired judges who work less than full-time and who are not counted in the number of regular judges allotted by Congress to each circuit and district court. The assignments are made by the chief judges of the circuit courts. (Each circuit and district court has a chief judge with responsibility for administrative matters. By statute, the chief judge is simply the most senior judge of the court, not yet 65 years of age, who has served as a judge for at least a year and is willing to accept the job.) In an occasional case of particular importance, all or a substantial number of the regular judges of a court of appeals will sit "en banc." The unsuccessful litigant in a district court can take an appeal, as a matter of right, to the court of appeals.

The Supreme Court of the United States has nine Justices. Its annual term begins in October and usually ends late in June. Each case is handled by the entire Court rather than by a panel. A quorum is six Justices. In the Court year designated as October Term, 1998 (ending in June 1999), the Court disposed of 7,045 of the 8,083 cases on its docket. In the Court year designated as October Term, 2001 (ending in June 2002), the Court disposed of 8,072 of the 9,176 cases on its docket.

---

18. The size of the Ninth Circuit has led to recurrent proposals that it be split in two by the creation of a new, Twelfth Circuit. The issue is complicated by politics—some believe proponents of the split are motivated more by distaste for the present Ninth Circuit's perceived liberal bias in cases dealing with environmental protection and constitutional rights than by legitimate concerns for sound judicial administration. The pros and cons of splitting the circuit for administrative reasons are reviewed at length in the recent report of a special commission created by Congress and chaired by retired Justice Byron R. White of the United States Supreme Court. Commission on Structural Alternatives for the Federal Courts of Appeals, *Final Report* 29–57 (1998), noted 113 Harvard Law Review 822 (2000). The Commission recommended against splitting the Ninth Circuit, and proposed instead that it be internally restructured in three adjudicative divisions. See A. Hellman, "The Unkindest Cut: the White Commission Proposal to Restructure the Ninth Circuit," 73 Southern California Law Review 377 (2000). Legislation has been introduced in Congress to implement the Commission's proposal, but the prospects for its enactment are uncertain.

Eighty-eight cases were argued and decided during the term; 85 were decided by full written opinions of the Court authored and signed by individual judges; the remaining 3 argued cases were disposed of by cursory "per curiam" decisions issued on behalf of the Court as a whole. Another 72 cases were reviewed and decided without oral argument.[19] The remaining 7,992 cases were disposed of by the Court simply refusing to exercise its jurisdiction, as the Court has discretion to do (and as it must do in order to have adequate time for deciding the important cases which it does choose to review).

ii. Basic Jurisdiction

Federal jurisdiction is intricate enough to require a complete course of its own. We will merely outline the most general forms of federal jurisdiction. One basic principle of federal jurisdiction should be learned now, however: for the most part, federal jurisdiction is the creation of Congress, not the Constitution, and is accordingly subject to Congressional modification.

At the top of the federal pyramid is the Supreme Court of the United States. Almost all of its business consists of reviewing the judgments of lower courts. These may be the judgments of state courts of last resort which dealt with questions of federal law, or they may be the judgments of lower federal courts. By "lower federal courts" we mean the federal circuit courts of appeals and district courts. As previously noted, the district courts are the trial courts of the federal system, and their judgments are generally appealed to the federal courts of appeals for the circuits in which they are located. In a few types of cases, which are becoming increasingly rare, the Supreme Court hears an appeal from a district court without any intermediate appeal to the circuit court. For the most part, however, the Supreme Court hears only cases which have already been appealed either to a state appellate court or to one of the 13 federal circuit courts of appeals.

We have previously indicated that the Supreme Court of the United States has the discretion to refuse to hear the vast majority of the cases in which its review is sought. This was not always the case. Until 1925, the Court heard most of its cases by means of a "writ of error," which functioned largely as an appeal as of right. In 1925, the Court's jurisdiction was revised by Congress to provide not only for appeals but also for writs of "certiorari." At the time, it was intended for the Court to have discretionary control only over cases subject to review by writ of certiorari; cases which met the more stringent criteria for an appeal were cases which the Court was supposed to hear automatically. Over the next several decades, however, the volume of appeals filed with the Court grew so unwieldy that the Court adopted procedures by which it disposed of most appeals just as summarily as it denied petitions for writs of

---

19. These caseload data were obtained online from Administrative Office of the U.S. Courts, *Judicial Business of the United States Courts*, Supplemental/Appendix Tables, Table A–1 <http://www.uscourts.gov/judbus2002/appendices/a01sep02.pdf> (visited Aug. 24, 2003).

certiorari, so that the distinction between review by appeal and by certiorari was reduced to little more than a technicality.[20] In 1988, Congress enacted a new statute that legitimated this development by expressly conferring upon the Court virtually plenary discretion over its own docket.

The jurisdiction of the federal courts of appeals, or circuit courts, is much simpler.[21] It consists principally of appeals from decisions by district courts, together with appeals from decisions by federal administrative agencies, such as the Interstate Commerce Commission and the National Labor Relations Board. In almost all of these cases, the courts of appeals have mandatory jurisdiction and cannot refuse to hear properly filed appeals. The rate of filing of appeals has increased drastically in all American appellate courts in the last two decades, and lacking any significant discretionary control over their dockets, many of the federal circuit courts have fallen substantially behind in their work.

The civil jurisdiction of the district courts is the most complex part of federal jurisdiction. The nationwide system of federal law is intertwined with highly variegated systems of state law in each of the fifty states, the District of Columbia, and territories such as Puerto Rico and Guam. Not all issues of federal law which arise in litigation give rise to the right to bring suit in a federal district court—of all questions of federal jurisdiction, the question of when a case "arises under" federal law for purposes of federal trial court jurisdiction is probably the most intractable. Besides these "arising under" cases, also called "federal question" cases, federal courts also have jurisdiction over civil cases involving maritime law (called "admiralty" jurisdiction) or involving parties from different states (called "diversity of citizenship" jurisdiction). The scope of the district courts' civil jurisdiction is further complicated by two facts: (1) most civil cases which qualify for federal jurisdiction can also be brought, at the plaintiffs' option, in the state courts; (2) some cases brought originally in state court can be "removed" to federal courts at the request of the defendants. By contrast, the district courts' criminal jurisdiction is relatively simple: with the exception of crimes by members of the military, all prosecutions for federal crimes are brought in federal district courts.[22]

20. Judges of the federal courts of appeals can also "certify" questions of law for binding decisions by the Supreme Court. The Supreme Court has strongly discouraged use of the certification device in all but truly extraordinary cases. The Court has exercised its certification jurisdiction only once in each of the past three decades.

21. An exception is the rather complex jurisdictional criteria of the United States Court of Appeals for the Federal Circuit, discussed in footnote 17, *supra*.

22. Prosecutions of misdemeanors (punishable by no more than a year's imprisonment) may be tried before federal magistrates, who are parajudicial assistants appointed by the judges of a federal district court. An appeal in such a case is heard by a regular district judge. Prosecutions for violations of military law are tried before the courts-martial of the military services, with a special system of appeal to courts of military review, the United States Court of Military Appeals, and ultimately (if certiorari is granted) the United States Supreme Court.

iii. Jurisdictional Diagrams

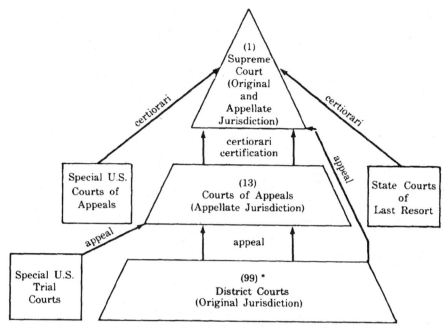

Federal Court Structure and Flow of Cases to the Supreme Court

* Includes 94 federal district courts in the 50 states, and the federal district courts for the District of Columbia, Puerto Rico, Guam, the Northern Mariana Islands, and the Virgin Islands.

[C1517]

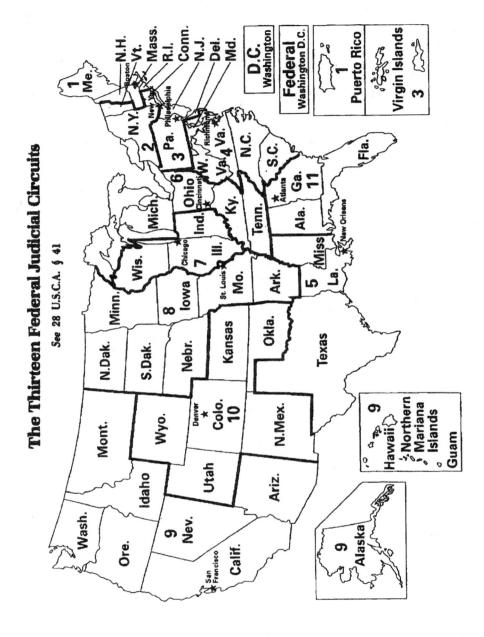

The Thirteen Federal Judicial Circuits

See 28 U.S.C.A. § 41

(d) The Constitutional Right to Jury Trial of Civil Actions in Federal Courts

AN INTRODUCTION TO THE CASE METHOD OF LEGAL INSTRUCTION

Throughout this book, summaries of actual cases and published court opinions are included in order to demonstrate the application of legal principles to concrete problems arising in the real world. Traditionally, law schools in the United States have used the "case method" as the fundamental mode of legal instruction.[23] This method is useful in demonstrating how the law evolves over time, which is one of the characteristics of common law systems. Also, the case method teaches students how courts interpret existing law, and thus teaches students to think like lawyers. This section uses the case method to illustrate the exercise of "federal question" jurisdiction by the federal judiciary and to illustrate the doctrine of the right to jury trial under the Seventh Amendment to the federal Constitution. (See Chapters III and IV, *infra*, for other examples of evolving lines of case law.)

ROGERS v. LOETHER

United States District Court, E.D. Wisconsin, 1970.
312 F. Supp. 1008.

REYNOLDS, DISTRICT JUDGE.

This is an action brought under Title VIII of the Civil Rights Act of 1968, 42 U.S.C. §§ 3601–3619, which prohibits discrimination in the rental of housing. Plaintiff claims that defendants discriminated against her by refusing to rent her an apartment because she is a Negro. Plaintiff requested injunctive relief restraining the rental of the subject apartment except to the plaintiff, money damages for loss incurred by the plaintiff due to the alleged discrimination, punitive damages in the amount of $1,000, and attorney's fees.

The court granted plaintiff's motion for a temporary restraining order on November 17, 1969, and, following an extended hearing, entered a preliminary injunction temporarily restraining the rental of the apartment pending final determination of the case. At a hearing on April 30, 1970, the Court, with consent of plaintiff, dissolved the preliminary injunction. Therefore, the only issues remaining in the suit are plaintiff's claim for compensatory and punitive damages and attorney's fees.

The defendants have requested a jury trial on these issues, and plaintiff has objected to this request. The parties have submitted briefs and argued to the court on this issue which is now before the court for decision.

---

23. *See generally* J. Feinman, "The Future History of Legal Education," 29 Rutgers Law Journal 475 (1998); J. Eagar, "The Right Tool for the Job: The Effective Use of Pedagogical Methods in Legal Education," 32 Gonzaga Law Review 389 (1997).

(handwritten margin note: beginning of argument)

(handwritten margin note: issue)

To warrant a jury trial, a claim must be of such a nature as would entitle a party to a jury at the time of the adoption of the Seventh Amendment. NLRB v. Jones & Laughlin Steel Corp., 301 U.S. 1 (1936).... The question before this court, therefore, is whether the cause of action under 42 U.S.C. §§ 3601–3919 is one recognized at common law which consequently requires a jury trial. I find that this cause of action is a statutory one invoking the equity powers of the court, by which the court may award compensatory and punitive money damages as an integral part of the final decree so that complete relief may be had. The action is not one in the nature of a suit at common law, and therefore there is no right to trial by jury on the issue of money damages in the case.

Defendant argues that the Seventh Amendment of the Constitution, Beacon Theatres, Inc. v. Westover, 359 U.S. 500 (1959); ... Dairy Queen, Inc. v. Wood, 369 U.S. 469 (1962); Harkless v. Sweeny Independent School District, 278 F. Supp. 632 (S.D. Texas 1968); and Ross v. Bernhard, 396 U.S. 531 (1970), require a jury trial on the issue of plaintiff's prayer for money damages due to the alleged discrimination.

(handwritten margin note: rejecting precedent)

Beacon [and] *Dairy Queen* ... hold that where equitable and legal claims are joined in the same cause of action, there is a right to trial by jury on the legal claims that must not be infringed by trying the legal issues as incidental to the equitable issues or by a court trial of common issues between the two. The Court in Swofford v. B & W, Inc., 336 F.2d 406, 414 (5th Cir. 1964) [(holding that the plaintiff in a patent-infringement case had a right to jury trial on the issue of compensatory damages, but not on the issues of discretionary treble damages and attorney's fees), *cert. denied*, 379 U.S. 962 (1965)], commented on these cases:

"... This is not to say, however, that they have converted typical non-jury claims, or remedies, into jury ones. Therefore, we reject a view that ... [they are] a catalyst which suddenly converts *any* money request into a money claim triable by jury."

The *Harkless* court granted a jury trial on the issue of [a] back pay award in an action brought under 42 U.S.C. § 1983 seeking reinstatement as teachers following a discharge allegedly based on racial discrimination. However, § 1983 expressly provides that persons acting under color of state law who deprive other persons of constitutional rights shall be liable "in an action at law." There is no such provision in 42 U.S.C. § 3612(c).

. . . .

The section of the statute dealing with remedies for violation of the act, 42 U.S.C. § 3612(c), provides:

"(c) *The court* (emphasis added) may grant as relief, as it deems appropriate, any permanent or temporary injunction, temporary restraining order or other order, and may award to the plaintiff actual damages and not more than $1,000 punitive damages...."

On its face, this statutory language seems to treat the actual damages issue as one for the trial judge rather than a jury. District courts in Hayes v. Seaboard Coast Line Railroad Co., 46 F.R.D. 49 (S.D. Ga.1969), and Cheatwood v. South Central Bell Telephone and Telegraph Co., 303 F. Supp. 754 (M.D. Ala.1969), have construed similar language in Title VII of the Civil Rights Act of 1964, 42 U.S.C. 2000e–5(g),[24] to mean that the issue of [a] back pay award in employment discrimination cases does not require jury determination.

Both *Hayes* and *Cheatwood* held that the money damages issue of back pay in an action under 42 U.S.C. § 2000e–5(g) of the 1964 Civil Rights Act was not a separate legal issue, but rather was a remedy the court could employ for violation of the statute in a statutory proceeding unknown at common law, and that there was no right to a trial by jury on that issue. As I have noted, the language of the remedial provisions of 42 U.S.C. § 2000e–5(g) of the Civil Rights Act of 1964 and 42 U.S.C. § 3612(c) of the Civil Rights Act of 1968 are very similar. The purpose of the two acts is similar. Title VII of the 1964 Act prohibits discrimination on the basis of race, color, religion, sex, or national origin by specified groups of employers, labor unions, and employment agencies. Title VIII of the 1968 Act prohibits discrimination on the basis of race, color, religion, or national origin in the sale or rental of housing by private owners, real estate brokers, and financial institutions. The award of money damages in a Title VIII action has the same place in the statutory scheme as does the award of back pay in a Title VII action. Determining the amount of a back pay award in a Title VII action can be as difficult a question of fact as determining the amount of money damages in a Title VIII action. . . .

An action under Title VIII is not an action at common law. The statute does not expressly provide for trial by jury of any issues in the action. In the absence of a clear mandate from Congress requiring a jury trial, I find that the similarities between the remedial provisions of the Civil Rights Acts of 1964 and 1968, in light of the undivided authority holding that the issue of money damages for back pay under Title VII of the 1964 Act is not an issue for the jury, compel the conclusion that the issue of compensatory and punitive money damages in an action under Title VIII of the 1968 Act is likewise an issue for the court. Accordingly, defendants' request for a jury trial must be denied.

Therefore, it is ordered that defendants' request for a jury trial be and it hereby is denied.

24. [Section 2000e–5(g) provides:] "If the court finds that the respondent has intentionally engaged in or is intentionally engaging in an unlawful employment practice charged in the complaint, *the court* may enjoin the respondent from engaging in such unlawful employment practice, and order such affirmative action as may be appropriate, which may include reinstatement or hiring of employees, with or without back pay (payable by the employer, employment agency, or labor organization, as the case may be, responsible for the unlawful employment practice). . . . " (Emphasis added.) [Footnote by the court.]

CURTIS v. LOETHER

Supreme Court of the United States, 1974.
415 U.S. 189, 94 S.Ct. 1005, 39 L.Ed.2d 260.

Mr. Justice Marshall delivered the opinion of the Court.

Section 812 of the Civil Rights Act of 1968, 82 Stat. 88, 42 U.S.C. § 3612, authorizes private plaintiffs to bring civil actions to redress violations of Title VIII, the fair housing provisions of the Act, and provides that "[t]he court may grant as relief, as it deems appropriate, any permanent or temporary injunction, temporary restraining order, or other order, and may award to the plaintiff actual damages and not more than $1,000 punitive damages, together with court costs and reasonable attorney fees...." The question presented in this case is whether the Civil Rights Act or the Seventh Amendment requires a jury trial upon demand by one of the parties in an action for damages and injunctive relief under this section.

Petitioner, a Negro woman, brought this action under § 812, claiming that respondents, who are white, had refused to rent an apartment to her because of her race, in violation of § 804(a) of the Act, 42 U.S.C. § 3604(a). In her complaint she sought only injunctive relief and punitive damages; a claim for compensatory damages was later added.[25] After an evidentiary hearing, the District Court granted preliminary injunctive relief, enjoining the respondents from renting the apartment in question to anyone else pending the trial on the merits. This injunction was dissolved some five months later with the petitioner's consent, after she had finally obtained other housing, and the case went to trial on the issues of actual and punitive damages.

Respondents made a timely demand for jury trial in their answer. The District Court, however, held that jury trial was neither authorized by Title VIII nor required by the Seventh Amendment, and denied the jury request. Rogers v. Loether, 312 F. Supp. 1008 (ED Wis.1970). After trial on the merits, the District Judge found that respondents had in fact discriminated against petitioner on account of her race. Although he found no actual damages, see n. [25], *supra*, he awarded $250 in punitive damages....

The Court of Appeals reversed on the jury trial issue. Rogers v. Loether, 467 F.2d 1110 (CA7 1972). After an extended analysis, the court concluded essentially that the Seventh Amendment gave respondents the right to a jury trial in this action, and therefore interpreted the statute to authorize jury trials so as to eliminate any question of its constitution-

---

25. Although the lower courts treated the action as one for compensatory and punitive damages, petitioner has emphasized in this Court that her complaint sought only punitive damages. It is apparent, however, that petitioner later sought to recover actual damages as well. The District Court's pretrial order indicates the judge's understanding, following a pretrial conference with counsel, that the question of actual damages would be one of the issues to be tried.... Petitioner in fact attempted to prove actual damages, ... but her testimony was excluded for failure to comply with a pretrial discovery order. The District Judge later dismissed the claim of actual damages for failure of proof. In these circumstances, it is irrelevant that the pleadings were never formally amended. Fed.Rules Civ.Proc. 15(b), 16. [Footnote by the Court.]

ality.] In view of the importance of the jury trial issue in the administration and enforcement of Title VIII and the diversity of views in the lower courts on the question, we granted certiorari, 412 U.S. 937 (1973).[26] [We affirm.]

The legislative history on the jury trial question is sparse, and what little is available is ambiguous. There seems to be some indication that supporters of Title VIII were concerned that the possibility of racial prejudice on juries might reduce the effectiveness of civil rights damages actions.[27] On the other hand, one bit of testimony during committee hearings indicates an awareness that jury trials would have to be afforded in damages actions under Title VIII.[28] Both petitioner and respondents have presented plausible arguments from the wording and construction of § 812. We see no point to giving extended consideration to these arguments, however, for we think it is clear that the Seventh Amendment entitles either party to demand a jury trial in an action for damages in the federal courts under § 812.[29]

The Seventh Amendment provides that "[i]n suits at common law, where the value in controversy shall exceed twenty dollars, the right of trial by jury shall be preserved." Although the thrust of the Amendment was to preserve the right to jury trial as it existed in 1791, it has long been settled that the right extends beyond the common-law forms of action recognized at that time. Mr. Justice Story established the basic principle in 1830:

> "The phrase 'common law,' found in this clause, is used in contradistinction to equity, and admiralty, and maritime jurisprudence.... By *common law*, [the Framers of the Amendment] meant ... not merely suits, which the *common* law recognized among its old and settled proceedings, but suits in which *legal* rights were to be ascertained and determined, in contradistinction to those where

---

26. Petitioner married while the case was pending before the Court, and her motion to change the caption of the case accordingly was granted. 414 U.S. 1140 (1974). [Footnote by the Court.]

27. *See, e.g.*, Hearings on Miscellaneous Proposals Regarding Civil Rights before Subcommittee No. 5 of the House Committee on the Judiciary, 89th Cong., 2d Sess., ser. 16, p. 1183 (1966). [Footnote by the Court.]

28. See Hearings on S. 3296 before the Subcommittee on Constitutional Rights of the Senate Committee on the Judiciary, 89th Cong., 2d Sess., pt. 2, p. 1178 (1966). [Footnote by the Court.]

29. We recognize, of course, the "cardinal principle that this Court will first ascertain whether a construction of the statute is fairly possible by which the [constitutional] question may be avoided." United States v. Thirty-Seven Photographs, 402 U.S. 363, 369 (1971), and cases there cited. In this case, however, the necessity for jury trial is so clearly settled by our prior Seventh Amendment decisions that it would be futile to spend time on the statutory issue, particularly since our result is not to invalidate the Civil Rights Act but only to direct that a certain form of procedure be employed in federal court actions under § 812.

Moreover, the Seventh Amendment issue in this case is in a very real sense the narrower ground of decision. Section 812(a) expressly authorizes actions to be brought "in appropriate State or local courts of general jurisdiction," as well as in the federal courts. The Court has not held that the right to jury trial in civil cases is an element of due process applicable to state courts through the Fourteenth Amendment. Since we rest our decision on Seventh Amendment rather than statutory grounds, we express no view as to whether jury trials must be afforded in § 812 actions in the state courts. [Footnote by the Court.]

equitable rights alone were recognized, and equitable remedies were administered. . . . In a just sense, the amendment then may well be construed to embrace all suits which are not of equity and admiralty jurisdiction, whatever might be the peculiar form which they may assume to settle legal rights." Parsons v. Bedford, 3 Pet. [28 U.S.] 433, 446–447 (1830) (emphasis in original).

Petitioner nevertheless argues that the Amendment is inapplicable to new causes of action created by congressional enactment. As the Court of Appeals observed, however, we have considered the applicability of the constitutional right to jury trial in actions enforcing statutory rights "as a matter too obvious to be doubted." 467 F.2d, at 1114. Although the Court has apparently never discussed the issue at any length, we have often found the Seventh Amendment applicable to causes of action based on statutes. See, e.g., Dairy Queen, Inc. v. Wood, 369 U.S. 469, 477 (1962) (trademark laws); Hepner v. United States, 213 U.S. 103, 115 (1909) (immigration laws). . . . Whatever doubt may have existed should now be dispelled. The Seventh Amendment does apply to actions enforcing statutory rights, and requires a jury trial upon demand, if the statute creates legal rights and remedies, enforceable in an action for damages in the ordinary courts of law.

NLRB v. Jones & Laughlin Steel Corp., 301 U.S. 1 (1937), relied on by petitioner, lends no support to her statutory-rights argument. The Court there upheld the award of back pay without jury trial in an NLRB unfair labor practice proceeding, rejecting a Seventh Amendment claim on the ground that the case involved a "statutory proceeding" and "not a suit at common law or in the nature of such a suit." Id., at 48. Jones & Laughlin merely stands for the proposition that the Seventh Amendment is generally inapplicable in administrative proceedings, where jury trials would be incompatible with the whole concept of administrative adjudication[30] and would substantially interfere with the NLRB's role in the statutory scheme. . . . But when Congress provides for enforcement of statutory rights in an ordinary civil action in the district courts, where there is obviously no functional justification for denying the jury trial right, a jury trial must be available if the action involves rights and remedies of the sort typically enforced in an action at law.

We think it is clear that a damages action under § 812 is an action to enforce "legal rights" within the meaning of our Seventh Amendment decisions. . . . A damages action under the statute sounds basically in tort—the statute merely defines a new legal duty, and authorizes the courts to compensate a plaintiff for the injury caused by the defendant's wrongful breach. . . . More important, the relief sought here—actual and punitive damages—is the traditional form of relief offered in the courts of law.[31]

---

30. "[T]he concept of expertise on which the administrative agency rests is not consistent with the use by it of a jury as fact finder." L. Jaffe, Judicial Control of Administrative Action 90 (1965). [Footnote by the Court.]

31. The procedural history of this case generated some question in the courts be-

We need not, and do not, go so far as to say that any award of monetary relief must necessarily be "legal" relief. *See, e.g.,* Mitchell v. Robert DeMario Jewelry, Inc., 361 U.S. 288 (1960) [(a discretionary back pay award may be regarded as an equitable remedy)]; Porter v. Warner Holding Co., 328 U.S. 395 (1946) [(a decree compelling one to disgorge profits or rents acquired illegally may be regarded as an equitable remedy)]. A comparison of Title VIII with Title VII of the Civil Rights Act of 1964, where the courts of appeals have held that jury trial is not required in an action for reinstatement and back pay,[32] is instructive, although we of course express no view on the jury trial issue in that context. In Title VII cases the courts of appeals have characterized back pay as an integral part of an equitable remedy, a form of restitution. But the statutory language on which this characterization is based—

> "[T]he court may enjoin the respondent from engaging in such unlawful employment practice, and order such affirmative action as may be appropriate, which may include, but is not limited to, reinstatement or hiring of employees, with or without back pay ..., or any other equitable relief as the court deems appropriate," 42 U.S.C. § 2000e–5(g) (1970 ed., Supp. II)—

contrasts sharply with § 812's simple authorization of an action for actual and punitive damages. In Title VII cases, also, the courts have relied on the fact that the decision whether to award back pay is committed to the discretion of the trial judge. There is no comparable discretion here: if a plaintiff proves unlawful discrimination and actual damages, he is entitled to judgment for that amount. Nor is there any sense in which the award here can be viewed as requiring the defendant to disgorge funds wrongfully withheld from the plaintiff. Whatever may be the merit of the "equitable" characterization in Title VII cases, there is surely no basis for characterizing the award of compensatory and punitive damages here as equitable relief.

We are not oblivious to the force of petitioner's policy arguments. Jury trials may delay to some extent the disposition of Title VIII damages actions. But Title VIII actions seeking only equitable relief will be unaffected, and preliminary injunctive relief remains available without a jury trial even in damages actions. Dairy Queen, Inc. v. Wood, 369

low as to whether the action should be viewed as one for damages and injunctive relief, or as one for damages alone, for purposes of analyzing the jury trial issue. The Court of Appeals concluded that the right to jury trial was properly tested by the relief sought in the complaint and not by the claims remaining at the time of trial. 467 F.2d, at 1118–1119. We need express no view on this question. If the action is properly viewed as one for damages only, our conclusion that this is a legal claim obviously requires a jury trial on demand. And if this legal claim is joined with an equitable claim, the right to jury trial on the legal claim, including all issues common to both claims, remains intact. The right cannot be abridged by characterizing the legal claim as 'incidental' to the equitable relief sought.... [Footnote by the Court.]

32. Johnson v. Georgia Highway Express, Inc., 417 F.2d 1122, 1125 (CA5 1969); Robinson v. Lorillard Corp., 444 F.2d 791, 802 (CA4), *cert. dismissed under Rule 60,* 404 U.S. 1006 (1971); *cf.* McFerren v. County Board of Education, 455 F.2d 199, 202–204 (CA6 1972); Harkless v. Sweeny Independent School District, 427 F.2d 319, 324 (CA5 1970), *cert. denied,* 400 U.S. 991 (1971).... [Footnote by the Court.]

U.S., at 479 n.20. Moreover, the statutory requirement of expedition of § 812 actions, 42 U.S.C. § 3614 (1970), applies equally to jury and non-jury trials. We recognize, too, the possibility that jury prejudice may deprive a victim of discrimination of the verdict to which he or she is entitled. Of course, the trial judge's power to direct a verdict, to grant judgment notwithstanding the verdict, or to grant a new trial provides substantial protection against this risk and respondents' suggestion that jury trials will expose a broader segment of the populace to the example of the federal civil rights laws in operation has some force. More fundamentally, however, these considerations are insufficient to overcome the clear command of the Seventh Amendment. The decision of the Court of Appeals must be affirmed.

Further References

Abraham, H.J., *The Judicial Process: An Introductory Analysis of the Courts of the United States, England, and France* (7th ed. 1998).

Baker, J.H., *An Introduction to English Legal History* (4th ed. 2002).

Baker, T.E., *Rationing Justice on Appeal: The Problems of the U.S. Courts of Appeals* (1994).

Hall, F.W., "The Common Law: An Account of Its Reception in the United States," 4 Vanderbilt Law Review 791 (1951).

Hellman, A.D., ed., *Restructuring Justice: The Innovations of the Ninth Circuit and the Future of the Federal Courts* (1990).

Kempin, F.G., *Historical Introduction to Anglo–American Law in a Nutshell* (3d ed. 1990).

Oakley, J.B., "The Screening of Appeals: The Ninth Circuit's Experience in the Eighties and Innovations for the Nineties," 1991 Brigham Young University Law Review 859.

Radcliffe, G.R.Y., and Cross, G., *The English Legal System* (6th ed. 1977).

Spence, G., "The History of the Court of Chancery," 2 *Select Essays in Anglo–American Legal History* 219 (1907–1909).

Thayer, J.B., "The Older Modes of Trial," 5 Harvard Law Review 45 (1891).

Thompson, R.S., and Oakley, J.B., "From Information to Opinion in Appellate Courts: How Funny Things Happen on the Way Through the Forum," 1986 Arizona State Law Journal 1.

Chapter III

STATUTES, CASE LAW, AND
JUDICIAL PRECEDENT

A. OVERVIEW

In Chapter I you were introduced to two formal sources of law: legislation and case law. You will recall that legislation is prescribed by some formally constituted law-making body, or by popular initiative, and (in the Anglo–American legal system at least) is generally prospective in application (that is, legislation makes rules of law to be applied in the future). The most familiar form of institution for enacting legislation is simply called a *legislature,* such as the Congress of the United States, the legislatures of the fifty states, and the Parliament of Great Britain. Laws enacted formally by legislatures are called *statutes.* Statutory law is illustrated in Section C of this Chapter.

So long as the legislature acts with the powers granted to it by the constitution which created it, its statutes are unquestionably *authoritative,* which is to say that judges have no choice but to decide lawsuits in accordance with applicable statutes. The application of statutes may raise difficult questions of statutory construction, which we will explore in Chapter VI. The constitutionality of statutes, although a matter of the greatest public significance, is a relatively rare problem for the practicing lawyer to encounter. Except for alerting you in Chapter I to the special way in which American constitutional law affects the process of legal classification, we will not attempt to present the basic principles of what American legislatures constitutionally can and cannot do.

In this chapter and the two which follow, we deal at length with the second of the formal sources of law: case law or "precedent," that is, the decisions by which judges have resolved previous lawsuits. The authoritative force of precedent is far more flexible than the authoritative force of statutes. This flexibility results from two circumstances.

First, judges do not typically decide cases with the sort of canonical language of general application which characterizes a statute. Although cases are normally decided on the basis of rules or general principles, judges will often articulate their decisions in language that focuses on the unique facts upon which the claims of the parties arise. A legislature, for instance, might provide that "any person who sells stock in an insolvent corporation without first disclosing to the purchaser that the corporation is insolvent, is liable to the purchaser of the stock for the refund of the purchase price." The decision of a court in a lawsuit for the return of the purchase price of stock bought by a purchaser who did not have the benefit of such a statute might hold only that, under the circumstances of that case, the sale of the stock without the disclosure to the purchaser of the fact of insolvency constituted fraud, and that under the relevant case law the commission of fraud made the seller liable to the purchaser for a refund of the purchase price of the stock. If another case arises in which the purchaser of stock in an insolvent corporation sues the seller of the stock for a refund, and the purchaser has only the previous decision, rather than a statute, to rely upon as establishing a legal right to the refund, a great deal will depend upon the analysis of the judicial ruling in the prior case. Was it held that any sale of worthless stock was fraudulent in the absence of disclosure? Or was the ruling confined to the particular kind of stock at issue in the prior case (mining stock, for instance), or to the particular kind of plaintiff in the prior case (a financially unsophisticated widow who had invested her life savings, for instance), or to the particular kind of defendant (a publicly-licensed stock broker, for instance)? There might be many other factual differences between the first case and the second.

Lawyers call reliance on these differences as a means of avoiding the authoritative effect of the prior decision the process of "distinguishing" a precedent. Because virtually all lawsuits arise on unique facts, virtually every precedent can arguably be "distinguished" from a subsequent case. Obviously some such distinctions are frivolous, because the factual difference is patently irrelevant to the legal rule announced in the prior case—as when the first case involves the operation of a red automobile in what is held to be a negligent manner, and the second case involves just the same sort of operation of a blue automobile. Equally obviously, the process of determining which distinctions are relevant and which are not is frequently more difficult. Suppose a court holds that a homeowner's insurance policy which excludes coverage of fire loss caused by the "unreasonably dangerous storage of inflammables in the home" does not obligate the insurance company to cover losses from a fire caused by a homeowner's storage of a can of gasoline in the kitchen. Does this precedent control a suit to enforce a similar insurance policy for a loss caused by the storage of a can of paint thinner in the garage?

The problem of determining whether a preceding judicial decision is really "on point" and not factually distinguishable from the legal dispute in which it is cited as a precedent has two dimensions. It involves not only the question of what the facts were in the preceding case, but also which of the facts of the preceding case were actually relied upon by the court in deciding the case. It also involves the question of whether the decision in the preceding case, if articulated in general terms which went beyond the facts actually then at issue, ought to be controlling in a subsequent case involving different facts. This second dimension calls for the determination of the *"ratio decidendi"* (a Latin phrase meaning "the reason for the decision") or the "holding" of the prior case. This problem will be discussed in detail in Chapter IV.

This leads us to the second fundamental reason for the flexibility of the authoritative force of precedent. Even when the controlling facts and *ratio decidendi* of a precedent are indisputably applicable to and dispositive of a subsequent lawsuit, an American court will not automatically follow that precedent—even if the court which decided the precedent is the very court which is later asked to follow it. This is not to say that American courts never follow precedent. They almost always do, and they frequently invoke the doctrine of *"stare decisis,"* which seems to say they must. This makes the doctrine of *stare decisis* a complex problem of American law, fascinating to study, but not easy to understand.

B. THE DOCTRINE OF *STARE DECISIS*

The term *stare decisis* is an abbreviation of the Latin phrase *"stare decisis et non quieta movere,"* which literally means "to stand by precedents and not to disturb settled points." As a legal term of art, *stare decisis* signifies the principle that, once a disputed point of law has been settled by a judicial decision, that decision will be followed in all subsequent cases. Differently expressed, *stare decisis* forecloses parties to a lawsuit from rearguing a point of law which has previously been argued and resolved in some prior lawsuit within the same legal system. It does not matter that the parties to the present lawsuit are not the same as the parties who argued the case in which the precedent was established.[1]

You should understand that the doctrine of *stare decisis is binding* to the extent that a lower court must follow the applicable precedent of a court with supervisory jurisdiction over it. Thus, a federal trial court is bound to follow the case law of the federal court of appeals for the circuit in which it is located, and all federal courts must follow the case law of the United States Supreme Court, as must state courts with respect to questions of federal law.

State courts are not bound by decisions of any federal court on nonfederal matters. Nor are they bound by decisions of federal courts, other than the Supreme Court, even on federal matters, although they will usually pay close attention to such decisions.

The most significant problem of *stare decisis* is the treatment by a court of its own precedent. Under the American doctrine of *stare decisis*, no court, state or federal, is bound absolutely by its own decisions. It

1. As you will learn in Civil Procedure, *"res judicata"* ("a thing which has been adjudicated") is the general term for the doctrine that particular parties may not relitigate some dispute which they personally have previously had settled by a court. In its specific applications the doctrine of *res judicata* bars relitigation of particular issues of fact or law as well as the more general contentions of a lawsuit, such as whether one party is liable to another for having caused a particular injury. Unlike the doctrine of *stare decisis*, the doctrine of *res judicata* is generally followed quite strictly by American courts.

may overrule its decisions, except where overruling would put the court out of line with decisions of a higher court by which it is bound.

In Thomas v. Washington Gas Light Co., 448 U.S. 261, 272 (1980), the following statement is found in the plurality opinion written by Justice Stevens:

> The doctrine of *stare decisis* imposes a severe burden on the litigant who asks us to disavow one of our precedents. For that doctrine not only plays an important role in orderly adjudication; it also serves the broader societal interests in evenhanded, consistent, and predictable application of legal rules. When rights have been created or modified in reliance on established rules of law, the arguments against their change have special force.

Justice Stevens points out in a footnote that *stare decisis* has a more limited application when the precedent rests on constitutional grounds, because correction of an earlier ill-advised decision through legislation is practically impossible.

E. BODENHEIMER, JURISPRUDENCE: THE PHILOSOPHY AND METHOD OF THE LAW

pp. 425–430 (Rev. ed. 1974).[2]

In a legal system where the rule of *stare decisis* is strictly and consistently applied, a precedent must not be disregarded or set aside, even though the rule or principle for which it is authority may seem archaic and wholly unreasonable to the judge called upon to apply it in a lawsuit. This element of the doctrine has frequently evoked criticism from laymen as well as from lawyers. A famous instance of lay criticism of the doctrine is an often-quoted passage from *Gulliver's Travels* by Jonathan Swift. "It is a maxim among ... lawyers," says Gulliver, "that whatever hath been done before may legally be done again: and therefore they take special care to record all the decisions formerly made against common justice and the general reason of mankind. These, under the name of precedents, they produce as authorities to justify the most iniquitous opinions; and the judges never fail of directing accordingly." Some jurists and judges have likewise charged that the doctrine of precedent produces excessive conservatism.

Since adherence to the doctrine of precedent obviously tends to freeze the law and to preserve the *status quo*, it must be asked what the advantages and meritorious features of the doctrine are. We may list the following five positive factors in support of the *stare decisis* principle:

(1) The doctrine introduces a modicum of certainty and calculability into the planning of private and business activities. It enables people to engage in trade and arrange their personal affairs with a certain amount of confidence that they will not become entangled in litigation. It gives them some basis for predicting how other members of the community

are likely to act toward them (assuming that such other members of the community comply with the law). Without this element of calculability, people would be uncertain of their rights, duties, and obligations, and they would be unable to ascertain what they might do without fear of coercive sanctions. Men would never know whether to settle or litigate a dispute if every established rule was liable to be overthrown from one day to the next, and litigation would be increased a thousandfold under such a state of affairs.

(2) *Stare decisis* provides attorneys counseling private parties with some settled basis for legal reasoning and the rendering of legal advice. A lawyer who does not have available to him the benefit of certain tools which are helpful to him in forecasting the probable outcome of litigation is of little use to his clients. In the words of Sir William Jones, "No man who is not a lawyer would ever know how to act and no lawyer would, in many instances, know how to advise, unless courts are bound by authority."

(3) The doctrine of *stare decisis* tends to operate as a curb on the arbitrariness of judges. It serves as a prop for weak and unstable judges who are inclined to be partial and prejudiced. By forcing them to follow (as a rule) established precedents, it reduces their temptation to render decisions colored by favor and bias. "If the doctrine of precedent were to be abolished in this country (where statutes have a relatively limited scope), the judges would be free to operate according to their individual whims and their private notions of right and wrong throughout the entire area of human relations not covered by statute." Such a condition would not be conducive to the maintenance of respect for the law and the preservation of public confidence in the integrity of the judiciary. One important reason why people are willing to accept judicial decisions as binding is that they are supposed to be based on an objective body of law and on impersonal reasoning free from subjective predilections— even though this condition may not always be fully realized in the practical operation of the legal system.

(4) The practice of following prior decisions facilitates dispatch of judicial business and thereby promotes efficient judicial administration. Following precedents saves the time and conserves the energy of judges and at the same time reduces the costs of litigation for the parties. It makes it unnecessary for the court to examine a legal problem *de novo* each time the problem is presented again. "The labor of judges," said Mr. Justice Cardozo, "would be increased almost to the breaking point if every past decision could be reopened in every case, and one could not lay one's own course of bricks on the secure foundation of the courses laid by others who had gone before him."

(5) The doctrine of precedent also receives support from the human sense of justice. The force of precedent in the law is heightened, in the words of Karl Llewellyn, by "that curious, almost universal sense of

justice which urges that all men are properly to be treated alike in like circumstances." If A was granted relief last month against an unwarranted interference with his privacy, it would be unjust to deny such relief to B this month if the facts shown by B are essentially the same as those that were presented by A a month ago.

In its relation to justice, however, the doctrine of precedent exhibits a weakness which has often been noted. A precedent controlling the decision of a court may be considered antiquated at the time when the problem arises again for decision. The prevailing notions of justice may have undergone a marked change in the interval between the earlier and the later decision. The first decision, reflecting perhaps the views of an earlier epoch of history, may have denied an action based on an invasion of the right to privacy. The decision may appear iniquitous to a modern judge, since our notions regarding infringement of personal privacy may in the meantime have become more sensitive and refined.

Assuming that there is a close relation between equality and justice, it must be realized that the equality contemplated by *stare decisis* is that between a *past* and a *present* decision. Justice, on the other hand, may require a modification of the standards of equality because of a change in social outlook. While *stare decisis* promotes equality in *time,* that is, equal treatment as between A litigating his case in 1760 and B obtaining a decision in a lawsuit occurring in 1960, justice may be more properly concerned with equality in *space,* with an equal treatment of two persons or two situations measured in terms of contemporary value judgments. Furthermore, the earlier decision may have been rendered by a weak or inept judge, so that considerations of justice and reasonableness might be adduced in favor of its overthrow on this ground.

What can the judge confronted with an outdated or unreasonable precedent do? May he disregard or set aside the precedent on the ground that it is repugnant to our contemporary notions of right and wrong? Or is he compelled to sacrifice justice to stability and adhere to the unwelcome precedent?

Prior to 1966, the highest courts of England and the United States took conflicting positions on this question. The British House of Lords decided in 1898 that it was absolutely bound by its own decisions. This principle was established in the case of London Street Tramways Co., Ltd. v. London County Council, in which the House of Lords ruled that "a decision of this House upon a question of law is conclusive, and ... nothing but an act of Parliament can set right that which is alleged to be wrong in a judgment of this House." In endeavoring to justify the rule, the Earl of Halsbury, who wrote the opinion in this case, made the following comments: "I do not deny that cases of individual hardship may arise, and there may be a current of opinion in the profession that such and such a judgment was erroneous; but what is that occasional interference with what is perhaps abstract justice as compared with the inconvenience—the disastrous inconvenience—of having each question subject to being reargued and the dealings of mankind rendered doubtful by reason of different decisions, so that in truth and in fact there would be no real final Court of Appeal?" In 1966, however, the House of Lords changed its position. Lord Chancellor Gardiner announced that "Their Lordships . . . recognise that too rigid adherence to precedent may lead to injustice in a particular case and also unduly restrict the proper development of the law. They propose, therefore, to modify their present practice and, while treating former decisions of this House as normally binding, to depart from a previous decision when it appears right to do so."[3]

In the United States, _stare decisis_ has never been considered an inexorable command, and the duty to follow precedent is held to be qualified by the right to overrule prior decisions. Although the inferior courts within a certain precinct of jurisdiction are considered bound by the decisions of the intermediate or highest appellate courts, the highest courts of the states, as well as the supreme federal court, reserve to themselves the right to depart from a rule previously established by them. In the interest of legal security, however, they will not lightly make use of this prerogative. "Adherence to precedent should be the rule and not the exception," said Mr. Justice Cardozo. Mr. Justice Brandeis observed: "_Stare decisis_ is usually the wise policy, because in most matters it is more important that the applicable rule be settled than that it be settled right." Nevertheless, the court will sometimes overrule its own decisions when it is necessary to avoid the perpetuation of pernicious error or where an earlier decision is wholly out of step with the exigencies of the time. On the whole, the United States Supreme Court will be less inclined to set aside a precedent which has become a well-established rule of property or commercial law than to overrule a case involving the validity of legislation under the federal Constitution. In the words of Chief Justice Stone, "The doctrine of _stare decisis,_ however appropriate or even necessary at times, has only a limited application in the field of constitutional law." In this area, it is particularly important to keep the law in accord with the dynamic flow of the social order, since correction of constitutional decisions by means of legislation is practically impossible.

It would seem that the American attitude toward precedents is preferable to the policy followed by the English House of Lords prior to 1966. Since the maintenance of stability is not the only goal of the legal order, the judges should be given authority to set aside former decisions which are hopelessly obsolete or thoroughly ill-advised and contrary to the social welfare. "If judges have woefully misinterpreted the mores of their day or if the mores of their day are no longer those of ours, they ought not to tie, in helpless submission, the hands of their successors." The same elasticity should be allowed to the judges with respect to precedents which represent an anomaly, do not fit into the structure of the legal system as a whole, or are at odds with some of its guiding principles. This last point was emphasized by Justice Frankfurter in Helvering v. Hallock, where he wrote: "We recognize that _stare decisis_

---

3. _See_ [1966] Weekly Law Reports 1234, 110 Solicitor's Journal 584 (1966); W. Barton Leach, "Revisionism in the House of Lords: The Bastion of Rigid Stare Decisis Falls," 80 Harvard Law Review 797 (1967).

embodies an important social policy. It represents an element of continuity in law and is rooted in the psychological need to satisfy reasonable expectations. But *stare decisis* is a principle of policy and not a mechanical formula of adherence to the latest decision, however recent and questionable, when such adherence involves collision with a prior doctrine more embracing in its scope, intrinsically sounder, and verified by experience." In granting courts the right to overrule their decisions, it should be made clear, however, that in exercising this right they should make certain that less harm will be done by rejecting a previous rule than by retaining it, even though the rule may be a questionable one. In every case involving the abandonment of an established precedent, the interest in a stable and continuous order of law must be carefully balanced against the advantages of improvement and innovation.

C. STATUTORY LAW AND CASE LAW

In this section, we will introduce you to the differences between statutory law and case law and we will explore the relationship between the two. In common law jurisdictions, the courts are often the first lawmakers to develop a rule of law. Legislatures may then enact statutes that announce a new rule that is in conflict with the judge-made rule of law. Because legislatures are superior to courts in the hierarchy of lawmakers, the impact of such legislation will be to overturn the judge-made rule of law. Also, because legislation usually operates prospectively, the impact of the legislation usually will be to overrule the judge-made rule of law prospectively. Often the common law judges will have refused to recognize a particular cause of action, and the legislature will have chosen to create the cause of action purely prospectively. When this happens, the plaintiff who was injured before the effective date of the statute will not be able to recover damages unless the court takes jurisdiction over the plaintiff's case and overrules the judge-made rule of law retroactively. In cases that are governed by a statute, it is the role of the judiciary to apply it to controversies that arise after the effective date of the statute. Once a court has interpreted the statute, that interpretation becomes a precedent that is binding in future cases. These principles are illustrated by the cases that appear below.

BALDWIN v. STATE

Supreme Court of Vermont, 1965.
125 Vt. 317, 215 A.2d 492.

Before HOLDEN, C. J., and SHANGRAW, BARNEY, SMITH and KEYSER, JJ.

HOLDEN, CHIEF JUSTICE.

The plaintiffs are husband and wife. The husband, Harold Baldwin, Sr., sues to recover for personal injuries sustained when the motor truck he was operating was struck by a railway locomotive, operated by the defendants, at a highway crossing. His complaint sets forth various duties owing from the defendants' failure to use reasonable care for his safety and others in approaching the grade crossing where the accident occurred.... There are other allegations that the defendants failed to maintain the railroad crossing in a safe condition for the protection of persons using the highway and especially the plaintiff who was unable to extricate himself and his vehicle from the crossing.

There is no allegation that Mrs. Baldwin was with her husband at the time of the accident. The standing of the plaintiff, Beatrice Baldwin, is based entirely on her claim that she is the wife of her co-plaintiff and that, as a result of the negligence of the defendants, she has been deprived of the consortium of her husband, the plaintiff, Harold Baldwin, Sr., to her damage in the amount of $25,000. The trial court dismissed the complaint of Mrs. Baldwin on motion of the defendants....

The elements which constitute the wife's claim for loss of consortium are not specified in the complaint. The plaintiffs' brief, however, makes it clear that the wife does not seek compensation for loss of her husband's support for she recognizes that her husband's loss of earning power is an element of recovery in his action. The definition relied upon by the plaintiff is that of her husband's affection, the conjugal society, aid and cooperation in every conjugal relation, as that term is defined in Woodhouse v. Woodhouse, 99 Vt. 91, 130 A. 758 [(1925)]. [In *Woodhouse*, the plaintiff-wife recovered damages against her parents-in-law for intentionally alienating the affections of her ex-husband by intermeddling in their marriage. The court held: "The gist of the action is the loss of consortium of the husband.... This includes his affection, his conjugal society, his aid and cooperation in every conjugal relation. It is not essential to the maintenance of the action that there should be any loss of service or any pecuniary loss whatever. Nor is the actionable character of the injury dependent upon separation or the physical absence of the husband. The wrong could be inflicted though the plaintiff was living with her husband at the time." 99 Vt. at 113, 130 A. at 769.]

There is no dispute that at common law a married woman had no right of action to sue for the loss of consortium of her husband. Since the Married Women's Act [of 1884] the wife can maintain an action for alienation of affections. Independent of property considerations, a remedy was afforded directly to the injured wife on the theory that the enticement or corruption of the minds and affections of one's consort is a civil wrong for which the offender is liable to the injured husband or wife. Knapp v. Wing, 72 Vt. 334, 338, 47 A. 1075[(1900)]. [In *Knapp*, the plaintiff-wife brought an intentional tort action for alienation of affections against her ex-husband's aunt, who allegedly had told her nephew that "he should never have a cent of her property as long as he lived with the plaintiff." *Id*. at 1076. The court held that the plaintiff had standing to sue the defendant for alienation of affections because the marriage contract "conferred upon her the right to his consortium" and "the deprivation of that right by acts of the defendant was a wrong for which the law should afford a remedy." *Id.* at 1076. The court recognized that it was announcing a new rule of law, but justified its decision on the following grounds: "It was a maxim of the common law that for every wrong the law provided an adequate redress; but the law was consistent in denying the wife an action against another woman for debauching her husband, or for alienating his affections from and depriving her of his society and support, for she had no legal existence separate from her husband, and consequently could not hold separate property.... It is now nearly a universal rule in those states in this country where the common-law disabilities of married women have been removed that this kind of action is maintainable." *Id.*]

In alienation cases, loss of consortium on the part of the injured spouse is the gist and essence of the wrong. The wrong is intentional and the element of punishment is involved....

In this jurisdiction the wife's remedy for disruption of the marriage relationship has been restricted to wrongs directly inflicted upon the marital obligation. Other wrongful acts which have indirectly accomplished this result, although done intentionally against the husband, were held not actionable at the suit of the wife. Nieberg v. Cohen, 88 Vt. 281, 92 A. 214 [(1914)]. [In *Nieberg*, the court refused to allow the plaintiff-wife to sue for loss of consortium caused indirectly by the defendants' alleged intentional false imprisonment of her husband. The court acknowledged that "the father, being entitled to the services of his children during their minority, may sue for any injury wrongfully inflicted upon his child which causes a loss of service," and that "a husband has a right to recover for any injury wrongfully inflicted upon his wife, physical or otherwise, which deprives him of her services." *Id.* at 217. But the court held that "the wife has no corresponding general right." *Id.* Consequently, a wife was deemed to have no cause of action for an indirectly-inflicted loss of consortium.]

Recognizing this restriction, the plaintiffs candidly call upon this Court to overrule the prevailing law as a proper exercise of the judicial function. It is said this is an essential step to keep the law apace with current mores and changing values. We are referred to several recent decisions in a minority of jurisdictions where the judicial process has been thus applied. Dini v. Naiditch, 20 Ill.2d 406, 891, 170 N.E.2d 881 [(1960)]; Montgomery v. Stephan, 359 Mich. 33, 101 N.W.2d 227, 232 [(1960)]; Hitaffer v. Argonne Co., 87 U.S. App. D.C. 57, 183 F.2d 811, 815 [(1950)].

. . . .

We recognize that our common law has afforded the husband a remedy for the loss of his wife's services and medical and other expenses resulting from her injury inflicted by the negligence of another.... These actions were grounded on loss of services and expenses incurred for medical care and assistance. We are not aware of any instance in this jurisdiction where the husband has been allowed a recovery separate and apart from these elements of damage.

The argument advanced in the cases upon which the plaintiffs rely to the effect that since the husband has a right of action, a wife should have equivalent recovery is not persuasive. Justice Schaefer's cogent dissent in *Dini v. Naiditch, supra,* 170 N.E.2d at 894, reminds us that it is no more than an historical accident that the husband's common law action survived the enactment of the Married Women's Act [because a wife may now sue in her own name to recover damages for her personal injuries, including the loss of her service capacity]. Survival has been by acquiescence and not because it has withstood critical analysis. In opposing the majority's departure from the common law rule to give the wife an independent action for loss of consortium, his opinion voices strong considerations against such recovery.

"Subject to legislative action, it is the function of a common-law court, in a case like this, to fix the boundaries within which an injury to one person gives another a right to recover damages. Each man's life is linked to the lives of many others, and an injury to one inevitably has its impact upon the lives of others. So far as I am aware, however, it has never been suggested that everyone who is adversely affected by an injury inflicted upon another should be allowed to recover his damages. It may be possible to argue that the relationship of husband and wife has distinctive characteristics that would justify a recovery which is denied to those who stand in other relationships to the injured person. But no such argument is advanced in the majority opinion, and it is hard to see why, for example, the wife of an injured man should be allowed a recovery that is denied to his children. If the boundaries of permissible recovery are to be extended, they should be extended upon a realistic appraisal of the factors involved, and not to achieve consistency with an outworn common-law cause of action." *Dini v. Naiditch, supra,* 170 N.E.2d at 894....

We hold that the complaint of the plaintiff, Beatrice Baldwin, fails to state a cause of action in negligence. We find no justification in established legal principle, precedent or policy to hold otherwise.... *Nieburg v. Cohen, supra,* 88 Vt. At 290;.... Restatement, Torts, § 695, Comment a. [*holding*]

Order dismissing the complaint of the plaintiff, Beatrice Baldwin, is affirmed. [*order*]

WHITNEY v. FISHER

Supreme Court of Vermont, 1980.
138 Vt. 468, 417 A.2d 934.

Before BARNEY, C.J., DALEY, BILLINGS and HILL, JJ., and SPRINGER, D.J., specially assigned.

BILLINGS, JUSTICE.

The sole issue in this case is whether as a matter of law a woman may recover for loss of consortium based on her husband's injuries. If so, [*issue*] the judgment below granting plaintiff, Donna Lee Whitney, such a recovery must be affirmed.

Facts

This action was commenced in 1976 upon a cause arising in 1973. On April 19, 1977, the legislature expressly authorized the bringing of an action for loss of consortium by either spouse with the enactment of 12 V.S.A. § 5431. [Section 5431 states: "An action for loss of consortium may be brought by either spouse." A companion statute abolished the common law cause of action for alienation of affections. 15 V.S.A. § 1001.]

The operational effect of statutory provisions with respect to their retroactivity is governed by 1 V.S.A. § 213, unless otherwise provided. This statute withholds retroactive effect from all enactments, except those relating to practice in court, competency of witnesses and amendments of process or pleading.... The provisions of 12 V.S.A. § 5431 simply create a substantive right and, therefore, are governed by the rule against retroactivity.

Failing to establish a cause of action under the statute, and since there appear to have been no prior enactments on the subject, the plaintiff's right is determined by the common law. The most recent Vermont case to fully consider the basis of a woman's right of action for loss of consortium is Baldwin v. State, 125 Vt. 317, 215 A.2d 492 (1965). There this Court, while acknowledging the right in a man, ... rejected the claim that a woman could also bring the action. The basis given by the court for that holding is that since the law recognizes no corresponding right in children, there is no reason to extend the availability of the action beyond the boundaries of an outworn common-law cause of action merely for the sake of consistency, unless some distinctive characteristic of the wife's status is shown to distinguish it from others. *Baldwin v. State, supra,* 125 Vt. at 320–21, 215 A.2d at 494 (quoting Dini v. Naiditch, 20 Ill.2d 406, 433, 170 N.E.2d 881, 884 (1960) (Schaefer, C.J., dissenting). This holding has since been applied without reexamination twice. *See* McAdam v. Wrisley, 134 Vt. 19, 20, 349 A.2d 886, 887 (1975); Herbert v. Layman, 125 Vt. 481, 486, 218 A.2d 706, 710 (1966). The only other Vermont case law on this subject would seem to be Nieberg v. Cohen, 88 Vt. 281, 92 A. 214 (1914), cited in *Baldwin v. State, supra,* 125 Vt. at 321, 215 A. at 494, for the proposition that since there was no "established legal principle, precedent or policy to hold otherwise," the Court would decline recognition of the right. Therefore, although this Court has heretofore declined to recognize a woman's right of action for loss of consortium, it has not foreclosed such recognition.

With respect to the rationale set forth in *Baldwin v. State, supra,* this Court long ago recognized that the action for loss of consortium is directed to the loss of affection, aid and cooperation in every conjugal relation, and conjugal society, as well as any pecuniary loss that might occur. Woodhouse v. Woodhouse, 99 Vt. 91, 113, 130 A. 758, 769 (1925).

Thus, while a child may have an interest in parental support, such an interest is different in kind from that protected by an action for loss of consortium because it does not have the breadth of the spousal interest....

Moreover, as numerous courts have recognized, there is substantial established principle, precedent and policy which compels this Court to reconsider the rule denying women a right of action for loss of consortium. *See* Annot., 36 A.L.R.3d 900 (1971). The plaintiff urges this Court to invoke the two-pronged test of the constitutionality of gender-based classifications under the equal protection clause of the Fourteenth Amendment to the United States Constitution. Recent United States Supreme Court decisions have required scrutiny of gender-based classifications to determine whether the classification serves "important governmental objectives" and whether the classification is "substantially related" to the attainment of those objectives. *See* ... Craig v. Boren, 429 U.S. 190 (1976)....

Inasmuch as the action for loss of consortium is for the remedy of injuries sustained by one who has been deprived of the affection, aid and cooperation in conjugal relations, conjugal society and support of another whom the law recognizes as a marital partner, ... it is difficult, indeed, to find any nonarbitrary distinction between the interests of the man and woman in their mutual society.... If there is a distinction between the society a woman can provide her husband and that which he provides her, it is wholly irrelevant to the availability of a right of action against those who interfere with that society, since that society requires the mutual participation of both spouses. There is no state of facts which reasonably may be conceived to justify a general rule denying a woman an action for loss of consortium, while recognizing the right in a man. Our prior cases cited herein for such a rule are hereby overruled insofar as they are inconsistent with this opinion. *holding*

Affirmed.

BARNEY, CHIEF JUSTICE, dissenting.

For reasons so cogently stated by Chief Justice Schaefer dissenting in Dini v. Naiditch, 20 Ill.2d 406, 431, 170 N.E.2d 881, 893 (1960), and cited in Baldwin v. State, 125 Vt. 317, 320, 215 A.2d 492, 494 (1965), I do not favor the concept of consortium damages as a separate item of recovery. Moreover, I find no compelling justification for disaffirming the holding in McAdam v. Wrisley, 134 Vt. 19, 20, 349 A.2d 886 (1975) [(a wife may not sue for loss of her husband's consortium)], particularly since this accident preceded both the enactment of 12 V.S.A. § 5431 (authorizing actions for loss of consortium by either spouse), and the *McAdam* holding....

DALEY, JUSTICE, dissenting.

Had the legislature intended 12 V.S.A. § 5431 to apply retroactively, they could have so stated. They did not, and therefore, as the majority appears to acknowledge, 1 V.S.A. § 213 bars retroactivity.... At the time these events occurred, plaintiff had no cause of action for loss of consortium. I would apply the law as it stood at that time, rather than create a cause of action out of thin air.

Notes and Questions

(1) The *Baldwin* opinion states that it is "an historical accident" that a husband can sue for loss of his wife's consortium, and refuses to grant a reciprocal right whereby a wife may sue for loss of her husband's consortium. Is there any justification for this discriminatory rule giving husbands greater rights than wives? Was there in 1965? If the Court had decided that such discrimination was intolerable, which should it have done: (A) extend the right to sue for loss of consortium to wives, or (B) end the "historical accident" by abrogating the right of husbands to sue for loss of consortium? For a history and contemporary analysis of loss-of-consortium suits by wives, *see* J. Bugg, "Torts—Recognition of Wife's Right to Husband's Consortium," 47 North Carolina Law Review 1006 (1969).

(2) The *Baldwin* opinion also states that "it is hard to see why, for example, the wife of an injured man should be allowed a recovery that is denied to his children." Does a wife's legal status more closely resemble a husband's status or a child's? How would you distinguish a wife's legal rights from a child's in a case like *Baldwin*? Do you see a constitutional issue lurking in this argument? In other words, is it permissible to classify husbands and wives differently with respect to the right to sue for loss of consortium? Is it any more (or less) permissible to classify spouses and children differently with respect to the right to sue for loss of consortium? What about classifications that distinguish between spouses and unmarried domestic partners, especially same-sex partners not permitted to marry? *See* L. Raisty, "Bystander Distress and Loss of Consortium: An Examination of the Relationship Requirements in Light of Romer v. Evans," 65 Fordham Law Review 2647 (1997).

(3) It is clear that *Whitney* overruled *Baldwin*. Is it clear *why*? Was the court indirectly giving effect to a change in statutory law? If so, is it fair to give statutes retroactive effect in pending cases? Or was the court overruling its own precedent? If so, does that mean that *Baldwin* was wrong when it was decided, and that Mrs. Baldwin was the victim of judicial error? Or does it mean that the court has changed its view of what the law should be? If so, is it fair to give retroactive effect to judicial changes in the common law? As a general rule, is it a good idea for courts to construe the Constitution in light of current legislative policy, or in some other way that is reflective of and responsive to public opinion?

NICHOLSON v. HUGH CHATHAM MEMORIAL HOSPITAL, INC.

Supreme Court of North Carolina, 1980.
300 N.C. 295, 266 S.E.2d 818.

CARLTON, JUSTICE.

Plaintiff presents the sole question whether under the law of North Carolina a wife has a cause of action for loss of consortium resulting [from a negligent injury to her husband. The Court of Appeals [,affirming the trial court's dismissal of plaintiff's complaint, correctly recognized the historical and common law rule in North Carolina and answered no. For reasons stated below, we reverse.

I.

At common law, consortium embraced those marital rights a husband had in respect to his wife.... Precisely what those rights were, however, has been open to various interpretations, ... and the term has been defined "sometimes in terms enormously complex as the judges followed the habit of lawyers of never using one word where two may be employed." Montgomery v. Stephan, 359 Mich. 33, 35, 101 N.W.2d 227, 228 (1960). Certainly, at common law the husband's action for loss of his wife's consortium was based on the understanding that his legal obligation to support his wife was balanced by her obligation to serve him.... This definition has been amended in other jurisdictions, however, so that the essence of consortium today has become the mutual right of a husband and wife to the society, companionship, comfort and affection of one another.... Unquestionably, this society and companionship includes a sexual component. *Cf.* Deems v. Western Maryland Railway Co., 247 Md. 95, 231 A.2d 514 (1967) (Consortium includes sexual relations); Ekalo v. Constructive Service Corporation of America, 46 N.J. 82, 215 A.2d 1 (1965) (Compensation for impotent husband is a measure of loss of consortium)....

At common law, a husband could sue negligent third parties for loss of his wife's consortium, but a wife had no comparable cause of action. Indeed, at common law, a wife could not even sue for her own personal injuries without joinder of her husband.... Hipp v. Dupont, 182 N.C. 9, 108 S.E. 318 (1921).... The reason for this inequity was that a wife was regarded as little more than a chattel in the eyes of the law. Only a husband could maintain an action for a wife's injuries and he could do so for the same reason he could maintain [an] action for injury to his horse, his slave or his other property. *Hipp v. Dupont, supra. See also* 3 W. Blackstone, Commentaries 143 (Lewis ed. 1897). All were his inferiors; none had capacity in themselves to sue.

The married women's provision in the North Carolina Constitution of 1868, Article X, section 6, abolished this unrealistic legal concept of married women, and provided that a wife's property no longer automatically became that of her husband upon marriage.... The legislature further clarified a wife's legal position in 1913 by [providing] that any damage for her own personal injuries could be recovered by a wife suing alone....

Even after passage of this legislation, it was clear that a husband could continue to maintain an action for loss of his wife's consortium, *see, e.g.*, ... Bailey v. Long, 172 N.C. 661, 90 S.E. 809 (1916). The question remained open, however, whether the married women's legislation in North Carolina gave a wife the equal right to sue for loss of her husband's consortium.

In *Hipp v. Dupont, supra*, this Court first considered the question and answered in the affirmative. There, plaintiff's husband sued and lost in a Virginia court for injuries he received as a result of his employment at defendant's chemical plant in Hopewell, Virginia [because he had assumed the risk of harm]. The family subsequently moved and plaintiff sued in North Carolina to recover [the] expenses incurred in maintaining her husband, for services performed in caring for her husband, for loss of his support and maintenance, for loss of his consortium and for her own mental anguish.

The Court in *Hipp* held that as a husband could continue to sue for loss of his wife's consortium, then by virtue of the married women's legislation and by virtue of logic and fairness, the plaintiff wife could maintain an action in her own behalf for loss of her husband's consortium.

This view did not last long. Four years later in Hinnant v. Tide Water Power Company, 189 N.C. 120, 126 S.E. 307 (1925), the Court expressly overruled *Hipp*, noting as it did so, that it joined the weight of authority in other jurisdictions.

In *Hinnant*, plaintiff's husband was injured by a train crash at 6:30 a.m. and died the following morning at 3:00 a.m. Plaintiff wife sued for mental shock and anguish, loss of support, and loss of her husband's "society, love and affection, his counsel and advice, his tender ministration in sickness, and the many comforts and pleasures which the marital relationship brings to those who are congenial with each other.". . . .

The judge instructed the jury that among other things, they could allow damages in the amount of fair compensation for plaintiff's loss of the society and companionship of her husband suffered between the time of his injury and the time of his death.

The jury awarded damages to plaintiff for loss of consortium. On appeal, this Court reversed the award and expressly overruled *Hipp v. Dupont*. In holding that a wife could no longer sue for loss of her husband's consortium, the Court gave four grounds for its decision. First, the Court emphasized that historically the wife had no action for consortium. The inference was that the married women's legislation had not changed that historical inability. Second, the Court emphasized that consortium included a predominant factor of service and that any attempt to separate that service element from society, companionship and affection was impossible. Thus, it held that a husband's right to recover loss of his wife's consortium was in actuality a right to recover for loss of her services. As the married women's acts had given the wife a right to recover for loss of her services in her own name, nothing compensable remained of a right to consortium. The inference of such a holding was that damages from loss of society and companionship rather than loss of service would be impossible to measure.

"Hinnant" reasoning

Third, the Court held that the wife's damages were too remote a consequence of a defendant's negligent injury of her husband to have been proximately caused by that injury. The Court apparently feared expansion of the cause of action so that unrelated third parties such as children, parents and employers would attempt to recover.

Fourth, the Court was concerned that to allow a wife's action for loss of consortium, particularly when the main component of that action was compensation for lost service, would allow double recovery. A husband, suing in his own behalf, would recover for loss of his services while a wife, suing for loss of consortium, would recover for loss of the selfsame services.

After *Hinnant*, a wife in North Carolina could not maintain an action for loss of consortium due to the negligence of third parties. The common law right of a husband to maintain such an action remained intact. That inequity was remedied in Helmstetler v. Duke Power Company, 224 N.C. 821, 32 S.E.2d 611 (1945). There plaintiff husband sued a defendant whose bus had seriously injured his wife. The Court affirmed summary judgment for defendant citing *Hinnant* and reasoning that because a wife had no cause of action for loss of consortium, a husband had no such cause of action either. Each spouse stood on a parity with each other and could recover for injuries done to each individually. Neither, however, could recover for loss of consortium due to negligent injuries to the other spouse.

Such has been the law in this jurisdiction since 1945. For the reasons stated below, however, we no longer consider this sound policy and expressly overrule *Hinnant* and *Helmstetler*.

II.

A close reading of both *Hinnant* and *Helmstetler* in the context of North Carolina law reveals several inconsistencies and anomalies. . . .

Taken together, *Hinnant* and *Helmstetler* strip both spouses of a right to recover for what can be a very real injury to the marital partnership. Such denuding contradicts the policy of modern law to expand liability in an effort to afford decent compensation as a measure to those injured by the wrongful conduct of others. Diaz v. Eli Lilly and Company, 364 Mass. 153, 302 N.E.2d 555 (1973); *Ekalo v. Constructive Service Corporation, supra*. The intent behind such a policy is presumptively to allow recourse for a definite injury to a legitimate interest, Millington v. Southeastern Elevator Company, 22 N.Y.2d 498, 293 N.Y.S.2d 305, 239 N.E.2d 897 (1968). . . . Thus to reason, as the *Helmstetler* Court did, that the action of the physically injured spouse alone is adequate compensation ignores the very real fact that the "uninjured" spouse's loss of conjugal fellowship deprives that spouse of sexual gratification and the possibility of children. Such deprivation can transform "a loving wife into a lonely nurse." *Ekalo v. Constructive Service, supra*, 46 N.J. at 84, 215 A.2d at 2.

Furthermore, the denial of a right to loss of consortium in cases such as this one is inconsistent with the rule in this jurisdiction that either spouse may sue for loss of consortium due to intentional torts by third parties. *See, e.g.*, Bishop v. Glazener, 245 N.C. 592, 96 S.E.2d 870 (1957) (Husband); Knighten v. McClain, 227 N.C. 682, 44 S.E.2d 79 (1947) (Wife). [The cited cases recognize a cause of action for alienation of affections.] True, intentional invasion of marital relationships can create tragic unhappiness and may all too frequently precipitate divorce. While lamentable in its result, such an intentional act, however, does not give rise to the awesome permanent deprivation one spouse faces when his or her marital partner is rendered a spectre of a former self.... We cannot believe total deprivation of a right of action, even though it extends to both husband and wife, is thus consistent with either our own law or sound public policy.... For this reason alone, reversal of *Helmstetler* seems warranted.

The basis for our change, however, does not rest here. A close reading of *Hinnant*, the case which began eliminating a cause of action for loss of consortium, indicates its reasoning is suspect on at least four grounds.

First, to hold by inference, as *Hinnant* seems to, that the married women's legislation does not create a right in the wife equal to that of her husband to sue for loss of consortium ignores the very purpose for which these acts were passed to remove common law disabilities against women and to equalize the rights of husbands and wives.... Indeed, this reasoning does not account for the holding of this Court that the married women's legislation gives a wife a right to sue for damages for loss of consortium due to intentional injuries....

Second, the *Hinnant* Court's presumption that service provides the totality of an action for consortium is no longer sound legal reasoning. In *Hinnant*, the Court itself acknowledged that in actions for intentional interference with consortium, "the loss of conjugal society and affection ... stand[s] out and [is] emphasized as the pre-eminent and possibly sole basis of recovery." 189 N.C. at 123, 126 S.E. at 309, quoting Marri v. Stamford Street Railroad Company, 84 Conn. 9, 78 A. 582 (1911). For the Court to conclude nevertheless that loss of service provided the totality of the measure of damages for loss of consortium illogically ignored this definition of consortium provided by cases involving intentional torts.

Nor was this concept of consortium necessarily historically accurate. The vast majority of commentators today either assert that consortium at common law included several severable interests, only one of which was service, *see, e.g.*, Lippman, The Breakdown of Consortium, 30 Colum.L.Rev. 651 (1930), or conclude that consortium is primarily limited to society, aid and affection.... Note: The Case of the Lonely Nurse: The Wife's Action for Loss of Consortium, 18 West. Res. L. Rev. 621 (1967).

Thus, while we recognize that consortium is difficult to define, we believe the better view is that it embraces service, society, companionship, sexual gratification and affection, and we so hold today. We do so in recognition of the many tangible and intangible benefits resulting from the loving bond of the marital relationship.

Third, the *Hinnant* Court's inference that damages in a consortium action are too remote to measure, again is no longer sound legal principle. The Court in *Hinnant* quoted *Marri v. Stamford Street Railroad Company, supra,* to the effect that where the injury was physical only to one spouse, there had been no actual injury to the affectionate feelings between the spouses. Common sense tells us this is not true. Indeed, experience with the North Carolina wrongful death statute, G.S. 28A–18–2(b), which does allow compensation for loss of consortium, indicates trial courts and juries recognize and can measure such damage to society, affection and companionship. Certainly the experience of other jurisdictions in awarding damages for loss of a husband's consortium has developed a respectable factoring of measure of loss ....

Finally, the *Hinnant* Court's fears of proximate causation and double recovery, while in themselves sound concerns, could have been dealt with in a fashion less draconian than totally denying a cause of action for loss of consortium. If a loss of consortium is seen not only as a loss of service but as a loss of legal sexual intercourse and general companionship, society and affection as well, by definition any damage to consortium is limited to the legal marital partner of the injured.[4] Strangers to the marriage partnership cannot maintain such an action, and there is no need to worry about extension of proximate causation to parties far removed from the injury.

In a similar vein, the prospect of double recovery can be virtually eliminated by limiting the action primarily to damage measures other than loss of services or support ....

A far sounder way to avoid double recovery in a suit against negligent third parties, however, is to compel joinder of one spouse's action for loss of consortium with the other spouse's action for personal injury. This solution is not unique; at least seven other American jurisdictions compel such joinder....

The reasons for requiring joinder are sound. Not only does joinder avoid the problem of double recovery, it recognizes that, in a very real sense, the injury involved is to the marriage as an entity....

We no longer believe the reasoning behind *Hinnant* and *Helmstetler* is sound. Defendants here, however, urge that if we are tempted to an "activist" role in dealing with the anomalies inherent in those decisions, we should rely on legislative action rather than forsake the "salutory doctrine of *stare decisis.*" The argument overlooks the fact that this

---

4. Because G.S. 14–184 makes fornication and adultery a misdemeanor in this State, the only sexual relationship the law protects is that between married partners. [Footnote by the court.]

entire area of the law has been developed by judicial decree. This Court created a wife's right to sue for loss of consortium due to negligence in *Hipp*, took that right away from the wife in *Hinnant* and eliminated the common law cause of action for the husband in *Helmstetler*. In view of such a history of judicial activity, we do not believe legislative fiat is necessary. We therefore overrule the holdings in *Hinnant* and *Helmstetler* and restore to both spouses a cause of action for loss of consortium due to the negligence of third parties.

In so holding, this jurisdiction once again returns to the mainstream of American legal thought. When this Court first decided *Hinnant* in 1925, it did so partly in response to a trend in other jurisdictions eliminating the cause of action. That trend has changed. Beginning in 1950 with Hitaffer v. Argonne Company, [87 U.S. App. D.C. 57, 183 F.2d 811, *cert. denied*, 340 U.S. 852 (1950)], 37 American jurisdictions, including 35 states, now recognize the right of either spouse to sue for loss of consortium due to the negligence of third parties. See, Annot., 36 A.L.R.3d 900 (1971 and Supp.1979) and cases cited therein.

For all these reasons, we hold that a spouse may maintain a cause of action for loss of consortium due to the negligent actions of third parties so long as that action for loss of consortium is joined with any suit the other spouse may have instituted to recover for his or her personal injuries.

The decision of the Court of Appeals is reversed, and this case is remanded to that court with instructions to remand to the trial court for further proceedings consistent with this opinion.

Reversed and remanded.

Notes and Questions

(1) The Restatement of Torts originally took the position that a wife was not entitled to recover for any harm caused to any of her marital interests by one who negligently injured her husband. Restatement of Torts § 695 (1938). But when the Restatement (Second) of Torts was published in the 1960's—at a time when the weight of authority was still slightly against such recovery—the American Law Institute adopted a new section 693, which stated in relevant part: "One who by reason of his tortious conduct is liable to one spouse for illness or other bodily harm is subject to liability to the other spouse for the resulting loss of the society and services of the first spouse, including impairment of capacity for sexual intercourse...."

(2) The rationale for recognizing the wife's cause of action for loss of consortium was poignantly stated by the Michigan Supreme Court in Montgomery v. Stephan, 359 Mich. 33, 101 N.W.2d 227, 229 (1960): "Were we to rule upon precedent alone, were stability the only reason for our being, we would have no trouble with this case. We would simply tell the woman to begone, and to take her shattered husband with her, that we need no longer be affronted by a sight so repulsive. In so doing,

we would have vast support from the dusty books. But dust the decision would remain in our mouths through the years ahead, a reproach to law and conscience alike. Our oath is to do justice, not to perpetuate error." The court concluded by saying: "The reasons for the old rule no longer obtaining, the rule falls with it. The obstacles to the wife's action were judge-invented and they are herewith judge-destroyed." 101 N.W.2d at 235.

COX v. HAWORTH

Supreme Court of North Carolina, 1981.
304 N.C. 571, 284 S.E.2d 322.

CARLTON, JUSTICE.

I.

Plaintiff filed suit on 15 July 1980 alleging that defendants had negligently performed a myelogram procedure on her husband, Alfred W. Cox, on or about 14 July 1978 and had performed the myelogram without his informed consent. She alleged that as a result of the myelogram procedure her husband developed spinal cord arachnoiditis that left him permanently disabled and sexually impotent. Because of his disability she has suffered the loss of her husband's general companionship and conjugal society and affection and has also suffered the loss of sexual gratification in her marriage. She prayed for damages "in excess of $10,000." In her complaint plaintiff requested that her claims be joined with the existing action filed by her husband against the same doctor on 20 May 1980 . . . .

Defendant Haworth moved to dismiss plaintiff's complaint for failure to state a claim for which relief may be granted because at the time of the alleged acts of negligence a claim for loss of consortium due to the negligence of third parties was not recognized under the laws of this state.

The motion to dismiss was . . . granted.

. . . . .

II.

On 3 June 1980, this Court announced its decision in Nicholson v. Hugh Chatham Memorial Hospital, Inc., 300 N.C. 295, 266 S.E.2d 818 (1980), and held that "a spouse may maintain a cause of action for loss of consortium due to the negligent actions of third parties so long as that action for loss of consortium is joined with any suit the other spouse may have instituted to recover for his or her personal injuries." . . . In so holding, this Court overruled longstanding case law which held that no action for loss of consortium exists. . . . Hinnant v. Tide Water Power Co., 189 N.C. 120, 126 S.E. 307 (1925) (wife has no right of action for loss of husband's consortium). Not before us in *Nicholson* was the question whether and to what extent the new rule applied to claims arising prior to the decision. We must now address this question. *issue*

A.

Under long-established North Carolina law, a decision of a court of supreme jurisdiction overruling a former decision is, as a general rule, retrospective in its operation. Mason v. A. E. Nelson Cotton Co., 148 N.C. 492, 62 S.E. 625 (1908); MacDonald v. University of North Carolina, 299 N.C. 457, 263 S.E.2d 578 (1980). This rule is based on the so-called "Blackstonian Doctrine" of judicial decision-making: courts merely discover and announce law; they do not create it; and the act of overruling is a confession that the prior ruling was erroneous and was never the law. People *ex rel*. Rice v. Graves, 242 App.Div. 128, 273 N.Y.S. 582 (1934), *aff'd*, 270 N.Y. 498, 200 N.E. 288, *cert. denied*, 298 U.S. 683 (1936) .... As stated by this Court in *Mason*, "the effect is not that the former decision is bad law, but that it never was the law." 148 N.C. at 510, 62 S.E. at 632. Under more recent decisions, however, courts have recognized that the question of retroactivity is one of judicial policy, and should be determined by a consideration of such factors as reliance on the prior decision, the degree to which the purpose behind the new decision can be achieved solely through prospective application, and the effect of retroactive application on the administration of justice. *See* Annot., ["Comment Note—Prospective or Retroactive Operation of Overruling Decision"], 10 A.L.R.3d 1371 [(1966)], at § 2. This Court has implicitly recognized that the decision on retroactivity involves a balancing of countervailing interests. *E.g.*, MacDonald v. University of North Carolina, 299 N.C. 457, 263 S.E.2d 578 (decision abolishing sovereign tort immunity applied prospectively because of vested contract rights); Rabon v. Rowan Memorial Hospital, Inc., 269 N.C. 1, 152 S.E.2d 485 (1967) (decision abolishing charitable immunity applied prospectively because of justified reliance on prior case law); State v. Bell, 136 N.C. 674, 49 S.E. 163 (1904) (contractual rights acquired by virtue of the prior construction will not be disturbed by a subsequent overruling decision)....

By overruling a prior decision, a court implicitly recognizes that the old rule has lost its viability and should no longer be the law. Unless compelling reasons, such as those noted above from our prior cases, exist for limiting the application of the new rule to future cases, we think that the overruling decision should be given retrospective effect.

Thus, we begin with the presumption of retroactivity and will apply the rule in *Nicholson* retroactively unless there exists a compelling reason for not doing so. Defendant contends there are three compelling reasons to apply *Nicholson* prospectively only: (1) because he justifiably relied on the prior case law, (2) because the purpose behind the *Nicholson* decision can be fully achieved through prospective application, and (3) because retroactive application of *Nicholson* would be unduly burdensome on the administration of justice.

Defendant first contends that in reliance on our decisions in *Hinnant* and *Helmstetler* he failed to procure insurance to protect against the additional risk of liability for loss of consortium. We find this argument unpersuasive. Justifiable failure to procure insurance has been accepted by this Court as a reason to limit the effect of an overruling decision only when the decision abolishes a common law immunity from tort liability. Rabon v. Rowan Memorial Hospital, Inc., 269 N.C. 1, 152 S.E.2d 485. Defendant cites to us cases from other jurisdictions accepting such a justifiable reliance argument, but these decisions, too, deal with the abolition of immunity: Molitor v. Kaneland Community Unit District No. 302, 18 Ill.2d 11, 163 N.E.2d 89 (1959), *cert. denied*, 362 U.S. 968 (1960) (abolition of tort immunity of school districts); Parker v. Port Huron Hospital, 361 Mich. 1, 105 N.W.2d 1 (1960) (abolition of charitable immunity); Spanel v. Mounds View School District No. 621, 264 Minn. 279, 118 N.W.2d 795 (1962) (abolition of school districts' tort immunity). When an immunity is abolished, the defendant suddenly becomes liable for all torts; when a new claim is recognized, the extent of liability increases. The difference between the fact of liability and the extent of liability is an important one. The former affects the decision whether to purchase insurance at all; the latter is merely one factor, among many, which is considered in deciding how much insurance to purchase. The effect of liability for loss of consortium on the decision of how much insurance to purchase is a matter of speculation and, in our opinion, would be minimal in comparison to other factors. We agree with the Supreme Court of Wisconsin that:

> The degree of reliance a tortfeasor might have placed on a wife's inability to recover consortium damages would be insignificant if existent. Certainly the tort was not committed with this in mind and the degree to which it may have influenced the decision whether or not to purchase liability insurance would be less than minimal. Nor will it effect (sic) the monetary limits of liability of the insurance carrier.

Fitzgerald v. Meissner & Hicks, Inc., 38 Wis.2d at 578, 157 N.W.2d at 598.

Neither can we agree with defendant's contention that the purpose behind the decision to allow an action for loss of consortium can be fully achieved through prospective application. The purpose of the *Nicholson* decision was to afford decent compensation to those injured by the wrongful conduct of others when the conduct impairs the service, society, companionship, sexual gratification and affection that is a vital part of the marital relationship. Nicholson v. Hugh Chatham Memorial Hospital, Inc., 300 N.C. at 300, 302, 266 S.E.2d at 821, 822. While prospective application will effectuate this policy with regard to future cases, it will not provide compensation for those injured prior to the *Nicholson* decision. The policy behind *Nicholson* is to compensate the loss of a legitimate interest; that policy can best be achieved by retroactive application.

We also reject defendant's contention that retroactive application of *Nicholson* will unduly burden the administration of justice. While we recognize that problems concerning joinder will arise, these questions are no different from those which arise in other civil cases. The guidance provided by our Rules of Civil Procedure concerning joinder is adequate to prevent an undue burden on the administration of justice. *See* Rules 13, 19, 20 & 21.

Our research reveals that most courts have chosen to give an overruling decision recognizing an action for loss of consortium retroactive effect.... Deems v. Western Maryland Railway Co., 247 Md. 95, 231 A.2d 514 (1967); Shepherd v. Consumers Co-operative Assoc., 384 S.W.2d 635 (Mo.1964) .... Our research revealed only one case in which the court refused to apply the new rule retroactively. In Thill v. Modern Erecting Co., 284 Minn. 508, 170 N.W.2d 865 (1969), the Minnesota Supreme Court limited its recognition of an action for loss of consortium to future cases, citing Spanel v. Mounds, 264 Minn. 279, 118 N.W.2d 795. *Spanel* limited the rule abolishing sovereign immunity to future cases because of justified reliance on prior case law. As discussed above, we reject the argument, as it applies to recognizing a claim for loss of consortium, that justified reliance dictates prospective application.

We conclude that there are no compelling reasons to limit the effect of *Nicholson* to causes of action accruing after the date it was decided. Our decision recognizing a claim for loss of consortium will be applied retrospectively to all cases or claims pending and not barred by judgment, settlement or the statute of limitations as of 3 June 1980.[5]

For the reasons stated above, we hold that plaintiff may pursue her claim for loss of consortium and remand the cause to the Superior Court, Guilford County, for further proceedings not inconsistent with this opinion.

HARRIS v. SHERMAN

Supreme Court of Vermont, 1998.
167 Vt. 613, 708 A.2d 1348.

Before AMESTOY, C.J., MORSE, JOHNSON and SKOGLUND, JJ., and ALLEN, C.J. (Ret.), Specially Assigned.

Plaintiff Shannon Harris appeals the Lamoille Superior Court's dismissal of her loss of consortium claim premised on personal injuries sustained by her husband John Harris. The court granted summary judgment for defendants and dismissed the claim because, at the time of the accident, Shannon and John were engaged to be married, but not yet legally wed. Plaintiff argues on appeal that 12 V.S.A. § 5431, which provides that "[a] loss of consortium [claim] may be brought by either spouse" affords relief not only to persons formally married at the time of

---

5. In Wall v. Stout, 310 N.C. 184, 205–06, 311 S.E.2d 571, 583–84 (1984), the Supreme Court of North Carolina held that this sentence referred to the direct tort victim's "cases or claims," since no loss-of-consortium claims could have been filed prior to June 3, 1980. The court also held that the accrual date for the three-year statute of limitations for a loss-of-consortium claim that was joined with a direct tort victim's claim based on a pre-*Nicholson* injury was June 3, 1980. Therefore, Mr. Wall, whose wife was injured in 1977, was permitted to proceed with his loss-of-consortium claim, even though he did not file his complaint until 1981.

injury, but also to persons engaged to be married at the time of the accident who marry prior to commencement of the action. . . .

The underlying facts are not in dispute. In May of 1995, John Harris allegedly sustained injury in an automobile accident with defendant, William Sherman. At the time of the accident, John and Shannon were engaged to be married; approximately two months later, they became legally wed. John Harris later sued defendants alleging negligent operation and maintenance of their automobile, and based on those injury claims, Shannon Harris claimed loss of consortium. Defendants moved for summary judgment on the consortium claim on the grounds that 12 V.S.A. § 5431 does not allow recovery for loss of consortium arising from injury sustained before marriage. Defendants argued that the loss of consortium statute was enacted for the sole purpose of extending to women the substantive right to claim for loss of consortium, *see* Whitney v. Fisher, 138 Vt. 468, 469, 417 A.2d 934, 935 (1980), and that the Legislature expressed no intention of otherwise extending or modifying the action's parameters. The superior court granted defendants' summary judgment motion and dismissed with prejudice plaintiff's loss of consortium claim, but did not otherwise explain its ruling. *See* V.R.C.P. 56 (summary judgment appropriate where no genuine issue of material fact exists and moving party is entitled to judgment as a matter of law). Plaintiff appeals.

Plaintiff contends that the superior court was wrong to dismiss her claim because the plain language of 12 V.S.A. § 5431 allows "either spouse" to bring a claim for loss of consortium and she is the spouse of the injured party. Her position is that if the Legislature did not specify a temporal requirement for when the marriage must be in existence it must have intended that no such limitation be imposed.

In construing statutes, courts have a duty to ascertain and effectuate the intent of the Legislature, . . . and where legislative intent can be ascertained on its face, the statute must be enforced according to its terms without resort to statutory construction. . . . Conversely, if the statute is ambiguous, we ascertain legislative intent through consideration of the entire statute, including its subject matter, effects and consequences, as well as the reason and spirit of the law. . . .

In the instant case, plaintiff correctly argues that 12 V.S.A. § 5431 provides a claim for loss of consortium to "either spouse," and that the statute is silent as to any temporal requirement for when the marriage must have been in existence. In light of this legislative silence, we must look beyond the plain language to determine legislative intent. Plaintiff argues that any ambiguity concerning the term "spouse" must be resolved in her favor, because § 5431 was enacted as a remedial statute, and thus should be interpreted in a light favorable to those persons it was designed to benefit. She contends that, when construed favorably toward her, the statute affords her a claim.

We find plaintiff's argument unpersuasive because, although § 5431 is remedial in nature, and thus entitled to a liberal construction, . . . we must look at the nature of the remedy enacted to determine its proper scope. The statute at issue was enacted to overrule the common law rule under which women could not recover for loss of consortium. *See Whitney*, 138 Vt. at 470, 417 A.2d at 935 (12 V.S.A. § 5431 created a substantive right in women to recover for loss of consortium based upon her husband's injuries). In all other respects, the statute indicates no legislative intent to modify the scope and application of a loss of consortium claim. Had the Legislature intended to modify the action's scope, it could have said so. "[G]reat care should be exercised by the court not to expand proper construction of a statute into judicial legislation." Murphy Motor Sales, Inc. v. First National Bank, 122 Vt. 121, 124, 165 A.2d 341, 343 (1960).

We have not before been asked to decide whether loss of consortium may be premised on injuries sustained prior to marriage. . . . The persuasive force of authority from other jurisdictions provides that there can be no loss of consortium recovery where the claimant was not married to the injured party at the time of the accident. *See, e.g.*, Doe v. Cherwitz, 518 N.W.2d 362, 365 (Iowa 1994); Gurliacci v. Mayer, 218 Conn. 531, 590 A.2d 914, 931–32 (1991). Miller v. Davis, 107 Misc.2d 343, 433 N.Y.S.2d 974, 975 (Sup.Ct.1980) (wife denied recovery when husband was injured on wedding day, causing postponement of marriage ceremony); Gillespie–Linton v. Miles, 58 Md.App. 484, 473 A.2d 947, 953 (1984) (spouse of an injured party could not recover where injury occurred four days prior to marriage); *see also* Restatement (Second) of Torts § 693 cmt. h (1977) (action for tortious harm to plaintiff's spouse is "applicable to parties to a valid marriage . . . subsisting at the time of the injury").

Plaintiff points to Bulloch v. United States, 487 F.Supp. 1078 (D.N.J.1980) [and] Sutherland v. Auch Inter–Borough Transit Co., 366 F.Supp. 127 (E.D.Pa.1973) . . . to support her contention that the rule should be otherwise. In each of these cases, the courts allowed loss of consortium damages premised on premarital injury. Plaintiff's authority, however, has either not been followed or has been repudiated, and is therefore unpersuasive. New Jersey state courts have rejected the result in *Bulloch*. *See* Leonardis v. Morton Chemical Co., 184 N.J.Super. 10, 445 A.2d 45, 46 (App.Div.1982) (loss of consortium claim not available unless formal marriage exists at time of injury; "We find no merit in and decline to follow Bulloch."). . . . Pennsylvania state courts have declined to follow *Sutherland*. *See, e.g.*, Rockwell v. Liston, 71 Pa.D. & C.2d 756, 757–58 (1975) (loss of consortium claim not available where spouse's injury occurred during engagement, but one month before formal marriage).

We hold that a spouse may bring a loss of consortium claim under 12 V.S.A. § 5431 only if the claimant was legally married to the injured party when that injury occurred. Vermont has long recognized the vital importance of marriage as a contract between spouses with attendant rights and obligations. . . . The significance of an engagement to be married is entirely personal, and carries no formal responsibilities or recognition by the state. We are mindful of the difficulty to be encountered if courts were required to determine which personal relationships were sufficiently harmed to merit recovery.

[Affirmed.] order

Notes and Questions

(1) In *Harris*, the court did not extend the loss of consortium law to spouses who were unmarried at the time of the tort. *Harris* is consistent with cases from other jurisdictions in the United States. *See* J.D. Lee & B. Lindahl, *Modern Tort Law: Liability and Litigation* § 29.16 (2d ed. 2003); Annot., "Recovery for Loss of Consortium Prior to Marriage," 5 American Law Reports 4th 300 (1981). So far, no courts have extended this right to same-sex couples. Do you think that same-sex couples would have a better chance of gaining the right to sue for loss of consortium if *Harris* had extended such a right to unmarried heterosexuals? What right to sue for loss of consortium should be recognized in a jurisdiction that permits same-sex couples to enter into a formal domestic partnership recognized by state law? *See generally* J.G. Culhane, "A 'Clanging Silence': Same-Sex Couples and Tort Law," 89 Kentucky Law Journal 911 (2001); W. Ellis, "Expanding Loss of Consortium in Vermont: Developing A New Doctrine," 12 Vermont Law Review 157 (1987).

(2) The Supreme Court of Vermont held, in Baker v. State, 170 Vt. 194, 744 A.2d 864, 81 A.L.R. 5th 627 (1999), that Vermont's marriage statute, which excluded same-sex couples from the opportunity to marry, was in violation of the Common Benefits Clause of the Vermont Constitution, which provides in relevant part:

> [G]overnment is, or ought to be, instituted for the common benefit, protection, and security of the people, nation, or community, and not for the particular emolument or advantage of any single person, family, or set of persons, who are a part only of that community....

Vt. Const. Ch. I, Art. 7. Specifically, the court held that same-sex couples are entitled to enjoy the benefits and protections which are afforded by Vermont law to married opposite-sex couples. The court allowed the unconstitutional marriage statute to remain in effect for a reasonable period of time to enable the legislature to consider and enact implementing legislation. The legislature enacted a "civil union" statute, effective July 1, 2000. 2000 Vermont Laws P.A.91 (H. 847). The statute specifically allows same-sex couples to sue for loss of consortium. *Id.* at § 1204(e)(2).

D.   THE PROBLEM OF RETROACTIVITY

The *Whitney* court had to decide whether to apply retroactively a statute recognizing a cause of action for loss of consortium. Both the *Cox* and *Whitney* courts had to decide whether to apply retroactively a judicial opinion overruling a prior precedent. As a general rule, civil statutes are applied prospectively and judicial opinions in civil cases are applied retroactively. Sometimes civil statutes are applied retroactively to cases that have not yet reached a final judgment, but the legislature must specify that it intends such a retroactive application in the text of the statute. *See* United States v. Schooner Peggy, 5 U.S. (1 Cranch) 103 (1801). When the statute is a criminal statute, the moral and political tradition of Western civilization condemns most instances of the retrospective application of the law as fundamentally unfair. People should, in principle, have the opportunity to inform themselves of the law and to conform their conduct to it in advance of incurring any liability.

This tradition is strongest with regard to rules of the criminal law, and the "ex post facto" clauses of Article I of the federal Constitution forbid either the federal or the state governments from giving criminal laws retroactive (also called retrospective) application. The constitutional constraints on retroactive application of laws affecting civil liabilities are somewhat weaker, but (as noted earlier) it nonetheless remains a general feature of legislation that it is enacted for prospective effect only—that is, it regulates only conduct which occurs after the date of enactment (or after a later effective date if the statute so specifies).

The decisions of judges may, of course, surprise the parties in many cases which do not overrule prior case law, but rather reach a decision on a particular subject for the first time, thereby filling in a gap in the pre-existing web of legislation and case law. In this situation, where the adverse parties to the law suit cannot have acted in reliance on the sort of authoritative pronouncement of the law which would have existed had there been a judicial precedent squarely in point, there has been little consternation among judges in applying their gap-filling decision retroactively; this means disposing of the case at hand even though that case involves conduct previous to their articulation of the authoritative and dispositive rule of law.

The truly difficult dilemma occurs when there is already an authoritative and dispositive rule of law in the form of a judicial precedent, but when that precedent is no longer just or rational given subsequent developments in the legal system and the society it serves. On the one hand, injustice will occur if the disfavored precedent is applied to dispose of the case at hand; on the other hand, a different sort of injustice will occur if the disfavored precedent is discarded and new law is applied retroactively to penalize individual conduct which was legally proper under the prior rule.

The traditional judicial solution to this problem consisted of giving overruling decisions retroactive application in fact, while avowing in principle that the law was not being applied retroactively at all. The central proposition of this solution was that the overruled precedent was mistaken, was never the law, and was therefore mistakenly relied upon by the losing litigant.

The *Graves* Case

This solution is well illustrated by People *ex rel*. Rice v. Graves, 242 App.Div. 128, 273 N.Y.S. 582 (1934). In 1928, the United States Supreme

Court had decided that a state had no right to tax income from copyright royalties. Long v. Rockwood, 277 U.S. 142 (1928). In 1932, this decision had been overruled. Fox Film Corp. v. Doyal, 286 U.S. 123 (1932). During the years 1928–1932, Elmer Rice, a dramatist living in New York, had received large royalties from his plays on which he had paid no New York income tax. In *People v. Graves*, the New York authorities demanded three years' back taxes from Mr. Rice on these royalties. The New York court, supporting the tax authorities, held Mr. Rice liable not only for the back taxes, but also for the payment of interest at six percent for being late. The court justified its decision on the following basis:

> The effect to be given to the action of a court of last resort, when it reverses itself, is a subject which has given rise to prolific litigation and has for centuries furnished a theme for philosophical discussion by jurists and text-writers. Out of the age-old discussion there have been developed two fundamentally opposing theories. According to one theory the decisions of the courts are always conclusive evidence of what the law is. Followers of the other school assert that the decisions are evidence, but not conclusive evidence, of the law. . . .

> A natural desire for stability in the law gave rise to a reliance on decided cases as far back as Bracton and the early Year Books of the fourteenth century. According to the orthodox theory of Blackstone, which still claims at least the nominal allegiance of most courts, a judicial decision is merely evidence of the law, not law itself; and when a decision is overruled, it does not become bad law; it never was the law, and the discredited decision will be viewed as if it had never been and the reconsidered pronouncement regarded as law from the beginning. Despite the expressed disapproval of some courts of repute and certain eminent writers, the prevailing doctrine is not that the law is changed by the overruling decision, but that the court was mistaken in its former decision, and that the law is, and always was, as expounded in the later decision. It should be said, however, that many leading English and American writers on jurisprudence characterize this theory of law as childish fiction and champion the doctrine that the rules which the judicial organs of the state lay down in deciding cases constitute law. However, according to the great weight of authority the theory that courts make law is unsound. The courts do not make law, but simply declare law. A judicial decision is but evidence of the law. An overruling decision does not change law, but impeaches the overruled decision as evidence of law. Adopting the theory that courts merely declare preexisting law, it logically follows that an overruling decision operates retroactively. Courts have generally given retroactive effect to decisions which have overruled earlier precedents.

> . . . Salmond, in his work on Jurisprudence (8th Ed.) p. 197, in discussing the retrospective effect of a later decision said: "The overruling of a precedent is not the abolition of an established rule

of law; it is an authoritative denial that the supposed rule of law has ever existed. The precedent is so treated not because it has made bad law, but because it has never in reality made any law at all. Hence it is that the overruling of a precedent, unlike the repeal of a statute, has retrospective operation. The decision is pronounced to have been bad *ab initio*. A repealed statute, on the contrary remains valid and applicable as to matters arising before the date of its repeal. The overruling of a precedent is analogous not to the repeal of a statute, but to the judicial rejection of a custom as unreasonable or as otherwise failing to conform to the requirements of customary law."

. . . .

We have not overlooked the relator's contention that a retrospective application of the decision in the *Fox Film Case* works an apparent hardship as to him. We concede as much. The answer to that argument, however, is that the hardship in question is no greater on the relator than was that suffered by the state by the erroneous decision in *Long v. Rockwood*. The ruling in that case deprived the state of revenue to which it was justly entitled. The construction in the instant case involves no hardship upon the relator beyond the payment of those taxes which he would have been required to pay in any event had the discredited decision in *Long v. Rockwood* never . . . been made.

Id. at 130–33, 134–35, 273 N.Y.S. at 586–88, 591.

The *Sunburst* Case

The converse approach to *People v. Graves*, one of complete prospectivity rather than complete retroactivity, was adopted by the Montana Supreme Court in the contemporaneous cases of Montana Horse Products Co. v. Great Northern Rwy. Co., 91 Mont. 194, 7 P.2d 919 (1932), and Sunburst Oil and Refining Co. v. Great Northern Rwy. Co., 91 Mont. 216, 7 P.2d 927 (1932). In both of these cases the shipper had paid freight charges which were later established, upon the shipper's complaint to the Montana Railroad Commission, to have been unreasonably high. The Commission, which under state law had the power to control railroad tariffs, in each case had ordered the rates reduced. The shippers had then filed suit in state court for refunds of the difference between the rates they had paid and the new rates established by the Commission. The trial courts had awarded the refunds on the authority of the Montana Supreme Court's decision in Doney v. Northern Pacific Rwy. Co., 60 Mont. 209, 199 P. 432 (1921), which had expressly held that shippers could sue for refunds of freight charges paid to railroads which were later held by the Commission to have been excessive. On Great Northern's appeals of these two judgments awarding refunds, the Supreme Court of Montana held that *Doney*'s rule of law regarding refunds was ill-advised, and *Doney* was pro tanto overruled. (The Latin phrase "pro tanto" literally means "by so much"; in this context it means "in this respect.'') The chief reason for overruling *Doney* was that the railroad commission's act of establishing new and lower rates was deemed to be a quasi-legislative act operative only in the future, so that the excess paid by the shippers in the past was not subject to refund.

Because the shippers had relied upon the *Doney* refund rule in paying rates subject to a later suit for a refund, and because *Doney* had similarly put railroads on notice that they might have to make refunds of charges subsequently found by the Commission to have been unreasonable, the Montana Supreme Court decided to make its decision to overrule the *Doney* refund rule purely prospective. In both cases the trial court's award of the refund was affirmed. Although the *Doney* rule was abrogated, that change in the law was not applied to the cases in which the change was announced.

For reasons that are not known, only one of these Montana cases was appealed to the United States Supreme Court. In Great Northern Rwy. Co. v. Sunburst Oil and Refining Co., 287 U.S. 358 (1932), the railroad argued that the traditional rule of complete retroactivity (such as applied in *Graves*) was constitutionally required as part of the ''due process of law'' required of the states by the 14th Amendment to the federal Constitution. The Court rejected this argument in an opinion by Justice Cardozo which can now be seen as the beginning of the modern trend away from unlimited retroactivity of case law.

> . . . This is not a case where a court in overruling an earlier decision has given to the new ruling a retroactive bearing, and thereby has made invalid what was valid in the doing. Even that may often be done, though litigants not infrequently have argued to the contrary. This is a case where a court has refused to make its ruling retroactive, and the novel stand is taken that the constitution of the United States is infringed by the refusal.

> We think the federal constitution has no voice upon the subject. A state in defining the limits of adherence to precedent may make a choice for itself between the principle of forward operation and that of relation backward. It may say that decisions of its highest court, though later overruled, are law none the less for intermediate transactions. Indeed there are cases intimating, too broadly, that it *must* give them that effect; but never has doubt been expressed that it *may* so treat them if it pleases, whenever injustice or hardship will thereby be averted. On the other hand, it may hold to the ancient dogma that the law declared by its courts had a Platonic or ideal existence before the act of declaration, in which event the discredited declaration will be viewed as if it had never been, and the reconsidered declaration as law from the beginning. The alternative is the same whether the subject of the new decision is common law or statute. The choice for any state may be determined by the juristic philosophy of the judges of her courts, their conceptions of law, its origin and nature. We review not the wisdom of their philosophies, but the legality of their acts. The State of Montana has

told us by the voice of her highest court that with these alternative methods open to her, her preference is for the first. In making this choice, she is declaring common law for those within her borders. The common law as administered by her judges ascribes to the decisions of her highest court a power to bind and loose that is unextinguished, for intermediate transactions, by a decision overruling them. As applied to such transactions we may say of the earlier decision that it has not been overruled at all. It has been translated into a judgment of affirmance and recognized as law anew. Accompanying the recognition is a prophecy, which may or may not be realized in conduct, that transactions arising in the future will be governed by a different rule. If this is the common law doctrine of adherence to precedent as understood and enforced by the courts of Montana, we are not at liberty, for anything contained in the constitution of the United States, to thrust upon those courts a different conception either of the binding force of precedent or of the meaning of the judicial process.

Id. at 364–66 (citations and footnotes omitted).

The *Linkletter* Case

The problem with the doctrine of complete retroactivity articulated in *Graves* is that it ignores what may have been quite legitimate reliance on the existing law as authoritatively declared by the courts—as might occur, for instance, if people lent money to a child, or a corporation, or a state agency, in reliance on an authoritative decision, later overruled, that such a loan gave rise to an enforceable debt. The opposite problem with the doctrine of complete prospectivity found constitutional in *Sunburst* is that a litigant who has succeeded in showing that a prior decision was wrong gets only the cold comfort that future litigants will not suffer the injustice of having the bad precedent applied to their detriment—the overruled case is applied, one last time, to the very litigant who has demonstrated its injustice. In a case like *Sunburst*, where the railroad was likely to be the future litigant most benefitted by the prospective overruling of *Doney*, the railroad cannot be said to have suffered any great harm. But in a more typical sort of case, where the litigant incurs substantial personal expense in successfully demonstrating why a precedent should be overruled, the only incentive for doing so is the hope of reaping the immediate benefit of the change in law.

This has led the federal courts, and many state courts, to adopt an intermediate rule of limited retroactivity, whereby the successful litigant in the case in which prior law is overruled does get the benefit of that decision, but the retroactive effect of the overruling on other litigants is not automatic. Generally, the change in law is also made applicable to all other lawsuits still in the process of litigation at the time the change in law is announced, and the hard question then becomes whether the change in law is also applicable to litigation already terminated. This is principally a problem with respect to the constitutional rights of persons convicted of crimes, because criminal convictions, unlike judgments of civil liability, remain subject to reexamination if it can later be shown that the convictions were obtained in violation of the defendants' constitutional rights.

It was in this context that the United States Supreme Court considered, in Linkletter v. Walker, 381 U.S. 618 (1965), whether state prisoners convicted through the use of illegally seized evidence were all entitled to new trials, even if their convictions had become final before the United States Supreme Court held, in Mapp v. Ohio, 367 U.S. 643 (1961), that illegally seized evidence was inadmissible in state criminal prosecutions. As the following excerpts show, Justice Clark's opinion for the Court in *Linkletter* sought to place the problem of *Mapp's* retroactivity in jurisprudential perspective before describing the elements of a balancing test to determine questions of retroactivity. 381 U.S. at 621–625, 627, 628–29, 639–40.

> Initially we must consider the term "retrospective" for the purposes of our opinion. A ruling which is purely prospective does not apply even to the parties before the court. *See, e.g.*, England v. Louisiana State Board of Medical Examiners, 375 U.S. 411 (1964). *See also* Great Northern R. Co. v. Sunburst Oil & Refining Co., 287 U.S. 358 (1932). However, we are not here concerned with pure prospectivity since we applied the rule announced in *Mapp* to reverse Miss Mapp's conviction. That decision has also been applied to cases still pending on direct review at the time it was rendered. Therefore, in this case, we are concerned only with whether the exclusionary principle enunciated in *Mapp* applies to state court convictions which had become final before rendition of our opinion.

> While to some it may seem "academic" it might be helpful to others for us to briefly outline the history and theory of the problem presented.

> At common law there was no authority for the proposition that judicial decisions made law only for the future. Blackstone stated the rule that the duty of the court was not to "pronounce a new law, but to maintain and expound the old one." 1 Blackstone, Commentaries 69 (15th ed. 1809). This Court followed that rule in Norton v. Shelby County, 118 U.S. 425 (1886), holding that unconstitutional action "confers no rights; it imposes no duties; it affords no protection; it creates no office; it is, in legal contemplation, as inoperative as though it had never been passed." At 442. The judge rather than being the creator of the law was but its discoverer. Gray, Nature and Sources of the Law 222 (1st ed. 1909). In the case of the overruled decision, *Wolf v. Colorado, supra*, here, it was thought to be only a failure at true discovery and was consequently never the law; while the overruling one, *Mapp,* was not "new law but an application of what is, and theretofore had been, the true law." Shulman, Retroactive Legislation, 13 Encyclopaedia of the Social Sciences 355, 356 (1934).

On the other hand, Austin maintained that judges do in fact do something more than discover law; they make it interstitially by filling in with judicial interpretation the vague, indefinite, or generic statutory or common-law terms that alone are but the empty crevices of the law. Implicit in such an approach is the admission when a case is overruled that the earlier decision was wrongly decided. However, rather than being erased by the later overruling decision it is considered as an existing juridical fact until overruled, and intermediate cases finally decided under it are not to be disturbed.

The Blackstonian view ruled English jurisprudence and cast its shadow over our own as evidenced by *Norton v. Shelby County, supra*. However, some legal philosophers continued to insist that such a rule was out of tune with actuality largely because judicial repeal ofttime did "work hardship to those who [had] trusted to its existence." Cardozo, Address to the N.Y. Bar Assn., 55 Rep.N.Y. State Bar Assn. 263, 296–297 (1932). The Austinian view gained some acceptance over a hundred years ago when it was decided that although legislative divorces were illegal and void, those previously granted were immunized by a prospective application of the rule of the case. Bingham v. Miller, 17 Ohio 445 (1848). And as early as 1863 this Court drew on the same concept in Gelpcke v. Dubuque, 1 Wall. [68 U.S.) 175 (1863). The Supreme Court of Iowa had repeatedly held that the Iowa Legislature had the power to authorize municipalities to issue bonds to aid in the construction of railroads. After the City of Dubuque had issued such bonds, the Iowa Supreme Court reversed itself and held that the legislature lacked such power. In *Gelpcke,* which arose after the overruling decision, this Court held that the bonds issued under the apparent authority granted by the legislature were collectible. "However we may regard the late [overruling] case in Iowa as affecting the future, it can have no effect upon the past." At 206. The theory was, as Mr. Justice Holmes stated in Kuhn v. Fairmont Coal Co., 215 U.S. 349, 371 (1910), "that a change of judicial decision after a contract has been made on the faith of an earlier one the other way is a change of the law." And in 1932 Mr. Justice Cardozo in Great Northern R. Co. v. Sunburst Oil & Refining Co., 287 U.S. 358, applied the Austinian approach in denying a federal constitutional due process attack on the prospective application of a decision of the Montana Supreme Court. He said that a State "may make a choice for itself between the principle of forward operation and that of relation backward." At 364. Mr. Justice Cardozo based the rule on the avoidance of "injustice or hardship" citing a long list of state and federal cases supporting the principle that the courts had the power to say that decisions though later overruled "are law none the less for intermediate transactions." At 364. Eight years later Chief Justice Hughes in Chicot County Drainage Dist. v. Baxter State Bank, 308 U.S. 371 (1940), in discussing the problem made it clear that the broad statements of *Norton, supra*, "must be taken with qualifications."

He reasoned that the actual existence of the law prior to the determination of unconstitutionality "is an operative fact and may have consequences which cannot justly be ignored. The past cannot always be erased by a new judicial declaration." He laid down the rule that the "effect of the subsequent ruling as to invalidity may have to be considered in various aspects." At 374.

. . . .

Under our cases it appears (1) that a change in law will be given effect while a case is on direct review, *Schooner Peggy, supra,* and (2) that the effect of the subsequent ruling of invalidity on prior final judgments when collaterally attacked is subject to no set "principle of absolute retroactive invalidity" but depends upon a consideration of "particular relations . . . and particular conduct[,] . . . of rights claimed to have become vested, of status, of prior determinations deemed to have finality"; and "of public policy in the light of the nature both of the statute and of its previous application." *Chicot County Drainage Dist. v. Baxter State Bank, supra,* at 374.

That no distinction was drawn between civil and criminal litigation is shown by the language used not only in *Schooner Peggy, supra,* and *Chicot County, supra,* but also in such cases as State v. Jones, 44 N.M. 623, 107 P.2d 324 (1940) and James v. United States, 366 U.S. 213 (1961). In the latter case, this Court laid down a prospective principle in overruling Commissioner v. Wilcox, 327 U.S. 404 (1946), "in a manner that will not prejudice those who might have relied on it." At 221. . . . Thus, the accepted rule today is that in appropriate cases the Court may in the interest of justice make the rule prospective. And "there is much to be said in favor of such a rule for cases arising in the future." Mosser v. Darrow, 341 U.S. 267, at 276 (dissenting opinion of Black, J.).

While the cases discussed above deal with the invalidity of statutes or the effect of a decision overturning long-established common-law rules, there seems to be no impediment—constitutional or philosophical—to the use of the same rule in the constitutional area where the exigencies of the situation require such an application. It is true that heretofore, without discussion, we have applied new constitutional rules to cases finalized before the promulgation of the rule. Petitioner contends that our method of resolving those prior cases demonstrates that an absolute rule of retroaction prevails in the area of constitutional adjudication. However, we believe that the Constitution neither prohibits nor requires retrospective effect. As Justice Cardozo said, "We think the federal constitution has no voice upon the subject."

Once the premise is accepted that we are neither required to apply, nor prohibited from applying, a decision retrospectively, we must then weigh the merits and demerits in each case by looking to the prior history of the rule in question, its purpose and effect, and whether retrospective operation will further or retard its operation. We believe that this approach is particularly correct with reference to the Fourth Amendment's prohibitions as to unreasonable searches and seizures. Rather than "disparaging" the Amendment we but apply the wisdom of Justice Holmes that "[t]he life of the law has not been logic: it has been experience." Holmes, The Common Law 5 (Howe ed. 1963).

. . . .

Nor can we accept the contention of petitioner that the *Mapp* rule should date from the day of the seizure there, rather than that of the judgment of this Court. The date of the seizure in *Mapp* has no legal significance. It was the judgment of this Court that changed the rule and the date of that opinion is the crucial date. In the light of the cases of this Court this is the better cutoff time. *See United States v. Schooner Peggy, supra.*

All that we decide today is that though the error complained of might be fundamental it is not of the nature requiring us to overturn all final convictions based upon it. After full consideration of all the factors we are not able to say that the *Mapp* rule requires retrospective application.

Id. at 621–25, 627–29, 639–40.

Developments Since *Linkletter*

A close reading of *Linkletter* suggests that the flexible rule on retroactivity enunciated by the Court was meant to apply only to situations where the judgment of a court had become final[6] and was subsequently challenged by a collateral attack, such as a petition for habeas corpus claiming that damning evidence at trial had been obtained by means later declared to be unconstitutional. The Court seemed to say, on the other hand, that a new rule of constitutional law changing the previous law should be applied to all cases on direct review that had not become final at the time the change of law was made.

For many years after *Linkletter* there was considerable ferment and inconsistency in the Supreme Court's decisions on the retroactive application of new rules of law. The Court wrestled with the issue in three discrete contexts that seemed to call for differentiated standards: civil cases in general, criminal cases involving direct appellate review of the judgment of conviction, and criminal cases involving postconviction review of an already final judgment that was collaterally attacked (often years after the underlying conviction) by means of the writ of habeas corpus. From this ferment clarity at last emerged.

In a civil case, the situation is uncomplicated by the opportunity for collateral attack on a final judgment. Once a civil judgment becomes

---

6. "Final" means that a judgment has been rendered, the availability of appeal has been exhausted, and the time for a petition for certiorari has elapsed (or a petition for certiorari has been denied).

final upon the completion of the process of direct appellate review, the doctrine of *res judicata* bars reconsideration of the judgment in light of subsequent changes in the applicable law. The Supreme Court has resolved that this calls for giving fully retrospective effect to any change in federal law in any case in which the appellate process has not been completed. "When this Court applies a rule of federal law to the parties before it, that rule is the controlling interpretation of federal law and must be given full retroactive effect in all cases still open on direct review and as to all events, regardless of whether such events predate or postdate our announcement of the rule." Harper v. Virginia Dept. of Taxation, 509 U.S. 86, 97 (1993).

The same rule applies to criminal cases still being litigated or appealed at the time the new rule of law is declared. But once a criminal conviction becomes final upon completion of the process of direct appellate review, the convicted party cannot invoke a change in the understanding of the law to undo his or her conviction by writ of habeas corpus—with two important but rarely applicable exceptions. A "new rule" will be applied retrospectively as the basis for habeas relief from an already final judgment of conviction if, but only if, (1) the new rule establishes a lack of substantive constitutional power to make criminal certain individual, private conduct, or (2) the new rule mandates a change in criminal procedure in some crucial and not merely technical way that is essential to the integrity and fundamental fairness of the criminal-justice system. Teague v. Lane, 489 U.S. 288, 307 (1989). This has led to a great deal of litigation in habeas corpus cases about when a new decision in fact announces a "new rule" or merely elaborates or extends the rule announced in an earlier decision. By and large, the Supreme Court has taken a quite strict view, from the perspective of hopeful habeas petitioners, classifying as a "new rule" (and hence one not available as the basis for retrospective habeas relief) any decision that goes beyond what was clearly compelled by precedent. *See* E. Chemerinsky, *Federal Jurisdiction* § 15.5.1, at 902–04 (4th ed. 2003).

This restrictive view has been codified and further circumscribed by Congress in a 1996 amendment to the habeas statute itself which forbids granting the writ unless the application of federal law by state courts was not only mistaken but also "contrary to" or "an unreasonable application of clearly established federal law, as determined by the Supreme Court of the United States." 28 U.S.C. § 2254(d)(1). In Williams (Terry) v. Taylor, 529 U.S. 362, 412–13 (2000), the majority construed the new statute as follows:

> [Section] 2254(d)(1) places a new constraint on the power of a federal habeas court to grant a state prisoner's application for a writ of habeas corpus with respect to claims adjudicated on the merits in state court. Under § 2254(d)(1), the writ may issue only if one of the following two conditions is satisfied—the state-court adjudication resulted in a decision that (1) "was contrary to ... clearly established Federal law, as determined by the Supreme Court of the United States," or (2) "involved an unreasonable application of ...

clearly established Federal law, as determined by the Supreme Court of the United States." Under the "contrary to" clause, a federal habeas court may grant the writ if the state court arrives at a conclusion opposite to that reached by this Court on a question of law or if the state court decides a case differently than this Court has on a set of materially indistinguishable facts. Under the "unreasonable application" clause, a federal habeas court may grant the writ if the state court identifies the correct governing legal principle from this Court's decisions but unreasonably applies that principle to the facts of the prisoner's case.

A parallel provision of the amended habeas statutes bars habeas relief on any grounds that the petitioner "failed" to present to the state courts in connection with the original prosecution or appeal, and which the state courts now refuse to entertain, unless based on "a new rule of constitutional law" made retroactive by *Teague* or involving facts that could not have been previously discovered in the exercise of due diligence, and unless the petitioner also shows essentially that any reasonable factfinder would conclude that the petitioner was innocent of the crime in question. 28 U.S.C. § 2254(e)(2). The Supreme Court has unanimously adopted a lenient construction of this provision, holding it inapplicable unless the petitioner "failed" to present the claim in a timely fashion to the state courts through "lack of diligence or some other fault," explaining that in this sense "[d]iligence ... depends upon whether the prisoner made a reasonable attempt, in light of the information available at the time, to investigate and pursue claims in state court." Williams (Michael) v. Taylor, 529 U.S. 420, 434–35 (2000).[7]

Notes and Questions

(1) In Gideon v. Wainwright, 372 U.S. 335 (1963), the Supreme Court recognized a right to the appointment of counsel for indigent defendants in felony cases. An earlier decision had held that the states were under an obligation to assign counsel to such defendants only under special circumstances, taking into account particularly the gravity of the crime and the complexity of the legal issues. Assume that the large majority of states, including the most populous ones, had recognized under their state constitutions, prior to the Supreme Court decision, a right to the appointment of counsel for indigents accused of any serious crime. Is this the sort of "new rule" that could be the basis for retrospective habeas relief under *Teague v. Lane*? Could a habeas petitioner who had unsuccessfully asserted a federal constitutional right to counsel at trial win retrospective habeas relief under *Gideon*, notwithstanding *Teague*? Notwithstanding new 28 U.S.C. § 2254(d)(1)?

(2) What about a habeas petitioner who, before *Gideon* was decided, had been tried and convicted in state court without the assistance of

---

7. The Supreme Court decided two habeas cases on the same day involving different petitioners, both named Williams, and the same prison warden, John Taylor. In the case construing § 2254(e)(2), the petitioner was Michael Wayne Williams. In the case construing § 2254(d)(1), the petitioner was Terry Williams.

counsel, having never requested counsel? Would habeas relief be barred by new § 2254(e)(2)?

(3) In Bowers v. Hardwick, 478 U.S. 186 (1986), a bare majority of five Justices held that a state had the constitutional power to criminalize private homosexual conduct. In Lawrence v. Texas, 539 U.S. ___, 123 S.Ct. 2472 (2003), a majority of five Justices plus one concurring Justice overruled *Bowers* and held that private homosexual conduct was a constitutionally protected right. Should someone imprisoned for the crime of private homosexual conduct be able to win immediate release, not withstanding that his or her conviction had already become final before *Lawrence* was decided? Would this be permitted under *Teague* and the amended habeas statute?

(4) Many contentious habeas cases involve the death penalty and the especially complex rules of federal constitutional law pertaining to capital cases. Should habeas relief be harder or easier to obtain when the state courts have erroneously but not unreasonably applied these complex rules in imposing and upholding a judgment sentencing the petitioner to death?

Further References

Alexander, L., "Constrained By Precedent," 63 Southern California Law Review 1 (1989).

Bradford, C.S., "Following Dead Precedent: The Supreme Court's Ill–Advised Rejection of Anticipatory Overruling," 59 Fordham Law Review 39 (1990).

Brenner, S. and Spaeth, H.J., *Stare Indecisis: The Alteration of Precedent on the Supreme Court, 1946–1992* (1995).

Caminker, E.H., "Why Must Inferior Courts Obey Superior Court Precedents?," 46 Stanford Law Review 817 (1994).

Cardozo, B.N., *The Nature of the Judicial Process* (1921), pp. 142–67.

Cross, R. and Harris, J.W., *Precedent in English Law* (4th ed. 1991), pp. 97–108, 228–32.

Douglas, W.O., "*Stare Decisis*," 49 Columbia Law Review 735 (1949).

Dworkin, R.M., *Law's Empire* (1986), Chapters 7–9.

Dworkin, R.M., *Taking Rights Seriously* (1977), Chapters 2–4.

Freed, T.E., "Is *Stare Decisis* Still the Lighthouse Beacon of Supreme Court Jurisprudence?: A Critical Analysis," 57 Ohio State Law Journal 1767 (1996).

Krent, H.J., "The Puzzling Boundary Between Criminal and Civil Retroactive Lawmaking," 84 Georgetown Law Journal 2143 (1996).

Leach, W.B., "Revisionism in the House of Lords: The Bastion of Rigid *Stare Decisis* Falls," 80 Harvard Law Review 797 (1967).

Lee, T.R., *"Stare Decisis* in Economic Perspective: An Economic Analysis of the Supreme Court's Doctrine of Precedent," 78 North Carolina Law Review 643 (2000).

Lee, T.R., *"Stare Decisis* in Historical Perspective: From the Founding Era to the Rehnquist Court," 52 Vanderbilt Law Review 647 (1999).

Lewis, A., *Gideon's Trumpet* (1964).

Matz, E., "The Nature of Precedent," 66 North Carolina Law Review 367 (1988).

Reynolds, W.L., *Judicial Process in a Nutshell* (3d ed. 2003).

Schaefer, W.V., "Prospective Rulings: Two Perspectives," 1982 *Supreme Court Review* 1.

Schauer, F., "Precedent," 39 Stanford Law Review 571 (1987).

Stephens, P. J., "The New Retroactivity Doctrine: Equality, Reliance and *Stare Decisis*," 48 Syracuse Law Review 1515 (1998).

Chapter IV

THE *RATIO DECIDENDI*
OF A CASE

A. OVERVIEW

The permutations of the doctrine of *stare decisis* and the problem of the retroactivity of decisions overruling precedent bear directly upon the rigor with which courts will examine a prior case to determine if it arose upon distinguishable facts, and upon the expansiveness or restrictiveness with which courts will construe the *ratio decidendi* of a purported precedent. The manipulation of both the factual distinctions and the holdings attributed to prior cases provides a covert way of affirming the authoritative force of case law in principle while evading it in practice. In this chapter and the next, we accordingly complement our discussion of the doctrine of *stare decisis* with materials on the determination of the *ratio decidendi* of a case, and on the role of logic and policy in the way judges reason from the *ratio decidendi* of a precedent to their decision of the case before them.

E. BODENHEIMER, JURISPRUDENCE: THE PHILOSOPHY AND METHOD OF THE LAW

pp. 432–435 (Rev. ed. 1974) [footnotes included].[1]

[N]ot every statement made in a judicial decision is an authoritative source to be followed in a later case presenting a similar situation. Only those statements in an earlier decision which may be said to constitute the *ratio decidendi* of that case are held to be binding, as a matter of general principle, in subsequent cases. Propositions not partaking of the character of *ratio decidendi* may be disregarded by the judge deciding the later case. Such nonauthoritative statements are usually referred to as *dicta* or (if they are quite unessential for the determination of the points at issue) *obiter dicta*.

---

1. Copyright © 1962, 1974 by the President and Fellows of Harvard College. Reprinted by permission of the publisher, Harvard University Press.

Unfortunately, the question as to what are the constituent elements and the scope of the *ratio decidendi* of a case is far from being settled. In the case of *Northwestern Life Ins. Co. v. Wright*,[2] the Supreme Court of Wisconsin stated its conception of the *ratio decidendi* of a case in the following language: "The key note of an adjudication is the ruling principle. The details showing the particular facts ruled by some particular principle are helpful; but, in the end, it is the principle, not the detail circumstances, commonly evidentiary only, which is the important feature as to whether an existing adjudication is a safe guide to follow in a case." It is widely conceded, however, that not every proposition of law formulated by a court in the course of a judicial opinion—even though it may have been the basis of the decision—possesses the authority belonging to the *ratio decidendi*. The principle of law enunciated by the court may have been much broader than was required for the decision of the case before it; and it is well established that in such situations the surplus not necessary to sustain the judgment must be regarded as a *dictum*. This qualification of the theory which identifies *ratio decidendi* with the ruling principle of a case is aptly brought out in the discussions of the problem by Sir John Salmond and Professor Edmund Morgan. Salmond points out that "a precedent . . . is a judicial decision which contains in itself a principle. The underlying principle which thus forms its authoritative element is often termed the *ratio decidendi*." He then goes on to say:

> . . . [C]ourts of justice . . . must take care in . . . [formulating] principles to limit themselves to the requirements of the case in hand. That is to say, they must not lay down principles which are not required for the due decision of the particular case, or which are wider than is necessary for this purpose. The only judicial principles which are authoritative are those which are thus relevant in their subject-matter and limited in their scope. All others, at the best, are of merely persuasive efficacy. They are not true *rationes decidendi*, and are distinguished from them under the name of *dicta* or *obiter dicta*, things said by the way.[3]

Morgan defined *ratio decidendi* in a similar fashion as "those portions of the opinion setting forth the rules of law applied by the court, the application of which was *required* for the determination of the issues presented."[4]

A substantially different theory as to what constitutes the *ratio decidendi* of a case was developed in England by Professor Arthur

2. 140 N.W. 1078, at 1081–1082 (1913).

3. John Salmond, "The Theory of Judicial Precedent," 16 Law Quarterly Review 376, at 387–388 (1900). *See also* Salmond, *Jurisprudence*, ed. G. Williams, 11th ed. (London, 1957), pp. 222–226.

4. Edmund M. Morgan, *Introduction to the Study of Law*, 2d ed. (Chicago, 1948), p. 155 (emphasis added); *see also* John C. Gray, *The Nature and Sources of the Law*, 2d ed. (New York, 1921), p. 261; Carleton K. Allen, *Law in the Making*, 6th ed. (Oxford, 1958), p. 247; Rupert Cross, *Precedent in English Law*, 2d ed. (Oxford, 1968), pp. 35–101.

Goodhart.[5] According to him, it is not the principle of law laid down in a decision which is the controlling element under the doctrine of *stare decisis*. In his opinion, the *ratio decidendi* is to be found by taking account of the facts treated as material by the judge who decided the case cited as a precedent, and of his decision as based on these facts.[6] Goodhart submits three main reasons for rejecting the proposition of law theory of the *ratio decidendi*. First, he points out, there may be no rule of law set forth in the opinion of the court. Second, the rule formulated by the judge may be too wide or too narrow. Third, in appellate courts the rules of law set forth by different judges in their separate opinions may have no relation to one another.

Goodhart's theory was, in its basic core, adopted by Professor Glanville Williams.[7] Williams explained that in the light of the actual practice of the courts, however, the phrase *"ratio decidendi* of a case" was slightly ambiguous, because it may mean either the rule that the judge who decided the case intended to lay down and apply to the facts, or the rule that a later court concedes him to have had the power to lay down. This is so because, as Williams rightly emphasizes, "courts do not accord to their predecessors an unlimited power of laying down wide rules."[8] This undeniable fact prompted Dean Edward Levi to take issue with Professor Goodhart on the ground that the later judge may quite legitimately find irrelevant the existence or absence of facts which the prior judge considered important. In the words of Levi, "It is not what the prior judge intended that is of any importance; rather it is what the present judge, attempting to see the law as a fairly consistent whole, thinks should be the determining classification. In arriving at this result he will ignore what the past thought important; he will emphasize facts which prior judges would have thought made no difference."[9]

A more radical point of view was advanced by Professors Sidney Post Simpson[10] and Julius Stone.[11] According to their approach, it is erroneous to assume that each decided case has its distinct *ratio decidendi*. They contend that practically each case has implicit in it a whole congeries of possible principles of decision. When a case is decided, no one can be certain which of the possible principles of decision is destined eventually to become the controlling one. In Stone's opinion, if there are ten facts stated in an opinion, as many general propositions will explain the decision as there are possible combinations of these facts. Only a study of a whole series of decisions on a particular problem of the law

---

5. *See* Goodhart, "Determining the *Ratio Decidendi* of a Case," 40 Yale Law Journal 161 (1930). A criticism of Goodhart's article is presented by R.N. Gooderson, *"Ratio Decidendi* and Rules of Law," 30 Canadian Bar Review 892 (1952).

6. Goodhart, p. 182.

7. Williams, *Learning the Law*, 8th ed. (London, 1969), p. 72: "The *ratio decidendi* of a case can be defined as the material facts of the case plus the decision thereon."

8. *Id.*, p. 69.

9. Edward H. Levi, *An Introduction to Legal Reasoning* (Chicago, 1949), p. 2.

10. "English Law in the Making," 4 Modern Law Review 121 (1940).

11. "Fallacies of the Logical Form in English Law," in *Interpretations of Modern Legal Philosophies*, ed. P. Sayre (New York, 1947), pp. 709–710; *cf. also* Stone, *Legal System and Lawyers' Reasonings* (Stanford, 1964), pp. 267–280.

will to some extent reveal what the fate of a particular precedent has been in the dynamic process of restricting, expanding, interpreting, reinterpreting, and reformulating a prior body of doctrine in the creative work of the courts.

If we ask ourselves what the presently prevailing attitude of the American courts toward the question of determining the *ratio decidendi* is, we must probably conclude that the views of Salmond and Morgan are accepted by most American judges as representing the most satisfactory approach. In other words, most judges will hold that the *ratio decidendi* of a case is to be found in the general principle governing an earlier decision, as long as the formulation of this general principle was necessary to the decision of the actual issue between the litigants.

NOTE BY THE EDITORS: REASONABLE APPLICATION OF THE *RATIO DECIDENDI*

The word "necessary," as used in the prevailing formulation of the *ratio decidendi* doctrine, should not be construed to mean "absolutely necessary." If "necessary" is defined in a radically restrictive sense, a court would always be justified in carving down a rule of law found in a judicial precedent to the narrowest range consistent with the factual situation. This would not be desirable. The rule or principle of law laid down by a court should not be unduly broad, but it should be broad enough to cover all situations that cannot, on any reasonable ground, be distinguished from the case at hand. This position is required by a fundamental axiom of justice, referred to in Chapter III, pursuant to which equal or essentially similar situations should be treated equally by the law.

The proper handling of the *ratio decidendi* doctrine, thus conceived, demands of the judge laying down a rule in a case of first impression a great deal of resourcefulness and imagination. The judge may easily miss the mark by stating the rule too broadly or too narrowly. In that event, a lower court generally bound by the decisions of the upper court is not obliged to accept the precise formulation of the rule by the upper court. It may whittle down the rule to exclude cases with different facts that are within the letter but not the spirit of the rule as originally formulated. Or it may expand the rule to cover situations that are not included in the rule as originally formulated, but should be included because they cannot be distinguished on reasonable grounds from the facts of the precedent. The Supreme Court of California has given expression to the principle implicit in the foregoing considerations by the following pronouncement: "Our statements of law remain binding on the trial and appellate courts of this state and must be applied wherever the facts of a case are not fairly distinguishable from the facts of the case in which we have declared the applicable principle of law." People v. Triggs, 8 Cal.3d 884, at 890–891, 506 P.2d 232, at 236, 106 Cal.Rptr. 408, at 412 (1973). This statement is not essentially different from the view of Morgan and Salmond, according to which the *ratio decidendi* of a case consists of the principle of law necessary to the determination of the issues before the court and, as the California Supreme Court has made clear, of issues that cannot be fairly distinguished from them.

The difficulties encountered by judges in hitting the nail on its head in a first attempt to state an adequately phrased rule or principle in an unprovided case may disappear in the course of time. After a number of efforts in articulating, revising, or limiting a legal prescription have been made, a properly formulated norm of law, subject perhaps to certain exceptions and qualifications, may emerge. It is often the case that such a norm will serve as a clear precedent to the courts of a jurisdiction for a considerable period of time.

Problems

(1) A left a legacy of $10,000 to B in his will. B, who had been informed by A of this testamentary bequest, murdered A shortly afterwards, because he was in need of money and wished to come into possession of the legacy immediately. He was convicted of intentional and premeditated homicide and sentenced to life imprisonment. Notwithstanding his conviction, he claimed the legacy of $10,000, for the benefit of his family, in a suit against C, the executor of A's estate. B's attorney asserted that there was no statute or judicial precedent barring B from taking the legacy. The trial court agreed with this argument and awarded the legacy to B.

On appeal by the executor, the Supreme Court of the state reversed the judgment, holding that B was not entitled to the legacy. The Court stated in its opinion that considerations of fundamental justice required the recognition of a principle to the effect that "no one shall be permitted to take advantage of his own wrong."

Some time thereafter D bequeathed $12,000 to E in his will. On a foggy day, E drove his car to a neighboring city; D was a guest in his car. Although driving within the legal speed limit, E used insufficient caution to control the speed of his car in the fog. The car ran into a truck and D was instantly killed. E was sentenced to two years' imprisonment for negligent homicide.

E brought suit against F, the executor of D's estate, to recover the legacy of $12,000. The attorney for the executor argued that E was not entitled to the legacy, since the trial court was bound by the holding of the state's Supreme Court to the effect that "no one shall be permitted to take advantage of his own wrong." He pointed out that the law had always viewed negligent homicide, just like intentional homicide, as a "wrong."

Should the trial court accept this argument? Or would the court be justified in distinguishing B's case and reaching the conclusion that E was entitled to the legacy?

(2) The Supreme Court of a state laid down a rule to the effect that overhanging branches of a tree may be cut off by a neighbor if they interfere with growth on his land or otherwise inconvenience him. Later, a case arose in a lower court of the state in which overhanging branches of a large rhododendron bush took sunlight away from some flowers

planted by the neighbor. The plaintiff invoked the authority of the Supreme Court case, but the defendant argued that the *ratio decidendi* of that case was limited to trees. What position should the trial court take?

B. THE EVOLUTION OF PRODUCTS LIABILITY AT COMMON LAW IN NEW YORK

The following sequence of cases focuses on the development of the law governing the liability of a manufacturer to a consumer for injuries caused by a negligently-manufactured product. It illustrates the way in which a prior precedent can be narrowed or broadened, depending upon a subsequent court's formulation of the *ratio decidendi* of the earlier case. As you read these materials, write down the *ratio decidendi* of each case immediately after reading it. Then compare your formulation with that made by the courts applying the rule of the case in subsequent decisions.

WINTERBOTTOM v. WRIGHT

Court of Exchequer, 1842.
10 M. & W. 109, 11 L.J.Ex. 415, 152 Eng.Rep. 402.

[The plaintiff was a mail coach driver who was injured when the coach broke down. The defendant had contracted with the Postmaster General to supply a number of coaches, including the coach in question, for the transport of mail. Under the terms of the contract, the defendant had promised the Postmaster General to keep the coaches in good repair. The plaintiff was employed by one Atkinson who, with knowledge of the defendant's contract, had contracted with the Postmaster General to supply horses and coachmen to operate the coaches. The plaintiff's declaration alleged that the defendant negligently failed to carry out his duties of maintenance and repair under the contract and that, as a consequence, the coach had become weakened and dangerous, causing the plaintiff's injuries.]

LORD ABINGER, C.B. I am clearly of opinion that the defendant is entitled to our judgment. We ought not to permit a doubt to rest upon this subject, for our doing so might be the means of letting in upon us an infinity of actions. This is an action of the first impression, and it has been brought in spite of the precautions which were taken, in the judgment of this Court in the case of Levy v. Langridge, [150 Eng.Rep. 863 (Ex. 1838); 150 Eng.Rep. 1458 (Ex. Ch. 1838)],[12] to obviate any notion that such an action could be maintained. We ought not to attempt

---

12. In Levy v. Langridge, 150 Eng.Rep. 1458 (Ex. Ch. 1838), the court allowed a boy who had been injured when a gun exploded in his hands to recover damages against the seller, who had sold the gun to the boy's father after making false representations that the gun had been produced by a reputable maker and that it was in good condition.

to extend the principle of that decision, which, although it has been cited in support of this action, wholly fails as an authority in its favour; for there the gun was bought for the use of the son, the plaintiff in that action, who could not make the bargain himself, but was really and substantially the party contracting. Here the action is brought simply because the defendant was a contractor with a third person; and it is contended that thereupon he became liable to everybody who might use the carriage. If there had been any ground for such an action, there certainly would have been some precedent of it; but with the exception of actions against innkeepers, ... no case of a similar nature has occurred in practice. That is a strong circumstance, and is of itself a great authority against its maintenance. It is however contended, that this contract being made on the behalf of the public by the Postmaster–General, no action could be maintained against him, and therefore the plaintiff must have a remedy against the defendant. But that is by no means a necessary consequence—he may be remediless altogether. There is no privity of contract between these parties; and if the plaintiff can sue, every passenger, or even any person passing along the road who was injured by the upsetting of the coach, might bring a similar action. Unless we confine the operation of such contracts as this to the parties who entered into them, the most absurd and outrageous consequences, to which I can see no limit, would ensue. Where a party becomes responsible to the public, by undertaking a public duty, he is liable, though the injury may have arisen from the negligence of his servant or agent. So in cases of public nuisances, whether the act was done by the party as a servant, or in any other capacity, you are liable to an action at the suit of any person who suffers. Those, however, are cases where the real ground of the liability is the public duty, or the commission of the public nuisance. There is also a class of cases in which the law permits a contract to be turned into a tort; but unless there has been some public duty undertaken, or public nuisance committed, they are all cases in which an action might have been maintained upon the contract. Thus, a carrier may be sued either in *assumpsit* or case; but there is no instance in which a party, who was not privy to the contract entered into with him, can maintain any such action. The plaintiff in this case could not have brought an action on the contract; if he could have done so, what would have been his situation, supposing the Postmaster–General had released the defendant? That would, at all events, have defeated his claim altogether. By permitting this action, we should be working this injustice, that after the defendant had done every thing to the satisfaction of his employer, and after all matters between them had been adjusted, and all accounts settled on the footing of their contract, we should subject them to be ripped open by this action of tort being brought against him.

ALDERSON, B. I am of the same opinion. The contract in this case was made with the Postmaster–General alone: and the case is just the same as if he had come to the defendant and ordered a carriage, and handed it at once over to Atkinson. If we were to hold that the plaintiff could sue in such a case, there is no point at which such actions would stop. The only safe rule is to confine the right to recover to those who enter into the contract: if we go one step beyond that, there is no reason why we should not go fifty. The only real argument in favour of the action is, that this is a case of hardship; but that might have been obviated, if the plaintiff had made himself a party to the contract. Then it is urged that it falls within the principle of the case of *Levy v. Langridge.* But the principle of that case was simply this, that the father having bought the gun for the very purpose of being used by the plaintiff, the defendant made representations by which he was induced to use it. There, a distinct fraud was committed on the plaintiff; the falsehood of the representation was also alleged to have been within the knowledge of the defendant who made it, and he was properly held liable for the consequences. How are the facts of that case applicable to those of the present? Where is the allegation of misrepresentation or fraud in this declaration? It shows nothing of the kind. Our judgment must therefore be for the defendant.

GURNEY, B., concurred.

ROLFE, B. The breach of the defendant's duty, stated in this declaration, is his omission to keep the carriage in a safe condition .... The duty, therefore, is shewn to have arisen solely from the contract; and the fallacy consists in the use of that word "duty." If a duty to the Postmaster–General be meant, that is true; but if a duty to the plaintiff be intended (and in that sense the word is evidently used), there was none. This is one of those unfortunate cases in which there certainly has been *damnum,* but is it *damnum absque injuria*; it is, no doubt, a hardship upon the plaintiff to be without a remedy, but, by that consideration we ought not to be influenced. Hard cases, it has been frequently observed, are apt to introduce bad law.

Judgment for the defendant.

THOMAS AND WIFE v. WINCHESTER

Court of Appeals of New York, 1852.
6 N.Y. 397, 57 Am.Dec. 455.

RUGGLES, CH. J., delivered the opinion of the court. This is an action brought to recover damages from the defendant for negligently putting up, labeling and selling as and for the extract of *dandelion,* which is a simple and harmless medicine, a jar of the extract of *belladonna,* which is a deadly poison; by means of which the plaintiff Mary Ann Thomas, to whom, being sick, a dose of dandelion was prescribed by a physician, and a portion of the contents of the jar, was administered as and for the extract of dandelion, was greatly injured, etc.

The facts proved were briefly these: Mrs. Thomas being in ill health, her physician prescribed for her a dose of dandelion. Her husband purchased what was believed to be the medicine prescribed, at the store of Dr. Foord, a physician and druggist in Cazenovia, Madison county, where the plaintiffs reside.

A small quantity of the medicine thus purchased was administered to Mrs. Thomas on whom it produced very alarming effects; such as coldness of the surface and extremities, feebleness of circulation, spasms of the muscles, giddiness of the head, dilation of the pupils of the eyes, and derangement of mind. She recovered however, after some time, from its effects, although for a short time her life was thought to be in great danger. The medicine administered was *belladonna, and not dandelion.* The jar from which it was taken was labeled "½ lb. dandelion, prepared by A. Gilbert, No. 108 John-street, N.Y. Jar 8 oz." . . . [Dr. Foord had purchased the jar from a druggist named Aspinwall, who had purchased the jar from the defendant "as extract of dandelion." The defendant had purchased the extract from a manufacturer of vegetable extracts for medicinal purposes. It was the defendant's employee, Gilbert, who had bottled the extract and who had put the label on the jar.] The extract of dandelion and the extract of belladonna resemble each other in color, consistency, smell and taste; but may on careful examination be distinguished the one from the other by those who are well acquainted with these articles. Gilbert's labels were paid for by Winchester and used in his business with his knowledge and assent.

The defendant's counsel moved for a nonsuit on the following grounds:

1. That the action could not be sustained, as the defendant was the remote vendor of the article in question: and there was no connection, transaction or privity between him and the plaintiffs, or either of them.

. . . .

[The judge denied the motion for nonsuit. He sent the case to the jury with instructions that, if the jury found that the defendant was negligent and that neither Aspinwall nor Foord was negligent, then the plaintiffs were entitled to recover damages. The jury returned a verdict for the plaintiffs.]

The case depends on the first point taken by the defendant on his motion for a nonsuit; and the question is, whether the defendant, being a remote vendor of the medicine, and there being no privity or connection between him and the plaintiffs, the action can be maintained.

If, in the labeling a poisonous drug with the name of a harmless medicine, for public market, no duty was violated by the defendant, excepting that which he owed to Aspinwall, his immediate vendee, in virtue of his contract of sale, this action cannot be maintained. If A builds a wagon and sells it to B, who sells it to C, and C hires it to D, who in consequence of the gross negligence of A in building the wagon is overturned and injured, D cannot recover damages against A, the builder. A's obligation to build the wagon faithfully arises solely out of his contract with B. The public have nothing to do with it. Misfortune to third persons, not parties to the contract, would not be a natural and necessary consequence of the builder's negligence; and such negligence is not an act imminently dangerous to human life.

. . . .

This was the ground on which the case of Winterbottom v. Wright, 10 Mees. & Welsb. 109, was decided. A contracted with the postmaster general to provide a coach to convey the mail bags along a certain line of road, and B and others also contracted to horse the coach along the same line. B and his co-contractors hired C, who was the plaintiff, to drive the coach. The coach, in consequence of some latent defect, broke down; the plaintiff was thrown from his seat and lamed. It was held that C could not maintain an action against A for the injury thus sustained. The reason of the decision is best stated by Baron Rolfe. A's duty to keep the coach in good condition was a duty to the postmaster general, with whom he made his contract, and not a duty to the driver employed by the owners of the horses.

But the case in hand stands on a different ground. The defendant was a dealer in poisonous drugs. Gilbert was his agent in preparing them for market. The death or great bodily harm of some person was the natural and almost inevitable consequence of the sale of belladonna by means of the false label.

Gilbert, the defendant's agent, would have been punishable for manslaughter if Mrs. Thomas had died in consequence of taking the falsely labeled medicine.... Although the defendant Winchester may not be answerable criminally for the negligence of his agent, there can be no doubt of his liability in a civil action, in which the act of the agent is to be regarded as the act of the principal.

In respect to the wrongful and criminal character of the negligence complained of, this case differs widely from those put by the defendant's counsel. No such imminent danger existed in those cases. In the present case the sale of the poisonous article was made to a dealer in drugs, and not to a consumer. The injury therefore was not likely to fall on him, or on his vendee who was also a dealer; but much more likely to be visited on a remote purchaser as actually happened. The defendant's negligence put human life in imminent danger. Can it be said that there was no duty on the part of the defendant, to avoid the creation of that danger by the exercise of greater caution? or that the exercise of that caution was a duty only to his immediate vendee, whose life was not endangered? The defendant's duty arose out of the nature of his business and the danger to others incident to its mismanagement. Nothing but mischief like that which actually happened could have been expected from sending the poison falsely labeled into the market; and the defendant is justly responsible for the probable consequences of the act. The duty of exercising caution in this respect did not arise out of the defendant's contract of sale to Aspinwall. The wrong done by the defendant was in putting the poison, mislabeled, into the hands of Aspinwall as an article of merchandise to be sold and afterwards used as the extract of dandelion, by some person then unknown. The owner of a horse and cart who leaves them unattended in the street is liable for any damage which may result from his negligence. Lynch v. Nurdin, 1 Q.B. 30, 113 Eng.Rep. 104 (1841); Illidge v. Goodwin, 5 Car. & P., 190, 172 Eng.Rep. 934 (1831).... The defendant's contract of sale to Aspinwall does not excuse the wrong done to the plaintiffs. It was a part of the means by which the wrong was effected. The plaintiffs' injury and their remedy would have stood on the same principle, if the defendant had given the belladonna to Dr. Foord without price, or if he had put it in his shop without his knowledge, under circumstances which would probably have led to its sale on the faith of the label.

In Longmeid v. Holliday, 6 Ex. 760, 155 Eng.Rep. 752 (1851) [(holding that the retail seller of a defectively manufactured lamp was not liable to the wife of the purchaser when the retailer had no knowledge of the defect)], the distinction is recognized between an act of negligence imminently dangerous to the lives of others, and one that is not so. In the former case, the party guilty of the negligence is liable to the party injured, whether there be a contract between them or not; in the latter, the negligent party is liable only to the party with whom he contracted, and on the ground that negligence is a breach of contract.

Judgment affirmed.

LOOP v. LITCHFIELD

Court of Appeals of New York, 1870.
42 N.Y. 351, 1 Am.Rep. 543.

HUNT, J. A piece of machinery already made and on hand, having defects which weaken it, is sold by the manufacturer to one who buys it for his own use. The defects are pointed out to the purchaser and are fully understood by him. This piece of machinery is used by the buyer for five years, and is then taken into the possession of a neighbor, who uses it for his own purposes. While so in use, it flies apart by reason of its original defects, and the person using it is killed. Is the seller, upon this state of facts, liable to the representatives of the deceased party? ... [The defendant had moved for a nonsuit on the ground that there was no privity between the defendant and the deceased. The trial court had denied the motion, and the jury had returned a verdict for the plaintiff. The jury's verdict had been reversed by the General Term.]

... [T]he appellants rely upon the case of Thomas v. Winchester, 6 N.Y. 397, 57 Am.Dec. 455, [which held that the defendant was liable because he had "put human life in imminent danger"] ....

The appellants seek to bring their case within [this principle] by asserting that the fly wheel in question was a dangerous instrument. Poison is a dangerous subject. Gunpowder is the same. A torpedo is a dangerous instrument, as is a spring gun, a loaded rifle or the like. They are instruments and articles in their nature calculated to do injury to mankind, and generally intended to accomplish that purpose. They are essentially, and in their elements, instruments of danger. Not so, however, an iron wheel, a few feet in diameter and a few inches in thickness, although one part may be weaker than another. If the article is abused by too long use, or by applying too much weight or speed, an injury may occur, as it may from an ordinary carriage wheel, a wagon axle, or the common chair in which we sit. There is scarcely an object in art or nature, from which an injury may not occur under such circumstances. Yet they are not in their nature sources of danger, nor can they, with any regard to the accurate use of language, be called dangerous instruments. That an injury actually occurred by the breaking of a carriage axle, the failure of the carriage body, the falling to pieces of a chair or sofa, or the bursting of a fly wheel, does not in the least alter its character.

. . . The injury in [*Thomas*] was a natural result of the act. . . . Not so here. The bursting of the wheel and the injury to human life was not the natural result or the expected consequence of the manufacture and sale of the wheel. Every use of the counterfeit medicines would be necessarily injurious, while this wheel was in fact used with safety for five years.

. . . .

Upon the facts as stated, assuming that the deceased had no knowledge of the defects complained of, and assuming that he was in the rightful and lawful use of the machine, I am of the opinion that the verdict cannot be sustained. The facts constitute no cause of action. . . .

All concur. Judgment [of the General Term] affirmed [on the ground that the trial court erred by not granting the defendant's motion for nonsuit].

DEVLIN v. SMITH

Court of Appeals of New York, 1882.
89 N.Y. 470, 42 Am.Rep. 311.

[The defendant Smith entered into a contract with the defendant Stevenson to erect a scaffold that was ninety feet high in the dome of a county courthouse. The deceased, an employee of Smith, was standing on the scaffold and preparing the dome for painting when he fell to his death due to a defect in the scaffold. At the first trial, the plaintiff (the deceased's widow) obtained a jury verdict against Stevenson, but it was reversed and a new trial was granted. At the second trial, the complaint was dismissed as to both defendants, and the plaintiff appealed.]

RAPALLO, J. Upon a careful review of all the testimony in this case, we are of opinion that there was sufficient evidence to require the submission to the jury of the question, whether the breaking down of the scaffold was attributable to negligence in its construction. . . . [Witnesses at the trial had testified that the portion of the scaffold at issue should have been secured with lashings, rather than with nails, which broke under pressure.]

The case was, therefore, one in which the jury might have found the evidence that the death was caused by the . . . negligent construction of the scaffold, and . . . the question is whether . . . either of the defendants should be held liable. . . .

[The court concluded that Smith was not at fault, and therefore not liable to the plaintiff, because he had hired an independent contractor, and he had not realized that the scaffold was defective due to the use of nails in its construction.]

If any person was at fault in the matter it was the defendant Stevenson [who knew that the brace in question was nailed to the ledger]. It is contended, however, that even if through his negligence the scaffold was defective, he is not liable in this action, because there was no privity between him and the deceased and he owed no duty to the deceased, his obligation and duty being only to Smith, with whom he contracted.

As a general rule the builder of a structure for another party, under a contract with him, or one who sells an article of his own manufacture, is not liable to an action by a third party who uses the same with the consent of the owner or purchaser, for injuries resulting from a defect therein, caused by negligence. The liability of the builder or manufacturer for such defects is, in general, only to the person with whom he contracted. But, notwithstanding this rule, liability to third parties has been held to exist when the defect is such as to render the article in itself imminently dangerous, and serious injury to any person using it is a natural and probable consequence of its use: as where a dealer in drugs carelessly labeled a deadly poison as a harmless medicine, it was held that he was liable not merely to the person to whom he sold it, but to the person who ultimately used it, though it had passed through many hands. This liability was held to rest not upon any contract or direct privity between him and the party injured, but upon the duty which the law imposes on every one to avoid acts in their nature dangerous to the lives of others. Thomas v. Winchester, 6 N.Y. 397, 57 Am.Dec. 455. In that case Mayor, etc. v. Cunliff, 2 N.Y. 165, was cited as an authority for the position that a builder is liable only to the party for whom he builds. Some of the examples there put by way of illustration were commented upon, and among others the case of one who builds a carriage carelessly and of defective materials, and sells it, and the purchaser lends it to a friend, and the carriage, by reason of its original defect, breaks down and the friend is injured, and the question is put, can he recover against the maker? The comments of Ruggles, Ch. J., upon this suppositious case, in *Thomas v. Winchester*, and the ground upon which he answers the question in the negative, show clearly the distinction between the two classes of cases. He says that in the case supposed, the obligation of the maker to build faithfully arises only out of his contract with the purchaser. The public have nothing to do with it. Misfortunes to third persons, not parties to the contract, would not be a natural and necessary consequence of the builder's negligence, and such negligence is not an act imminently dangerous to human life.

Applying these tests to the question now before us, the solution is not difficult. Stevenson undertook to build a scaffold ninety feet in height, for the express purpose of enabling the workmen of Smith to stand upon it to paint the interior of the dome. Any defect or negligence in its construction, which should cause it to give way, would naturally result in these men being precipitated from that great height. A stronger case, where misfortune to third persons not parties to the contract would be a natural and necessary consequence of the builder's negligence, can hardly be supposed, nor is it easy to imagine a more apt illustration of a case where such negligence would be an act imminently dangerous to human life. These circumstances seem to us to bring the case fairly within the principle of *Thomas v. Winchester*.

. . . .

Loop v. Litchfield (42 N.Y. 351, 1 Am.Rep. 543) was decided upon the ground that the wheel which caused the injury was not in itself a dangerous instrument, and that the injury was not a natural consequence of the defect or one reasonably to be anticipated. . . .

We think there should be a new trial as to the defendant Stevenson, and that it will be for the jury to determine whether the death of the plaintiff's intestate was caused by negligence on the part of Stevenson in the construction of the scaffold.

The judgment should be affirmed . . . as to the defendant Smith, and reversed as to the defendant Stevenson, and a new trial ordered as to him. . . .

STATLER v. GEORGE A. RAY MFG. CO.

Court of Appeals of New York, 1909.
195 N.Y. 478, 88 N.E. 1063.

Hiscock, J.

This action was brought to recover damages for personal injuries sustained through the explosion of a large coffee urn, whereby the plaintiff and another were severely scalded and a third person killed. The defendant was engaged in manufacturing and vending such urns for use in hotels. They were constructed in what was called a 'battery of three.' The central urn or boiler was equipped with a coil of pipe through which steam was driven, whereby water was heated which was siphoned into the urn on either side where the coffee was made. In the case of the appliance in question, the central urn was of considerable diameter, and perhaps three or four feet in height, and on the occasion of practically its first use its bottom was partially driven out by force of steam and water and the accident to plaintiff caused. The defendant did not sell this urn to the plaintiff, but to a jobber, who in turn sold the same to a company of which plaintiff was an officer. Thus there were no contractual relations between the parties to this action, but plaintiff instituted and thus far has succeeded in his action on the theory that defendant well knew the purposes for which its urn was to be used; that the latter was of such a character inherently that, when applied to the purposes for which it was designed, it was liable to become a source of great danger to many people if not carefully and properly constructed; that the defendant negligently and carelessly constructed it so that it was imminently dangerous when employed as intended to be; and that as the natural and direct result of this negligent and heedless conduct the urn exploded and the plaintiff was injured.

... We think further that there was evidence which permitted a jury to say that the defendant, knowing the uses for which the urn was intended when it marketed the same, was guilty of, and of course chargeable with knowledge of, defective and unsafe construction. This leaves on this branch of the case simply the question whether a manufacturer and vendor of such an inherently dangerous appliance as this was may be made liable to a third party on the theory invoked by plaintiff, and we think that this question must be regarded as settled in the latter's favor by the following authorities: Thomas v. Winchester, 6 N. Y. 397, 57 Am. Dec. 455; ... Huset v. Case Threshing Machine Co., 120 Fed. 865, 872, 57 C. C. A. 237 [(8th Cir. 1903)]....

[Torgesen v. Schultz, 192 N.Y. 156, 84 N.E. 956 (1908)] is the last decision by this court on this general subject. That action was one by the plaintiff to recover against the defendant for personal injuries caused by the bursting of a siphon bottle of aerated water filled and put on the market by the latter. The plaintiff enjoyed no contractual relation whatever with the defendant, and the action was maintained on the same principles urged in this action. It was in that case in substance held that if a vendor had knowledge that the bottles used for aerated water, when charged at a certain pressure were liable to explode unless first subjected to an adequate test, and there was evidence that the test used by such vendor was insufficient to render it reasonably certain that bottles charged at such pressure would not explode when used as customers might be expected to use them [(e.g., customers might be expected to place the bottles in contact with ice, especially in hot weather)], the question of the defendant's negligence should be submitted to the jury. The action thus was based upon no contractual relation, but upon the ground of negligence. As the basis in part at least of the decision, Judge Willard Bartlett, writing in behalf of the court, quoted with approval the rule laid down by Lord Justice Cotton in Heaven v. Pender, L. R. (11 Q. B. D.) 503 [(1883)] [(holding a dock owner who was also the builder of defective scaffolding located on his dock liable to a ship's painter who was standing on the scaffolding when it broke because the builder had constructed the scaffolding with scorched ropes)] as follows: 'Any one who leaves a dangerous instrument, as a gun, in such a way as to cause danger, or who without due warning supplies to others for use an instrument or thing which to his knowledge, from its construction or otherwise, is in such a condition as to cause danger, not necessarily incident to the use of such an instrument or thing, is liable for injury caused to others by reason of his negligent act.' This rule distinctly recognizes the principle that, in the case of an article of an inherently dangerous nature, a manufacturer may become liable for a negligent construction which, when added to the inherent character of the appliance, makes it imminently dangerous, and causes or contributes to an injury not necessarily incident to the use of such an article if properly constructed, but naturally following from a defective construction.

While thus we should not hesitate to affirm the judgment on its general merits, we find that errors were committed in rulings on evidence which are so pronounced and in the aggregate at least so important and prejudicial to the rights of the defendant that they cannot be overlooked.

. . . .

The judgment appealed from should be reversed, and a new trial granted. . . .

GRAY, WERNER, WILLARD BARTLETT, and CHASE, JJ., concur. VANN, J., concurs in result. CULLEN, C. J., absent.

MacPHERSON v. BUICK MOTOR CO.

Court of Appeals of New York, 1916.
217 N.Y. 382, 111 N.E. 1050.

CARDOZO, J. The defendant is a manufacturer of automobiles. It sold an automobile to a retail dealer. The retail dealer re-sold to the plaintiff. While the plaintiff was in the car, it suddenly collapsed. He was thrown out and injured. One of the wheels was made of defective wood, and its spokes crumbled into fragments. The wheel was not made by the defendant; it was bought from another manufacturer. There is evidence, however, that its defects could have been discovered by reasonable inspection, and that inspection was omitted. There is no claim that the defendant knew of the defect and willfully concealed it. . . . The charge is one, not of fraud, but of negligence. The question to be determined is whether the defendant owed a duty of care and vigilance to any one but the immediate purchaser. [The trial court entered a judgment in favor of the plaintiff upon a jury verdict. The intermediate appellate court affirmed the trial court's judgment.]

The foundations of this branch of the law, at least in this state, were laid in Thomas v. Winchester, 6 N.Y. 397, 57 Am.Dec. 455. A poison was falsely labeled. The sale was made to a druggist, who in turn sold to a customer. The customer recovered damages from the seller who affixed the label. "The defendant's negligence," it was said, "put human life in imminent danger." A poison falsely labeled is likely to injure any one who gets it. Because the danger is to be foreseen, there is a duty to avoid the injury. Cases were cited by way of illustration in which manufacturers were not subject to any duty irrespective of contract. The distinction was said to be that their conduct, though negligent, was not likely to result in injury to any one except the purchaser. We are not required to say whether the chance of injury was always as remote as the distinction assumes. Some of the illustrations might be rejected today. The principle of the distinction is for present purposes the important thing.

Thomas v. Winchester became quickly a landmark of the law. In the application of its principle there may at times have been uncertainty or even error. There has never in this state been doubt or disavowal of the principle itself. The chief cases are well known, yet to recall some of them will be helpful. Loop v. Litchfield, 42 N.Y. 351, 1 Am.Rep. 543, is the earliest. It was the case of a defect in a small balance wheel used on a circular saw. The manufacturer pointed out the defect to the buyer, who wished a cheap article and was ready to assume the risk. The risk can hardly have been an imminent one, for the wheel lasted five years before it broke. In the meanwhile the buyer had made a lease of the machinery. It was held that the manufacturer was not answerable to the lessee. *Loop v. Litchfield* was followed in Losee v. Clute, 51 N.Y. 494, 10 Am.Rep. 638, the case of the explosion of a steam boiler. That decision has been criticised (Thompson on Negligence, 233, Shearman & Redfield on Negligence [6th ed.], § 117); but it must be confined to its special facts. It was put upon the ground that the risk of injury was too remote. The buyer in that case had not only accepted the boiler, but had tested it. The manufacturer knew that his own test was not the final one. The finality of the test has a bearing on the measure of diligence owing to persons other than the purchaser....

These early cases suggest a narrow construction of the rule. Later cases, however, evince a more liberal spirit. First in importance is Devlin v. Smith, 89 N.Y. 470, 42 Am.Rep. 311. The defendant, a contractor, built a scaffold for a painter. The painter's servants were injured. The contractor was held liable. He knew that the scaffold, if improperly constructed, was a most dangerous trap. He knew that it was to be used by the workmen. He was building it for that very purpose. Building it for their use, he owed them a duty, irrespective of his contract with their master, to build it with care.

From *Devlin v. Smith* we pass over intermediate cases and turn to the latest case in this court in which *Thomas v. Winchester* was followed. That case is Statler v. Ray Mfg. Co., 195 N.Y. 478, 480, 88 N.E. 1063. The defendant manufactured a large coffee urn. It was installed in a restaurant. When heated, the urn exploded and injured the plaintiff. We held that the manufacturer was liable. We said that the urn "was of such a character inherently that, when applied to the purposes for which it was designed, it was liable to become a source of great danger to many people if not carefully and properly constructed."

It may be that *Devlin v. Smith* and *Statler v. Ray Mfg. Co.* have extended the rule of *Thomas v. Winchester*. If so, this court is committed to the extension. The defendant argues that things imminently dangerous to life are poisons, explosives, deadly weapons—things whose normal function it is to injure or destroy. But whatever the rule in *Thomas v. Winchester* may once have been, it has no longer that restricted meaning. A scaffold (*Devlin v. Smith, supra*) is not inherently a destructive instrument. It becomes destructive only if imperfectly constructed. A large coffee urn (*Statler v. Ray Mfg. Co., supra*) may have within itself, if negligently made, the potency of danger, yet no one thinks of it as an implement whose normal function is destruction....

. . . . .

We hold, then, that the principle of *Thomas v. Winchester* is not limited to poisons, explosives, and things of like nature, to things which in their normal operation are implements of destruction. If the nature of a thing is such that it is reasonably certain to place life and limb in peril when negligently made, it is then a thing of danger. Its nature gives warning of the consequences to be expected. If to the element of danger there is added knowledge that the thing will be used by persons other than the purchaser, and used without new tests, then, irrespective of contract, the manufacturer of this thing of danger is under a duty to make it carefully. That is as far as we are required to go for the decision of this case. There must be knowledge of a danger, not merely possible, but probable. It is possible to use almost anything in a way that will make it dangerous if defective. That is not enough to charge the manufacturer with a duty independent of his contract. Whether a given thing is dangerous may be sometimes a question for the court and sometimes a question for the jury. There must also be knowledge that in the usual course of events the danger will be shared by others than the buyer. Such knowledge may often be inferred from the nature of the transaction. But it is possible that even knowledge of the danger and of the use will not always be enough. The proximity or remoteness of the relation is a factor to be considered. We are dealing now with the liability of the manufacturer of the finished product, who puts it on the market to be used without inspection by his customers. If he is negligent, where danger is to be foreseen, a liability will follow. We are not required at this time to say that it is legitimate to go back of the manufacturer of the finished product and hold the manufacturers of the component parts. To make their negligence a cause of imminent danger, an independent cause must often intervene; the manufacturer of the finished product must also fail in his duty of inspection. It may be that in those circumstances the negligence of the earlier members of the series is too remote to constitute, as to the ultimate user, an actionable wrong.... We leave that question open. We shall have to deal with it when it arises. The difficulty which it suggests is not present in this case. There is here no break in the chain of cause and effect. In such circumstances, the presence of a known danger, attendant upon a known use, makes vigilance a duty. We have put aside the notion that the duty to safeguard life and limb, when the consequences of negligence may be foreseen, grows out of contract and nothing else. We have put the source of the obligation where it ought be. We have put its source in the law.

From this survey of the decisions, there thus emerges a definition of the duty of a manufacturer which enables us to measure this defendant's liability. Beyond all question, the nature of an automobile gives warning of probable danger if its construction is defective. This automobile was designed to go fifty miles an hour. Unless its wheels were sound and strong, injury was almost certain. It was as much a thing of danger as a defective engine for a railroad. The defendant knew of the danger. It knew also that the car would be used by persons other than the buyer. This was apparent from its size; there were seats for three persons. It was apparent also from the fact that the buyer was a dealer in cars, who bought to resell. The maker of this car supplied it for the use of purchasers from the dealer just as plainly as the contractor in *Devlin v. Smith* supplied the scaffold for use by the servants of the owner. The dealer was indeed the one person of whom it might be said with some approach to certainty that by him the car would not be used. Yet the defendant would have us say that he was the one person whom it was under a legal duty to protect. The law does not lead us to so inconsequent a conclusion. Precedents drawn from the days of travel by stage coach do not fit the conditions of travel today. [Cardozo later noted that *Winterbottom v. Wright* had not been overruled.] The principle that the danger must be imminent does not change, but the things subject to the principle do change. They are whatever the needs of life in a developing civilization require them to be.

.   .   .   .

There is nothing anomalous in a rule which imposes upon A, who has contracted with B, a duty to C and D and others according as he knows or does not know that the subject matter of the contract is intended for their use. . . .

In this view of the defendant's liability there is nothing inconsistent with the theory of liability on which the case was tried. It is true that the court told the jury that "an automobile is not an inherently dangerous vehicle." The meaning, however, is made plain by the context. The meaning is that danger is not to be expected when the vehicle is well constructed. The court left it to the jury [which returned a verdict for the plaintiff] to say whether the defendant ought to have foreseen that the car, if negligently constructed, would become "imminently dangerous." Subtle distinctions are drawn by the defendant between things inherently dangerous and things imminently dangerous, but the case does not turn upon these verbal niceties. If danger was to be expected as reasonably certain, there was a duty of vigilance, and this whether you call the danger inherent or imminent. In varying forms that thought was put before the jury. We do not say that the court would not have been justified in ruling as a matter of law that the car was a dangerous thing. If there was any error, it was none of which the defendant can complain.

We think the defendant was not absolved from a duty of inspection because it bought the wheels from a reputable manufacturer. It was not merely a dealer in automobiles. It was a manufacturer of automobiles. It was responsible for the finished product. It was not at liberty to put the finished product on the market without subjecting the component parts to ordinary and simple tests .... Under the charge of the trial judge nothing more was required of it. The obligation to inspect must vary with the nature of the thing to be inspected. The more probable the danger, the greater the need of caution. There is little analogy between this case and Carlson v. Phenix Bridge Co., 132 N.Y. 273, 30 N.E. 750, where the defendant bought a tool for a servant's use. The making of tools was not the business in which the master was engaged. Reliance on the skill of the manufacturer was proper and almost inevitable. But that is not the defendant's situation. Both by its relation to the work and by the nature of its business, it is charged with a stricter duty.

The judgment should be affirmed . . . .

WILLARD BARTLETT, Ch. J. (dissenting).

The plaintiff was injured in consequence of the collapse of a wheel of an automobile manufactured by the defendant corporation which sold it to a firm of automobile dealers in Schenectady, who in turn sold the car to the plaintiff. The wheel was purchased by the Buick Motor Company, ready made, from the Imperial Wheel Company of Flint, Michigan, a reputable manufacturer of automobile wheels which had furnished the defendant with eighty thousand wheels, none of which had proved to be made of defective wood prior to the accident in the present case. The defendant relied upon the wheel manufacturer to make all necessary tests as to the strength of the material therein and made no such tests itself. The present suit is an action for negligence brought by the subvendee of the motor car against the manufacturer as the original vendor. The evidence warranted a finding by the jury that the wheel which collapsed was defective when it left the hands of the defendant. The automobile was being prudently operated at the time of the accident and was moving at a speed of only eight miles an hour. There was no allegation or proof of any actual knowledge of the defect on the part of the defendant or any suggestion that any element of fraud or deceit or misrepresentation entered into the sale.

The theory upon which the case was submitted to the jury by the learned judge who presided at the trial was that, although an automobile is not an inherently dangerous vehicle, it may become such if equipped with a weak wheel; and that if the motor car in question, when it was put upon the market was in itself inherently dangerous by reason of its being equipped with a weak wheel, the defendant was chargeable with a knowledge of the defect so far as it might be discovered by a reasonable inspection and the application of reasonable tests. This liability, it was further held, was not limited to the original vendee, but extended to a subvendee like the plaintiff, who was not a party to the original contract of sale.

I think that these rulings, which have been approved by the Appellate Division, extend the liability of the vendor of a manufactured article further than any case which has yet received the sanction of this court. It has heretofore been held in this state that the liability of the vendor of a manufactured article for negligence arising out of the existence of defects therein does not extend to strangers injured in consequence of such defects but is confined to the immediate vendee. The exceptions to this general rule which have thus far been recognized in New York are cases in which the article sold was of such a character that danger to life or limb was involved in the ordinary use thereof; in other words, where the article sold was inherently dangerous. As has already been pointed out, the learned trial judge instructed the jury that an automobile is not an inherently dangerous vehicle.

The late Chief Justice Cooley of Michigan, one of the most learned and accurate of American law writers, states the general rule thus: 'The general rule is that a contractor, manufacturer, vendor, or furnisher of an article is not liable to third parties who have no contractual relations with him for negligence in the construction, manufacture, or sale of such article.' (2 Cooley on Torts (3d ed.), 1486.)

. . . .

... The character of the exception to the general rule limiting liability for negligence to the original parties to the contract of sale, was ... clearly stated by Judge Hiscock, writing for the court in Statler v. Ray Manufacturing Co. (195 N.Y. 478, 482) where he said that 'in the case of an article of an inherently dangerous nature, a manufacturer may become liable for a negligent construction which, when added to the inherent character of the appliance, makes it imminently dangerous, and causes, or contributes to a resulting injury not necessarily incident to the use of such an article of properly constructed, but naturally following from a defective construction.' In that case the injuries were inflicted by the explosion of a battery of steam-driven coffee urns, constituting an appliance liable to become dangerous in the course of ordinary usage.

. . . .

I do not see how we can uphold the judgment in the present case without overruling what has been so often said by this court and other courts of like authority in reference to the absence of any liability for negligence on the part of the original vendor of an ordinary carriage to any one except his immediate vendee. The absence of such liability was the very point actually decided in the English case of *Winterbottom v. Wright (supra)*, and the illustration quoted from the opinion of Chief Judge Ruggles in *Thomas v. Winchester (supra)* [regarding the wagon] assumes that the law on the subject was so plain that the statement would be accepted almost as a matter of course. In the case at bar the defective wheel on an automobile moving only eight miles an hour was not any more dangerous to the occupants of the car than a similarly defective wheel would be to the occupants of a carriage drawn by a horse at the same speed; and yet unless the courts have been all wrong on this question up to the present time there would be no liability to strangers to the original sale in the case of the horse-drawn carriage.

. . . .

Hiscock, Chase and Cuddeback, JJ., concur with Cardozo, J., and Hogan, J., concurs in result; Willard Bartlett, Ch. J., reads dissenting opinion; Pound, J., not voting.

Judgment affirmed.

Further References

Coleman, B., "Lord Denning & Justice Cardozo: The Judge as Poet-Philosopher," 32 Rutgers Law Journal 485 (2001).

Collier, C.W., "Precedent and Legal Authority: A Critical History," 1988 Wisconsin Law Review 771.

Cross, R. & Harris, J.W., *Precedent in English Law* (4th ed. 1991), pp. 39–96.

Dworkin, R.M., *Taking Rights Seriously* (1977), pp. 110–23.

Friedman, L., *Creative Uncertainty: American Law in the Twentieth Century* (2002).

Goldberg, J.C.P. & Zipursky, B.C., "The Moral of MacPherson," 146 University of Pennsylvania Law Review 1733 (1998).

Kaufman, A.L., *Cardozo* (1998).

Levi, E.H., *An Introduction to Legal Reasoning* (1949), pp. 1–19.

MacCormick, N., *Legal Reasoning and Legal Theory* (2d ed. 1994).

Ohrenschall, J.C., "Diverse Views of What Constitutes the Principle of Law of a Case," 36 University of Colorado Law Review 377 (1964).

Radin, M., "Case Law and *Stare Decisis*: Concerning *Prajudizienrecht in Amerika*," 33 Columbia Law Review 199 (1933).

Williams, G.L., *Learning the Law* (11th ed. 1982), pp. 67–79.

Chapter V

LOGIC AND POLICY IN LEGAL REASONING

A. THEORETICAL PERSPECTIVES

Under the doctrine of *stare decisis*, each judicial decision forms a precedent to be followed in subsequent cases. Judicial opinions are therefore often characterized as syllogisms. The previously-established precedent is the major premise, the proposition stating the crucial facts in the case before the court is the minor premise, and the judge's decision is the conclusion. The first excerpt in this chapter demonstrates how judicial opinions can be cast into syllogistic form.

P.E. TREUSCH, "THE SYLLOGISM," IN J. HALL, READINGS IN JURISPRUDENCE

pp. 539–548 (1938) [footnotes omitted].[1]

I. THE CATEGORICAL SYLLOGISM

1. *Proposition Defined.*

Legal rules, findings of fact, and decisions may be stated in the form of propositions. A proposition is the verbal expression of a thought. Grammatically, it is a sentence in which something (the "predicate") is asserted or denied of something else (the "subject"). Where this relation is unconditionally asserted or denied the proposition is said to be in "categorical" form. The subject (S) and the predicate (P) are known as the "terms", and the relation between them is always expressed by some form of the verb "to be," called the "copula" (C). Thus the rule, An oral conveyance of real estate (S) is (C) invalid (P), is a proposition in categorical form, as is the finding of fact, This conveyance of real estate (S) is (C) oral (P). Similarly, if a decision is taken as asserting or denying that a legal consequence should be applied to a given fact situation, the legal consequence may be stated as the predicate, and the given fact situation to which such consequence is held applicable or inapplicable

1. Copyright © 1938 by Bobbs–Merrill Co. Reprinted by permission.

may be stated as the subject of a categorical proposition; *e.g.*, This conveyance of real estate (S) is (C) invalid (P).

. . . .

2. *Syllogism Defined.*

Suppose it becomes necessary to decide whether a given conveyance of real estate is valid or not. The conveyance is an oral one. Moreover, there is a rule of law in the jurisdiction to the effect that all oral conveyances of real estate are invalid. An opinion might then appear in the form of the syllogism:

Oral conveyances of real estate are invalid

This conveyance is an oral conveyance of real estate

Therefore, this conveyance is invalid.

Here the term *this conveyance* is related to the term *invalid* by reason of a known relation of each of these terms to a common third term, *oral conveyance of real estate.* The common term is called the "middle term." *This conveyance,* which appears as the subject of the conclusion is known as the "minor term," and *invalid,* which appears as [the] predicate, is the "major term."

There are three propositions in any syllogism, called, in order, "major premise," "minor premise" and "conclusion." The major premise relates the major term to the middle term, as the minor premise relates the minor term to the middle term. The conclusion, as indicated, relates the minor term as subject to the major term as predicate.

Symbolically, if S, M, and P are taken to represent the minor, middle, and major terms respectively and the letter *a* to indicate that the proposition is universal and affirmative, the above syllogism assumes the following form: MaP
SaM
SaP

Judicial opinions sometimes fall into clear syllogistic form; *e.g.*,

One has a right to the fruits of   (All M is P)
his labor (i.e., Fruits of labor
are the property of their authors)

Private correspondence is a   (All S is M)
fruit of the author's labor

Therefore, private correspon-   (All S is P)
dence is the property of the
author.

. . . .

Rarely, however, do judicial opinions spell out such syllogistic reasoning explicitly. Attention has been called to this by Mr. Justice

Holmes' eloquent phrase "the inarticulate major premise." Frequently a rule of law is such a commonplace that while a court may be conscious of each premise, the style of juristic writing bars a cumbersome elaboration. Often it is argued "a promise given for what the promisor is already bound to do is without consideration and void." All such opinions can be expressed in complete syllogistic form:

[A promise without consideration is void].

A promise given for what the promisor is already bound to do is without consideration.

[Therefore, such a promise] is void.

. . . .

The conclusion of a syllogism is formally correct if it follows necessarily from the premises regardless of their material sense and thus regardless of the factual truth of the conclusion; *e.g.*

All men are penguins.

Ghandi is a man.

Therefore, Ghandi is a penguin.

or

All men are mortal.

Charley McCarthy is a man.

Therefore, Charley McCarthy is mortal.

Although the major premise or the minor premise be false in fact, the conclusion in each case follows necessarily from the accepted premises and is formally correct.

O.W. HOLMES, THE COMMON LAW

pp. 1–2, 35–36 (1909).

... The life of the law has not been logic: it has been experience. The felt necessities of the time, the prevalent moral and political theories, intuitions of public policy, avowed or unconscious, even the prejudices which judges share with their fellow men, have had a good deal more to do than the syllogism in determining the rules by which men should be governed. The law embodies the story of a nation's development through many centuries, and it cannot be dealt with as if it contained only the axioms and corollaries of a book of mathematics. In order to know what it is, we must know what it has been, and what it tends to become. We must alternately consult history and existing theories of legislation. But the most difficult labor will be to understand the combination of the two into a new product at every stage....

. . . .

[I]n substance the growth of the law is legislative. And this in a deeper sense than that what the courts declare to have always been the law is in fact new. It is legislative in its grounds. The very considerations which judges most rarely mention, and always with an apology, are the secret root from which the law draws all the juices of life. I mean, of course, considerations of what is expedient for the community concerned. Every important principle which is developed by litigation is in fact and at bottom the result of more or less definitely understood views of public policy; most generally, to be sure, under our practices and traditions, the unconscious result of instinctive preferences and inarticulate convictions, but none the less traceable to views of public policy in the last analysis. And as the law is administered by able and experienced men, who know too much to sacrifice good sense to a syllogism, it will be found that, when ancient rules maintain themselves in the way that has been and will be shown in this book, new reasons more fitted to the time have been found for them, and that they gradually receive a new content, and at last a new form, from the grounds to which they have been transplanted.

... The truth is, that the law is always approaching, and never reaching, consistency. It is forever adopting new principles from life at one end, and it always retains old ones from history at the other, which have not yet been absorbed or sloughed off. It will become entirely consistent only when it ceases to grow.

L.G. BOONIN, "CONCERNING THE RELATION OF LOGIC TO LAW"

17 Journal of Legal Education 155–160, 165–166 (1965) [footnotes omitted].[2]

Questions concerning the relation of logic to law have been of perplexing concern to legal theorists, jurists, and others seeking to understand and make intelligible the basic structure of the law. The problems which have arisen concerning their relation have been due largely to a failure to clarify conceptually the nature of "legal logic." The purpose of this article is both to explain how some of this confusion concerning the relation of logic to law arose, and to introduce certain distinctions as a way of clarifying their relation.

I

Very broadly speaking, and with some notable exceptions, the general legal theory which prevailed from the time of Blackstone until the Twentieth Century treated the law as a coherent and complete rational system. It was thought to contain legal rules, principles, standards, and maxims, by the application of which one could deductively arrive at the appropriate decision in any given case. The rules and principles were sometimes conceived as eternal and unchanging natural laws, at other times as the historically authentic "living law" embedded in the customs of society, and again as simply the valid enactments of the sovereign. These three representative views as to the source and criteria of the validity of legal rules are, respectively, natural law doctrine, historical jurisprudence, and legal positivism. While proponents of these varying views disagreed as to the criteria of valid law, there seems to have been general agreement in the view of the law as coherent and complete, and of the judicial process as essentially a deductive application of existing rules of law.

While this conception of the law may appear more fitting for a legal system based on a code developed by legal authorities consciously seeking to systematize the law, it was also a widely held view of Anglo-American legal theorists. These theorists were in some way able to reconcile this conception of the law with the fact that in Anglo-American law legal decisions are authoritative sources of legal rules and law grows, to a large extent, out of such legal decisions.

Law was even compared with mathematics and the judge was considered a kind of geometrician, which implied that judges' decisions were as bound by rules and as logically necessary as mathematical proofs. In addition, legal decisions were justified as logically following from the application of those principles and rules. An important corollary of this view of the law was that there is as little justification for holding the judiciary responsible for judicial decisions as for holding mathematicians personally responsible for simply deriving what is implicit within a given mathematical system. The judge's function is simply to apply existing principles of law, whether such principles be conceived in terms of natural law, living law or valid legislative enactments. The judiciary does not make or create law, but rather finds it and applies it. Even cases in which a judge reverses a previous interpretation of the law are not to be characterized as changing the law. What is being done in such cases is simply to restore the "true" rule and remove its previous misinterpretation. That this "traditional theory" did permeate the conception of law until recently can be gathered from the reflections of an American lawyer:

> In days that men of my generation can remember, it was popular for lawyers to assert that judges do not make the law; they merely find it as it already exists in law books and other source material of recognized authority. This notion went unchallenged and exercised a dominant influence over the practical life of the law.... That it is a myth is now generally recognized. The breakdown of its effect on the law, not yet complete but far enough advanced to be unmistakable, represents a major change in the climate of professional legal opinion within my generation.

II

It is perhaps fair to identify the beginnings of the systematic attack on the rational deductive model of the law in the United States with the writings and legal opinions of Justice Oliver Wendell Holmes. Holmes can best be understood in the context of the general "revolt against formalism" that occurred in various disciplines at the turn of the century. The influence on Holmes of the doctrines of evolution and pragmatism is unmistakable. Holmes was even a participant in the "Metaphysical Club" of C.S. Pierce. His concern with legal history and the evolution and development of legal principles made it difficult for him to conceive the law as based on eternal and unchanging rational principles. His pragmatic concern with the operative effects and consequences of legal doctrine is clearly expressed in his famous address, "The Path of the Law."

> What constitutes the law? You will find some text writers telling you that it is something different from what is decided by the courts of Massachusetts or England, that it is a system of reason, that it is a deduction from principles of ethics or admitted axioms or what not, which may or may not coincide with the decisions. But if we take the view of our friend the bad man we shall find that he does not care two straws for the axioms or deductions, but that he does want to know what the Massachusetts or English courts are likely to do in fact. I am much of his mind. The prophecies of what the courts will do in fact, and nothing more pretentious, are what I mean by the law.

It is this concern with the actual consequences and operative effects of legal doctrine, as opposed to the mere formal normative content, that becomes the central concern of the movement called "legal realism." ...

. . . .

III

While the traditional view of the judicial process was apparently widely expressed, one can perhaps raise questions as to how literally it was meant. In a way, it seems implausible that anyone with the least familiarity with the judicial process could have conceived it in such a simple manner. While the traditional theory may appear more plausible in a period characterized by relatively stable conditions, as opposed to one in which great changes and developments are clearly evident, it is still difficult to see how one could literally believe the law to be a coherent and complete system, and the judicial process to be only a logical application of existing rules of law. Professor Cooperrider has made the plausible suggestion that the traditional theory was not intended as an accurate descriptive account of the judicial process:

> ... I am also inclined to doubt that it is sound to think of it as a conscious attempt at scientific description. It did, however, represent a view which at one time was generally held as to the *attitude* which the judge should bring to his task: that it should be his *objective* to deal with the case before him in that way which was indicated by an interpretation of existing authorities, rather than in that way which seemed to him on the facts to be the fairest or most desirable from a social point of view. It called for the subordination of his judgment to that of the collectivity of his predecessors, for a primary reliance on a reasoned extrapolation of accumulated experience.

According to this interpretation, the traditional theory represents more a practical regulative *ideal* of how the judicial process *ought* to be conceived by the judiciary than a theoretical analysis of its actual structure and functioning. If this analysis adequately explains why the traditional theory was, and perhaps to some extent still is, deeply embedded in the legal consciousness, it of course does not constitute a justification for it. Part of the message of contemporary jurisprudence is that the judge does, to some extent, unavoidably exercise a creative "legislative" choice, and that he has the responsibility to exercise it in an intelligent manner. To conceal the inevitable elements of discretion involved in the judicial process behind a theory which denies their existence cannot contribute to a responsible use of that discretion. The attack on the traditional theory has been valuable and important in making us sensitive to the variety and complexity of values involved in the judicial process. It has also led, unfortunately, to some confusion concerning the relation of logic to law.

IV

The attack on the conception of law as a coherent and complete system has often shifted into an attack on logic itself. One can find numerous instances in legal literature and legal opinions in which logic is deprecated and its value questioned. One of Justice Holmes' most famous remarks has often been employed by those objecting to logic in the law:

> The life of the law has not been logic: it has been experience. The felt necessities of the time, the prevalent moral and political theories, intuitions of public policy, avowed or unconscious, even the prejudices which judges share with their fellow men, have had a good deal more to do than the syllogism in determining the rules by which men should be governed.

While this statement is perhaps susceptible to more than one interpretation, Holmes can be construed as making two points which are essentially sound and true. First, that the changes and development of legal rules and principles cannot be fully explained and made intelligible in terms of purely logical analysis of legal concepts. Second, that such logical analysis is not a sufficient tool for rationally deciding legal controversies.

Whether Holmes intended it or not, his remark has been repeated in many contexts that import a sharp antithesis between "logic" and "experience." Holmes himself appears to adopt this interpretation elsewhere when he says:

> ... [T]he whole outline of the law is the resultant of a conflict at every point between logic and good sense—the one striving to work fiction out to consistent results, the other restraining and at last overcoming that effort when the results become too manifestly unjust.

. . . . .

Logic is concerned with the general and formal principles of valid reasoning. Legal logic is correspondingly concerned with the particular principles of legally sound and valid reasoning and decision-making. The whole body of authoritative legal material constitutes a complex network in terms of which legal inferences can be made and evaluated. It is this material sense of legal logic that underlies most of the remarks of legal theorists concerning the relation of logic to law.

When legal theorists say that the law is not logical, one of the main things they mean is that the law is not a wholly consistent and complete system. A legal system is open-textured in the sense that new rules and principles can be created and old ones changed. In addition, it is often the case that competing rules have applicability to the same set of facts. To say that the law is not wholly logical is a way of saying that judges are not merely tools for deriving legal conclusions. Judges exercise a creative function in various ways. The basic problem is one of setting up rational standards to guide judges in exercising their creative functions. This is a fundamental problem for normative jurisprudence.

NOTE BY THE EDITORS: TYPES OF LEGAL REASONING

Deductive Reasoning. Treusch describes a type of reasoning generally referred to as "deductive reasoning." This category of reasoning is appropriate when a rule of law clearly covers the facts of a litigated case and is therefore applied by the judge through the use of syllogistic logic. You have seen an illustration of deductive reasoning in the *Harris* case, *supra* Chapter III, involving a claim brought under the Vermont statute which allows spouses to recover for loss of consortium and filed by a woman who was married to the tort victim at the time that she filed her complaint, but not at the time of the tort.

Inductive Reasoning. In some cases, no ready-made rule is available to guide the judge, but the judge may be able to distill a pertinent rule or principle from a string of earlier decisions. The earlier cases may have been decided on extremely narrow grounds, yet the judge may find implicit in them a general principle fit to serve as a rule of decision in the case at bar. In that event, the judge is said to derive a general rule from particular instances by the method of inductive reasoning. Thus, a sequence of cases might show that the courts, without spelling out a comprehensive general principle, had granted injunctions or damages to homeowners who had been seriously inconvenienced by noisy blasting operations, or noxious smells, or the barking of dogs in a nearby kennel. From these decisions, a judge could derive a rule to the effect that a homeowner is entitled to protection against nuisances interfering with the enjoyment of his property rights. You have seen an illustration of inductive reasoning in the line of products liability cases that you read in Chapter IV involving plaintiffs who were not in privity with the manufacturer of the product.

Reasoning by Analogy. This form of reasoning involves the extension of a legal rule to a fact situation not covered by its express words, but deemed to be within the purview of a policy principle underlying the rule. If there is a rule, for example, that the executor of a will is precluded from bringing an action outside of the state of his appointment, this rule might be extended by analogy to an administrator of an estate. This extension would be predicated on the rationale, held to be implicit in the rule in question, that the authority of court-appointed functionaries to act in a representative capacity should be confined to the jurisdictional limits of the state in which they are performing official acts. Reasoning by analogy is widely used in relation to judicial precedent, and will be illustrated by the first two cases in this Chapter.

Dialectical Reasoning. This type of reasoning is used by judges and lawyers in the following groups of cases: (1) novel problems in which no suitable rule or principle is provided by the law (*see, e.g., Guy v. Livesey, supra* Chapter II); (2) instances in which a rule or precedent covering the case at hand exists, but where the court rejects its application as unsound, either generally or at least in the context of the litigated facts (*see, e.g., Whitney v. Fisher, supra* Chapter III); and (3) situations where two or more competing rules or major premises are available for the determination of an issue, among which a genuine choice must be made (*see, e.g.,* the *Hynes* cases, *infra* Chapter IV). In these three types of cases, it is impossible for the court to dispose of the controversy by means of an analytic form of argumentation, that is, by deduction, induction, or analogy.

In these situations, judges or lawyers will rely on arguments that they deem to be plausible, reasonable, and convincing. A careful evaluation of points speaking for and against the contemplated solution is frequently an important part of the process. In other words, a balance sheet of opposing considerations is drawn up, and a comparison of their relative weight and utility in the light of the problem to be solved is undertaken. The result finally reached will usually gain in persuasiveness if it rests not only on a single ground, but is strengthened by the cumulative force of a number of reasons.

In some cases, the courts use complex or mixed modes of reasoning. For example, when the words of a statute are ambiguous, a simple deductive application of the statute is not possible. If the legislative history of the statute throws a clear light on the meaning of an ambiguous term, a two-step form of recovery becomes necessary, i.e., an induction from the legislative history clarifying the ambiguous term combined with a deduction from the text of the clarified statute. If the legislative history is also unclear or ambiguous, dialectical reasoning becomes necessary in order to determine which of two or more interpretations is the most persuasive one.

Problems

(1) A loans a valuable painting to B for an indefinite period of time. B sells the painting to C. A causes B to be indicted for larceny. B is sentenced to a term in prison. The conviction is based on a state statute reading as follows: "Whoever unlawfully appropriates a chattel belonging to another is guilty of larceny and shall be punished by imprisonment not exceeding five years or by a fine."

Some time thereafter E took a car belonging to D for the purpose of stealing a ride to a neighboring town. Upon arrival he abandoned the car. It was restored to D a week later. D, having been seriously inconvenienced by the temporary loss of the car, caused E to be indicted for larceny. E was acquitted. The court took the position that the drafters of the larceny statute had in mind a permanent acquisition of a chattel by the thief. A merely temporary use of a car belonging to another, even though unlawful, was not in the court's view within the meaning of the term "appropriate."

What type of legal reasoning was used by the court in this case?

(2) In Muskopf v. Corning Hospital District, 55 Cal.2d 211, 11 Cal.Rptr. 89, 359 P.2d 457 (1961), the Supreme Court of California overruled earlier decisions recognizing the doctrine of sovereign immunity, a doctrine that denied the responsibility of the state for tortious acts committed by its agents. The court pointed out that the principle of sovereign immunity originated in England as a personal prerogative of the Stuart kings, was thoughtlessly received into American law, became riddled with exceptions in the course of time, and caused many serious and unnecessary injustices. The court referred to the argument made on behalf of the state that the rule has existed for such a long time that only the legislature can abolish it. The court countered this argument by stating that not only the courts, but also the legislature, had imposed many restrictions on the doctrine, implying by this statement that ever-increasing dissatisfaction with the doctrine had marked its history in this century. For these reasons the court concluded that the doctrine should be abandoned because it was obsolete and thoroughly unfair.

What type of legal reasoning was used by the court in this case?

B. LOGIC AND POLICY IN JUDICIAL OPINIONS

BORER v. AMERICAN AIRLINES, INC.

Supreme Court of California, 1977.
19 Cal.3d 441, 138 Cal.Rptr. 302, 563 P.2d 858.

TOBRINER, ACTING CHIEF JUSTICE.

In Rodriguez v. Bethlehem Steel Corp. (1974) 12 Cal.3d 382, 115 Cal.Rptr. 765, 525 P.2d 669, we held that a married person whose spouse had been injured by the negligence of a third party may maintain a cause of action for loss of "consortium." We defined loss of "consortium" as the "loss of conjugal fellowship and sexual relations" (12 Cal.3d at p. 385, 115 Cal.Rptr. at p. 766, 525 P.2d at p. 670), but ruled that the term included the loss of love, companionship, society, sexual relations, and household services. Our decision carefully avoided resolution of the question whether anyone other than the spouse of a negligently injured person, such as a child or a parent, could maintain a cause of action analogous to that upheld in *Rodriguez*. We face that issue today: the present case presents a claim by nine children for the loss of the services, companionship, affection and guidance of their mother; the companion case of Baxter v. Superior Court, 19 Cal.3d 441, 138 Cal.Rptr. 315, 563

P.2d 871 presents the claim of a mother and father for the loss of the companionship and affection of their 16–year–old son.

. . . .

Since this appeal arises following a trial court order sustaining a demurrer to plaintiffs' complaint without leave to amend, we focus first on the specific allegations of plaintiffs' complaint. Plaintiffs, the nine children of Patricia Borer, allege that on March 21, 1972, the cover on a lighting fixture at the American Airlines Terminal at Kennedy Airport fell and struck Patricia. Plaintiffs further assert that as a result of the physical injuries sustained by Patricia, each of them has been "deprived of the services, society, companionship, affection, tutelage, direction, guidance, instruction and aid in personality development, all with its accompanying psychological, educational and emotional detriment, by reason of Patricia Borer being unable to carry on her usual duties of a mother." The complaint sets forth causes of action based upon negligence, breach of warranty, and manufacture of a defective product; it names as defendants American Airlines, two companies which manufactured and assembled the lighting fixture, and various fictitious defendants. Each plaintiff seeks damages of $100,000.

. . . .

Rodriguez ... does not compel the conclusion that foreseeable injury to a legally recognized relationship necessarily postulates a cause of action; instead it clearly warns that social policy must at some point intervene to delimit liability. Patricia Borer, for example, foreseeably has not only a husband (who has a cause of action under *Rodriguez*) and the children who sue here, but also parents whose right of action depends upon our decision in the companion case of *Baxter v. Superior Court*; foreseeably, likewise, she has brothers, sisters, cousins, inlaws, friends, colleagues, and other acquaintances who will be deprived of her companionship. No one suggests that all such persons possess a right of action for loss of Patricia's consortium; all agree that somewhere a line must be drawn. As stated by Judge Breitel in Tobin v. Grossman (1969) 24 N.Y.2d 609, 619, 301 N.Y.S.2d 554, 561, 249 N.E.2d 419, 424: "Every injury has ramifying consequences, like the ripplings of the waters, without end. The problem for the law is to limit the legal consequences of wrongs to a controllable degree."

The decision whether to limit liability for loss of consortium by denying a cause of action in the parent-child context, or to permit that action but deny any claim based upon more remote relationships, is thus a question of policy....

In the first instance, strong policy reasons argue against extension of liability to loss of consortium of the parent-child relationship. Loss of consortium is an intangible, nonpecuniary loss; monetary compensation will not enable plaintiffs to regain the companionship and guidance of a mother; it will simply establish a fund so that upon reaching adulthood, when plaintiffs will be less in need of maternal guidance, they will be unusually wealthy men and women. To say that plaintiffs have been "compensated" for their loss is superficial; in reality they have suffered a loss for which they can never be compensated; they have obtained, instead, a future benefit essentially unrelated to that loss.

. . . .

A second reason for rejecting a cause of action for loss of parental consortium is that, because of its intangible character, damages for such a loss are very difficult to measure. Plaintiffs here have prayed for $100,000 each, yet by what standard could we determine that an award of $10,000 was inadequate, or one of $500,000 excessive?

. . . .

Plaintiffs point out that similar policy arguments could be, and to some extent were, raised in *Rodriguez,* and that our decision to uphold the wife's action for loss of consortium rejected those arguments. We do not, however, read *Rodriguez* as holding that arguments based upon the intangible character of damages and the difficulty of measuring such damages do not merit consideration. Such a holding would imply an indefinite extension of liability for loss of consortium to all foreseeable relationships, a proposition *Rodriguez* plainly repudiates.

Rodriguez, then, holds no more than that in the context of a spousal relationship, the policy arguments against liability do not suffice to justify a holding denying a cause of action. Plaintiffs contend, however, that no adequate ground exists to distinguish a cause of action for loss of spousal consortium from one for loss of parental consortium. We reject the contention for three reasons.

First, as *Rodriguez* pointed out, the spousal action for loss of consortium rests in large part on the "impairment or destruction of the sexual life of the couple." (12 Cal.3d 382, 405, 115 Cal.Rptr. 765, 780, 525 P.2d 669, 684.) No similar element of damage appears in a child's suit for loss of consortium.

Second, actions by children for loss of parental consortium create problems of multiplication of actions and damages not present in the spousal context. . . .

The instant case illustrates the point. Patricia Borer has nine children, each of whom would possess his own independent right of action for loss of consortium. Even in the context of a consolidated action, the assertion of nine independent causes of action for the children in addition to the father's claim for loss of consortium and the mother's suit for ordinary tort damages, demonstrates the extent to which recognition of plaintiffs' asserted cause of action will multiply the tort liability of the defendant.

Finally, the proposition that a spouse has a cause of action for loss of consortium, but that a child does not, finds overwhelming approval in the decisions of other jurisdictions. Over 30 states, a clear majority of those who have decided the question, now permit a *spousal* suit for loss of consortium. *No* state permits a child to sue for loss of parental consortium. That claim has been presented, at latest count, to 18 jurisdictions, and rejected by all of them.

. . . .

In summary, we do not doubt the reality or the magnitude of the injury suffered by plaintiffs. We are keenly aware of the need of children for the love, affection, society and guidance of their parents; any injury which diminishes the ability of a parent to meet these needs is plainly a family tragedy, harming all members of that community. We conclude, however that taking into account all considerations which bear on this question, including the inadequacy of monetary compensation to alleviate that tragedy, the difficulty of measuring damages, and the danger of imposing extended and disproportionate liability, we should not recognize a nonstatutory cause of action for the loss of parental consortium.

The judgment is affirmed.

[JUSTICE MOSK dissented.]

HAY v. MEDICAL CENTER HOSPITAL OF VERMONT

Supreme Court of Vermont, 1985.
145 Vt. 533, 496 A.2d 939.

Before HILL, UNDERWOOD, PECK and GIBSON, JJ., and LARROW, J. (Ret.), Specially Assigned.

UNDERWOOD, JUSTICE.

This case presents this Court with a question we have not heretofore had an opportunity to consider: does a minor child have a cause of action for the loss of consortium of a parent who is alive, but who is alleged to be permanently comatose? . . .

. . . .

[Mary's husband, Walter, filed a complaint for loss of consortium and her two children filed a complaint for loss of society and companionship.]

We note that the claims . . ., though independent causes of action, are each derivative of the underlying claim of Mary Hay, and therefore the viability of each of these damage claims is wholly dependent upon Mary Hay's cause of action against these same defendants.

The trial court [ruled that] . . . "a minor has no recognizable cause of action for damages for loss of physical training, moral training, intellectual training, affection, society, love, protection, and companionship from a living parent who was allegedly rendered totally disabled through the negligence of the defendants."[3] . . . def

---

3. It is assumed by the trial court in its legal conclusions, and by the litigants in their pleadings, briefs and oral arguments, that Mary Hay has not deceased and is therefore not legally dead even though she remains in a permanently comatose condition. See 18 V.S.A. § 5218 (Supp.1984). [Footnote by the court.]

I

We must first decide whether we will judicially recognize a minor child's cause of action for a claimed loss of parental consortium when the parent has been tortiously injured but has not deceased. It is clear that recovery of a loss of consortium is an action recognized at common law. Whitney v. Fisher, 138 Vt. 468, 470, 417 A.2d 934, 935 (1980) . . . .

As an element of common law, the doctrine permitting recovery for loss of spousal consortium was initially created and developed by courts of law. Berger v. Weber, 411 Mich. 1, 17, 303 N.W.2d 424, 427 (1981); Theama v. City of Kenosha, 117 Wis.2d 508, 521, 344 N.W.2d 513, 519 (1984). In the context of the present contested cause of action, we agree with the Wisconsin Supreme Court when it stated:

> [T]he rule denying recovery for the loss of society and companionship was created by the courts and not the legislature, and it is, therefore, as much our duty as the legislature's to change that law if it no longer meets society's needs.

Theama, supra, 117 Wis.2d at 519, 344 N.W.2d at 518; *accord* Ferriter v. Daniel O'Connell's Sons, Inc., 381 Mass. 507, 516, 413 N.E.2d 690, 695–96 (1980); Ueland v. Reynolds Metals Co., 103 Wash.2d 131, 135, 691 P.2d 190, 193 (1984). Thus, it is clear that this Court has the authority to make changes in the common law, should we deem it appropriate to do so.

II

In considering the merits of recognizing a child's claim for loss of parental consortium, we first look to analogous areas of existing Vermont law. Under the provisions of Vermont's wrongful death statutes, 14 V.S.A. §§ 1491–1492, a minor child may recover "such damages as are just, with reference to the pecuniary injuries resulting from [the death of a parent]. . . ." 14 V.S.A. § 1492(b) (Supp.1984). In a case involving minor children whose father had been killed, this Court held that the loss of the children's mental, moral and physical training by their dead father was properly included in the term "pecuniary loss." Hoadley v. International Paper Co., 72 Vt. 79, 83–84, 47 A. 169, 171 (1899). Although such a definition of "pecuniary loss" may be more limited than the recovery of "parental consortium" sought by David Hay in the present case, it is inappropriate that a minor child may recover such a loss if a parent is killed, but not if the parent is rendered permanently comatose. *Accord Berger, supra,* 411 Mich. at 15, 303 N.W.2d at 426; *Ueland, supra,* 103 Wash.2d at 133, 691 P.2d at 192 . . . .

David Hay also argues that because either spouse may recover for loss of consortium in the event of the [injury] of the other spouse, a minor child should be able to recover for loss of parental consortium upon the [injury] of either parent. We recognize that there is indeed a difference between spousal and parental consortium:

Sexual relations [however] are but one element of the spouse's consortium action. The other elements—love, companionship, affection, society, comfort, services and solace—are similar in both relationships and in each are deserving of protection.

Berger, supra, 411 Mich. at 14, 303 N.W.2d at 426. Not only are the losses suffered by a parent and a child similar in many respects, but the child is in a uniquely difficult position to make up for the loss of a parent.

[W]hile an adult is capable of seeking out new relationships in an attempt to fill in the void of his or her loss, a child may be virtually helpless in seeking out a new adult companion. Therefore, compensation through the courts may be the child's only method of reducing his or her deprivation of the parent's society and companionship.

Theama, supra, 117 Wis.2d at 516, 344 N.W.2d at 516.

Defendants point out that this Court appears to have rejected the concept of parental consortium. *Whitney v. Fisher, supra,* 138 Vt. at 470–71, 417 A.2d at 936; *Baldwin v. State, supra,* 125 Vt. at 320–21, 215 A.2d at 494. It must be pointed out that the asserted denial of parental consortium in *Whitney* was contained only in a quoted passage from a dissent by Chief Justice Schaefer in *Dini v. Naiditch,* 20 Ill.2d 406, 433, 170 N.E.2d 881, 894 (1960). Chief Justice Shaefer's dissent was cited in *Whitney, supra,* and *Baldwin, supra,* only insofar as it provided support (in the absence of a statute) for denying a wife recovery for loss of consortium upon the [injury] of her husband. This Court has never denied a child recovery for loss of parental consortium, and to the extent that *Whitney, supra,* implies otherwise, it is in error. We find that prior Vermont law presents no obstacle to our recognition of a cause of action for loss of parental consortium on behalf of the instant minor child.

III

A.

The defendants have raised a series of objections to the recognition of the right of a minor child to recover for the loss of parental consortium. The first of these objections concerns whether there is a duty on the part of the defendants to the minor child of the plaintiff. The defendants contend that recovery for loss of parental consortium is precluded by the fact that the injury to the minor child is too remote, and therefore unforeseeable.... As stated earlier, consortium claims may be initiated independently by either spouse but are derivative actions and are therefore distinguishable from the underlying negligence claims in the principal action. *See* ... Love, Tortious Interference with the Parent–Child Relationship: Loss of an Injured Person's Society and Companionship, 51 Ind.L.J. 590, 628–33 (1976)....

... The question of remoteness concerns only the relationship between the tortfeasor and the "primary tort victim." *Berger, supra,* 411 Mich. at 15–16, 303 N.W.2d at 426–27; *Theama, supra,* 117 Wis.2d at

527, 344 N.W.2d at 522. We also note that we see little difference in terms of remoteness between the situation of a spouse seeking to recover for loss of consortium, and that of a minor child similarly seeking recovery for loss of consortium.

B.

Defendants also raise several potential procedural problems. The first of these problems is the possibility of increased litigation as a result of such recognition. It is axiomatic that whenever a new cause of action is recognized, there is the potential for increased litigation. Making the courts available for the consideration of such claims is the natural object of such recognition. In an era of ever-increasing caseloads in both the trial and appellate courts of this state, and where our society is being increasingly criticized for its propensity for litigation, the recognition of a new cause of action is not a step which we take lightly. However, it is the rights of the new class of plaintiffs, and the desire to see justice made available within our legal system, which are of paramount importance. . . .

Defendants also object on the ground that recognition of the contested cause of action will result in multiple lawsuits arising from the same incident, because the various minor children and other recognized plaintiffs could bring independent lawsuits. We agree that this could present a problem, and we therefore hold that a minor child's claim for the loss of parental consortium must be joined with the injured parent's claim whenever feasible. . . .

. . . .

C.

Defendants have raised a number of objections based upon problems concerning damages. We agree that damages for the loss of parental consortium are speculative and uncertain, but this does not provide sufficient grounds for refusal to recognize such a cause of action. . . .

Defendants also claim that monetary damages are an insufficient compensation for a minor child's loss of a parent. We agree that no amount of money can ever take the place of a lost parent. We reject, however, the sentiment, expressed by the California Supreme Court, that recovery for loss of parental consortium "will simply establish a fund so that upon reaching adulthood, when plaintiffs will be less in need of maternal guidance, they will be unusually wealthy men and women." Borer v. American Airlines, Inc., 19 Cal.3d 441, 447, 563 P.2d 858, 862, 138 Cal.Rptr. 302, 306 (1977). Although monetary damages may be an inadequate compensation for the loss of a parent, we are satisfied that monetary damages can help to ease the loss, and should therefore be made available. "Although a monetary award may be a poor substitute for the loss of a parent's society and companionship, it is the only workable way that our legal system has found to ease the injured party's tragic loss." *Theama, supra,* 117 Wis.2d at 523, 344 N.W.2d at 520 . . . .

Finally, defendants contend that the allowance of a claim for loss of parental consortium will result in a double recovery of damages. The recognition of a separate cause of action on behalf of a minor child, however, will allow juries to properly allocate losses among the separate claims of multiple plaintiffs. We are confident in the ability of the trial court judges to give adequate jury instructions concerning the computation and allocation of damages, and of juries to follow such instructions. . . . The trial courts can protect the record for review by submitting written interrogatories or special verdicts to the jury. In cases where a jury fails to follow a trial court's instructions and returns a verdict with inappropriate damages, the defendants have an opportunity to request the correction of any such error. . . . We also note that the provision for separate recovery for the minor child "guarantees that the award will be utilized for the child's benefit and not by the parent for other purposes." *Theama, supra*, 117 Wis.2d at 524, 344 N.W.2d at 520–21. . . .

D.

Defendants suggest that this Court should defer to the legislature and refrain from recognizing the cause of action at issue in the present case. For the reasons set forth below, we do not feel obliged to await legislative recognition of a cause of action which we find to be appropriate, merely because it is novel. . . .

It is the role of this Court to adapt the common law to the changing needs and conditions of the people of this state:

> That court best serves the law which recognizes that the rules of law which grew up in a remote generation may, in the fullness of experience, be found to serve another generation badly, and which discards the old rule when it finds that another rule of law represents what should be according to the established and settled judgment of society, and no considerable property rights have become vested in reliance upon the old rule. It is thus great writers upon the common law have discovered the source and method of its growth, and in its growth found its health and life. It is not and it should not be stationary. Change of this character should not be left to the legislature.

B. Cardozo, The Nature of the Judicial Process 151–52 (1921) (quoting Dwy v. Connecticut Co., 89 Conn. 74, 99, 92 A. 883, 891 (1915) (Wheeler, J., concurring)). . . .

The argument that this Court should prohibit the present claim for parental consortium from going to a jury because the issue is more appropriate for legislative resolution is wholly unpersuasive; such an argument ignores our responsibility to face a difficult legal question and accept judicial responsibility for a needed change in the common law. This Court has often met changing times and new social demands by expanding outmoded common law concepts. *See, e.g.*, R. & E. Builders, Inc. v. Chandler, 144 Vt. 302, 476 A.2d 540 (1984) (rejected common law

rule that wife's legal existence merged with that of husband) ...;
Zaleskie v. Joyce, 133 Vt. 150, 333 A.2d 110 (1975) (expanded common
law to include strict products liability) ...; O'Brien v. Comstock Foods,
Inc., 125 Vt. 158, 212 A.2d 69 (1965) (rejecting privity as a defense for
injuries to consumer) ....

The foregoing serves to illustrate that this Court has frequently met
new and difficult problems head-on, using common law principles. Many
of these cases have produced change which would have a profound effect
on social and business relationships.... When confronted with these
difficult and complex issues, this Court did not shirk its duty and retreat
into the safe haven of deference to the legislature. It is the responsibility
of the courts to balance competing interests and to allocate losses arising
out of human activities. One of the principal purposes of the law of torts
is to compensate people for injuries they sustain as a result of the
negligent conduct of others....

When the conditions and needs of a society have changed, judges
must adapt the common law to those new conditions. The main characteristic of the common law is its dynamism,

> which allows it to grow and to tailor itself to meet changing needs
> within the doctrine of *stare decisis*, which, if correctly understood,
> was not static and did not forever prevent the courts from reversing
> themselves or from applying principles of common law to new
> situations as the need arose.

Bielski v. Schulze, 16 Wis.2d 1, 11, 114 N.W.2d 105, 110 (1962) (footnote
omitted).

We also realize that in instances where the legislature has acted to
change the common law of this state, the question of whether the new
cause of action it created fully covers the situation it intended to address
is not always certain. For example, in 1977, the legislature expressly
authorized a wife to bring an action for the loss of the consortium of her
husband. 12 V.S.A. § 5431 (added 1977, No. 43). It did not, however,
determine whether a wife could exercise the right to bring such a suit for
a cause of action arising prior to the effective date of the statute. This
Court, in *Whitney v. Fisher, supra,* had to grapple with the question of
whether the Vermont courts should recognize a cause of action for a
wife's loss of spousal consortium where her cause of action arose prior to
the enactment of 12 V.S.A. § 5431.

It must also be noted that our recognition of a new cause of action
for the loss of parental consortium, as in the present case, in no way
precludes the legislature from also addressing the subject; it is still free
to act. The legislature may ratify, limit or reject our holding....

E.

. . . .

For the reasons cited herein, we recognize that a minor child has the
right to sue for damages for the loss of parental consortium when the

parent has been rendered permanently comatose. While we recognize that the weight of legal precedent favors nonrecognition of such a cause of action, we choose to follow what appears to be a growing trend in this area of the law. Whether we are the first state—or the fiftieth state—to adopt a specific legal proposition, our decision inevitably will be based upon what we deem to be in the best interests of justice and of the citizens of the State of Vermont at the time the question is presented to us. . . .

Reversed and remanded for further proceedings consistent with the views expressed herein.

LARROW, JUSTICE (Ret.), Specially Assigned, dissenting. . . . I am authorized to say that JUSTICE PECK joins with me in this dissenting opinion.

[Justices Larrow and Peck dissented primarily on the ground that Mary Hay was in fact "legally dead" under 81 V.S.A. § 5218, and therefore it was the wrongful death statute that ought to control the case.]

Questions

If an adult child in Vermont were to sue for loss of society and companionship, what arguments would each party advance before the Vermont Supreme Court? *See generally* Annot., "Adult Child's Right of Action for Loss of Parental Consortium," 2002 American Law Reports 5th 1.

If parents in Vermont were to sue for loss of their injured child's society and companionship, what arguments would each party advance before the Vermont Supreme Court? *See generally* Annot., "Parent's Right to Recover for Loss of Consortium in Connection with Injury to Child," 54 American Law Reports 4th 112 (1987).

NOTE BY THE EDITORS: DUTY OF CARE OWED BY LANDOWNERS

When reading the next two cases, you should know that, at common law, the duty of a landowner to a stranger regarding risks created by a dangerous condition on his or her property varied, depending upon whether the stranger was located on or off the premises. A landowner was required to exercise reasonable care to see that strangers using an adjacent public highway or waterway passed by safely. By contrast, he or she owed no duty of care whatsoever to trespassers who came upon the property without an invitation. *See generally* D.B. Dobbs, The Law of Torts §§ 231–32 (2000).

HYNES v. NEW YORK CENTRAL R.R. CO.

Supreme Court of New York, Appellate Division, 1919.
188 App.Div. 178, 176 N.Y.S. 795.

[The decedent was a 16–year-old boy who had swum across the Spuyten Devil Creek, or the United States Ship Canal, from the Manhattan bank to the Bronx County bank. He had climbed upon the defendant's wooden-faced bulkhead, and then had walked out on a spring board projecting over the water. It was a 2" x 12" plank that was spiked down on the bulkhead, from which it ran back about 4 feet, so that the shore end was on land. About 11 feet of the plank hung over the water. As the decedent was about to dive off the end of the plank, electric wires fell from the pole maintained by the defendant along its railroad track. One of the wires struck the decedent; others, falling on the plank, broke it off at the bulkhead; the deceased was thrown into the water and died. The plank had been there for about three years, but it was not clear who had placed it there. Employees of the defendant and others had used it. Warnings that the defendant's property was not a thoroughfare had been posted near the water front. The jury had returned a verdict for the decedent's estate, but the trial court judge had set aside the verdict and ordered a new trial because the deceased was a trespasser.]

PUTNAM, J.: The complaint alleged defendant's neglect in improperly erecting, constructing and maintaining its poles and appurtenances and the wires attached thereto, and in failing to secure said wires and repair the poles, appurtenances and wires, with the result that the same fell.

The learned court rightly held that the deceased was a trespasser. The plank was part of defendant's property, and was so annexed as to become part of the realty. Decedent's entry upon defendant's close from the waters of the ship canal was an unlawful intrusion. On this plank, he was still a trespasser—even when he stepped outward across defendant's technical boundary line and stood near the outer end, over the waters of the ship canal.

Appellant's point that defendant did not own the extremity of this plank, because it projected over the waterway, is against ancient doctrines, that such an object, supported from the place of annexation, carries the title to the whole thing so annexed, even if it protrudes over and across a vertical boundary line. This applies to tree branches which overhang a neighbor's land. (Masters v. Pollie, (1619) 2 Roll's Rep. 141.)[4] In Hoffman v. Armstrong (48 N.Y. 201) such an instance of an overhanging branch led the court to declare that "if an adjoining owner should build his house so as to overhang it, such an encroachment would not give the owner of the land the legal title to the part so overhanging." (p. 203). In support of which is cited Aiken v. Benedict (39 Barb. 400), which held that ejectment would not lie in such a case. While the owner of land so overhung may cut off the branches above his land (Lemon v. Webb, L.R. (1895) A.C. 1), he cannot, in removing the nuisance, appropriate the materials, and convert to his use the severed branches, or fruit thereon. . . .

4. In Masters v. Pollie, 2 Rolle 141 (1619), the plaintiff brought an action of trespass, alleging that the defendant had carried away his timber. The defendant replied that the timber came from a tree that was partly on his land. The Court found that the main part of the tree was on the plaintiff's land, and that some roots only extended into the defendant's land. On the basis of these facts the Court found that the tree belonged to the plaintiff, and that defendant was not entitled to any part of the timber which the plaintiff had cut into boards.

The plank cannot be held an unlawful interference with navigation, in view of the apparent shallowness of the water and the circumstances that neither the Federal nor the State authorities had taken any steps for its removal. . . .

The owner of a wharf, pier or like projection, even if run out beyond the proper exterior line, has a good right against all private intruders or trespassers. (Wetmore v. Atlantic White Lead Co., 37 Barb. 70; Wetmore v. Brooklyn Gaslight Co., 42 N.Y. 384.)[5] As Grover, J. said in the case last cited, the State may have a remedy, but this "gives the plaintiff no right of entry upon such land for any purpose" (p. 393). . . .

In another view, an argument that the extremity of such plank was not defendant's property cannot aid the plaintiff, since, for all that here appears, the entire plank was in defendant's possession; and such possession, even without legal title, is good against an intruder committing a trespass. . . . Beardslee v. New Berlin, L. & P., 207 N.Y. 34, 41.

This complaint was for breach of duty whereby the poles and wires broke and "fell to the ground." The suggestion that plaintiff might recover in analogy to a like accident to a boy swimming in the canal, I think cannot apply. The duty toward persons passing in the fairway, whether in vessels or swimming, is widely different from the duty to one intruding against warning signs, and wrongfully occupying defendant's property. Therefore, the fall of defendant's wires, not being a willful or wanton injury, violated no duty which defendant owed to the deceased.

The order setting aside the verdict for plaintiff and granting a new trial should be affirmed, with costs.

JENKS, P.J., KELLY, J., concurred; JAYCOX J. read for reversal, with whom BLACKMAR, J. concurred.

JAYCOX, J., dissenting:

The plaintiff's intestate was not a trespasser in the sense which brings him within the operation of the rule that the owner of the premises owes no duty to trespassers. Ordinarily it clearly appears that the accident would not have happened but for the trespass. In this case, however, the falling wires would have been as fatal to this boy swimming in the river at that point as standing upon a plank attached to the defendant's premises. If a wagon of the defendant had been left standing in the highway, and the plaintiff's intestate had climbed into that wagon, and while there had been killed by the defendant's wires falling into the highway, there would have been no question as to the plaintiff's right to recover. The situation is exactly analogous to the situation involved in this action. The boy's death was not caused by a defect in the premises

---

5. In Wetmore v. Atlantic White Lead Co., 37 Barb. (N.Y.) 70 (1862), the defendant owned a wharf extending into the public river. The construction and maintenance of the wharf had been authorized by a legislative act of the State of New York. The plaintiff attempted to unload one of his ships at the wharf and was prevented from doing so by the defendant. He sued for damages. The Court held that the wharf was the exclusive property of the defendant, although it extended into the public stream, and that the plaintiff had no easement for its use.

upon which he trespassed, but by the negligence of the defendant, which permitted its wires to fall into the navigable waters of the river. If the boy's death had been caused by the breaking of the plank upon which he was standing, the reasoning of the prevailing opinion herein would apply.

I dissent.

HYNES v. NEW YORK CENTRAL R.R. CO.

Court of Appeals of New York, 1921.
231 N.Y. 229, 131 N.E. 898.

CARDOZO, J. On July 8, 1916, Harvey Hynes, a lad of sixteen, swam with two companions from the Manhattan to the Bronx side of the Harlem River or United States Ship Canal, a navigable stream. Along the Bronx side of the river was the right of way of the defendant, the New York Central railroad, which operated its trains at that point by high tension wires, strung on poles and cross-arms. Projecting from the defendant's bulkhead above the waters of the river was a plank or springboard from which boys of the neighborhood used to dive. One end of the board had been placed under a rock on the defendant's land, and nails had been driven at its point of contact with the bulkhead. Measured from this point of contact the length behind was five feet; the length in front eleven. The bulkhead itself was about three and a half feet back of the pier line as located by the government. From this it follows that for seven and a half feet the springboard was beyond the line of the defendant's property, and above the public waterway. Its height measured from the stream was three feet at the bulkhead, and five feet at its outermost extremity. For more than five years swimmers had used it as a diving board without protest or obstruction.

On this day Hynes and his companions climbed on top of the bulkhead intending to leap into the water. One of them made the plunge in safety. Hynes followed to the front of the springboard, and stood poised for his dive. At that moment a cross-arm with electric wires fell from the defendant's pole. The wires struck the diver, flung him from the shattered board, and plunged him to his death below. His mother, suing as administratrix, brings this action for her damages. Thus far the courts have held that Hynes at the end of the springboard above the public waters was a trespasser on the defendant's land. They have thought it immaterial that the board itself was a trespass, an encroachment on the public ways. They have thought it of no significance that Hynes would have met the same fate if he had been below the board and not above it. The board, they have said, was annexed to the defendant's bulkhead. By force of such annexation, it was to be reckoned as a fixture, and thus constructively, if not actually, an extension of the land. The defendant was under a duty to use reasonable care that bathers swimming or standing in the water should not be electrocuted by wires falling from its right of way. But to bathers diving from the springboard, there was no duty, we are told, unless the injury was the product of mere willfulness or wantonness .... Without wrong to them, cross arms might be left to rot; wires highly charged with electricity might sweep them from their stand, and bury them in the subjacent waters. In climbing on the board, they became trespassers and outlaws. The conclusion is defended with much subtlety of reasoning, with much insistence upon its inevitableness as a merely logical deduction. A majority of the court are unable to accept it as the conclusion of the law.

We assume, without deciding, that the springboard was a fixture, a permanent improvement of the defendant's right of way. Much might be said in favor of another view. We do not press the inquiry, for we are persuaded that the rights of bathers do not depend upon these nice distinctions. Liability would not be doubtful, we are told, had the boy been diving from a pole, if the pole had been vertical. The diver in such a situation would have been separated from the defendant's freehold. Liability, it is said, has been escaped because the pole was horizontal. The plank when projected lengthwise was an extension of the soil. We are to concentrate our gaze on the private ownership of the board. We are to ignore the public ownership of the circumambient spaces of water and of air. Jumping from a boat or a barrel, the boy would have been a bather in the river. Jumping from the end of a springboard, he was no longer, it is said, a bather, but a trespasser on a right of way.

Rights and duties in systems of living law are not built upon such quicksands.

Bathers in the Harlem river on the day of this disaster were in the enjoyment of a public highway, entitled to reasonable protection against destruction by the defendant's wires. They did not cease to be bathers entitled to the same protection while they were diving from encroaching objects or engaging in the sports that are common among swimmers. Such acts were not equivalent to an abandonment of the highway, departure from its proper uses, a withdrawal from the waters, and an entry upon land. A plank of private right has been interposed between the river and the air, but the public ownership was unchanged in the space below it and above. The defendant does not deny that it would have owed a duty to this boy if he had been leaning against the springboard with his feet upon the ground. He is said to have forfeited protection as he put his feet upon the plank. Presumably the same result would follow if the plank had been a few inches above the surface of the water instead of a few feet. Duties are thus supposed to arise and to be extinguished in alternate zones or strata. Two boys walking in the country or swimming in a river stop to rest for a moment along the side of the road or the margin of the stream. One of them throws himself beneath the overhanging branches of the tree. The other perches himself on a bough a foot or so above the ground (Hoffman v. Armstrong, 48 N.Y. 201). Both are killed by falling wires. The defendant would have us say that there is a remedy for the representatives of one, and none for the representatives of the other. We may be permitted to distrust the logic that leads to such conclusions.

The truth is that every act of Hynes, from his first plunge into the river until the moment of his death, was in the enjoyment of the public waters, and under cover of the protection which his presence in those waters gave him. The use of the springboard was not an abandonment of his rights as a bather. It was a mere by-play, an incident, subordinate and ancillary to the execution of his primary purpose, the enjoyment of the highway. The by-play, the incident, was not the cause of the disaster. Hynes would have gone to his death if he had been below the springboard or beside it (Laidlaw v. Sage, 158 N.Y. 73, 97). The wires were not stayed by the presence of the plank. They followed the boy in his fall, and overwhelmed him in the waters. The defendant assumes that the identification of ownership of a fixture with ownership of land is complete in every incident. But there are important elements of difference. Title to the fixture, unlike title to the land, does not carry with it rights of ownership *usque ad coelum*. There will hardly be denial that a cause of action would have arisen if the wires had fallen on an aeroplane proceeding above the river, though the location of the impact could be identified as the space above the springboard. The most that the defendant can fairly ask is exemption from liability where the use of the fixture is itself the efficient peril. That would be the situation, for example, if the weight of the boy upon the board had caused it to break and thereby thrown him into the river. There is no such causal connection here between his position and his injuries. We think there was no moment when he was beyond the pale of the defendant's duty—the duty of care and vigilance in the storage of destructive forces.

This case is a striking instance of the dangers of "a jurisprudence of conceptions" (Pound, Mechanical Jurisprudence, 8 Columbia Law Review 605, 608, 610), the extension of a maxim or a definition with relentless disregard of consequences to "a dryly logical extreme." The approximate and relative become the definite and absolute. Landowners are not bound to regulate their conduct in contemplation of the presence of trespassers intruding upon private structures. Landowners are bound to regulate their conduct in contemplation of the presence of travelers upon the adjacent public ways. There are times when there is little trouble in marking off the field of exemption and immunity from that of liability and duty. Here structures and ways are so united and commingled, superimposed upon each other, that the fields are brought together. In such circumstances, there is little help in pursuing general maxims to ultimate conclusions. They have been framed *alio intuitu*. They must be reformulated and readapted to meet exceptional conditions. Rules appropriate to spheres which are conceived of as separate and distinct cannot both be enforced when the spheres become concentric. There must then be readjustment or collision. In one sense, and that a highly technical and artificial one, the diver at the end of the springboard is an intruder on the adjoining lands. In another sense, and one that realists will accept more readily, he is still on public waters in the exercise of public rights. The law must say whether it will subject him to the rule of the one field or of the other, of this sphere or of that. We think that considerations of analogy, of convenience, of policy, and of justice, exclude him from the field of the defendant's immunity and exemption, and place him in the field of liability and duty (Beck v. Carter, 68 N.Y. 283; Jewhurst v. City of Syracuse, 108 N.Y. 303; McCloskey v. Buckley, 223 N.Y. 187, 192.)

The judgment of the Appellate Division and that of the Trial Term should be reversed, and a new trial granted, with costs to abide the event.

HOGAN, POUND, and CRANE, JJ., concur; HISCOCK, CH. J., CHASE and McLAUGHLIN, JJ., dissent.

Further References

Bodenheimer, E., "A Neglected Theory of Legal Reasoning," 21 Journal of Legal Education 373 (1969).

Cross, R. & Harris, J.W., *Precedent in English Law* (4th ed. 1991), pp. 186–207.

Hathaway, O.A., "Path Dependence in the Law: The Course and Pattern of Change in a Common Law System," 86 Iowa Law Review 601 (2001).

Joseph, H.W.B., *An Introduction to Logic* (2d ed. 1916), pp. 249–86.

Kaufman, A.L., "Benjamin Cardozo as Paradigmatic Tort Lawmaker," 49 De Paul Law Review 281 (1999).

Newman, J.O., "Between Legal Realism and Neutral Principles: The Legitimacy of Institutional Values," 72 California Law Review 200 (1984).

Patterson, E.W., "Logic in the Law," 90 University of Pennsylvania Law Review 875 (1942).

Perelman, C., *Justice, Law, and Argument: Essays on Moral and Legal Reasoning* (1980), pp. 125–35, 163–74.

Posner, R.A., *Cardozo: A Study in Reputation* (1990), pp. 48–55 (discussing *Hynes*).

Posner, R.A., "Legal Formalism, Legal Realism, and the Interpretation of Statutes and the Constitution," 37 Case Western Reserve Law Review 179, 180–90 (1986).

Schwartz, G.T., "Cardozo as Tort Lawmaker," 49 De Paul Law Review 305 (1999).

Sherwin, E., "A Defense of Analogical Reasoning in Law," 66 University of Chicago Law Review 1179 (1999).

Sunstein, C.R., "On Analogical Reasoning," 106 Harvard Law Review 741 (1993).

Chapter VI

FUNDAMENTALS OF STATUTORY INTERPRETATION

A. OVERVIEW

In this chapter, we will turn our attention to legislation. You will recall that legislation is more authoritative than judicial precedent. A statute supersedes any prior inconsistent case law, and a judge is not free to disregard or "overrule" a statute except upon a finding of unconstitutionality. Nor can a judge alter the language of a statute in the same way that he or she can modify the rule of a prior case by reformulating its *ratio decidendi*.

The application of statutes to individual fact situations by a process of deductive reasoning is often rendered difficult by the substantial indeterminacy inherent in human language; words in many instances are inexact symbols of communication. For this and other reasons—among them the limited range of human imagination—statutes are rarely capable of identifying in precise terms the results intended by the legislature in all cases that might conceivably arise under them.

As we have already seen, case law cannot be applied mechanistically or formalistically. There will often be some doubt about the more appropriate formulation of the *ratio decidendi,* and considerations of policy, justice, and stare decisis may pull judicial decisionmakers in different directions. We now explore the parallel problems of statutory interpretation. While the greater authoritativeness of legislation keeps the judiciary under tighter rein when interpreting statutes than when applying precedent, excessive formalism may be as dangerous in the former situation as in the latter.

H.L.A. HART, THE CONCEPT OF LAW
pp. 123–26 (1st ed. 1961).[1]

Even when verbally formulated general rules are used, uncertainties as to the form of behaviour required by them may break out in

1. Copyright © 1961 by Oxford University Press. Reprinted by permission. The second edition of this classic work, published posthumously in 1994, reprints the origi-

particular concrete cases.... In all fields of experience, not only that of rules, there is a limit, inherent in the nature of language, to the guidance which general language can provide.... Canons of "interpretation" cannot eliminate, though they can diminish, these uncertainties; for these canons are themselves general rules for the use of language, and make use of general terms which themselves require interpretation. They cannot, any more than other rules, provide for their own interpretation....

. . . .

Whichever device, precedent or legislation, is chosen for the communication of standards of behaviour, these, however smoothly they work over the great mass of ordinary cases, will, at some point where their application is in question, prove indeterminate; they will have what has been termed an *open texture*. So far we have presented this, in the case of legislation, as a general feature of human language; uncertainty at the borderline is the price to be paid for the use of general classifying terms in any form of communication concerning matters of fact.... It is, however, important to appreciate why, apart from this dependence on language as it actually is, with its characteristics of open texture, we should not cherish, even as an ideal, the conception of a rule so detailed that the question of whether it applied or not to a particular case was always settled in advance, and never involved, at the point of actual application, a fresh choice between open alternatives. Put shortly, the reason is that the necessity for such choice is thrust upon us because we are men, not gods. It is a feature of the human predicament (and so of the legislative one) that we labour under two connected handicaps whenever we seek to regulate, unambiguously and in advance, some sphere of conduct by means of general standards to be used without further official direction on particular occasions. The first handicap is our relative ignorance of fact: the second is our relative indeterminacy of aim....

... When we are bold enough to frame some general rule of conduct (e.g. a rule that no vehicle may be taken into the park), the language used in this context fixes necessary conditions which anything must satisfy if it is to be within its scope, and certain clear examples of what is certainly within its scope may be present to our minds. They are the paradigm, clear cases (the motor-car, the bus, the motor-cycle); and our aim in legislating is so far determinate because we have made a certain choice. We have initially settled the question that peace and quiet in the park is to be maintained at the cost, at any rate, of the exclusion of these things. On the other hand, until we have put the general aim of peace in the park into conjunction with those cases which we did not, or perhaps could not, initially envisage (perhaps a toy motor-car electrically propelled) our aim is, in this direction, indeterminate. We have not settled,

nal text with minor revisions and slight variations in pagination, and adds a postscript replying to critics.

because we have not anticipated, the question which will be raised by the unenvisaged case when it occurs: whether some degree of peace in the park is to be sacrificed to, or defended against, those children whose pleasure or interest it is to use these things. When the unenvisaged case does arise, we confront the issues at stake and can then settle the question by choosing between the competing interests in the way which best satisfies us. In doing so we shall have rendered more determinate our initial aim, and shall incidentally have settled a question as to the meaning, for the purposes of this rule, of a general word.

Different legal systems, or the same system at different times, may either ignore or acknowledge more or less explicitly such a need for the further exercise of choice in the application of general rules to particular cases. The vice known to legal theory as formalism or conceptualism consists in an attitude to verbally formulated rules which both seeks to disguise and to minimize the need for such choice, once the general rule has been laid down.

NOTE BY THE EDITORS: THE HART/DWORKIN DEBATE

For an earlier but no less eloquent presentation of Professor Hart's views on the role of judges in construing legislation, *see* H.L.A. Hart, "Positivism and the Separation of Law and Morals," 71 Harvard Law Review 593, 606–15 (1958). For a complex and engaging counterpoint to Hart's analysis of how judges faced by "the unenvisaged case" are to "settle the question by choosing between the competing interests," see R.M. Dworkin, "Hard Cases," 88 Harvard Law Review 1057, 1082–87 (1975). The approaches of Professors Hart and Dworkin are compared in J.B. Oakley, "Taking Wright Seriously: Of Judicial Discretion, Jurisprudents, and the Chief Justice," 4 Hastings Constitutional Law Quarterly 789, 801–09 (1977). For a comprehensive restatement of Professor Dworkin's approach, see R.M. Dworkin, *Law's Empire* (1986). Professor Hart replied in the postscript to *The Concept of Law* (2d ed. 1994), at pp. 238–76.

Problems

Professor Hart, in the preceding excerpt, refers to an ordinance, apparently enacted by a municipality, which prohibits the taking of vehicles into a public park. In your opinion, would the ordinance apply to the following facts?

(1) A child seeks to take his large, battery-powered toy automobile into the park. The toy is designed for use upon a sidewalk. The sidewalks of the park are used by many pedestrians.

(2) A child has been injured in the park and her father calls for an ambulance. The ambulance seeks to enter the park in order to pick up the child at the place of injury.

B. BASIC APPROACHES TO STATUTORY INTERPRETATION

As the preceding materials demonstrate, judges do more than apply statutes—they interpret them. Over the centuries, Anglo–American courts have taken different approaches to the task of statutory interpretation.

1. HISTORICAL INTRODUCTION

The ancient Roman law, in its period of maturity, took a liberal attitude toward the interpretation of statutes. If the application of a broadly-phrased statute to a particular combination of facts led to a serious injustice, a judge was under no constraint to follow the words but could disregard them. This was in effect an application of Aristotelian equity. Conversely, when the words of a statute did not fit a particular case but the policy rationale behind the statute clearly covered it, the courts applied the statute by analogy. The Roman pattern has been widely followed in the orbit of the modern civil law.

Samuel Thorne has shown that, during certain periods of English medieval history, the position of the common law toward the construction of statutes was similar to the general attitude of the Roman and civil law. S. Thorne, *A Discourse upon the Exposition & Understandings of Statutes* (1942). Statutes were sometimes extended to situations that they did not expressly cover. Conversely, if the application of a broadly phrased statute to a particular complex of facts led to a hardship or injustice, a judge was under no constraint to follow the words of the statute. In the early fourteenth century, the freedom with which statutes were treated by common-law judges was so great that a substantial rewriting of statutory law by the judiciary was not at all uncommon. In the words of Thorne, statutes were viewed as "suggestions of policy to be treated with an easy unconcern as to their precise content." While this freedom of interpretation was gradually curbed and far-reaching extensions of statutory norms came to be looked upon as improper, the emerging doctrine of the equity of the statute still permitted a liberal interpretation of legislation according to its purpose and the use of analogy within moderate limits. The reporter Plowden stated in 1573 that "the intent of statutes is more to be regarded and pursued than the precise letter of them, for oftentimes things which are within the words of statutes, are out of the purview of them, which purview extends no further than the intent of the makers of the Act, and the best way to construe an Act of Parliament is according to the intent rather than according to the words."

In the eighteenth century, Blackstone, in his *Commentaries on the Laws of England,* still recognized the doctrine of the equity of the statute. He pointed out that judges are under no obligation to follow the words of a statute if its application to a particular case would lead to an unreasonable result not foreseen by the legislature. However, it seems that Blackstone did not favor the method of applying statutes by analogy.[2]

2. DESCRIPTION OF THREE BASIC APPROACHES

The three fundamental approaches to statutory interpretation under Anglo–American law, as articulated by the English courts, are set forth below:

(a) The Literal Rule

The "literal rule" or "plain meaning" approach to statutory interpretation has been described as follows:

> If the language of a statute be plain, admitting of only one meaning, the Legislature must be taken to have meant and intended what it has plainly expressed, and whatever it has in clear terms enacted must be enforced though it should lead to absurd or mischievous results.

Lord Atkinson in Vacher & Sons, Ltd. v. London Society of Compositors, [1913] App. Cas. 107, 121 (House of Lords).

(b) The Golden Rule

The "plain meaning" rule sometimes leads to harsh results. Consequently, the "golden rule" emerged as an alternative approach to statutory interpretation.

> But it is to be borne in mind that the office of the Judges is not to legislate, but to declare the expressed intention of the Legislature, even if that intention appears to the Court injudicious; and I believe that it is not disputed that what Lord Wensleydale used to call the golden rule is right, viz., that we are to take the whole statute together, and construe it all together, giving the words their ordinary signification, unless when so applied they produce an inconsistency, or an absurdity or inconvenience so great as to convince the Court that the intention could not have been to use them in their ordinary signification, and to justify the Court in putting on them some other signification which, though less proper, is one which the court thinks the words will bear.

Lord Blackburn in River Wear Commissioners v. Adamson, [1876–77] 2 App.Cas. 743, 764–65 (House of Lords, 1877).

(c) The Purposive Approach

In the 1990's, the English Courts embraced the "purposive approach" to statutory interpretation:

2. G. Williams, *Learning the Law* (11th ed. 1982), p. 102. For a statement of contemporary basic rules of statutory interpretation in England, see F. Bennion, *Statutory Interpretation* (4th ed. 2002); R. Cross, *Statutory Interpretation* (3d ed. 1995), pp. 48–68; C. Manchester, D. Salter, P. Moodie, & B. Lynch, *Exploring the Law: The Dynamics of Precedent and Statutory Interpretation* (1996), at pp. 30–67.

The days have long passed when the courts adopted a strict-constructionist view of interpretation which required them to adopt the literal meaning of the language. The courts now adopt a purposive approach which seeks to give effect to the true purpose of legislation and are prepared to look at much extraneous material that bears upon the background against which the legislation was enacted.

Lord Griffiths in Pepper v. Hart, [1993] 1 All E.R. 42, 50 (House of Lords, 1992).

NOTE BY THE EDITORS: THE CASE OF THE SPELUNCEAN EXPLORERS

The plain meaning and purposive approaches to statutory interpretation are classically illustrated by Professor Lon Fuller's fictional account of a debate among the judges of an imaginary state's highest court, which appears in the Appendix, *infra*. L. Fuller, "The Case of the Speluncean Explorers," 62 Harvard Law Review 616 (1949), *reprinted in* 112 Harvard Law Review 1851 (1999). *See* D.L. Shapiro, "The Case of the Speluncean Explorers: A Fiftieth Anniversary Symposium," 112 Harvard Law Review 1834 (1999). *See also* P. Suber, *The Case of the Speluncean Explorers: Nine New Opinions* (1998); W.N. Eskridge, "The Case of the Speluncean Explorers: Twentieth–Century Statutory Interpretation in a Nutshell," 61 George Washington Law Review 1731 (1993); N.R. Cahn, *et al.*, "The Case of the Speluncean Explorers: Contemporary Proceedings," 61 George Washington Law Review 1754 (1993).

Which of the three basic approaches to statutory interpretation was applied in each of the following cases?

UNITED STATES v. KIRBY

Supreme Court of the United States, 1868.
74 U.S. (7 Wall.) 482, 19 L.Ed. 278.

[This case arose under the Act of Congress of March 3, 1825, providing for the conviction of any person who "shall knowingly and willfully obstruct or retard the passage of the mail, or of any driver ... carrying the same." The Court held that the statute had no application to a sheriff who arrested a mailman upon a warrant issued by a state court, thereby retarding delivery of the mail.]

All laws should receive a sensible construction. General terms should be so limited in their application as not to lead to injustice, oppression, or an absurd consequence. It will always, therefore, be presumed that the legislature intended exceptions to its language which would avoid results of this character. The reason of the law in such cases should prevail over its letter.

HOLY TRINITY CHURCH v. UNITED STATES

Supreme Court of the United States, 1892.
143 U.S. 457, 12 S.Ct. 511, 36 L.Ed. 226.

[This case involved an 1885 statute making it "unlawful for any person, company, partnership, or corporation, in any manner whatsoever, to ... in any way assist or encourage the ... migration of any alien ... into the United States ... under contract or agreement ... made previous to the ... migration of such alien ... to perform labor or service of any kind in the United States. ..." The defendant church was a corporation which had entered into a contract with an Englishman to come to the United States to act as its pastor. The trial court judge found that the church had violated the 1885 act and imposed a fine payable to the United States because "where the terms of a statute are plain, unambiguous, and explicit, the courts are not at liberty to go outside of the language to search for a meaning which it does not reasonably bear in the effort to ascertain and give effect to what may be imagined to have been or not to have been the intention of Congress." 36 F. 303, 304 (C.C.S.D.N.Y. 1888). The Supreme Court reversed.]

It must be conceded that the act of the corporation is within the letter of this section, for the relation of rector to his church is one of service, and implies labor on the one side with compensation on the other. Not only are the general words labor and service both used, but also, as it were to guard against any narrow interpretation, and emphasize a breadth of meaning, to them is added "of any kind;" and, further, as noticed by the Circuit Judge in his opinion, the fifth section, which makes specific exceptions, among them professional actors, artists, lecturers, singers and domestic servants, strengthens the idea that every other kind of labor and service was intended to be reached by the first section. While there is great force to this reasoning, we cannot think Congress intended to denounce with penalties a transaction like that in the present case. It is a familiar rule, that a thing may be within the letter of the statute and yet not within the statute, because not within its spirit, nor within the intention of its makers. This has been often asserted, and the reports are full of cases illustrating its application. This is not the substitution of the will of the judge for that of the legislator, for frequently words of general meaning are used in a statute, words broad enough to include an act in question, and yet a consideration of the whole legislation, or of the circumstances surrounding its enactment, or of the absurd results which follow from giving such broad meaning to the words, makes it unreasonable to believe that the legislator intended to include the particular act. . . .

. . . .

Again, another guide to the meaning of a statute is found in the evil which it is designed to remedy; and for this the court properly looks at contemporaneous events, the situation as it existed, and as it was pressed upon the attention of the legislative body. . . . The situation which called for this statute was briefly but fully stated by Mr. Justice Brown when, as District Judge, he decided the case of United States v. Craig, 28 F. 795, 798: "The motives and history of the act are matters of common knowledge. It has become the practice for large capitalists in this country to contract with their agents abroad for the shipment of great numbers of an ignorant and servile class of foreign laborers, under contracts, by which the employer agreed, upon the one hand, to prepay their passage, while, upon the other hand, the laborers agreed to work after their arrival for a certain time at a low rate of wages. The effect of this was to break down the labor market, and to reduce other laborers engaged in like occupations to the level of the assisted immigrant. The evil finally became so flagrant that an appeal was made to Congress for relief by the passage of the act in question, the design of which was to raise the standard of foreign immigrants, and to discountenance the migration of those who had not sufficient means in their own hands or those of their friends, to pay their passage."

It appears, also, from the petitions, and in the testimony presented before the committees of Congress, that it was this cheap unskilled labor which was making the trouble, and the influx of which Congress sought to prevent. It was never suggested that we had in this country a surplus of brain toilers, and, least of all, that the market for the services of Christian ministers was depressed by foreign competition. Those were matters to which the attention of Congress, or of the people, was not directed. So far, then, as the evil which was sought to be remedied interprets the statute, it also guides us to an exclusion of this contract from the penalties of the act.[3]

CAMINETTI v. UNITED STATES

Supreme Court of the United States, 1917.
242 U.S. 470, 37 S.Ct. 192, 61 L.Ed. 442.

[This case involved the construction of the "White Slave Traffic Act" of 1910, otherwise known as the Mann Act. In 1917, the statute made it a crime to transport or assist the transportation of, in interstate commerce, "any woman or girl for the purpose of prostitution or debauchery, or for any other immoral purpose." Caminetti had been convicted under that Act of transporting a woman from Sacramento to Reno for "immoral purposes." The proof at trial established only that Caminetti had induced the woman to travel to Reno to have an affair with him, and that the couple had indeed engaged in sexual relations. For this, Caminetti was fined $1,500 and sentenced to imprisonment for 18 months. His appeal was premised on the argument that Congress had intended only to outlaw the use of channels of interstate commerce for "purposes of prostitution" (*i.e.*, for purposes of commercial, as opposed to noncommercial, sexual relations). With one justice not participating,

---

3. There is a scholarly debate as to whether the Court misread the legislative history in the Holy Trinity case. *Compare* A. Vermeule, "Legislative History and the Limits of Judicial Competence: The Untold Story of Holy Trinity Church," 50 Stanford Law Review 1833 (1998) (yes), *with* C. Chomsky, "Unlocking the Mysteries of Holy Trinity: Spirit, Letter, and History in Statutory Interpretation," 100 Columbia Law Review 901 (2000) (no). More recently, it has been suggested that the Court might have known at the time when it decided *Holy Trinity* in 1892 that Congress had, in 1891, enacted an amendment to the 1885 statute which prospectively expanded the exception for "professional actors, artists, singers, and lecturers" to include "ministers of any religious denomination," "persons belonging to any recognized profession," and "professors for colleges and seminaries." H.P. Southerland, "Theory and Reality in Statutory Interpretation," 15 Saint Thomas Law Review 1, 36 (2002) (citing the Act of March 3, 1891, 26 Stat. 1084, at §§ 5, 12).

five members of the Court affirmed Caminetti's conviction. The three dissenters invoked *Holy Trinity Church,* and relied heavily on the legislative history of the Act, which showed concern exclusively with the interstate transportation of women for purposes of commercial prostitution, as reflected in the name "White Slave Traffic Act," under which the statute was enacted. The majority did not mention *Holy Trinity Church* and rejected the dissenters' arguments as follows:]

It is elementary that the meaning of a statute must, in the first instance, be sought in the language in which the act is framed, and if that is plain, and if the law is within the constitutional authority of the law-making body which passed it, the sole function of the courts is to enforce it according to its terms. . . .

Where the language is plain and admits of no more than one meaning the duty of interpretation does not arise and the rules which are to aid doubtful meanings need no discussion. . . . There is no ambiguity in the terms of this act. It is specifically made an offense to knowingly transport or cause to be transported, etc., in interstate commerce, any woman or girl for the purpose of prostitution or debauchery, or for "any other immoral purpose," or with the intent and purpose to induce any such woman or girl to become a prostitute or to give herself up to debauchery, or to engage in any other immoral practice.

Statutory words are uniformly presumed, unless the contrary appears, to be used in their ordinary and usual sense, and with the meaning commonly attributed to them. To cause a woman or girl to be transported for the purposes of debauchery, and for an immoral purpose, to-wit, becoming a concubine or mistress, for which Caminetti [was] convicted, . . . would seem by the very statement of the facts to embrace transportation for purposes denounced by the act, and therefore fairly within its meaning.

While such immoral purpose would be more culpable in morals and attributed to baser motives if accompanied with the expectation of pecuniary gain, such considerations do not prevent the lesser offense against morals of furnishing transportation in order that a woman may be debauched, or become a mistress or a concubine, from being the execution of purposes within the meaning of this law. To say the contrary would shock the common understanding of what constitutes an immoral purpose when those terms are applied, as here, to sexual relations.

. . . .

. . . It is true that § 8 of the act provides that it shall be known and referred to as the "White Slave Traffic Act," and the report accompanying the introduction of the same into the House of Representatives set forth the fact that a material portion of the legislation suggested was to meet conditions which had arisen in the past few years, and that the legislation was needed to put a stop to a villainous interstate and international traffic in women and girls. Still, the name given to an act by way of designation or description, or the report which accompanies it, cannot change the plain import of its words. If the words are plain, they give meaning to the act, and it is neither the duty nor the privilege of the courts to enter speculative fields in search of a different meaning.

Reports to Congress accompanying the introduction of proposed laws may aid the courts in reaching the true meaning of the legislature in cases of doubtful interpretation .... But, as we have already said, and it has been so often affirmed as to become a recognized rule, when words are free from doubt, they must be taken as the final expression of the legislative intent, and are not to be added to or subtracted from by considerations drawn from titles or designating names or reports accompanying their introduction, or from any extraneous source. In other words, the language being plain, and not leading to absurd or wholly impracticable consequences, it is the sole evidence of the ultimate legislative intent.[4]

UNITED STATES v. AMERICAN TRUCKING ASS'NS

Supreme Court of the United States, 1940.
310 U.S. 534, 60 S.Ct. 1059, 84 L.Ed. 1345.

[This case called for a determination of "the power of the Interstate Commerce Commission under the Motor Carrier Act of 1935 to establish reasonable requirements with respect to the qualifications and maximum hours of service of employees of motor carriers, other than employees whose duties affect safety of operation." When Congress enacted the Motor Carrier Act, it sought to ensure "efficient and economical movement in interstate commerce," and it also sought to ensure "safety of operation." The Act assigned certain tasks to the Interstate Commerce Commission for purposes of advancing Congress's objectives: "It shall be the duty of the Commission ... to regulate common carriers by motor vehicle ..., and to that end the Commission may establish reasonable requirements with respect to continuous and adequate service, transpor-

---

4. For a detailed discussion of the facts in *Caminetti* (two defendants who were married men in their mid-twenties and who were friends, rode on a train across a state line with two unmarried women who were nineteen and twenty years of age and who were friends, after the foursome had double-dated for a number of months) and of the political factors surrounding the decision to prosecute (Caminetti was the son of a prominent Democrat who had just been appointed Commissioner of Immigration by President Wilson and the federal prosecutor was a holdover Republican still serving in the new Democratic administration), see D.J. Langum, *Crossing over the Line: Legislating Morality and the Mann Act* (1994). There is a scholarly debate as to whether the Court incorrectly interpreted the Mann Act in *Caminetti*, especially in light of the fact that it would have been difficult (as a political matter) for Congress to have voted

to overturn the Court's holding. *Id.* at 136–37. For a discussion of the political factors surrounding the decision to prosecute in this case, see L. Carter, *Reason in Law* (5th ed. 1998), at pp. 158–61.

The Mann Act was amended in 1986 to eliminate the reference to "white slavery." *Id.* at 73. The text of the revised statute provides: "Whoever knowingly transports any individual in interstate ... commerce ..., with intent that such individual engage in prostitution, or in any sexual activity for which any person can be charged with a criminal offense, ... shall be fined under this title or imprisoned not more than 10 years, or both." 18 U.S.C. § 2421. For a fictional case based on an alleged violation of the amended Mann Act, see W.N. Eskridge, "The Case of the Amorous Defendant: Criticizing Absolute *Stare Decisis* for Statutory Cases," 88 Michigan Law Review 2450 (1990).

tation of baggage and express, uniform systems of accounts, records, and reports, . . . qualifications and maximum hours of service of employees, and safety of operation and equipment." Shortly after the approval of the Act, the Commission fixed maximum hours of service for "employees whose function in the operation of motor vehicles make such regulations desirable because of safety considerations" at 60 hours per week. It left undecided the extent of its jurisdiction over other employees. Subsequently, Congress enacted the Fair Labor Standards Act of 1938, which set 40 hours per week at the normal rate of pay as the maximum number of hours of service for most employees, but which exempted employees who were governed by the Motor Carrier Act of 1935. The Commission then concluded that its power over employees was limited to the promotion of safe operation, and therefore it further concluded that it had jurisdiction to establish hours of work and qualifications for drivers, but it did not have jurisdiction over other employees of motor carriers. The Wage and Hour Division of the Department of Labor agreed.

The plaintiffs, an organization of motor carriers subject to regulation under the Act as well as various common carriers by motor vehicle, filed a petition with the Commission, seeking an exercise of the Commission's jurisdiction "with respect to qualifications and maximum hours of service of all employees of common carriers," and not just of truck drivers. The Commission denied the petition. The plaintiffs then filed this action in a three-judge district court to compel the Commission to take jurisdiction over all employees of common carriers by motor vehicle. At the hearing, the plaintiffs argued that the plain meaning of the 1935 Act required the Commissioner to exercise jurisdiction over all employees of common carriers by motor vehicle. The Commissioner responded that, under the plaintiff's interpretation of the statute, the Commission would have "to prescribe qualifications for stenographers, clerks, accountants, [and] mechanics, . . . of whose duties and qualifications it [had] no special knowledge." In this function, its determination "would not be based upon considerations of transportation," but upon "social and economic considerations" as to which it had no special expertise.

The three-judge court, by a 2–1 vote, held that the Commission was in error in denying jurisdiction and that an order should be made requiring it to exercise jurisdiction. The majority ruled that "the language of the disputed section is so plain as to permit of only one interpretation," and therefore it refused to consider the legislative history. The Supreme Court of the United States granted a direct right of appeal and reversed the lower court by a 5–4 vote. The dissenters said that "the decree should be affirmed for the reasons stated in the opinion of the district court." The majority, by contrast, said:]

In the broad domain of social legislation few problems are enmeshed with the difficulties that surround a determination of what qualifications an employee shall have and how long his hours of work may be. Upon the proper adjustment of these factors within an industry and in relation to competitive activities may well depend the economic success of the enterprises affected as well as the employment and efficiency of the workers. The Motor Carrier Act lays little emphasis upon the clause we are called upon now to construe, 'qualifications and maximum hours of service of employees.' None of the words are defined by ... the Act. They are a part of an elaborate enactment drawn and passed in an attempt to adjust a new and growing transportation service to the needs of the public. To find their content, they must be viewed in their setting.

In the interpretation of statutes, the function of the courts is easily stated. It is to construe the language so as to give effect to the intent of Congress. There is no invariable rule for the discovery of that intention. To take a few words from their context, and with them thus isolated to attempt to determine their meaning, certainly would not contribute greatly to the discovery of the purpose of the draftsmen of a statute, particularly in a law drawn to meet many needs of a major occupation.[5]

There is, of course, no more persuasive evidence of the purpose of a statute than the words by which the legislature undertook to give expression to its wishes. Often these words are sufficient in and of themselves to determine the purpose of the legislation. In such cases we have followed their plain meaning.[6] When that meaning has led to absurd or futile results, however, this Court has looked beyond the words to the purpose of the act.[7] Frequently, however, even when the plain meaning did not produce absurd results but merely an unreasonable one 'plainly at variance with the policy of the legislation as a whole' this Court has followed that purpose, rather than the literal words. When aid to construction of the meaning of words, as used in the statute, is available, there certainly can be no 'rule of law' which forbids its use,[8] however clear the words may appear on 'superficial examination.' The interpretation of the meaning of statutes, as applied to justiciable controversies, is exclusively a judicial function. This duty requires one body of public servants, the judges, to construe the meaning of what another body, the legislators, has said. Obviously there is danger that the courts' conclusion as to legislative purpose will be unconsciously influenced by the judges' own views or by factors not considered by the enacting body. A lively appreciation of the danger is the best assurance of escape from its threat but hardly justifies an acceptance of a literal interpretation dogma which withholds from the courts available information for reaching a correct conclusion. Emphasis should be laid, too, upon the necessity for appraisal of the purposes as a whole of Congress in

5. *Cf*.... Radin, "Statutory Interpretation," 43 Harvard Law Review 863 [(1930)]; Landis, "A Note on Statutory Interpretation," 43 Harvard Law Review 886 [(1930)].... [Footnote by the Court.]

6. ... Caminetti v. United States, 242 U.S. 470, 490 [(1917)].... [Footnote by the Court.]

7. ... Sorrells v. United States, 287 U.S. 435, 446 [(1932)].... [Footnote by the Court.]

8. Boston Sand & Gravel Co. v. United States, 278 U.S. 41, 48 [(1928) (J. Holmes) ("It is said that when the meaning of language is plain we are not to resort to evidence in order to raise doubts. That is rather an axiom of experience than a rule of law and does not preclude consideration of persuasive evidence if it exists.")]. [Footnote by the Court.]

analyzing the meaning of clauses or sections of general acts. A few words of general connotation appearing in the text of statutes should not be given a wide meaning, contrary to a settled policy, 'excepting as a different purpose is plainly shown.'

The language here under consideration, if construed as appellees contend, gives to the Commission a power of regulation as to qualifications and hours of employees quite distinct from the settled practice of Congress. That policy has been consistent in legislating for such regulation of transportation employees in matters of movement and safety only. The Hours of Service Act imposes restrictions on the hours of labor of employees 'actually engaged in or connected with the movement of any train.' The Seamen's Act limits employee regulations under it to members of ships' crews. . . . It is stated by appellants in their brief with detailed citations . . . that at the time of the passage of the Motor Vehicle Act 'forty states had regulatory measures relating to the hours of service of employees' and every one 'applied exclusively to drivers or helpers on the vehicles.' In the face of this course of legislation, coupled with the supporting interpretation of the two administrative agencies concerned with its interpretation, the Interstate Commerce Commission and the Wage and Hour Division, it cannot be said that the word 'employee' as used in Section 204(a) is so clear as to the workmen it embraces that we would accept its broadest meaning. The word, of course, is not a word of art. It takes color from its surroundings and frequently is carefully defined by the statute where it appears.

We are especially hesitant to conclude that Congress intended to grant the Commission other than the customary power to secure safety in view of the absence in the legislative history of the Act of any discussion of the desirability of giving the Commission broad and unusual powers over all employees. The clause in question was not contained in the bill as introduced. . . . It was presented on the Senate Floor as a committee amendment following a suggestion of the Chairman of the Legislative Committee of the Commission, Mr. McManamy. The committee reports and the debates contain no indication that a regulation of the qualifications and hours of service of all employees was contemplated; in fact the evidence points the other way. . . . When suggesting the addition of the clause, the Chairman of the Commission's Legislative Committee said: '. . . it relates to safety.' In the House the member in charge of the bill characterized the provisions as tending 'greatly to promote careful operation for safety on the highways,' and spoke with assurance of the Commission's ability to 'formulate a set of reasonable rules . . . including therein maximum labor-hours service on the highway.' And in the report of the House Committee a member set out separate views criticizing the delegation of discretion to the Commission and proposing an amendment providing for an eight-hour day for 'any employee engaged in the operation of such motor vehicle.'

. . . . .

It is important to remember that the Commission has three times concluded that its authority was limited to securing safety of operation. The first interpretation was made on December 29, 1937, when the Commission stated: '. . . until the Congress shall have given us a more particular and definite command in the premises, we shall limit our regulations concerning maximum hours of service to those employees whose functions in the operation of motor vehicles make such regulations desirable because of safety considerations.' This expression was half a year old when Congress enacted the Fair Labor Standards Act . . . . Under the circumstances it is unlikely indeed that Congress would not have explicitly overruled the Commission's interpretation had it intended to exempt others than employees who affected safety from the Labor Standards Act.

. . . .

Our conclusion, in view of the circumstances set out in this opinion, is that the meaning of employees in [the Motor Carrier Act of 1935] is limited to those employees whose activities affect the safety of operation. The Commission has no jurisdiction to regulate the qualifications or hours of service of any others. The decree of the district court is accordingly reversed and it is directed to dismiss the complaint of the appellees.[9]

C. INTRINSIC AIDS: LINGUISTIC CANONS OF STATUTORY CONSTRUCTION

In attempting to ascertain the intent of the legislature, English and American courts have developed various "canons" of statutory construction. *See generally* R. Cross, *Statutory Interpretation* (3d ed. 1995), at pp. 38–43, 113–41; K. Llewellyn, "Remarks on the Theory of Appellate Decision and the Rules or Canons About How Statutes Are to be Construed," 3 Vanderbilt Law Review 395 (1950). These canons of construction are simply a specialized body of precedent derived from cases in which the courts have engaged in the process of interpreting legislation. It should be noted that the generality of these canons, coupled with their interpretative function, has prompted the courts to treat them more as persuasive principles than as binding rules of law. The most frequently invoked canons are described below. Consider how they might have been applied to the cases in Chapter VI, Section B.

1. EXPRESSIO UNIUS EST EXCLUSIO ALTERIUS

The canon *expressio unius est exclusio alterius* means that "the expression of one thing is the exclusion of another." When the legisla-

---

9. In 1937, the Supreme Court of the United States "upheld the constitutionality of key enactments of the New Deal," and "three years later, in *United States v. American Trucking Associations*, it discarded the plain meaning rule." H.W. Baade, " 'Original Intent' in Historical Perspective: Some Critical Glosses," 69 Texas Law Review 1001, 1087 (1991). Mr. Justice Frankfurter in 1948 listed "no fewer than 131 Supreme Court cases relying on legislative history, handed down between . . . 1939 and . . . 1948," and found that "a federal government department or agency (or an independent regulatory commission) was a party to 105 of the 131 cases . . . ." *Id.* at 1088.

ture creates a list of specific items, for example, the implication is that it intended to exclude all other items from the list. In Townsley v. County of Ozaukee, 60 Wis. 251, 18 N.W. 840 (1884), the plaintiff, a county surveyor of the defendant county, presented to the board of supervisors a claim against the county for fuel and stationery used in his office. A Wisconsin statute enumerated a number of county officers, not including the county surveyor, who were entitled to be supplied with fuel and stationery by the county. The Supreme Court of Wisconsin disallowed the plaintiff's claim on the ground that the statute, by not mentioning county surveyors, meant to exclude them from the benefit provided.

In Tennessee Valley Authority v. Hill, 437 U.S. 153 (1978), the United States Supreme Court upheld an injunction against the completion of the Tellico Dam in order to prevent the extinction of the snail darter, a fish of three-inch size without food value and existing only in relatively small numbers. The Court deemed the injunction required by the Endangered Species Act of 1973, which provided in Section 7 that federal departments and agencies should utilize their authority in furtherance of the Act by carrying out programs for the conservation of endangered species and "by taking such action necessary to insure that actions authorized, funded, or carried out by them do not jeopardize the continued existence of such endangered species...." The Court said: "This language admits of no exception."

The Act was passed seven years after construction of the dam had commenced, and Congress had continued appropriations for Tellico, with full awareness of the snail darter problem. After citing some examples of on-going projects which Congress realized would in some way be altered by passage of the Act, the Court, in an opinion by Chief Justice Burger, continued:

> ... The plain intent of Congress ... was to halt and reverse the trend toward species extinction, whatever the cost....
>
> . . . .
>
> One might dispute the applicability of these examples to the Tellico Dam by saying that in this case the burden on the public through the loss of millions of unrecoverable dollars would greatly outweigh the loss of the snail darter. But neither the Endangered Species Act nor Art. III of the Constitution provides federal courts with authority to make such fine utilitarian calculations. On the contrary, the plain language of the Act, buttressed by its legislative history, shows clearly that Congress viewed the value of endangered species as "incalculable." Quite obviously, it would be difficult for a court to balance the loss of a sum certain—even $100 million— against a congressionally declared "incalculable" value, even assuming we had the power to engage in such a weighing process, which we emphatically do not.
>
> In passing the Endangered Species Act of 1973, Congress was also aware of certain instances in which exceptions to the statute's broad sweep would be necessary. Thus, § 10, 16 U.S.C. § 1539, creates a number of limited "hardship exemptions," none of which

would even remotely apply to the Tellico Project. In fact, there are no exemptions in the Endangered Species Act for federal agencies, meaning that under the maxim *expressio unius est exclusio alterius,* we must presume that these were the only "hardship cases" Congress intended to exempt.

Id. at 187–88. Reliance by the defendant on the *Holy Trinity Church* case, *supra*, Section B of this Chapter, was held unjustified by the Chief Justice on the ground that the principle of that case was to apply only in "rare and exceptional circumstances," and only when there was "something to make plain the intent of Congress that the letter of the statute is not to prevail." *Id.* at 187 n.33. He emphasized that, in this case, there was "nothing to support the assertion that the literal reading of Section 7 should not apply." *Id.*

Justices Powell, Blackmun, and Rehnquist dissented. Justice Powell argued that nothing in the language of the Act called for its retrospective application to projects nearing completion, and that this interpretation of Congressional intent was corroborated by the continuation of appropriations for Tellico subsequent to the passage of the Act. He also rejected Chief Justice Burger's narrow construction of the holding in *Holy Trinity Church* and said that a "literal application of a statute which would lead to absurd consequences is to be avoided whenever a reasonable application can be given which is consistent with the legislative purpose." *Id.* at 205 n.14.

After the decision was handed down, Congress overturned it and ordered the completion of the dam.

2. NOSCITUR A SOCIIS

Noscitur a sociis translates as "a thing is known by its associates." This canon directs a judge to determine the meaning of a word by looking at the other words which surround it in a statutory text. R. Cross, *Statutory Interpretation* (3d ed. 1995), at pp. 138–39; Gutierrez v. Ada, 528 U.S. 250 (2000).

In Jarecki v. G.D. Searle & Co., 367 U.S. 303 (1961), manufacturers of drugs (*e.g.*, Dramamine) and photographic devices (*e.g.*, Polaroid cameras) claimed that they were entitled to the same favorable income tax treatment as Congress had afforded to the oil, gas and mining industries for "income resulting from exploration, discovery or prospecting, or any combination of the foregoing." The Court rejected their argument, saying: "We look first to the face of the statute. 'Discovery' is a word usable in many contexts and with various shades of meaning. Here, however, it does not stand alone, but gathers meaning from the words around it. . . . The three words in conjunction . . . all describe income-producing activity in the oil and gas and mining industries, but it is difficult to conceive of any other industry to which they all apply. . . . The maxim *noscitur a sociis*, that a word is known by the company it keeps, while not an inescapable rule, is often wisely applied where a word is capable of many meanings in order to avoid the giving of unintended breadth to the Acts of Congress." *Id.* at 307.

In Babbitt v. Sweet Home Chapter of Communities for a Great Oregon, 515 U.S. 687 (1995), the plaintiffs, who were loggers in the Pacific Northwest, brought a declaratory judgment action against the Secretary of the Interior, asking the court to construe the Endangered Species Act, which makes it unlawful for any person to "take" any endangered or threatened species. The defendant had promulgated a regulation that defined the statutory term "take" so as to include "significant habitat modification or degradation where it actually kills or injures wildlife." *Id.* at 690. The plaintiffs alleged that the application of this regulation to the northern spotted owl and the red cockaded woodpecker had injured them economically and they claimed that the Secretary had exceeded his statutory authority by promulgating the regulation. The statute defined the term "take" as meaning "to harass, harm, pursue, hunt, shoot, wound, kill, trap, capture, or collect." The plaintiffs asserted that the statutory definition encompassed only "direct injuries," and the Court of Appeals had accepted the plaintiffs' argument, based on the *noscitur a sociis* canon. The Supreme Court reversed, emphasizing the fact that the Court of Appeals had erroneously employed *noscitur a sociis* to give "harm" the same meaning as other words in the definition, "thereby denying it of independent meaning." *Id.* at 702. Once the Court had separated the word "harm" from the other words in the definition of "take," it went on to hold that the word "harm" provided authorization for the defendant's regulation, which prohibited "indirect injuries."

3. EJUSDEM GENERIS

Under the *ejusdem generis* rule, "when particular words of description are used, followed by general words, the latter are to be limited in their meaning so as to embrace only a class of the things indicated by the particular words." State ex rel. School Dist. of Sedalia v. Harter, 188 Mo. 516, 520, 87 S.W. 941, 944 (1905).

In United States v. Alpers, 338 U.S. 680 (1950), the question was whether the shipment of obscene phonograph records in interstate commerce was prohibited by a provision in the Federal Criminal Code which made illegal the interstate shipment of any "obscene ... book, pamphlet, picture, motion-picture film, paper, letter, writing, print, or other matter of indecent character." The Court of Appeals for the Ninth Circuit had invoked the rule of *ejusdem generis*. Since the specific words "book, pamphlet, etc." appearing in the statute refer to objects comprehensible by sight only, the Court of Appeals had construed the general words "other matter of indecent character" to be limited to matter of the same genus. The Ninth Circuit had held phonograph records to be excluded from the scope of the statute, since phonograph records are comprehended by the sense of hearing. The United States Supreme Court disagreed. The Court stated that the rule of *ejusdem generis,* when properly applied, was a useful canon of construction. But, in the opinion of the Court, "it is to be resorted to not to obscure and defeat the intent and purpose of Congress, but to elucidate its words and effectuate its intent. It cannot be employed to render general words meaningless." *Id.* at 682. The Court deemed controlling in the present case the obvious purpose of Congress to prohibit the interstate shipment of obscene material.

NOTE BY THE EDITORS: THRUST AND PARRY

Karl Llewellyn observed that, for every canon of statutory interpretation, there is a counter-canon. Specifically, with reference to the canons described above, he said: 1) "Expression of one thing excludes another," but "the language may fairly comprehend many different cases where some only are expressly mentioned by way of example"; 2) "General terms are to receive a general construction," but "they may be limited by specific terms with which they are associated"; and 3) "It is a general rule of construction that where general words follow an enumeration they are to be held as applying only to persons and things of the same general kind or class specifically mentioned," but "general words must operate on something," and *ejusdem generis* "is only an aid in getting the meaning and does not warrant confining the operations of a statute within narrower limits than were intended." K. Llewellyn, "Remarks on the Theory of Appellate Decision and the Rules or Canons About How Statutes Are to be Construed," 3 Vanderbilt Law Review 395, 405–06 (1950).

NOTE BY THE EDITORS: THE SURVIVAL OF THE CANONS

Although Llewellyn's devastating critique of the canons of statutory construction might have been expected to bring about their gradual demise, contemporary commentators have observed their "puzzling persistence." *See, e.g.,* G.P. Miller, "Pragmatics and the Maxims of Interpretation," 1990 Wisconsin Law Review 1179. Miller's article shows that "some of these maxims have endured across a wide variety of legal systems" (*e.g.,* the systems for interpreting sacred Hindu texts and Judeo–Christian texts) and that "the insights captured by the maxims reflect common sense methods of interpreting utterances in ordinary conversation, as formalized by Grice's theory of implicatures." *Id.* at 1225. (Paul Grice was a linguistic philosopher who proposed a system of maxims for interpreting language in conversational settings that are remarkably similar in form to many of the leading canons of statutory interpretation.) Miller suggests that "the maxims often do reflect reasonable inferences about legislative meaning," and that "their apparent inconsistency and indeterminacy stems from the fact that the implicatures arising from the maxims are always cancelable and often have to be weighed against one another to determine which implicature is the strongest in a given case." *Id.* Therefore, Miller says: "Despite Llewellyn's apparent coup de grâce, the maxims survive." *Id.* For additional contemporary commentary on the canons of statutory interpretation, see W.N. Eskridge, *Dynamic Statutory Interpretation* (1994), at pp. 275–306 ("canons came back in style in the 1980's") (clustering canons into three categories: textual canons; extrinsic source canons; and substantive canons); W.N. Eskridge, P. Frickey & E. Garrett, *Legislation and Statutory Interpretation*

(2000), at pp. 249–86; W.N. Eskridge, "Norms, Empiricism and Canons in Statutory Interpretation," 66 University of Chicago Law Review 671 (1999); A. Vermeule, "Interpretive Choice," 75 New York University Law Review 74 (2000). *See also* J. Manning, "Legal Realism and the Canons' Revival," 5 Green Bag 2d 283 (2002) ("Many scholars still subscribe to Llewellyn's basic insight. The real news, however, is, first, that a large and growing number of academics (and academics-turned-judges) now believe in the utility of canons of construction ..., and, second, that the newly faithful cover a broad philosophical spectrum. Modern textualists, who tend to be formalist in orientation, understandably favor the use of canons, particularly the traditional linguistic canons.... Perhaps more surprisingly, a number of prominent pragmatists have concurred.... [T]hese scholars ... have sought to revive a basic idea ... that a system of established rules of construction might make the process of statutory interpretation more predictable, effective, and even legitimate.")

D. LEGISLATIVE HISTORY AND OTHER EXTRINSIC AIDS

In addition to the linguistic canons of statutory construction, which serve as intrinsic guides to ascertaining legislative intent, the courts often rely on extrinsic aids, such as legislative history. The law review articles and cases in this section demonstrate that there is a difference of opinion regarding the appropriateness of relying on extrinsic aids to ascertain legislative intent.

M. RADIN, "STATUTORY INTERPRETATION"
43 Harvard Law Review 863, 870–871 (1930).[10]

That the intention of the legislature is undiscoverable in any real sense is almost an immediate inference from a statement of the proposition. The chances that of several hundred men each will have exactly the same determinate situations in mind as possible reductions of a given determinable, are infinitesimally small. The chance is still smaller that a given determinate, the litigated issue, will not only be within the minds of all these men but will be certain to be selected by all of them as the present limit to which the determinable should be narrowed. In an extreme case, it might be that we could learn all that was in the mind of the draftsman, or of a committee of half a dozen men who completely approved of every word. But when this draft is submitted to the legislature and at once accepted without a dissentient voice and without debate, what have we then learned of the intentions of the four or five hundred approvers? Even if the contents of the minds of the legislature were uniform, we have no means of knowing that content except by the external utterances or behavior of these hundreds of men, and in almost every case the only external act is the extremely ambiguous one of acquiescence, which may be motivated in literally hundreds of ways, and which by itself indicates little or nothing of the pictures which the statutory descriptions imply. It is not impossible that this knowledge could be obtained. But how probable it is, even venturesome mathematicians will scarcely undertake to compute.

And if it were discoverable, it would be powerless to bind us. What gives the intention of the legislature obligating force? ... [The] function [of the legislature] is not to impose their will even within limits on their fellow-citizens, but to "pass statutes," which is a fairly precise operation. That is, they make statements in general terms of undesirable and desirable situations, from which flow certain results.

J.M. LANDIS, "A NOTE ON STATUTORY INTERPRETATION"

43 Harvard Law Review 886, 888–892 (1930) [footnotes omitted].[11]

The assumption that the meaning of a representative assembly attached to the words used in a particular statute is rarely discoverable, has little foundation in fact. The records of legislative assemblies once opened and read with a knowledge of legislative procedure often reveal the richest kind of evidence. To insist that each individual legislator besides his aye vote must also have expressed the meaning he attaches to the bill as a condition precedent to predicating an intent on the part of the legislature, is to disregard the realities of legislative procedure. Through the committee report, the explanation of the committee chairman, and otherwise, a mere expression of assent becomes in reality a concurrence in the expressed views of another. A particular determinate thus becomes the common possession of the majority of the legislature, and as such a real discoverable intent.

Legislative history similarly affords in many instances accurate and compelling guides to legislative meaning. Successive drafts of the same act do not simply succeed each other as isolated phenomena, but the substitution of one for another necessarily involves an element of choice often leaving little doubt as to the reasons governing such a choice. The voting down of an amendment or its acceptance upon the statement of its proponent again may disclose real evidence of intent. Changes made in the light of earlier statutes and their enforcement, acquiescence in a known administrative interpretation, the use of interpreted language borrowed from other sources, all give evidence of a real and not a fictitious intent, and should be deemed to govern questions of construction. The real difficulty is twofold: that strong judges prefer to override the intent of the legislature in order to make law according to their own views, and that barbaric rules of interpretation too often exclude the opportunity to get at legislative meaning in a realistic fashion. The latter, originating at a time when records of legislative assemblies were not in existence, deserve no adherence in these days of carefully kept journals, debates, and reports. Unfortunately they persist with that tenaciousness characteristic of outworn legal rules. Strong judges are always with us; no science of interpretation can ever hope to curb their propensities. But the effort should be to restrain their tendencies, not to give them free rein in the name of scientific jurisprudence.

. . . To ignore legislative processes and legislative history in the processes of interpretation, is to turn one's back on whatever history may reveal as to the direction of the political and economic forces of our time.

SCHWEGMANN BROS. v. CALVERT DISTILLERS CORP.

Supreme Court of the United States, 1951.
341 U.S. 384, 395–96, 71 S.Ct. 745, 751, 95 L.Ed. 1035.

MR. JUSTICE JACKSON, with whom MR. JUSTICE MINTON joins, concurring.

. . . .

Resort to legislative history is only justified where the face of the Act is inescapably ambiguous, and then I think we should not go beyond Committee reports, which presumably are well considered and carefully prepared. I cannot deny that I have sometimes offended against that rule. But to select casual statements from floor debates, not always distinguished for candor or accuracy, as a basis for making up our minds what law Congress intended to enact is to substitute ourselves for the Congress in one of its important functions. The Rules of the House and Senate, with the sanction of the Constitution, require three readings of an Act in each House before final enactment. That is intended, I take it, to make sure that each House knows what it is passing and passes what it wants, and that what is enacted was formally reduced to writing. It is the business of Congress to sum up its own debates in its legislation. Moreover, it is only the words of the bill that have presidential approval, where that approval is given. It is not to be supposed that, in signing a bill the President endorses the whole Congressional Record. For us to undertake to reconstruct an enactment from legislative history is merely to involve the Court in political controversies which are quite proper in the enactment of a bill but should have no place in its interpretation.

Moreover, there are practical reasons why we should accept whenever possible the meaning which an enactment reveals on its face. Laws are intended for all of our people to live by; and the people go to law offices to learn what their rights under those laws are. . . . Aside from a few offices in the larger cities, the materials of legislative history are not available to the lawyer who can afford neither the cost of acquisition, the cost of housing, or the cost of repeatedly examining the whole congressional history. Moreover, if he could, he would not know any way of anticipating what would impress enough members of the Court to be controlling. To accept legislative debates to modify statutory provisions is to make the law inaccessible to a large part of the country.

By and large, I think our function was well stated by MR. JUSTICE HOLMES: "We do not inquire what the legislature meant; we ask only what the statute means." Holmes, Collected Legal Papers, 207....

R. POSNER, "ECONOMICS, POLITICS, AND THE READING OF STATUTES AND THE CONSTITUTION"

49 University of Chicago Law Review 263, 274–75 (1982) [footnotes omitted].[12]

[There are] two recurrent issues in the use of legislative history to interpret statutes. The first is whether it is proper to use legislative history at all, and if so, which parts of that history to use. Because legislators vote on the statutory language rather than on the legislative history, they cannot be presumed to have assented to all that has been said, either in the committee reports or on the floor, about a bill that becomes law.

This matters, however, only if one holds the unrealistic view that each enacted bill reflects the convictions of a majority of legislators voting for it. If instead it is assumed that some unknown fraction of all bills are passed at the behest of politically powerful interest groups, it is not so clear that each member of the legislative majority behind a particular bill has studied the details of the bill he voted for. It may be more realistic to assume that he assented to the deal struck by the sponsors of the bill. The terms of the deal presumably are stated accurately in the committee reports and in the floor comments of the sponsors (otherwise the sponsors will have difficulty striking deals in the future), though not necessarily by opponents of the bill, who may take the floor or write minority opinions in committees to create a specious legislative history that they hope will influence judicial interpretation of the statute.

This picture is especially persuasive if we assume a considerable amount of "log rolling"—that is, vote trading—in the legislative process. Log rolling implies that legislators often vote without regard to their personal convictions. This process makes it unrealistic to demand that each legislator assent only to those aspects of statutory meaning that are fixed in the language of the bill, divorced from the intentions of its sponsors as reflected in their statements in the committee reports and on the floor.

My analysis is also germane to the question what weight to give post-enactment expressions of legislative intent. The answer it suggests, which is also the traditional answer, is that such expressions should be given little or no weight. The deal is struck when the statute is enacted. If courts paid attention to subsequent expressions of legislative intent not embodied in any statute, they would be unraveling the deal that had been made; they would be breaking rather than enforcing the legislative contract. Nor, if one takes seriously the interest group theory of politics,

12. Copyright © 1982 by The University of Chicago. Reprinted by permission.

can subsequent expressions of legislative understanding be treated simply as impartial interpretations of the law; they are as likely to be a gambit in the practice of interest group politics.

PEPPER v. HART

House of Lords of the United Kingdom, 1992.
[1993]   1 All E.R. 42.

LORD BROWNE-WILKINSON

. . . .

Under present law, there is a general rule that reference to Parliamentary material as an aid to statutory construction is not permissible (the exclusionary rule).... The exclusionary rule was probably first stated by Willes, J. in Miller v. Taylor (1769) 4 Burr. 2303, 2332 ....

... This rule has now been relaxed so as to permit reports of commissioners, including law commissioners, and white papers to be looked at for the purpose solely of ascertaining the mischief which the statute is intended to cure but not for the purpose of discovering the meaning of the words used by Parliament to effect such cure ....

. . . .

Mr. Lester submitted that the time has come to relax the rule .... Other common law jurisdictions have abandoned the rule without adverse consequences. Although the practical reasons for the rule (difficulty in getting access to Parliamentary material and the cost and delay in researching it) are not without substance, they can be greatly exaggerated: experience in commonwealth countries which have abandoned the rule does not suggest that the drawbacks are substantial, provided that the court keeps a tight control on the circumstances in which references to Parliamentary material are allowed.

On the other side, the Attorney General submitted that the existing rule had a sound constitutional and practical basis. If statements by Ministers as to the intent or effect of an Act were allowed to prevail, this would contravene the constitutional rule that Parliament is "sovereign only in respect of what it expresses by the words used in the legislation it has passed." ... It is for the courts alone to construe such legislation. It may be unwise to attach importance to ministerial explanations which are made to satisfy the political requirements of persuasion and debate, often under pressure of time and business....

My Lords, I have come to the conclusion that, as a matter of law, there are sound reasons for making a limited modification to the existing rule (subject to strict safeguards) .... In my judgment, ... reference to Parliamentary material should be permitted as an aid to the construction of legislation which is ambiguous or obscure or the literal meaning of which leads to an absurdity. Even in such cases references in court to Parliamentary material should only be permitted where such material clearly discloses the mischief aimed at or the legislative intention lying behind the ambiguous or obscure words. In the case of statements made in Parliament, as at present advised, I cannot foresee that any statement other than the statement of the Minister or other promoter of the Bill is likely to meet these criteria.

. . . .

. . . Attempts to introduce material which does not satisfy those tests should be met by orders for costs made against those who have improperly introduced the material. Experience in the United States of America, where legislative history has for many years been much more generally admissible than I am now suggesting, shows how important it is to maintain strict control over the use of such material. . . .

. . . .

In sum, I do not think that the practical difficulties arising from a limited relaxation of the rule are sufficient to outweigh the basic need for the courts to give effect to the words enacted by Parliament in the sense that they were intended by Parliament to bear. Courts are frequently criticized for their failure to do that. This failure is due not to cussedness but to ignorance of what Parliament intended by the obscure words of the legislation. The courts should not deny themselves the light which Parliamentary materials may shed on the meaning of the words Parliament has used and thereby risk subjecting the individual to a law which Parliament never intended to enact.

. . . .

E. CONTEMPORARY APPROACHES TO STATUTORY INTERPRETATION IN THE UNITED STATES

WEST VIRGINIA UNIVERSITY HOSPITALS, INC. v. CASEY

Supreme Court of the United States, 1991.
499 U.S. 83, 111 S.Ct. 1138, 113 L.Ed.2d 68.

JUSTICE SCALIA delivered the opinion of the Court.

This case presents the question whether fees for services rendered by experts in civil rights litigation may be shifted to the losing party pursuant to 42 U.S.C. § 1988, which permits the award of "a reasonable attorney's fee."

I

Petitioner West Virginia University Hospitals, Inc. (WVUH), operates a hospital in Morgantown, W.Va., near the Pennsylvania border. The hospital is often used by Medicaid recipients living in southwestern Pennsylvania. In January 1986, Pennsylvania's Department of Public Welfare notified WVUH of new Medicaid reimbursement schedules for services provided to Pennsylvania residents by the Morgantown hospital. In administrative proceedings, WVUH unsuccessfully objected to the new reimbursement rates on both federal statutory and federal constitutional grounds. After exhausting administrative remedies, WVUH filed suit in Federal District Court under 42 U.S.C. § 1983.[13] Named as defendants (respondents here) were Pennsylvania Governor Robert Casey and various other Pennsylvania officials.

Counsel for WVUH employed Coopers & Lybrand, a national accounting firm, and three doctors specializing in hospital finance to assist in the preparation of the lawsuit and to testify at trial. WVUH prevailed at trial in May 1988. The District Court subsequently awarded fees pursuant to 42 U.S.C. § 1988,[14] including over $100,000 in fees attributable to expert services. The District Court found these services to have been "essential" to presentation of the case—a finding not disputed by respondents.

Respondents appealed both the judgment on the merits and the fee award. The Court of Appeals for the Third Circuit affirmed as to the former, but reversed as to the expert fees, disallowing them except to the extent that they fell within the $30–per-day fees for witnesses prescribed by 28 U.S.C. § 1821(b). 885 F.2d 11 (1989). WVUH petitioned this Court for review of that disallowance....

II

Title 28 U.S.C. § 1920 provides:

"A judge or clerk of any court of the United States may tax as costs the following:

"(1) Fees of the clerk and marshal;

"(2) Fees of the court reporter for all or any part of the stenographic transcript necessarily obtained for use in the case;

"(3) Fees and disbursements for printing and witnesses; ...

"(6) Compensation of court appointed experts, compensation of interpreters, and salaries, fees, expenses, and costs of special interpretation services under section 1828 of this title."

Title 28 U.S.C. § 1821(b) limits the witness fees authorized by § 1920(3) as follows: "A witness shall be paid an attendance fee of $30 per day for each day's attendance. A witness shall also be paid the attendance fee for the time necessarily occupied in going to and returning from the place of attendance...."[15] In Crawford Fitting Co. v. J.T. Gibbons, Inc., 482 U.S. 437 (1987), we held that these provisions

---

13. Section 1983 provides: "Every person who, ... [under color of state law], subjects ... any citizen of the United States or other person within the jurisdiction thereof to the deprivation of any rights, privileges, or immunities secured by the constitution and laws, shall be liable to the party injured in an action at law, suit in equity, or other proper proceeding for redress."

14. Title 42 U.S.C. § 1988 provides in relevant part: "In any action or proceeding

to enforce a provision of sections 1981, 1982, 1983, 1985, and 1986 of this title, ... the court, in its discretion, may allow the prevailing party, other than the United States, a reasonable attorney's fee as part of the costs." [Footnote by the Court.]

15. Section 1821(b) has since been amended to increase the allowable per diem from $30 to $40.... [Footnote by the Court.]

define the full extent of a federal court's power to shift litigation costs absent express statutory authority to go further. "[W]hen," we said, "a prevailing party seeks reimbursement for fees paid to its own expert witnesses, a federal court is bound by the limits of § 1821(b), absent contract or explicit statutory authority to the contrary." *Id.,* at 439. "We will not lightly infer that Congress has repealed §§ 1920 and 1821, either through [Federal Rule of Civil Procedure] 54(d) or any other provision not referring explicitly to witness fees." *Id.,* at 445.

As to the testimonial services of the hospital's experts, therefore, *Crawford Fitting* plainly requires, as a prerequisite to reimbursement, the identification of "explicit statutory authority." WVUH argues, however, that some of the expert fees it incurred in this case were unrelated to expert *testimony,* and that as to those fees the § 1821(b) limits, which apply only to witnesses in attendance at trial, are of no consequence. We agree with that, but there remains applicable the limitation of § 1920.... None of the categories of expenses listed in § 1920 can reasonably be read to include fees for services rendered by an expert employed by a party in a nontestimonial advisory capacity. The question before us, then, is—with regard to both testimonial and nontestimonial expert fees—whether the term "attorney's fee" in § 1988 provides the "explicit statutory authority" required by *Crawford Fitting.*

III

The record of statutory usage demonstrates convincingly that attorney's fees and expert fees are regarded as separate elements of litigation cost. While some fee-shifting provisions, like § 1988, refer only to "attorney's fees," *see, e.g.,* Civil Rights Act of 1964, 42 U.S.C. § 2000e–5(k), many others explicitly shift expert witness fees *as well as* attorney's fees. In 1976, just over a week prior to the enactment of § 1988, Congress passed those provisions of the Toxic Substances Control Act, 15 U.S.C. §§ 2618(d), 2619(c)(2), which provide that a prevailing party may recover "the costs of suit and reasonable fees for attorneys *and expert witnesses.*" (Emphasis added.) ...

... The Equal Access to Justice Act (EAJA), the counterpart to § 1988 for violation of federal rights by federal employees, states that " 'fees and other expenses' [as shifted by § 2412(d)(1)(A)] includes the reasonable expenses of expert witnesses ... and reasonable attorney fees." 28 U.S.C. § 2412(d)(2)(A). At least 34 statutes in 10 different titles of the United States Code explicitly shift attorney's fees *and* expert witness fees.

. . . .

We think this statutory usage shows beyond question that attorney's fees and expert fees are distinct items of expense. If, as WVUH argues, the one includes the other, dozens of statutes referring to the two separately become an inexplicable exercise in redundancy.

IV

WVUH argues that at least in pre–1976 *judicial* usage the phrase "attorney's fees" included the fees of experts. To support this proposition, it relies upon two historical assertions: first, that pre–1976 courts, when exercising traditional equitable discretion in shifting attorney's fees, taxed as an element of such fees the expenses related to expert services; and second, that pre–1976 courts shifting attorney's fees pursuant to statutes identical in phrasing to § 1988 allowed the recovery of expert fees. We disagree with these assertions. The judicial background against which Congress enacted § 1988 mirrored the statutory background: expert fees were regarded not as a subset of attorney's fees, but as a distinct category of litigation expense.

. . . .

. . . [W]here the courts' holdings treated attorney's fees and expert fees the same (*i.e.*, granted both or denied both), their analysis discussed them as separate categories of expense. *See, e.g.*, Wolf v. Frank, 477 F.2d 467, 480 (CA5 1973) ("The reimbursing of plaintiffs' costs for attorney's fees *and* expert witness fees is supported . . . by well established equitable principles") (emphasis added) . . .; Bebchick v. Pub. Util. Comm'n, 115 U.S.App.D.C. 216, 233, 318 F.2d 187, 204 (1963) ("It is also our view that reasonable attorneys' fees for appellants, . . . reasonable expert witness fees, and appropriate litigation expenses, should be paid by [appellee]") . . . . We have found no support for the proposition that, at common law, courts shifted expert fees *as an element of* attorney's fees.

Of arguably greater significance than the courts' treatment of attorney's fees *versus* expert fees at common law is their treatment of those expenses under statutes containing fee-shifting provisions similar to § 1988. WVUH contends that in some cases courts shifted expert fees as well as the statutorily authorized attorney's fees—and thus must have thought that the latter included the former. We find, however, that the practice, at least in the overwhelming majority of cases, was otherwise.

Prior to 1976, the leading fee-shifting statute was the Clayton Act, 38 Stat. 731, as amended, 15 U.S.C. § 15 (shifting "the cost of suit, including a reasonable attorney's fee"). As of 1976, four Circuits (six Circuits, if one includes summary affirmances of district court judgments) had held that this provision did not permit a shift of expert witness fees. . . . No court had held otherwise. Also instructive is pre–1976 practice under the federal patent laws, which provided, 35 U.S.C. § 285, that "[t]he court in exceptional cases may award reasonable attorney fees to the prevailing party." Again, every court to consider the matter as of 1976 thought that this provision conveyed no authority to shift expert fees. . . .

. . . .

In sum, we conclude that at the time this provision was enacted neither statutory nor judicial usage regarded the phrase "attorney's fees" as embracing fees for experts' services.

V

WVUH suggests that a distinctive meaning of "attorney's fees" should be adopted with respect to § 1988 because this statute was meant to overrule our decision in Alyeska Pipeline Service Co. v. Wilderness Society, 421 U.S. 240 (1975). As mentioned above, prior to 1975 many courts awarded expert fees and attorney's fees in certain circumstances pursuant to their equitable discretion. In *Alyeska,* we held that this discretion did not extend beyond a few exceptional circumstances long recognized by common law. Specifically, we rejected the so-called "private attorney general" doctrine recently created by some lower federal courts, *see, e.g.,* La Raza Unida v. Volpe, 57 F.R.D. 94, 98–102 (ND Cal.1972), which allowed equitable fee shifting to plaintiffs in certain types of civil rights litigation. 421 U.S., at 269. WVUH argues that § 1988 was intended to restore the pre-*Alyeska* regime—and that, since expert fees were shifted then, they should be shifted now.

Both chronology and the remarks of sponsors of the bill that became § 1988 suggest that at least some members of Congress viewed it as a response to *Alyeska. See, e.g.,* S.Rep. No. 94–1011, pp. 4, 6 (1976). It is a considerable step, however, from this proposition to the conclusion the hospital would have us draw, namely, that § 1988 should be read as a reversal of *Alyeska* in all respects.

By its plain language and as unanimously construed in the courts, § 1988 is both broader and narrower than the pre-*Alyeska* regime. Before *Alyeska,* civil rights plaintiffs could recover fees pursuant to the private attorney general doctrine only if private enforcement was necessary to defend important rights benefiting large numbers of people, and cost barriers might otherwise preclude private suits. . . . Section 1988 contains no similar limitation—so that in the present suit there is no question as to the propriety of shifting WVUH's *attorney's* fees, even though it is highly doubtful they could have been awarded under pre-*Alyeska* equitable theories. In other respects, however, § 1988 is not as broad as the former regime. It is limited, for example, to violations of specified civil rights statutes—which means that it would not have reversed the outcome of *Alyeska* itself, which involved not a civil rights statute, but the National Environmental Policy Act of 1969, 42 U.S.C. § 4321 *et seq.* Since it is clear that, in many respects, § 1988 was not meant to return us precisely to the pre-*Alyeska* regime, the objective of achieving such a return is no reason to depart from the normal import of the text.

WVUH further argues that the congressional purpose in enacting § 1988 must prevail over the ordinary meaning of the statutory terms. It quotes, for example, the House Committee Report to the effect that "the judicial remedy [must be] full and complete," H.R.Rep. No. 94–1558, p. 1 (1976), and the Senate Committee Report to the effect that "[c]itizens must have the opportunity to recover what it costs them to vindicate [civil] rights in court," S.Rep. No. 94–1011, *supra,* at 2. As we have observed before, however, the purpose of a statute includes not only what it sets out to change, but also what it resolves to leave alone.... The best evidence of that purpose is the statutory text adopted by both Houses of Congress and submitted to the President. Where that contains a phrase that is unambiguous—that has a clearly accepted meaning in both legislative and judicial practice—we do not permit it to be expanded or contracted by the statements of individual legislators or committees during the course of the enactment process. *See* United States v. Ron Pair Enterprises, Inc., 489 U.S. 235, 241 (1989) ("[W]here, as here, the statute's language is plain, 'the sole function of the court is to enforce it according to its terms' "), quoting Caminetti v. United States, 242 U.S. 470, 485 (1917). Congress could easily have shifted "attorney's fees and expert witness fees," or "reasonable litigation expenses," as it did in contemporaneous statutes; it chose instead to enact more restrictive language, and we are bound by that restriction.

WVUH asserts that we have previously been guided by the "broad remedial purposes" of § 1988, rather than its text, in a context resolving an "analogous issue": In Missouri v. Jenkins, 491 U.S. 274, 285 (1989), we concluded that § 1988 permitted separately billed paralegal and law clerk time to be charged to the losing party. The trouble with this argument is that *Jenkins* did *not* involve an "analogous issue," insofar as the relevant considerations are concerned. The issue there was not, as WVUH contends, whether we would permit our perception of the "policy" of the statute to overcome its "plain language." It was not remotely plain in *Jenkins* that the phrase "attorney's fee" did not include charges for law clerk and paralegal services. Such services, like the services of "secretaries, messengers, librarians, janitors, and others whose labor contributes to the work product," *id.,* at 285, had traditionally been included in calculation of the lawyers' hourly rates. Only recently had there arisen "the 'increasingly widespread custom of separately billing for [such] services,' " *id.,* at 286 (quoting from Ramos v. Lamm, 713 F.2d 546, 558 (CA10 1983)). By contrast, there has never been, to our knowledge, a practice of including the cost of expert services within attorneys' hourly rates. There was also no record in *Jenkins*—as there is a lengthy record here—of statutory usage that recognizes a distinction between the charges at issue and attorney's fees. We do not know of a single statute that shifts clerk or paralegal fees separately.... In other words, *Jenkins* involved a respect in which the term "attorney's fees" (giving the losing argument the benefit of the doubt) was genuinely ambiguous; and we resolved that ambiguity not by invoking some policy that supersedes the text of the statute, but by concluding that charges of this sort had traditionally been included in attorney's fees and that separate billing should make no difference. The term's application to expert fees is not ambiguous; and if it were the means of analysis employed in *Jenkins* would lead to the conclusion that since such fees have not traditionally been included within the attorney's hourly rate they are not attorney's fees.

WVUH's last contention is that, even if Congress plainly did not include expert fees in the fee-shifting provisions of § 1988, it would have done so had it thought about it. Most of the pre-§ 1988 statutes that explicitly shifted expert fees dealt with environmental litigation, where the necessity of expert advice was readily apparent; and when Congress later enacted the EAJA, the federal counterpart of § 1988, it explicitly included expert fees. Thus, the argument runs, the 94th Congress simply forgot; it is our duty to ask how they would have decided had they actually considered the question. *See* Friedrich v. Chicago, 888 F.2d 511, 514 (CA7 1989) (awarding expert fees under § 1988 because a court should "complete ... the statute by reading it to bring about the end that the legislators would have specified had they thought about it more clearly").

This argument profoundly mistakes our role. Where a statutory term presented to us for the first time is ambiguous, we construe it to contain that permissible meaning which fits most logically and comfortably into the body of both previously and subsequently enacted law. *See* 2 J. Sutherland, *Statutory Construction* § 5201 (3d F. Horack ed.1943). We do so not because that precise accommodative meaning is what the lawmakers must have had in mind (how could an earlier Congress know what a later Congress would enact?), but because it is our role to make sense rather than nonsense out of the *corpus juris*. But where, as here, the meaning of the term prevents such accommodation, it is not our function to eliminate clearly expressed inconsistency of policy and to treat alike subjects that different Congresses have chosen to treat differently. The facile attribution of congressional "forgetfulness" cannot justify such a usurpation. Where what is at issue is not a contradictory disposition within the same enactment, but merely a difference between the more parsimonious policy of an earlier enactment and the more generous policy of a later one, there is no more basis for saying that the earlier Congress forgot than for saying that the earlier Congress felt differently. In such circumstances, the attribution of forgetfulness rests in reality upon the judge's assessment that the later statute contains the *better* disposition. But that is not for judges to prescribe. We thus reject this last argument for the same reason that Justice Brandeis, writing for the Court, once rejected a similar (though less explicit) argument by the United States:

> "[The statute's] language is plain and unambiguous. What the Government asks is not a construction of a statute, but, in effect, an enlargement of it by the court, so that what was omitted, presumably by inadvertence, may be included within its scope. To supply omissions transcends the judicial function." Iselin v. United States, 270 U.S. 245, 250–251 (1926).[16]

16. WVUH at least asks us to guess the preferences of the *enacting* Congress. Jus-tice Stevens apparently believes our role is to guess the desires of the *present* Congress, or of Congresses yet to be. "Only time will tell," he says, "whether the Court, with its literal reading of § 1988, has correctly interpreted the will of Congress" .... The implication is that today's holding will be proved wrong if Congress amends the law to conform with his dissent. We think not. The "will of Congress" we look to is not a will evolving from Session to Session, but a will expressed and fixed in a particular enactment. Otherwise, we would speak not of "interpreting" the law but of "intuiting" or

For the foregoing reasons, we conclude that § 1988 conveys no authority to shift expert fees. When experts appear at trial, they are of course eligible for the fee provided by § 1920 and § 1821—which was allowed in the present case by the Court of Appeals.

The judgment of the Court of Appeals is affirmed.

JUSTICE MARSHALL, dissenting.

As JUSTICE STEVENS demonstrates, the Court uses the implements of literalism to wound, rather than to minister to, congressional intent in this case. That is a dangerous usurpation of congressional power when any statute is involved. It is troubling for special reasons, however, when the statute at issue is clearly designed to give access to the federal courts to persons and groups attempting to vindicate vital civil rights. . . .

JUSTICE STEVENS, with whom JUSTICE MARSHALL and JUSTICE BLACKMUN join, dissenting.

Since the enactment of the Statute of Wills in 1540,[17] careful draftsmen have authorized executors to pay the just debts of the decedent, including the fees and expenses of the attorney for the estate. Although the omission of such an express authorization in a will might indicate that the testator had thought it unnecessary, or that he had overlooked the point, the omission would surely not indicate a deliberate decision by the testator to forbid any compensation to his attorney.

In the early 1970's, Congress began to focus on the importance of public interest litigation, and since that time, it has enacted numerous fee-shifting statutes. In many of these statutes, which the majority cites at length, . . . Congress has expressly authorized the recovery of expert witness fees as part of the costs of litigation. The question in this case is whether, notwithstanding the omission of such an express authorization in 42 U.S.C. § 1988, Congress intended to authorize such recovery when it provided for "a reasonable attorney's fee as part of the costs." In my view, just as the omission of express authorization in a will does not preclude compensation to an estate's attorney, the omission of express authorization for expert witness fees in a fee-shifting provision should not preclude the award of expert witness fees. We should look at the way in which the Court has interpreted the text of *this statute* in the past, as well as *this statute's* legislative history, to resolve the question before us, rather than looking at the text of the many other statutes that the majority cites in which Congress expressly recognized the need for compensating expert witnesses.

I

Under . . . the broad view of "a reasonable attorney's fee" articulated by this Court, expert witness fees are a proper component of an award under § 1988. Because we are not interpreting these words for the first

---

"predicting" it. Our role is to say what the law, as hitherto enacted, *is;* not to forecast what the law, as amended, *will be.* [Footnote by the Court.]

17.   32 Hen. VIII, ch. 1 (1540). [Footnote by the Court.]

time, they should be evaluated in the context that this and other courts have already created.[18]

. . . .

In *Jenkins,* the Court acknowledged that the use of paralegals instead of attorneys reduced the cost of litigation, and " 'by reducing the spiraling cost of civil rights litigation, further[ed] the policies underlying civil rights statutes.' " *Id.,* at 288. If attorneys were forced to do the work that paralegals could just as easily perform under the supervision of an attorney, such as locating and interviewing witnesses or compiling statistical and financial data, then "it would not be surprising to see a greater amount of such work performed by attorneys themselves, thus increasing the overall cost of litigation." *Id.,* at 288, n.10.

This reasoning applies equally to other forms of specialized litigation support that a trial lawyer needs and that the client customarily pays for, either directly or indirectly. Although reliance on paralegals is a more recent development than the use of traditional expert witnesses, both paralegals and expert witnesses perform important tasks that save lawyers' time and enhance the quality of their work product. In this case, it is undisputed that the District Court correctly found that the expert witnesses were "essential" and "necessary" to the successful prosecution of the plaintiff's case, and that their data and analysis played a pivotal role in the attorney's trial preparation. Had the attorneys attempted to perform the tasks that the experts performed, it obviously would have taken them far longer than the experts and the entire case would have been far more costly to the parties. . . .

In *Jenkins,* we interpreted the award of "a reasonable *attorney's* fee" to cover charges for paralegals and law clerks, even though a paralegal or law clerk is not an attorney. Similarly, the federal courts routinely allow an attorney's travel expenses or long-distance telephone calls to be awarded, even though they are not literally part of an "attorney's *fee,*" or part of "costs" as defined by 28 U.S.C. § 1920. To allow reimbursement of these other categories of expenses, and yet not to include expert witness fees, is both arbitrary and contrary to the broad remedial purpose that inspired the fee-shifting provision of § 1988.

II

The Senate Report on the Civil Rights Attorney's Fees Awards Act of 1976 explained that the purpose of the proposed amendment to 42 U.S.C. § 1988 was "to remedy anomalous gaps in our civil rights laws created by the United States Supreme Court's recent decision in Alyeska Pipeline Service Co. v. Wilderness Society, 421 U.S. 240 (1975), and to

---

18. My view, as I have expressed in the past, is that we should follow Justice Cardozo's advice to the judge to "lay [his] own course of bricks on the secure foundation of the courses laid by others who had gone before him." B. Cardozo, *The Nature of the Judicial Process* 149 (1921). [Footnote by the Court.]

achieve consistency in our civil rights laws."[19] S.Rep. No. 94–1011, p. 1 (1976), 1976 U.S.Code Cong. & Admin.News 5909. The Senate Committee on the Judiciary wanted to level the playing field so that private citizens, who might have little or no money, could still serve as "private attorneys general" and afford to bring actions, even against state or local bodies, to enforce the civil rights laws. The Committee acknowledged that "[i]f private citizens are to be able to assert their civil rights, and if those who violate the Nation's fundamental laws are not to proceed with impunity, then citizens must have the opportunity to recover *what it costs them* to vindicate these rights in court." *Id.,* at 2, 1976 U.S.Code Cong. & Admin.News 5910 (emphasis added). According to the Committee, the bill would create "no startling new remedy," but would simply provide "the technical requirements" requested by the Supreme Court in *Alyeska,* so that courts could "continue the practice of awarding attorneys' fees which had been going on for years prior to the Court's May decision." *Id.,* at 6, 1976 U.S.Code Cong. & Admin.News 5913.

To underscore its intention to return the courts to their pre-*Alyeska* practice of shifting fees in civil rights cases, the Senate Committee's Report cited with approval not only several cases in which fees had been shifted, but also all of the cases contained in Legal Fees, Hearings before the Subcommittee on Representation of Citizen Interests of the Senate Committee on the Judiciary, 93d Cong., 1st Sess., pt. 3, pp. 888–1024, 1060–1062 (1973) (hereinafter Senate Hearings). *See* S.Rep. No. 94–1011, at 4, n.3. The cases collected in the 1973 Senate Hearings included many in which courts had permitted the shifting of costs, including expert witness fees. At the time when the Committee referred to these cases, though several were later reversed, it used them to make the point that prior to *Alyeska,* courts awarded attorney's fees and costs, including expert witness fees, in civil rights cases, and that they did so in order to encourage private citizens to bring such suits. It was to this pre-*Alyeska* regime, in which courts could award expert witness fees along with attorney's fees, that the Senate Committee intended to return through the passage of the fee-shifting amendment to § 1988.

The House Report expressed concerns similar to those raised by the Senate Report. It noted that "[t]he effective enforcement of Federal civil rights statutes depends largely on the efforts of private citizens" and that the House bill was "designed to give such persons effective access to the judicial process . . . ." H.R.Rep. No. 94–1558, p. 1 (1976). The House Committee on the Judiciary concluded that "civil rights litigants were suffering very severe hardships because of the *Alyeska* decision," and that the case had had a "devastating impact" and had created a

---

19. In Alyeska Pipeline Service Co. v. Wilderness Society, 421 U.S. 240 (1975), the Court held that courts were not free to fashion new exceptions to the American Rule, according to which each side assumed the cost of its own attorney's fees. The Court reasoned that it was not the Judicia-ry's role "to invade the legislature's province by redistributing litigation costs . . . ," *id.,* at 271, and that it would be "inappropriate for the Judiciary, without legislative guidance, to reallocate the burdens of litigation. . . . " *Id.,* at 247. [Footnote by the Court.]

"compelling need" for a fee-shifting provision in the civil rights context. *Id.*, at 2–3.

According to both Reports, the record of House and Senate subcommittee hearings, consisting of the testimony and written submissions of public officials, scholars, practicing attorneys, and private citizens, and the questions of the legislators, makes clear that both committees were concerned with preserving access to the courts and encouraging public interest litigation.[20]

It is fair to say that throughout the course of the hearings, a recurring theme was the desire to return to the pre-*Alyeska* practice in which courts could shift fees, including expert witness fees, and make those who acted as private attorneys general whole again, thus encouraging the enforcement of the civil rights laws.

The case before us today is precisely the type of public interest litigation that Congress intended to encourage by amending § 1988 to provide for fee shifting of a "reasonable attorney's fee as part of the costs." Petitioner, a tertiary medical center in West Virginia near the Pennsylvania border, provides services to a large number of Medicaid recipients throughout Pennsylvania. In January 1986, when the Pennsylvania Department of Public Welfare notified petitioner of its new Medicaid payment rates for Pennsylvania Medicaid recipients, petitioner believed them to be below the minimum standards for reimbursement specified by the Social Security Act. Petitioner successfully challenged the adequacy of the State's payment system under 42 U.S.C. § 1983.

This Court's determination today that petitioner must assume the cost of $104,133 in expert witness fees is at war with the congressional purpose of making the prevailing party whole. As we said in . . . *Jenkins,* petitioner's recovery should be "comparable to what 'is traditional with attorneys compensated by a fee-paying client.' S.Rep. No. 94–1011, p. 6 (1976), U.S.Code Cong. & Admin.News 1976, pp. 5908, 5913." 491 U.S., at 286.

III

In recent years the Court has vacillated between a purely literal approach to the task of statutory interpretation and an approach that seeks guidance from historical context, legislative history, and prior cases identifying the purpose that motivated the legislation. Thus, for example, in Christiansburg Garment Co. v. EEOC, 434 U.S. 412 (1978),

---

20. A frequently expressed concern was the need to undo the damage to public interest litigation caused by *Alyeska. See, e.g.,* Awarding of Attorneys' Fees, Hearings before the Subcommittee on Courts, Civil Liberties, and the Administration of Justice of the House Committee on the Judiciary, 94th Cong., 1st Sess., 2, 41, 42, 43, 54, 82–85, 87, 90–92, 94, 103, 119–121, 123–125, 134, 150, 153–155, 162, 182–183, 269, 272–273, 370, 378–395, 416–418 (1975) (hereinafter House Hearings). Many who testified expressed the view that attorneys needed fee-shifting provisions so that they could afford to work on public interest litigation, *see, e.g., id.,* at 66–67, 76, 78–79, 80, 89, 124–125, 137–142, 146, 158–159, 276–277, 278–280, 306–308. . . . The Senate Hearings also examined the average citizen's lack of access to the legal system. *See, e.g.,* Senate Hearings, pts. 1, 2, pp. 1–2, 3–4, 273. . . . [Footnote by the Court.]

we rejected a "mechanical construction," *id.,* at 418, of the fee-shifting provision in § 706(k) of Title VII of the Civil Rights Act of 1964 that the prevailing defendant had urged upon us. Although the text of the statute drew no distinction between different kinds of "prevailing parties," we held that awards to prevailing plaintiffs are governed by a more liberal standard than awards to prevailing defendants. That holding rested entirely on our evaluation of the relevant congressional policy and found no support within the four corners of the statutory text. Nevertheless, the holding was unanimous and, to the best of my knowledge, evoked no adverse criticism or response in Congress.

On those occasions, however, when the Court has put on its thick grammarian's spectacles and ignored the available evidence of congressional purpose and the teaching of prior cases construing a statute, the congressional response has been dramatically different. It is no coincidence that the Court's literal reading of Title VII, which led to the conclusion that disparate treatment of pregnant and nonpregnant persons was not discrimination on the basis of sex, *see* General Electric Co. v. Gilbert, 429 U.S. 125 (1976), was repudiated by the 95th Congress[21] . . . .

In the domain of statutory interpretation, Congress is the master. It obviously has the power to correct our mistakes, but we do the country a disservice when we needlessly ignore persuasive evidence of Congress' actual purpose and require it "to take the time to revisit the matter" and to restate its purpose in more precise English whenever its work product suffers from an omission or inadvertent error. As Judge Learned Hand explained, statutes are likely to be imprecise.

> "All [legislators] have done is to write down certain words which they mean to apply generally to situations of that kind. To apply these literally may either pervert what was plainly their general meaning, or leave undisposed of what there is every reason to suppose they meant to provide for. Thus it is not enough for the judge just to use a dictionary. If he should do no more, he might come out with a result which every sensible man would recognize to be quite the opposite of what was really intended; which would contradict or leave unfulfilled its plain purpose." L. Hand, How Far Is a Judge Free in Rendering a Decision?, in *The Spirit of Liberty* 103, 106 (I. Dilliard ed.1952).

The Court concludes its opinion with the suggestion that disagreement with its textual analysis could only be based on the dissenters' preference for a "better" statute. . . . It overlooks the possibility that a different view may be more faithful to Congress' command. The fact that Congress has consistently provided for the inclusion of expert witness fees in fee-shifting statutes when it considered the matter is a weak reed on which to rest the conclusion that the omission of such a provision

21. *See* Pregnancy Discrimination Act of 1978, Pub.L. 95–555, 92 Stat. 2076, 42 U.S.C. § 2000e(k) (overturning General Electric Co. v. Gilbert, 429 U.S. 125 (1976)). [Footnote by the Court.]

represents a deliberate decision to forbid such awards. Only time will tell whether the Court, with its literal reading[22] of § 1988, has correctly interpreted the will of Congress with respect to the issue it has resolved today.

I respectfully dissent.[23]

NOTE BY THE EDITORS: THE UNITED STATES SUPREME COURT'S USE OF LEGISLATIVE HISTORY

Empirical studies of the United States Supreme Court's use of legislative history show that the Court gradually became more willing to look at legislative history during the twentieth century until the time that Justice Scalia joined the Court in 1986. J.L. Carro & A.R. Brann, "Use of Legislative Histories by the United States Supreme Court: A Statistical Analysis," 9 J. Legis. 282 (1982); N.S. Zeppos, "The Use of Authority in Statutory Interpretation: An Empirical Analysis," 70 Texas Law Review 1073 (1992) (random sample of Supreme Court terms between 1890 and 1990). *See also*, P.M. Wald, "Some Observations on the Use of Legislative History in the 1981 Supreme Court Term," 68 Iowa Law Review 195 (1983) (Supreme Court cited legislative history in virtually every statutory interpretation case). Between 1986 and 1998, the Court's use of legislative history declined significantly. M.H. Koby, "The Supreme Court's Declining Reliance on Legislative History: The Impact of Justice Scalia's Critique," 36 Harvard Journal on Legislation 369 (1999) (updating the study by Carro and Brann by looking at the period from 1980 to 1998). *See also*, T.W. Merrill, "Textualism and the Future of the *Chevron* Doctrine," 72 Washington University Law Quarterly 351 (1994) (in the 1992 term, the Court used legislative history in only 18 percent of its statutory cases); P.M. Wald, "The

---

22. Seventy years ago, Justice Cardozo warned of the dangers of literal reading, whether of precedents or statutes:

> "[Some judges'] notion of their duty is to match the colors of the case at hand against the colors of many sample cases spread out upon their desk. The sample nearest in shade supplies the applicable rule. But, of course, no system of living law can be evolved by such a process, and no judge of a high court, worthy of his office, views the function of his place so narrowly. If that were all there was to our calling, there would be little of intellectual interest about it. The man who had the best card index of the cases would also be the wisest judge. It is when the colors do not match, when the references in the index fail, when there is no decisive precedent, that the serious business of the judge begins." *The Nature of the Judicial Process*, at 20–21.

[Footnote by the Court.]

23. When Congress enacted the Civil Rights Act of 1991, amending Section 1981 (which prohibits race-based employment

discrimination), it added the following sentence to Section 1988: "In awarding an attorney's fee under subsection (b) of this section in any action or proceeding to enforce a provision of section 1981 or 1981a of this title, the court, in its discretion, may include expert fees as part of the attorney's fee." 42 U.S.C. § 1988 (c). Section 1988 (c) makes no explicit reference to Section 1983, and the Supreme Court has not yet ruled on the question of whether the 1991 Act should be construed to overturn *West Virginia Hospitals* in the context of Section 1983 actions. For a recommendation that Congress should "should extend the scope of the changes effected by the Civil Rights Act of 1991 ... to encompass all awards of a 'reasonable attorney's fee' under § 1988," see S. Cameron, "Civil Rights Plaintiffs' Recovery of Expenses for Experts as Litigated Costs Under 42 U.S.C. § 1988," 66 Temple Law Review 857, 861 (1993). For a discussion of how to litigate in the shadow of *West Virginia Hospitals*, see R.J. Gregory, "Overcoming Text in the Age of Textualism: A Practitioner's Guide to Arguing Cases of Statutory Interpretation," 35 Akron L. Rev. 451 (2002).

Sizzling Sleeper: The Use of Legislative History in Construing Statutes in the 1988–1989 Term of the United States Supreme Court," 39 American University Law Review 277, 298 (1990) (the Court cited legislative history in 75 percent of its statutory cases).

NOTE BY THE EDITORS: THE ROLE OF JUSTICE BREYER ON THE UNITED STATES SUPREME COURT

Justice Breyer has influenced the Supreme Court's approach to statutory interpretation since he joined the Court in 1994. Prior to that date, he wrote an article based on his experience as former Chief Counsel to the Senate Judiciary Committee. S. Breyer, "On the Uses of Legislative History in Interpreting Statutes," 65 Southern California Law Review 845 (1992). In the article, Breyer suggests that it is appropriate to consider "institutional intent." He also suggests that the best evidence of a "busy Congress's" institutional intent is expressed in committee reports, which are written by the "expert" members (and staffers) of a committee and which are then read and relied upon by the other members of Congress, who do not have the time or the resources to research the implications of a particular bill. When Justice Breyer joined the Court, "his [busy Congress] perspective, fueled with personal experience and a vision of the larger implications, influenced the Court's turnaround from the peak of textualism . . . in a series of cases developing the new concept." C. Tiefer, "The Reconceptualization of Legislative History in the Supreme Court," 2000 Wisconsin Law Review 205, 225 (2000). Justice Thomas usually (but not always) joins with Justice Scalia, who is the staunchest proponent of textualism. A. Scalia, "Common Law Courts in a Civil Law System: The Role of the United States Federal Courts in Interpreting the Constitution and Laws," in *A Matter of Interpretation: Federal Courts and the Law* (Amy Gutmann, ed. 1997). Justice Stevens often joins with Justice Breyer in opposing Justice Scalia's textualism. That leaves the five swing voters on the issue (Justices Rehnquist, O'Connor, Kennedy, Ginsburg, and Souter) free "to settle into an agnostic position between theories," which allows those Justices "to implement their pragmatic sensibilities." *Id.* at 272–73. All of the Justices except for Justices Scalia and Thomas will now "readily rel[y] on drafting history and conference reports as guides to Congress's intent." *Id.* at 232.

NOTE BY THE EDITORS: THE STATE COURTS' USE OF LEGISLATIVE HISTORY

State courts have become increasingly likely to consider legislative history due to the increased availability of documentary legislative materials. J.R. Torres & S. Windsor, "State Legislative Histories: A Select, Annotated Bibliography," 85 Law Library Journal 545 (1993). In fact, in March of 2003, the Connecticut Supreme Court held: "In performing the process of statutory interpretation, we do not follow the plain meaning rule in whatever formulation it may appear." State v. Courchesne, 262 Conn. 537, 570, 816 A.2d 562, 582 (2003). The majority of the court said that, for at least two reasons, it "disagreed" with the plain meaning rule as a "useful rubric for the process of statutory interpretation." *Id.* First, the rule is "fundamentally inconsistent with the purposive and contextual nature of legislative language." *Id.* Second, application of the plain meaning rule "necessarily requires the court to engage in a threshold determination of whether the language is ambiguous," and this requirement, in turn, "leaves the court open to the criticism of being result-oriented in interpreting statutes." *Id.* at 571, 816 A.2d at 583. To emphasize the second point, the Connecticut court quoted Circuit City Stores, Inc. v. Adams, 532 U.S. 105, 133 (2001) (Stevens, J., dissenting): "Justice Ahron Barak of the Supreme Court of Israel has perceptively noted [that] the 'minimalist' judge who 'holds that the purpose of the statute may be learned only from its language' has more discretion than the judge 'who will seek guidance from every reliable source.' "*Id.* at 573 n.28, 816 A.2d at 584 n.28.

The dissenters in *Courchesne*, who had adhered to the plain meaning doctrine, dissented again on the issue of statutory interpretation in a subsequent case because "the principle of stare decisis does not apply to the approach to statutory interpretation adopted by the majority in *Courchsene*." Mandell v. Gavin, 262 Conn. 659, 672, 816 A.2d 619, 626 (2003). The dissenters took the position that an "approach to statutory interpretation" is "not a rule of substantive law," but rather is a "principle" of "judicial philosophy," and "judicial philosophy is a matter of individual conscience and is not subject to majority rule by the members of this court." *Id.* at 672–73, 816 A.2d at 627 (2003). At that point, the Connecticut legislature stepped in and passed the following statute, which the governor signed on June 26, 2003: "[Effective October 1, 2003] the meaning of a statute shall, in the first instance, be ascertained from the text of the statute itself and its relationship to other statutes. If, after examining such text and considering such relationship, the meaning of such text is plain and unambiguous and does not yield absurd or unworkable results, extratextual evidence of the meaning of the statute shall not be considered." Public Act No. 03–154.

The Connecticut state legislature is unique in that it has "mandated" the use of a particular approach to statutory interpretation. It is also unique in that it has expressed a preference for the "plain meaning" rule. Several other state legislatures have enacted statutes which "suggest" the use of the "purpose approach" to statutory interpretation. In Texas, for example, the legislature enacted a statute in 1985 that says: "In construing a statute, whether or not the statute is considered ambiguous on its face, a court may consider among other matters the: (1) object sought to be attained; (2) circumstances under which the statute was enacted; (3) legislative history; (4) common law or statutory provisions, including laws on the same or similar subjects; (5) consequences of a particular construction; (6) administrative construction of the statute; and (7) title (caption), preamble, and emergency provision." Tex. Gov't Code Ann. § 311.023 (Vernon 1998).

The National Conference of Commissioners on Uniform State Laws promulgated the Uniform Statutory Construction Act in 1965. In 1975, its name was changed to the Model Statutory Construction Act. That Act was adopted by Colorado, Iowa, and Wisconsin, and many of its individual provisions can be found in the statutes of over 43 other states. The Model Act was revised in 1995, and now it is called the Uniform Statute and Rule Construction Act. New Mexico is one state that has adopted the 1995 Act. The Prefatory Note to the 1995 Act says that "all of the generally recognized theories of construction have been justifiably criticized," and "[t]his Act, therefore, does not require a construer to follow any particular theory of construction, but sets forth a process to be followed by a construer with an open mind." Section 18 (a) of the 1995 Act, entitled "Principles of Construction," provides that "[a] statute or rule is construed, if possible, to: (1) give effect to its objective and purpose; (2) give effect to its entire text; and (3) avoid an unconstitutional, absurd, or unachievable result." The Prefatory Note also states that "this Act assists courts" in construing statutes, and therefore it is "not a legislative infringement of the judiciary's special function of construing a statute; it is merely an aid to the courts in performing that function." The Prefatory Note then concludes: "The existence and use of statutory construction acts for over a century without successful challenge further demonstrates that these acts do not violate the fundamental constitutional principle of separation of powers."

F. SUBSTANTIVE CANONS OF STATUTORY CONSTRUCTION: CRIMINAL LAW

In addition to the linguistic canons of statutory interpretation, federal and state courts have developed substantive canons of statutory interpretation, which are presumptions that arise due to the subject matter of the statute. These canons differ from the linguistic canons in that they are not value-neutral. Rather, they are based on policies that advance the objectives of a particular area of the law, such as criminal law, which is the topic featured in this section. The application of substantive canons of statutory interpretation may vary from one jurisdiction to another, and may vary over time.

When a court applies a criminal statute, there is a "presumption" that the penal law will be construed strictly. The general thrust of this rule of statutory interpretation is to preclude criminal convictions and, therefore, it is often called the "rule of lenity." The United States Supreme Court explained the reason for the rule in United States v. Wiltberger, 18 U.S. 76 (1820) (Marshall, C.J.):

> The rule that penal laws are to be construed strictly is perhaps not much less old than construction itself. It is founded on the tenderness of the law for the rights of individuals; and on the plain principle that the power of punishment is vested in the legislative, not in the judicial department. It is the legislature, not the Court, which is to define a crime, and ordain its punishment.

Id. at 95.

McBOYLE v. UNITED STATES

Supreme Court of the United States, 1931.
283 U.S. 25, 51 S.Ct. 340, 75 L.Ed. 816.

Mr. Justice Holmes delivered the opinion of the Court.

The petitioner was convicted of transporting from Ottawa, Illinois, to Guymon, Oklahoma, an airplane that he knew to have been stolen, and was sentenced to serve three years' imprisonment and to pay a fine of $2,000. The judgment was affirmed by the Circuit Court of Appeals for the Tenth Circuit. 43 F.2d 273. A writ of certiorari was granted by this Court on the question whether the National Motor Vehicle Theft Act applies to aircraft. Act of October 29, 1919, c. 89, 41 Stat. 324, U.S. Code, title 18, § 408 (18 USCA § 408). That Act provides: 'Sec. 2. That when used in this Act: (a) The term 'motor vehicle' shall include an automobile, automobile truck, automobile wagon, motor cycle, or any other self-propelled vehicle not designed for running on rails; ... Sec. 3. That whoever shall transport or cause to be transported in interstate or foreign commerce a motor vehicle, knowing the same to have been stolen, shall be punished by a fine of not more than $5,000, or by imprisonment of not more than five years, or both.'

Section 2 defines the motor vehicles of which the transportation in interstate commerce is punished in Section 3. The question is the meaning of the word 'vehicle' in the phrase 'any other self-propelled vehicle not designed for running on rails.' No doubt etymologically it is possible to use the word to signify a conveyance working on land, water or air.... But in everyday speech 'vehicle' calls up the picture of a thing moving on land.... [H]ere, the phrase under discussion calls up the popular picture. For after including automobile truck, automobile wagon and motor cycle, the words 'any other self-propelled vehicle not designed for running on rails' still indicate that a vehicle in the popular sense, that is a vehicle running on land, is the theme. It is a vehicle that runs, not something, not commonly called a vehicle, that flies. Airplanes were well known in 1919 when this statute was passed, but it is admitted that they were not mentioned in the reports or in the debates in Congress. It is impossible to read words that so carefully enumerate the different forms of motor vehicles and have no reference of any kind to aircraft, as including airplanes under a term that usage more and more precisely confines to a different class....

Although it is not likely that a criminal will carefully consider the text of the law before he murders or steals, it is reasonable that a fair warning should be given to the world in language that the common world will understand, of what the law intends to do if a certain line is passed. To make the warning fair, so far as possible the line should be clear. When a rule of conduct is laid down in words that evoke in the common mind only the picture of vehicles moving on land, the statute should not be extended to aircraft simply because it may seem to us that a similar policy applies, or upon the speculation that if the legislature had thought of it, very likely broader words would have been used....

Judgment reversed.[24]

24. In 1948, Congress amended the National Motor Vehicle Theft Act to provide that: "Whoever transports in interstate or foreign commerce a motor vehicle *or air-* *craft*, knowing the same to have been stolen, shall be fined ... or imprisoned, or both." 62 Stat. 806, 18 U.S.C.A. § 2312 (emphasis added).

MOSKAL v. UNITED STATES

Supreme Court of the United States, 1990.
498 U.S. 103, 111 S.Ct. 461, 112 L.Ed.2d 449.

JUSTICE MARSHALL delivered the opinion of the Court.

The issue in this case is whether a person who knowingly procures genuine vehicle titles that incorporate fraudulently tendered odometer readings receives those titles "knowing [them] to have been *falsely made.*" 18 U.S.C. § 2314 (emphasis added)....

I

Petitioner Raymond Moskal participated in a "title-washing" scheme. Moskal's confederates purchased used cars in Pennsylvania, rolled back the cars' odometers, and altered their titles to reflect those lower mileage figures. The altered titles were then sent to an accomplice in Virginia, who submitted them to Virginia authorities. Those officials, unaware of the alterations, issued Virginia titles incorporating the false mileage figures. The "washed" titles were then sent back to Pennsylvania, where they were used in connection with car sales to unsuspecting buyers. Moskal played two roles in this scheme: He sent altered titles from Pennsylvania to Virginia; he received "washed" titles when they were returned.

The Government indicted and convicted Moskal under 18 U.S.C. § 2314 for receiving two washed titles, each recording a mileage figure that was 30,000 miles lower than the true number. Section 2314 imposes fines [of no more than $10,000] or imprisonment [of no more than ten years] on anyone who, "with unlawful or fraudulent intent, transports in interstate ... commerce any falsely made, forged, altered, or counterfeited securities ..., knowing the same to have been falsely made, forged, altered or counterfeited." [The statute defined "securities" to include any "valid ... motor vehicle title." 18 U.S.C. § 2311.] On appeal, Moskal maintained that the washed titles were nonetheless genuine and thus not "falsely made." The Court of Appeals disagreed, finding that "the purpose of the term 'falsely made' was to ... prohibit the fraudulent introduction into commerce of falsely made documents regardless of the precise method by which the introducer or his confederates effected their lack of authenticity." ...

Notwithstanding the narrowness of this issue, we granted certiorari to resolve a divergence of opinion among the Courts of Appeals.... *See* United States v. Sparrow, 635 F.2d 794 (CA10 1980) (en banc), *cert. denied,* 450 U.S. 1004 (1981) (washed automobile titles are not "falsely made" within the meaning of § 2314)....

II

... Moskal acknowledges that he could have been charged with violating [§ 2314] when he sent the Pennsylvania titles to Virginia, since those titles were "altered" within the meaning of § 2314. But he insists that he did not violate the provision in subsequently receiving the washed titles from Virginia because, although he was participating in a fraud (and thus no doubt had the requisite intent under § 2314), the washed titles themselves were not "falsely made." He asserts that when a title is issued by appropriate state authorities who do not know of its falsity, the title is "genuine" or valid as the state document it purports to be and therefore not "falsely made."

Whether a valid title that contains fraudulently tendered odometer readings may be a "falsely made" security for purposes of § 2314 presents a conventional issue of statutory construction, and we must therefore determine what scope Congress intended § 2314 to have. Moskal, however, suggests a shortcut in that inquiry. Because it is *possible* to read the statute as applying only to forged or counterfeited securities, and because *some* courts have so read it, Moskal suggests we should simply resolve the issue in his favor under the doctrine of lenity....

In our view, this argument misconstrues the doctrine. We have repeatedly "emphasized that the 'touchstone' of the rule of lenity 'is statutory ambiguity.'" Bifulco v. United States, 447 U.S. 381, 387 (1980), quoting Lewis v. United States, 445 U.S. 55, 65 (1980)....

Because the meaning of language is inherently contextual, we have declined to deem a statute "ambiguous" for purposes of lenity merely because it was *possible* to articulate a construction more narrow than that urged by the Government.... Nor have we deemed a division of judicial authority automatically sufficient to trigger lenity.... If that were sufficient, one court's unduly narrow reading of a criminal statute would become binding on all other courts, including this one. Instead, we have always reserved lenity for those situations in which a reasonable doubt persists about a statute's intended scope even *after* resort to "the language and structure, legislative history, and motivating policies" of the statute. *Bifulco v. United States, supra,* 447 U.S. at 387; *see also* United States v. Bass, 404 U.S. 336, 347 (1971) (court should rely on lenity only if, "[a]fter 'seiz[ing] every thing from which aid can be derived,'" it is "left with an ambiguous statute," quoting United States v. Fisher, 2 Cranch [6 U.S.] 358, 386 (1805) (Marshall, C.J.)). Examining these materials, we conclude that § 2314 unambiguously applies to Moskal's conduct.

A

"In determining the scope of a statute, we look first to its language," ... giving the "words used" their "ordinary meaning." ... We think that the words of § 2314 are broad enough, on their face, to encompass washed titles containing fraudulently tendered odometer readings. Such titles are "falsely made" in the sense that they are made to contain false, or incorrect, information.

Moskal resists this construction of the language on the ground that the state officials responsible for issuing the washed titles did not know that they were incorporating false odometer readings. We see little merit in this argument. As used in § 2314, "falsely made" refers to the character of the securities being transported. In our view, it is perfectly consistent with ordinary usage to speak of the security as *being* "falsely made" regardless of whether the party responsible for the physical production of the document *knew* that he was making a security in a manner that incorporates false information. Indeed, we find support for this construction in the nexus between the *actus reus* and *mens rea* elements of § 2314. Because liability under the statute depends on *transporting* the "falsely made" security with unlawful or fraudulent intent, there is no reason to infer a scienter requirement for the act of falsely making itself.

Short of construing "falsely made" in this way, we are at a loss to give *any* meaning to this phrase independent of the other terms in § 2314, such as "forged" or "counterfeited." By seeking to exclude from § 2314's scope any security that is "genuine" or valid, Moskal essentially equates "falsely made" with "forged" or "counterfeited." His construction therefore violates the established principle that a court should " 'give effect, if possible, to every clause and word of a statute.' " ...

Our conclusion that "falsely made" encompasses genuine documents containing false information is supported by Congress' purpose in enacting § 2314. Inspired by the proliferation of interstate schemes for passing counterfeit securities, see 84 Cong.Rec. 9412 (statement of Sen. O'Mahoney), Congress in 1939 added the clause pertaining to "falsely made, forged, altered or counterfeited securities" as an amendment to the National Stolen Property Act. 53 Stat. 1178. Our prior decisions have recognized Congress' "general intent" and "broad purpose" to curb the type of trafficking in fraudulent securities that often depends for its success on the exploitation of interstate commerce. In United States v. Sheridan, 329 U.S. 379 (1946), we explained that Congress enacted the relevant clause of § 2314 in order to "com[e] to the aid of the states in detecting and punishing criminals whose offenses are complete under state law, but who utilize the channels of interstate commerce to make a successful getaway and thus make the state's detecting and punitive processes impotent." ... This, we concluded, "was indeed one of the most effective ways of preventing further frauds." ...

We think that "title-washing" operations are a perfect example of the "further frauds" that Congress sought to halt in enacting § 2314. As Moskal concedes, his title-washing scheme is a clear instance of fraud involving securities. And as the facts of this case demonstrate, title washes involve precisely the sort of fraudulent activities that are dispersed among several States in order to elude state detection.

Moskal draws a different conclusion from this legislative history. Seizing upon the references to counterfeit securities, petitioner finds no evidence that "the 1939 amendment had anything at all to do with odometer rollback schemes." ... We think petitioner misconceives the inquiry into legislative purpose by failing to recognize that Congress sought to attack a category of fraud. At the time that Congress amended the National Stolen Property Act, counterfeited securities no doubt constituted (and may still constitute) the most prevalent form of such interstate fraud. The fact remains, however, that Congress did not limit the statute's reach to "counterfeit securities" but instead chose the broader phrase "falsely made, forged, altered, *or* counterfeited securities," which was consistent with its purpose to reach a class of frauds that exploited interstate commerce.

. . . .

Our precedents concerning § 2314 specifically reject constructions of the statute that limit it to *instances* of fraud rather than the *class* of fraud encompassed by its language. For example, in *United States v. Sheridan, supra,* the defendant cashed checks at a Michigan bank, drawn on a Missouri account, with a forged signature. The Court found that such conduct was proscribed by § 2314. In reaching that conclusion, the Court noted Congress' primary objective of reaching counterfeiters of corporate securities but nonetheless found that the statute covered check forgeries "done by 'little fellows' who perhaps were not the primary aim of the congressional fire." ... "Whether or not Congress had in mind primarily such small scale transactions as Sheridan's," we held, "his operation was covered literally and we think purposively. Had this not been intended, appropriate exception could easily have been made." ...

. . . .

To summarize our conclusions as to the meaning of "falsely made" in § 2314, we find both in the plain meaning of those words and in the legislative purpose underlying them ample reason to apply the law to a fraudulent scheme for washing vehicle titles.[25]

B

Petitioner contends that such a reading of § 2314 is nonetheless precluded by a further principle of statutory construction. "[W]here a federal criminal statute uses a common-law term of established meaning without otherwise defining it, the general practice is to give that term its common-law meaning." United States v. Turley, 352 U.S. 407, 411 (1957). Petitioner argues that, at the time Congress enacted the relevant clause of § 2314, the term "falsely made" had an established common-law meaning equivalent to forgery. As so defined, "falsely made" excluded authentic or genuine documents that were merely false in content.

---

25. Because of this conclusion, we have no trouble rejecting Moskal's suggestion that he did not have fair notice that his conduct could be prosecuted under § 2314. Moskal's contention that he was "entitled to rely" on one Court of Appeals decision holding that washed titles were not "falsely made" is wholly unpersuasive. See United States v. Rodgers, 466 U.S. 475, 484 (1984) (existence of conflicting decisions among courts of appeals does not support application of the doctrine of lenity where "review of th[e] issue by this Court and decision against the position of the [defendant are] reasonably foreseeable"). [Footnote by the Court.]

Petitioner maintains that Congress should be presumed to have adopted this common-law definition when it amended the National Stolen Property Act in 1939 and that § 2314 therefore should be deemed not to cover washed vehicle titles that merely contain false odometer readings. We disagree for two reasons.

First, Moskal has failed to demonstrate that there was, in fact, an "established" meaning of "falsely made" at common law. Rather, it appears that there were divergent views on this issue in American courts. Petitioner and respondent agree that many courts interpreted "falsely made" to exclude documents that were false only in content. The opinion in United States v. Wentworth, 11 F. 52 (CCNH 1882), typifies that view. There, the defendants were prosecuted for having "falsely made" affidavits that they submitted to obtain a pension. The defendants did sign the affidavits, but the facts recited therein were false. The court concluded that this would support a charge of perjury but not false making because "to falsely make an affidavit is one thing; to make a false affidavit is another." . . .

But the *Wentworth* view—that "falsely made" excluded documents "genuinely" issued by the person purporting to make them and false only in content—was not universal. For example, in United States v. Hartman, 65 F. 490 (ED Mo.1894), the defendant procured a "notary certificate" containing falsehoods. Finding that this conduct fell within the conduct proscribed by a statute barring certain falsely made, forged, altered, or counterfeited writings, the judge stated:

> "I cannot conceive how any significance can be given to the words 'falsely make' unless they shall be construed to mean the statements in a certificate which in fact are untrue. 'Falsely' means in opposition to the truth. 'Falsely makes' means to state in a certificate that which is not true. . . ." *Id.,* at 491.

Other common-law courts, accepting the equation of "falsely making" with "forgery," treated as "forged" otherwise genuine documents fraudulently procured from innocent makers. In State v. Shurtliff, 18 Me. 368 (1841), a landowner signed a deed conveying his farm under the misapprehension that the deed pertained to a different land parcel. Although this deed was "genuine" in the sense that the owner had signed it, the court held it was "falsely made" by the *grantee,* who had tendered this deed for the owner's signature instead of one previously agreed upon by the parties. . . . In concluding that the deed was falsely made, the court explained: "[I]t is not necessary, that the act [of falsely making] should be done, in whole or in part, by the hand of the party charged. It is sufficient if he cause or procure it to be done." . . . *See also* Annot., Genuine Making of Instrument for Purpose of Defrauding as Constituting Forgery, 41 A.L.R. 229, 247 (1926).

This plurality of definitions of "falsely made" substantially undermines Moskal's reliance on the "common-law meaning" principle. That rule of construction, after all, presumes simply that Congress accepted the *one* meaning for an undefined statutory term that prevailed at common law. Where, however, no fixed usage existed at common law, we think it more appropriate to inquire which of the common-law readings of the term best accords with the overall purposes of the statute rather than to simply assume, for example, that Congress adopted the reading that was followed by the largest number of common-law courts....

Our second reason for rejecting Moskal's reliance on the "common-law meaning" rule is that, as this Court has previously recognized, Congress' general purpose in enacting a law may prevail over this rule of statutory construction....

... The position of those common-law courts that defined "falsely made" to exclude documents that are false only in content does not accord with Congress' broad purpose in enacting § 2314—namely, to criminalize trafficking in fraudulent securities that exploits interstate commerce. We conclude, then, that it is far more likely that Congress adopted the common-law view of "falsely made" that encompasses "genuine" documents that are false in content.

. . . .

For all of the foregoing reasons, the decision of the Court of Appeals is affirmed.

Justice Souter took no part in the consideration or decision of this case.

Justice Scalia, with whom Justice O'Connor and Justice Kennedy join, dissenting.

Today's opinion succeeds in its stated objective of "resolv[ing] a divergence of opinion among the Courts of Appeals" ... regarding the application of 18 U.S.C. § 2314. It does that, however, in a manner that so undermines generally applicable principles of statutory construction that I fear the confusion it produces will far exceed the confusion it has removed.

I

The Court's decision rests ultimately upon the proposition that, pursuant to "ordinary meaning," a "falsely made" document includes a document which is genuinely what it purports to be, but which contains information that the maker knows to be false, or even information that the maker does not know to be false but that someone who causes him to insert it knows to be false. It seems to me that such a meaning is quite *extra*-ordinary. Surely the adverb preceding the word "made" naturally refers to the manner of making, rather than to the nature of the product made. An inexpensively made painting is not the same as an inexpensive painting. A forged memorandum is "falsely made"; a memorandum that contains erroneous information is simply "false."

One would not expect general-usage dictionaries to have a separate entry for "falsely made," but some of them do use precisely the phrase "to make falsely" to define "forged." *See, e.g.,* Webster's New International Dictionary 990 (2d ed. (1945); Webster's Third New International

Dictionary 891 (1961). The Court seeks to make its interpretation plausible by the following locution: "Such titles are 'falsely made' in the sense that they are made to contain false, or incorrect, information." ... This sort of word-play can transform virtually anything into "falsely made." Thus: "The building was falsely made in the sense that it was made to contain a false entrance." This is a far cry from "ordinary meaning."

That "falsely made" refers to the manner of making is also evident from the fifth clause of § 2314, which forbids the interstate transportation of "any tool, implement, or thing used or fitted to be used in falsely making, forging, altering, or counterfeiting any security or tax stamps." This obviously refers to the tools of counterfeiting, and not to the tools of misrepresentation.

The Court maintains, however, that giving "falsely made" what I consider to be its ordinary meaning would render the term superfluous, offending the principle of construction that if possible each word should be given some effect.... The principle is sound, but its limitation ("if possible") must be observed. It should not be used to distort ordinary meaning. Nor should it be applied to the obvious instances of iteration to which lawyers, alas, are particularly addicted—such as "give, grant, bargain, sell, and convey," "aver and affirm," "rest, residue, and remainder," or "right, title, and interest." *See generally* B. Garner, A Dictionary of Modern Legal Usage 197–200 (1987). The phrase at issue here, "falsely made, forged, altered, or counterfeited," is, in one respect at least, uncontestedly of that sort. As the United States conceded at oral argument, and as any dictionary will confirm, "forged" and "counterfeited" mean the same thing.... Since iteration is obviously afoot in the relevant passage, there is no justification for extruding an unnatural meaning out of "falsely made" simply in order to avoid iteration. The entire phrase "falsely made, forged, altered, or counterfeited" is self-evidently not a listing of differing and precisely calibrated terms, but a collection of near synonyms which describes the product of the general crime of forgery.

. . . .

V

I feel constrained to mention, though it is surely superfluous for decision of the present case, the so-called rule of lenity—the venerable principle that "before a man can be punished as a criminal under the federal law his case must be plainly and unmistakably within the provisions of some statute." ... As JUSTICE MARSHALL explained some years ago:

"This principle is founded on two policies that have long been part of our tradition. First, a 'fair warning should be given to the world in language that the common world will understand, of what the law intends to do if a certain line is passed. To make the warning fair, so far as possible the line should be clear.' McBoyle v. United States,

283 U.S. 25, 27 (1931) (Holmes, J.) ... Second, because of the seriousness of criminal penalties, and because criminal punishment usually represents the moral condemnation of the community, legislatures and not courts should define criminal activity. This policy embodies 'the instinctive distaste against men languishing in prison unless the lawmaker has clearly said they should.' H. Friendly, Mr. Justice Frankfurter and The Reading of Statutes, in Benchmarks, 196, 209 (1967)." United States v. Bass, 404 U.S. 336, 347–349 (1971).

"Falsely made, forged, altered, or counterfeited" had a plain meaning in 1939 .... If the rule of lenity means anything, it means that the Court ought not do what it does today: use an ill-defined general purpose to override an unquestionably clear term of art, and (to make matters worse) give the words a meaning that even one unfamiliar with the term of art would not imagine. The temptation to stretch the law to fit the evil is an ancient one, and it must be resisted. As Chief Justice Marshall wrote:

> "The case must be a strong one indeed, which would justify a Court in departing from the plain meaning of words, especially in a penal act, in search of an intention which the words themselves did not suggest. To determine that a case is within the intention of a statute, its language must authorize us to say so. It would be dangerous, indeed, to carry the principle that a case which is within the reason or mischief of a statute, is within its provisions, so far as to punish a crime not enumerated in the statute, because it is of equal atrocity, or of kindred character, with those which are enumerated." United States v. Wiltberger, 5 Wheat. 76, 96, 5 L.Ed. 37 (1820) [(holding that a federal criminal statute which prohibited murder "upon the high seas, or in any river," but which prohibited manslaughter only "upon the high seas," did not apply to the manslaughter of a seaman on board a ship in the mouth of a river)].

For the foregoing reasons, I respectfully dissent.[26]

G. SUBSTANTIVE CANONS OF STATUTORY CONSTRUCTION: CIVIL LAW

In this section, the focus will shift from substantive canons governing criminal law to substantive canons governing civil law. When a court construes a civil statute, it is common for the court to apply an old English maxim that "statutes in derogation of the common law will not be extended" by the judiciary. But that canon can be countered by an

---

26. For a discussion of Justice Scalia's invocation of the "rule of lenity" as part of his "plain meaning" approach to statutory interpretation, see S. Newland, "The Mercy of Scalia: Statutory Construction and the Rule of Lenity," 29 Harvard Civil Rights–Civil Liberties Law Review 197 (1994) (Justice Scalia applies the rule of lenity without first referring to legislative history; "Justice Scalia's mercy therefore lies in his willingness to employ the rule of lenity more liberally to resolve statutory ambiguity in favor of a criminal defendant.")

equally old English maxim that "such acts will be liberally construed if their nature is remedial." K. Llewellyn, "Remarks on the Theory of Appellate Decision and the Rules or Canons About How Statutes Are to be Construed," 3 Vanderbilt Law Review 395, 401–02 (1950).

The cases in this section address the question of whether a survivor of a decedent may bring an action for "wrongful death" and, if so, what damages are recoverable. Because the common law did not recognize such a cause of action (see *Higgins v. Butcher, supra,* at Chapter II.B.3.), claims for wrongful death in both England and the United States are predominantly statutory causes of action. The first wrongful death statute was adopted in England in the mid-nineteenth century, and it was known as Lord Campbell's Act. The Act allowed the jury to award "[d]amages as they may think proportioned to the injury resulting from such death." Lord Campbell's Act, 1846, 9 & 10 Vict., ch. 93. The action lay where the deceased himself could have sued had he survived with regard to the statute of limitations. Despite the breadth of the text of the Act, the English courts construed the statute narrowly to say that wrongful death damages must be based on "pecuniary loss." When legislatures in the United States passed wrongful death statutes modeled upon Lord Campbell's Act in the 1800's and in the early 1900's, courts construing those statutes often imposed the English "pecuniary loss" limitation. In modern times, those same courts have been revisiting the question of whether such a narrow interpretation of wrongful death statutes is appropriate.

VAN BEECK v. SABINE TOWING CO.

Supreme Court of the United States, 1937.
300 U.S. 342, 57 S.Ct. 452, 81 L.Ed. 685.

Mr. Justice Cardozo delivered the opinion of the Court.

The Merchant Marine Act of 1920[27] (. . . 46 U.S.C. § 688 . . .) gives a cause of action for damages to the personal representative of a seaman who has suffered death in the course of his employment by reason of his employer's negligence. The question is whether the liability abates where the beneficiary of the cause of action, in this case the mother of the seaman, dies during the pendency of a suit in her behalf.

27. The Merchant Marine Act of 1920 authorized negligence actions by seamen against their employers and it provided in relevant part that "in the case of the death of any seaman as a result of personal injury [in the course of employment] the personal representative of such seaman may maintain an action for damages at law with the right of trial by jury, and in such action all statutes of the United States conferring or regulating the right of action for death in the case of railway employees shall be applicable." The Federal Employer's Liability Act (45 U.S.C. § 51), regulating the right of action for death in the case of railway em- ployees, provided in relevant part that a common carrier engaged in interstate commerce "shall be liable" in damages "to any person suffering injury while he is employed by such carrier in such commerce," or, "in the case of the death of such employee, to his or her personal representative, for the benefit of the surviving widow or husband and children of such employee; and, if none, then of such employee's parents; and, if none, then of the next of kin dependent upon such employee, for such injury or death [resulting from the employer's negligence]."

[A tugboat sank in the Gulf of Mexico just off the coast of Texas, causing the death of all on board, including the second mate, Edward C. Van Beeck, who died unmarried, leaving a mother and several brothers. The mother was the sole beneficiary of the statutory wrongful death cause of action. She died in July, 1931, and a brother of the deceased was appointed as her successor. A Commissioner recommended damages in the sum of $700 for the losses that the mother had suffered up until the time of her death, but the trial court dismissed the claim on the ground that the wrongful death action abated at her death. The intermediate appellate court affirmed, and the Supreme Court granted certiorari "[t]o settle the meaning of an important act of Congress."]

The statutory cause of action to recover damages for death ushered in a new policy and broke with old traditions. Its meaning is likely to be misread if shreds of the discarded policy are treated as still clinging to it and narrowing its scope. The case of *Higgins v. Butcher*[28] ... is the starting point of the rule, long accepted in our law, though at times with mutterings of disapproval, that, in an action of tort, damages are not recoverable by any one [including a representative of the decedent's estate] for the death of a human being.... The explanation has been found at times in the common-law notion that trespass as a civil wrong is drowned in a felony.[29] As to the adequacy of this explanation, grave doubt has been expressed.[30] None the less, the rule as to felony merger seems to have coalesced, even if in a confused way, with the rule as to abatement,[31] and the effect of the two in combination was to fasten upon the law a doctrine which it took a series of statutes to dislodge.

The adoption of Lord Campbell's Act in 1846 (9 & 10 Vict. c. 93), giving an action to the executor for the use of wife, husband, parent, or child, marks the dawn of a new era. In this country, statutes substantially the same in tenor followed in quick succession in one state after another, till today there is not a state of the union in which a remedy is lacking. Congress joined in the procession, first with the Employers' Liability Act for railway employees (45 U.S.C. §§ 51–59), next with the Merchant Marine Act of 1920 for seamen and their survivors (46 U.S.C. § 688), and again with an act of the same year (... 46 U.S.C. §§ 761,

28. In Higgins v. Butcher, 80 Eng. Rep. 61 (K.B. 1606), *supra*, at Chapter II.B.3., the court rejected a husband's claim for his wife's wrongful death because the offense had become "an offense of the crown, being converted into a felony, and that drowns the particular offense, and private wrong ...."

29. Admiralty Commissioners v. S. S. Amerika, (1917) A.C. 38, 43, 47, 60. [Footnote by the Court.] [In *S.S. Amerika*, a master sued for the wrongful death of his servants in an admiralty action. The House of Lords refused to recognize a common law (as opposed to a statutory) wrongful death action. It reaffirmed the holding in Higgins v. Butcher, 80 Eng. Rep. 61 (K.B. 1606) and

rested its rationale on the felony-merger doctrine. For an explanation of the felony-merger doctrine, see D.J. Seipp, "The Distinction Between Crime and Tort in the Early Common Law," 76 Boston University Law Review 59 (1996), describing the differences in medieval England between a "writ of trespass," an "appeal of felony" (brought by a private prosecutor), and an "indictment of felony" (brought by a public prosecutor).]

30. Holdsworth, [*A History of English Law*], Vol. 3, Appendix VIII; also Vol. 3, pp. 332–336.... [Footnote by the Court.]

31. *Higgins v. Butcher, supra; Admiralty Commissioners v. S. S. Amerika, supra* .... [Footnote by the Court.]

762), not limited to seamen, which states the legal consequences of death upon the high seas.

. . . The statutes thus referred to as a standard display a double aspect. . . . One is for the wrong to the injured person, and is confined to his personal loss and suffering before he died, while the other is for the wrong to the beneficiaries, and is confined to their pecuniary loss through his death. It is loss of this last order, and no other, that is the subject of the present suit. So far as the record shows, the seaman died at once upon the sinking of the vessel. . . .

Viewing the cause of action as one to compensate a mother for the pecuniary loss caused to her by the negligent killing of her son, we think the mother's death does not abate the suit, but that the administrator may continue it, for the recovery of her loss up to the moment of her death, though not for anything thereafter, the damages when collected to be paid to her estate. Such is the rule in many of the state courts in which like statutes are in force. . . . When we remember that under the death statutes an independent cause of action is created in favor of the beneficiaries for their pecuniary damages, the conclusion is not difficult that the cause of action once accrued is not divested or extinguished by the death of one or more of the beneficiaries thereafter, but survives, like a cause of action for injury to a property right or interest, to the extent that the estate of the deceased beneficiary is proved to be impaired. . . .

. . . .

Death statutes have their roots in dissatisfaction with the archaisms of the law which have been traced to their origin in the course of this opinion. It would be a misfortune if a narrow or grudging process of construction were to exemplify and perpetuate the very evils to be remedied. There are times when uncertain words are to be wrought into consistency and unity with a legislative policy which is itself a source of law, a new generative impulse transmitted to the legal system. "The Legislature has the power to decide what the policy of the law shall be, and if it has intimated its will, however indirectly, that will should be recognized and obeyed."[32] Its intimation is clear enough in the statutes now before us that their effects shall not be stifled, without the warrant of clear necessity, by the perpetuation of a policy which now has had its day.

The decree should be reversed and the cause remanded for further proceedings in accord with this opinion.

MOBIL OIL CORP. v. HIGGINBOTHAM

Supreme Court of the United States, 1978.
436 U.S. 618, 98 S.Ct. 2010, 56 L.Ed.2d 581.

MR. JUSTICE STEVENS delivered the opinion of the Court.

This case involves death on the high seas. . . .

Petitioner used a helicopter in connection with its oil drilling operations in the Gulf of Mexico about 100 miles from the Louisiana shore. On

---

32. Per Holmes, Circuit Justice, in Johnson v. United States (C.C.A.) 163 F. 30, 32. . . . [Footnote by the Court.]

August 15, 1967, the helicopter crashed outside Louisiana's territorial waters, killing the pilot and three passengers. In a suit brought by the passengers' widows, in their representative capacities, the District Court accepted admiralty jurisdiction [on the ground that the helicopter was the functional equivalent of a crewboat] and found that the deaths were caused by petitioner's negligence. The court awarded damages equal to the pecuniary losses suffered by the families of two passengers.[33] Although the court valued the two families' loss of society at $100,000 and $155,000, it held that the law did not authorize recovery for this loss.[34] The Court of Appeals reversed, holding that the plaintiffs were entitled to claim damages for loss of society. We granted certiorari limited to this issue. . . .

I

In 1877, the steamer *Harrisburg* collided with a schooner in Massachusetts coastal waters. The schooner sank, and its first officer drowned. Some five years later, his widow brought a wrongful-death action against the *Harrisburg*. This Court held that admiralty afforded no remedy for wrongful death in the absence of an applicable state or federal statute. *The Harrisburg*, 119 U.S. 199 [(1886)]. . . .

In 1920, Congress repudiated the rule of *The Harrisburg* for maritime deaths occurring beyond the territorial waters of any State. It passed the Death on the High Seas Act (hereinafter sometimes DOHSA),[35] creating a remedy in admiralty for wrongful deaths more than three miles from shore. This Act limits the class of beneficiaries to the decedent's "wife, husband, parent, child, or dependent relative," establishes a two-year period of limitations, allows suits filed by the victim to continue as wrongful-death actions if the victim dies of his injuries while suit is pending, and provides that contributory negligence will not bar recovery. With respect to damages, the statute declares: "The recovery . . . shall be a fair and just compensation for the pecuniary loss sustained by the persons for whose benefit the suit is brought. . . ."

In the half century between 1920 and 1970, deaths on the high seas gave rise to federal suits under DOHSA, while those in territorial waters were largely governed by state wrongful-death statutes. . . .

. . . .

33. 360 F.Supp. 1140 (W.D.La.1973). One family received $362,297, the other $163,400. . . . [Footnote by the Court.]

34. The former figure [of $362,297] included $50,000 for one widow and $50,000 for her only daughter. The latter figure [of $163,400] included $25,000 for the second widow and for each of two minor children, as well as $20,000 for each of four older children. 360 F.Supp., at 1144–1148. [Footnote by the Court.]

35. 41 Stat. 537, 46 U.S.C. § 761 et seq. [Footnote by the Court.]

II

. . . .

As the divergence of views among the States discloses, there are valid arguments both for and against allowing recovery for loss of society. Courts denying recovery cite two reasons: (1) that the loss is "not capable of measurement by any material or pecuniary standard," and (2) that an award for the loss "would obviously include elements of passion, sympathy and similar matters of improper character." 1 S. Speiser, Recovery for Wrongful Death, § 3:49 (2d ed. 1975). Courts allowing the award counter: (1) that the loss is real, however intangible it may be, and (2) that problems of measurement should not justify denying all relief. . . .

In this case, however, we need not pause to evaluate the opposing policy arguments. Congress has struck the balance for us. It has limited survivors to recovery of their pecuniary losses. Respondents argue that Congress does not have the last word on this issue—that admiralty courts have traditionally undertaken to supplement maritime statutes and that such a step is necessary in this case to preserve the uniformity of maritime law. Neither argument is decisive.

. . . It is true that the measure of damages in coastal waters will differ from that on the high seas, but even if this difference proves significant, a desire for uniformity cannot override the statute.

We realize that, because Congress has never enacted a comprehensive maritime code, admiralty courts have often been called upon to supplement maritime statutes. The Death on the High Seas Act, however, announces Congress' considered judgment on such issues as the beneficiaries, the limitations period, contributory negligence, survival, and damages. . . . The Act does not address every issue of wrongful-death law, . . . but when it does speak directly to a question, the courts are not free to "supplement" Congress' answer so thoroughly that the Act becomes meaningless.

. . . Congress did not limit DOHSA beneficiaries to recovery of their pecuniary losses in order to encourage the creation of nonpecuniary supplements. . . . There is a basic difference between filling a gap left by Congress' silence and rewriting rules that Congress has affirmatively and specifically enacted. In the area covered by the statute, it would be no more appropriate to prescribe a different measure of damages than to prescribe a different statute of limitations, or a different class of beneficiaries. Perhaps the wisdom we possess today would enable us to do a better job of repudiating *The Harrisburg* than Congress did in 1920, but even if that be true, we have no authority to substitute our views for those expressed by Congress in a duly enacted statute.

Accordingly, the judgment of the Court of Appeals is reversed, and the case is remanded for further proceedings consistent with this opinion.

It is so ordered.

Mr. Justice Brennan took no part in the consideration or decision of this case.

Mr. Justice Marshall, with whom Mr. Justice Blackmun joins, dissenting.

. . . .

... By enacting DOHSA, Congress sought to "bring our maritime law into line with the laws of those enlightened nations which confer a right of action for death at sea." S.Rep.No.216, 66th Cong., 1st Sess., 4 (1919); H.R.Rep.No.674, 66th Cong., 2d Sess., 4 (1920)....

The Court today uses this ameliorative, remedial statute as the foundation of a decision denying a remedy. It purports to find, in the section of DOHSA that provides for "fair and just compensation for the pecuniary loss sustained," 46 U.S.C. § 762, a "considered judgment" by Congress that recovery must be limited to pecuniary loss.... Nothing in this section, however, states that recovery must be so limited; certainly Congress was principally concerned, not with limiting recovery, but with ensuring that those suing under DOHSA were able to recover at least their pecuniary loss. As Representative Montague stated in the House debate, the Act was meant to provide a cause of action "in cases where there is now no remedy." 59 Cong.Rec. 4486 (1920)....

Although recognizing that DOHSA was a response to *The Harrisburg*, ... the majority opinion otherwise ignores the legislative history of the Act. The fundamental premise of the opinion—that Congress meant to "[limit] survivors to recovery of their pecuniary losses" ...—is simply assumed....

. . . .

Accordingly, I dissent.

CLYMER v. WEBSTER

Supreme Court of Vermont, 1991.
156 Vt. 614, 596 A.2d 905.

Before Gibson, Dooley and Morse, JJ. and Barney, C.J. (Ret.) and Springer, District Judge (Ret.), Specially Assigned.

Gibson, Justice.

This appeal concerns the remedies available to the parents and the administrator of the estate of Jane Clymer, an adult decedent, in an action against two commercial vendors that served alcohol to a patron who thereafter drove his car and struck and killed the decedent....

I.

On September 14, 1985, after being served alcohol at The Rotisserie Restaurant and at Wesson's Diner, Theron Webster drove his car and struck Jane Clymer, an eighteen-year-old college student, while she was pushing her bicycle along the side of Route 116 in the town of Williston. Ms. Clymer suffered massive brain damage, but was kept alive until her parents arrived the next morning, when she was pronounced brain dead and allowed to expire. Theron Webster was charged with and pled guilty to DWI-death resulting.

In a complaint filed in July of 1986, plaintiffs alleged negligence against Theron Webster, and a Dram Shop Act violation against the commercial vendors and certain of the vendors' employees, seeking compensatory damages for medical and funeral expenses, ... loss of companionship, ... and loss of means of support.... Plaintiffs eventually settled with Theron Webster, and the court dismissed him from the action .... After several rulings that limited the damages recoverable by plaintiffs "to medical and funeral expenses and lost services and guidance," the court dismissed the action with prejudice and entered judgment for the defendants on the ground that those damages did not exceed the $120,000 plaintiffs had already recovered from the negligent driver.

On appeal, plaintiffs argue that the trial court erred by denying their claims for (1) damages for deprivation of love, affection and society (loss of companionship) under ... the Wrongful Death Act [WDA] ....

. . . .

III.

The WDA allows the decedent's personal representative to recover "such damages as are just, with reference to the pecuniary injuries resulting from such death," on behalf of decedent's spouse and next of kin. 14 V.S.A. § 1492(b).[36] A 1976 amendment to § 1492(b) added a provision that "where the decedent is a minor child, the term pecuniary injuries shall also include the loss of love and companionship of the child and for destruction of the parent-child relationship in such amount as under all the circumstances of the case, may be just." Because the WDA was "designed to allay the harsh common law rule denying liability due to the death of the victim," it is remedial in nature and must be construed liberally....

A.

The question confronting us herein is whether the WDA permits a parent to recover damages for the loss of companionship resulting from the death of an adult child. The 1976 amendment recognizes a right of recovery for loss-of-companionship damages when the decedent is a minor child, but it makes no mention of adult children. Although we cannot be certain as to the reason for the omission, the legislative history of the amendment suggests that the Legislature was more concerned with clarifying the scope of damages available to the relatives of minor decedents than limiting the damages available upon the death

---

36. The Survival Statutes, 14 V.S.A. §§ 1451–1453, allow a decedent's estate to recover for injuries sustained by the decedent prior to his or her death ...; the decedent's death need not result from the injury as with wrongful death actions. [Footnote by the court.]

of an adult decedent. See H. 58 (1975 Vt., Bien.Sess.) (sponsor's statement of purpose: "the purpose of this bill [is] to provide guidelines for the compensation to parents for the death of a minor child"); *cf.* Caledonian Record Publishing Co. v. Walton, 154 Vt. 15, 25, 573 A.2d 296, 302 (1990) (a proviso may be added to an existing statute to exclude a possible misunderstanding of its extent).

In any case, the amendment neither expressly nor implicitly precludes a plaintiff who is seeking compensation for the death of an adult child from showing that, under the circumstances of a particular case, he or she is entitled to loss-of-companionship damages. In accordance with our analysis hereinafter, we do not believe the statute should be narrowly construed to foreclose the recovery of loss-of-companionship damages for parents of decedent adult children. As previously noted, the WDA is to be liberally construed. The negative inference that defendants would have us adopt—that loss-of-companionship damages are not available to a parent of a deceased adult child—does not rise to the level of "plain meaning" so as to require us to hold otherwise, and we decline to do so. *Cf.* McAllister v. AVEMCO Ins. Co., 148 Vt. 110, 112, 528 A.2d 758, 759 (1987) (Court will expand plain meaning of statute by implication only when necessary to make statute effective).

At first glance, our rules of statutory construction seem to work in favor of defendants. For instance, normally "we must presume that all language is inserted in a statute advisedly" . . .; thus, one might argue that permitting pecuniary damages for the death of both a minor and an adult child, in effect, interprets the amendment as if the word "minor" were not there. Moreover, the use of the word "also" in the amendment evidences a recognition that pecuniary injuries did not formerly include what is bestowed by the amendment. . . . Perhaps defendants' strongest argument is summed up in the Latin phrase "*expressio unius est exclusio alterius*"—the expression of one thing is the exclusion of another. . . . Pursuant to this maxim, the inclusion of the term "a minor child" in the amendment evidences an intention to exclude an adult child. . . .

On the other hand, such canons are routinely discarded when they do not further a statute's remedial purposes. See Herman & MacLean v. Huddleston, 459 U.S. 375, 387 n.23 (1983); *see also* Hardesty v. Andro Corp., 555 P.2d 1030, 1036 (Okla.1976) (*expressio unius* maxim is "to be applied with great caution, is not of universal application, and is not conclusive as to the meaning of a statute"); *cf.* State v. Baldwin, 140 Vt. 501, 511, 438 A.2d 1135, 1140 (1981) ("Rules of construction are not laws, hard and inflexible, which *must* be applied in a given situation simply because it is possible to do so."). As noted, the Legislature passed the 1976 amendment, not to limit the damages available to the relatives of adult decedents, but rather to further the remedial purposes of the WDA by developing the definition of pecuniary injuries.

By 1976, in Vermont, as elsewhere, the case law concerning the nature and extent of pecuniary loss available under the WDA was in a state of gradual intermittent development. Although no Vermont case had held that relational damages available for the death of a parent or spouse were also available for the death of a child, a parent could recover any reasonable "financial loss which the evidence shows will probably be caused by the death." It had already long been established that pecuniary loss was not restricted to loss of services, see Lazelle v. Town of Newfane, 70 Vt. 440, 445, 41 A. 511, 512 (1898) [action by adult son for wrongful death of his mother in which the plaintiff sought to recover for pecuniary losses above and beyond the loss of service which his mother had provided to his family while she was living with them] (pecuniary injury includes lost "intellectual and moral training and proper nurture of a child") [quoting from Tilley v. Hudson River Railroad Co., 24 N.Y. 471, 86 Am. Dec. 297 (1862) (action by minor child for death of minor child's mother)], and that damages resulting from a child's death need not be restricted to damages accruing during the decedent's minority. D'Angelo v. Rutland Ry. Light & Power Co., 100 Vt. 135, 137–39, 135 A. 598, 599 (1927).

We believe that rather than intending to restrict the development of case law recognizing that pecuniary loss is more than loss of services, the 1976 amendment intended to further that development by ensuring that such damages would be available for the death of a minor child. Because the type of damages available to adult decedents is not essential to the principal remedial purpose of the amendment, we shall not adopt the negative implication of the amendment argued by the defendants. The amendment does not expressly restrict the damages available under the WDA, which must be construed with its remedial purposes in mind. The following statement by Justice Cardozo, though made in a different factual setting, is equally relevant here:

> Death statutes have their roots in dissatisfaction with the archaisms of the law.... It would be a misfortune if a narrow or grudging process of construction were to exemplify and perpetuate the very evils to be remedied. Van Beeck v. Sabine Towing Co., 300 U.S. 342, 350–51 (1937).

Having concluded that the 1976 amendment did not foreclose an award of loss-of-companionship damages to relatives of adult decedents, we now consider whether such damages constitute "pecuniary injury."

At common law, despite the fact that the courts allowed recovery for wrongful injury, a civil action for wrongful death was not permitted.... Lord Campbell's Act, the predecessor of the American wrongful death acts, was adopted in England in the mid-nineteenth century to correct this anomaly. The act allowed the jury to award "Damages as they may think proportioned to the Injury resulting from such Death." Lord Campbell's Act, 1846, 9 & 10 Vict., ch. 93. The English courts held, however, that damages under the act must be based on pecuniary loss—a limitation imposed in many of the American wrongful death statutes, including Vermont's....

Many early cases, reflecting nineteenth-century social conditions when children were valued largely for their capacity to contribute to the family income, resulted in minimal awards representing the monetary loss occasioned by the parents' deprivation of their child's services. *See, e.g.*, Allen v. Moore, 109 Vt. 405, 409, 199 A. 257, 258 (1938) ($200 verdict for wrongful death of 17–year-old daughter not grossly inadequate). Nonetheless, early on, this Court approvingly cited language stating that pecuniary damages should include " 'all pecuniary loss of every kind which the circumstances of the particular case establish with reasonable certainty will be suffered by the beneficiary of the statute in the future.' " *D'Angelo*, 100 Vt. at 138, 135 A. at 599 (quoting Bond v. United R.R., 159 Cal. 270, 277, 113 P. 366, 369 (1911)). Further, as in most jurisdictions, this Court did not always construe the term "pecuniary loss" in its strictest sense. *See, e.g.*, *Lazelle*, 70 Vt. at 445, 41 A. at 512 (citing with approval cases that allowed damages for a child's loss of intellectual and moral training and proper nurture, as well as a widow's loss of her husband's care and protection).

By the early 1960s, some courts were rejecting the child-labor measure of pecuniary loss,[37] and expanding its scope to include loss of companionship. *See, e.g.*, Wycko v. Gnodtke, 361 Mich. 331, 340, 105 N.W.2d 118, 122–23 (1960) (the human companionship between individual family members "has a definite, substantial, and ascertainable pecuniary value") .... In recent years, a clear majority of jurisdictions with statutes limiting wrongful death recovery to pecuniary loss have expanded the scope of such loss to encompass loss of companionship of a child. *See, e.g.*, Bullard v. Barnes, 102 Ill.2d 505, 512, 515, 82 Ill.Dec. 448, 452, 454, 468 N.E.2d 1228, 1232, 1234 (1984); Sanchez v. Schindler, 651 S.W.2d 249, 252–53 (Tex. 1983). Further, many courts have refused to limit recovery for loss of companionship to situations where the decedent is a minor child. *See, e.g.*, Grandstaff v. City of Borger, 767 F.2d 161, 172 (5th Cir. 1985) (Texas law allows parents to recover for loss of companionship, and no distinction is made based on whether the decedent is an adult or a minor child); ... Ballweg v. City of Springfield, 114 Ill.2d 107, 120, 102 Ill.Dec. 360, 366, 499 N.E.2d 1373, 1379 (1986) (presumption of loss of society pertains to cases where decedent is adult child) ....

We now hold that the loss of the comfort and companionship of an adult child is a real, direct and personal loss that can be measured in pecuniary terms. Children have an intrinsic value to their parents regardless of who is supporting whom at the time of death. Whether the decedent child is an adult or a minor, society recognizes the destruction of the parents' investment in affection, guidance, security and love....

In some cases, the close, familial ties that unite a minor child with his or her parents may dissipate as the child becomes an adult. Nonetheless, the WDA does not preclude the parents of an adult child from showing that the death of their child did in fact injure them by depriving them of the society of that child. Every case must stand upon its own

---

37. Under this approach, pecuniary loss consisted of the financial burden upon the parents that resulted from loss of the child's services. [Footnote by the court.]

facts and circumstances. In determining whether and what amount of damages are appropriate for loss of companionship, the court or jury should consider the physical, emotional, and psychological relationship between the parents and the child. Accordingly, among other things, the factfinder should examine the living arrangements of the parties, the harmony of family relations, and the commonality of interests and activities.... Prior cases contrary to our holding herein are overruled.

. . . .

Reversed and remanded.

HILL v. CITY OF GERMANTOWN

Supreme Court of Tennessee, 2000.
31 S.W.3d 234.

HOLDER, J., delivered the opinion of the court, in which ANDERSON, C.J., and BIRCH and BARKER, JJ., joined.

We granted this appeal to determine ... whether Jordan v. Baptist Three Rivers Hosp., 984 S.W.2d 593 (Tenn.1999) applies retroactively to this case to permit loss of consortium damages to be awarded to the plaintiffs....

BACKGROUND

. . . .

[The plaintiffs were two men who had been married to two women who were killed in an automobile accident in 1995 arising out of a high-speed police chase. The plaintiffs sued the City of Germantown for failing to adequately train the newly-hired police officer who had conducted the chase. In a bench trial, the court found for the plaintiffs and assessed pecuniary damages at $401,249.32 and $621,071.46, refusing to award damages for loss of consortium. The plaintiffs each recovered the maximum amount permitted by the Governmental Tort Liability Act of $130,000 per claimant.]

... The Court of Appeals affirmed the trial court's rulings in all respects. It held ... that at the time Plaintiffs' causes of actions accrued, loss of consortium damages were unavailable in Tennessee in wrongful death actions. In so holding, the Court of Appeals held that our decision in Jordan v. Baptist Three Rivers Hosp., 984 S.W.2d 593 (Tenn.1999), allowing such damages in wrongful death actions, could not be applied retroactively....

ANALYSIS

. . . .

II. LOSS OF CONSORTIUM

Plaintiffs contend that the trial court erred in failing to award damages for loss of consortium.... Defendants claim that Plaintiffs received the maximum allowable award under the GTLA and are therefore precluded from further recovery, rendering any claim for consortium moot.

Plaintiffs claim damages under the Tennessee wrongful death statute. We thoroughly discussed the nature of Tennessee's wrongful death damages statute, Tenn.Code Ann. § 20–5–113, in Jordan v. Baptist Three Rivers Hosp., 984 S.W.2d 593 (Tenn.1999)....

... In *Jordan*, we held that loss of consortium damages were recoverable by the decedent's family as part of the pecuniary value of the decedent's life.

Prior to *Jordan*, however, Tennessee case law prohibited consortium damages in wrongful death suits.... The cause of action in this case arose on April 11, 1995, the date of the accident, almost four years before *Jordan* was released. Accordingly, we must determine if *Jordan* should be applied retroactively.

Jordan involved the overruling of prior judicial construction of a statute. In civil cases, judicial decisions overruling prior cases generally are given retrospective effect. *See, e.g.,* Perez v. McConkey, 872 S.W.2d 897, 906 (Tenn.1994) (applying abolition of assumption of the risk doctrine retroactively) .... Retrospective effect will be "denied only if such an application would work a hardship upon those who have justifiably relied upon the old precedent." Marshall v. Marshall, 670 S.W.2d 213, 215 (Tenn.1984) ....

Nevertheless, we expressly held in Blank v. Olsen, 662 S.W.2d 324 (Tenn.1983), that "in the absence of ... an expressed intent [to make it retroactive,] the rule is ... that the decision overruling a *judicial construction of a statute* will not be given retroactive effect." *Id.* at 325 (emphasis added).... We cited with approval authority from other jurisdictions that had held "a judicial interpretation of a statute becomes a part of the statute itself" and that "[a] change in the judicial view of the law by a subsequent decision could not amount to more than a change in the law by legislation, and, of course, could act prospectively only....

Recent unpublished decisions of the Court of Appeals have declined to apply *Jordan* retroactively. Each of these holdings was based on a correct interpretation and application of *Blank* and turned largely on the fact that we included no language in *Jordan* directing that our holding was to be applied retroactively.

We are constrained to note, however, that the absence of language directing the retroactivity of the *Jordan* decision was a product of oversight rather than the result of a judicial decision to limit *Jordan* to prospective application only. As the issue of retroactivity of *Jordan* is now squarely before us, we take the opportunity, within *Blank's* rule, to correct our oversight....

We held in *Blank* that a judicial decision overturning a prior judicial construction of a statute could not be applied retroactively "in the absence of ... expressed intent." ... We now express that intent. We hold that *Jordan* applies retroactively to: (1) all cases tried or retried after the date of our decision in *Jordan;* and (2) to all cases pending on appeal in which the issue decided in *Jordan* was raised at an appropriate time. We are aware that our holding will require retrial of some cases and the expenditure of additional judicial resources. Still, we cannot perpetuate denial of retroactive application of *Jordan* when that result was not our intention.

In this case, Plaintiffs' claims for loss of consortium were properly pleaded in the trial court and raised on appeal. The issue of loss of consortium damages is therefore properly before us. Retroactive application of *Jordan,* however, would not increase Plaintiffs' damages. In *Jordan* we expressly stated, "This holding does not create a new cause of action but merely refines the term 'pecuniary value.' " ... Pursuant to our statute, loss of consortium damages in a wrongful death claim are wholly contained within the award for wrongful death. Plaintiffs have each received $130,000, the maximum allowable award under the GTLA per injured person.... Loss of consortium damages could not increase the total amount of the award. Accordingly, we decline to remand these cases to the trial court to consider the issue of inclusion of loss of consortium damages in the pecuniary value of the decedents' lives.

CONCLUSION

... We ... hold that *Jordan* applies retroactively to: (1) all cases tried or retried after January 25, 1999, the date of our decision in *Jordan;* and (2) to all cases pending on appeal in which the issue decided in *Jordan* was raised at an appropriate time. Because Appellants have received the maximum amount of damages that may be awarded under the GTLA, however, we decline to remand for the purpose of application of *Jordan* in these cases. Accordingly, the decision of the Court of Appeals is affirmed in part and reversed in part.

DROWOTA, [J.,] not participating.

H.   REASONING FROM STATUTES BY ANALOGY

In Chapter V, we observed that courts sometimes resolve a controversy by referring to an analogous judicial precedent. The following excerpt suggests that civil (as opposed to criminal) statutes could be used in precisely the same manner.

R. POUND, "COMMON LAW AND LEGISLATION"
21 Harvard Law Review 383, 385–386 (1908).[38]

Four ways may be conceived of in which courts in such a legal system as ours might deal with a legislative innovation. (1) They might

---

38. Copyright © 1907, 1908 by Harvard Law Review Association. Reprinted by permission.

receive it fully into the body of the law as affording not only a rule to be applied but a principle from which to reason, and hold it, as a later and more direct expression of the general will, of superior authority to judge-made rules on the same general subject; and so reason from it by analogy in preference to them. (2) They might receive it fully into the body of the law to be reasoned from by analogy the same as any other rule of law, regarding it, however, as of equal or co-ordinate authority in this respect with judge-made rules upon the same general subject. (3) They might refuse to receive it fully into the body of the law and give effect to it directly only; refusing to reason from it by analogy but giving it, nevertheless, a liberal interpretation to cover the whole field it was intended to cover. (4) They might not only refuse to reason from it by analogy and apply it directly only, but also give to it a strict and narrow interpretation, holding it down rigidly to those cases which it covers expressly. The fourth hypothesis represents the orthodox common law attitude toward legislative innovations. Probably the third hypothesis, however, represents more nearly the attitude toward which we are tending. The second and first hypotheses doubtless appeal to the common law lawyer as absurd. He can hardly conceive that a rule of statutory origin may be treated as a permanent part of the general body of the law. But it is submitted that the course of legal development upon which we have entered already must lead us to adopt the method of the second and eventually the method of the first hypothesis.

NOTE BY THE EDITORS: ANALOGICAL USE OF STATUTES

Despite the possibility of using statutes as analogous precedents, most courts "have rejected the civil law notion that the general principles drawn from statutes may be made use of as bases for analogy in the decision of cases which do not fall within the broadest possible meaning of statutory language." H.W. Jones, "Statutory Doubts and Legislative Intention," 40 Columbia Law Review 957, 974 (1940). On the other hand, certain commentators have encouraged common law judges to follow the example set by their civil law counterparts. *See, e.g.*, G. Calebresi, *A Common Law for the Age of Statutes* (1982); J. Frank, "Civil Law Influences on Common Law," 104 University of Pennsylvania Law Review 887, 889–91 (1956). One statute that frequently has been applied by analogy is the Uniform Commercial Code (U.C.C.), which you will study extensively in your Contracts course. *See, e.g.*, New England Savings Bank v. Lopez, 227 Conn. 270, 630 A.2d 1010 (1993) (extending U.C.C. to real property transactions); Justice E.A. Peters, "Common Law Judging in a Statutory World: An Address," 43 University of Pittsburgh Law Review 995 (1982); R.F. Williams, "Statutes as Sources of Law Beyond Their Terms," 50 George Washington Law Review 554 (1982); Note, "The Uniform Commercial Code as a Premise of Judicial Reasoning," 65 Columbia Law Review 880 (1965).

Further References

Bell, B., "R–E–S–P–E–C–T: Respecting Legislative Judgments in Interpretative Theory," 78 North Carolina Law Review 1253 (2000).

Buzbee, W.W. & Schapiro, R.A., "Legislative Record Review," 54 Stanford Law Review 87 (2001).

Buzbee, W.W., "The One–Congress Fiction in Statutory Interpretation," 149 University of Pennsylvania Law Review 171 (2000).

Dougherty, V.M., "Absurdity and the Limits of Literalism: Defining the Absurd Result in Principle in Statutory Interpretation," 44 American University Law Review 127 (1994).

Eskridge, W.N., Jr., *Dynamic Statutory Interpretation* (1994).

Eskridge, W.N., Jr., "All About Words: Early Understandings of the 'Judicial Power' in Statutory Interpretation, 1776–1806," 101 Columbia Law Review 990 (2001).

Eskridge, W.N., Jr., "Overriding Supreme Court Statutory Interpretation Decisions," 101 Yale Law Journal 331 (1991).

Eskridge, W.N., Jr., "Textualism, The Unknown Ideal?" 96 Michigan Law Review 1509 (1998).

Farber, D.A., "Do Theories of Statutory Interpretation Matter? A Case Study," 94 Northwestern Law Review 1409 (2000).

Farber, D.A., "The Inevitability of Practical Reason: Statutes, Formalism, and the Rule of Law," 45 Vanderbilt Law Review 533 (1992).

Frank, J.N., "Words and Music: Some Remarks on Statutory Interpretation," 47 Columbia Law Review 1259 (1947).

Frankfurter, F., "Some Reflections on the Reading of Statutes," 47 Columbia Law Review 527 (1947).

Frickey, P.P., "From the Big Sleep to the Big Heat: The Revival of Theory in Statutory Interpretation," 77 Minnesota Law Review 241 (1992).

Gebbia–Pinetti, K.M., "Statutory Interpretation, Democratic Legitimacy and Legal System Values," 21 Seton Hall Legislative Journal 233 (1997).

Greenawalt, K., *Statutory Interpretation: 20 Questions* (1999).

Greenawalt, K., "Are Mental States Relevant for Statutory and Constitutional Interpretation?" 85 Cornell Law Review 1609 (2000).

Healy, M.P., "Legislative Intent and Statutory Interpretation in England and the United States: An Assessment of the Impact of *Pepper v. Hart*," 35 Stanford Journal of International Law 231 (1999).

Hurst, J.W., *Dealing With Statutes* (1982).

Manning, J.F., "Deriving Rules of Statutory Interpretation from the Constitution," 101 Columbia Law Review 1648 (2001).

Manning, J.F., "Textualism and the Equity of the Statute," 101 Columbia Law Review 1 (2001).

Manning, J.F., "The Absurdity Doctrine," 116 Harvard Law Review 2387 (2003).

Mikva, A.J., & Lane, E., *An Introduction to Statutory Interpretation and the Legislative Process* (1997).

Molot, J.T., "The Judicial Perspective in the Administrative State: Reconciling Modern Doctrines of Defense with the Judiciary's Structural Role," 53 Stanford Law Review 1 (2000).

Noah, L., "Diving Regulatory Intent: The Place for a 'Legislative History' of Agency Rules," 51 Hastings Law Journal 255 (2000).

Posner, R.A., "Legal Formalism, Legal Realism and the Interpretation of Statutes and the Constitution," 37 Case Western Reserve Law Review 179 (1986).

Posner, R.A., "Statutory Interpretation—in the Classroom and in the Courtroom," 50 University of Chicago Law Review 800 (1983).

Popkin, W.D., "An 'Internal' Critique of Justice Scalia's Theory of Statutory Interpretation," 76 Minnesota Law Review 1133 (1992).

Scalia, A., "Common Law Courts in a Civil Law System: The Role of the United States Federal Courts in Interpreting the Constitution and Laws," in *A Matter of Interpretation: Federal Courts and the Law* (Amy Gutmann, ed. 1997).

Schacter, J.S., "Metademocracy: The Changing Structure of Legitimacy in Statutory Interpretation," 108 Harvard Law Review 593 (1995).

Schacter, J.S., "The Confounding Common Law Originalism in Recent Supreme Court Statutory Interpretation: Implications for the Legislative History Debate and Beyond," 51 Stanford Law Review 1 (1998).

Schauer, F., "Statutory Construction and the Coordinating Function of Plain Meaning," 1990 Supreme Court Review 231.

Shapiro, D.L., "Continuity and Change in Statutory Interpretation," 67 New York University Law Review 921 (1992).

Siegel, J.R., "What Statutory Drafting Errors Teach Us about Statutory Interpretation," 69 George Washington Law Review 309 (2001).

Spiropoulos, A.C., "A Defense of Substantive Canons of Construction," 2001 Utah Law Review 915.

Sunstein, C.R., "Interpreting Statutes in the Regulatory State," 103 Harvard Law Review 405 (1989).

Thorne, S., *A Discourse upon the Exposition & Understandings of Statutes* (1942), pp. 1–99 (discussing the early English history).

Tiersma, P.M., "A Message in a Bottle: Text, Autonomy, and Statutory Interpretation," 76 Tulane Law Review 431 (2001).

Appendix

THE CASE OF THE SPELUNCEAN EXPLORERS[a1]

In the Supreme Court of Newgarth, 4300
Lon L. Fuller[a2]

The defendants, having been indicted for the crime of murder, were convicted and sentenced to be hanged by the Court of General Instances of the County of Stowfield. They bring a petition of error before this Court. The facts sufficiently appear in the opinion of the Chief Justice.

Truepenny, C. J. The four defendants are members of the Speluncean Society, an organization of amateurs interested in the exploration of caves. Early in May of 4299 they, in the company of Roger Whetmore, then also a member of the Society, penetrated into the interior of a limestone cavern of the type found in the Central Plateau of this Commonwealth. While they were in a position remote from the entrance to the cave, a landslide occurred. Heavy boulders fell in such a manner as to block completely the only known opening to the cave. When the men discovered their predicament they settled themselves near the obstructed entrance to wait until a rescue party should remove the detritus that prevented them from leaving their underground prison. On the failure of Whetmore and the defendants to return to their homes, the Secretary of the Society was notified by their families. It appears that the explorers had left indications at the headquarters of the Society concerning the location of the cave they proposed to visit. A rescue party was promptly dispatched to the spot.

The task of rescue proved one of overwhelming difficulty. It was necessary to supplement the forces of the original party by repeated increments of men and machines, which had to be conveyed at great expense to the remote and isolated region in which the cave was located. A huge temporary camp of workmen, engineers, geologists, and other experts was established. The work of removing the obstruction was several times frustrated by fresh landslides. In one of these, ten of the workmen engaged in clearing the entrance were killed. The treasury of the Speluncean Society was soon exhausted in the rescue effort, and the sum of eight hundred thousand frelars, raised partly by popular subscription and partly by legislative grant, was expended before the imprisoned men were rescued. Success was finally achieved on the thirty-second day after the men entered the cave.

a1. A reprint of Lon L. Fuller, The Case of the Speluncean Explorers, 62 Harv. L. Rev. 616 (1949). Copyright © 1949 & 1999, The Harvard Law Review Association and The Estate of Lon L. Fuller. Reprinted by permission.

a2. Carter Professor of General Jurisprudence, Harvard Law School.

Since it was known that the explorers had carried with them only scant provisions, and since it was also known that there was no animal or vegetable matter within the cave on which they might subsist, anxiety was early felt that they might meet death by starvation before access to them could be obtained. On the twentieth day of their imprisonment it was learned for the first time that they had taken with them into the cave a portable wireless machine capable of both sending and receiving messages. A similar machine was promptly installed in the rescue camp and oral communication established with the unfortunate men within the mountain. They asked to be informed how long a time would be required to release them. The engineers in charge of the project answered that at least ten days would be required even if no new landslides occurred. The explorers then asked if any physicians were present, and were placed in communication with a committee of medical experts. The imprisoned men described their condition and the rations they had taken with them, and asked for a medical opinion whether they would be likely to live without food for ten days longer. The chairman of the committee of physicians told them that there was little possibility of this. The wireless machine within the cave then remained silent for eight hours. When communication was re-established the men asked to speak again with the physicians. The chairman of the physicians' committee was placed before the apparatus, and Whetmore, speaking on behalf of himself and the defendants, asked whether they would be able to survive for ten days longer if they consumed the flesh of one of their number. The physicians' chairman reluctantly answered this question in the affirmative. Whetmore asked whether it would be advisable for them to cast lots to determine which of them should be eaten. None of the physicians present was willing to answer the question. Whetmore then asked if there were among the party a judge or other official of the government who would answer this question. None of those attached to the rescue camp was willing to assume the role of advisor in this matter. He then asked if any minister or priest would answer their question, and none was found who would do so. Thereafter no further messages were received from within the cave, and it was assumed (erroneously, it later appeared) that the electric batteries of the explorers' wireless machine had become exhausted. When the imprisoned men were finally released it was learned that on the twenty-third day after their entrance into the cave Whetmore had been killed and eaten by his companions.

From the testimony of the defendants, which was accepted by the jury, it appears that it was Whetmore who first proposed that they might find the nutriment without which survival was impossible in the flesh of one of their own number. It was also Whetmore who first proposed the use of some method of casting lots, calling the attention of the defendants to a pair of dice he happened to have with him. The defendants were at first reluctant to adopt so desperate a procedure, but after the conversations by wireless related above, they finally agreed on the plan proposed by Whetmore. After much discussion of the mathematical problems involved, agreement was finally reached on a method of determining the issue by the use of the dice.

Before the dice were cast, however, Whetmore declared that he withdrew from the arrangement, as he had decided on reflection to wait for another week before embracing an expedient so frightful and odious. The others charged him with a breach of faith and proceeded to cast the dice. When it came Whetmore's turn, the dice were cast for him by one of the defendants, and he was asked to declare any objections he might have to the fairness of the throw. He stated that he had no such objections. The throw went against him, and he was then put to death and eaten by his companions.

After the rescue of the defendants, and after they had completed a stay in a hospital where they underwent a course of treatment for malnutrition and shock, they were indicted for the murder of Roger Whetmore. At the trial, after the testimony had been concluded, the foreman of the jury (a lawyer by profession) inquired of the court whether the jury might not find a special verdict, leaving it to the court to say whether on the facts as found the defendants were guilty. After some discussion, both the Prosecutor and counsel for the defendants indicated their acceptance of this procedure, and it was adopted by the court. In a lengthy special verdict the jury found the facts as I have related them above, and found further that if on these facts the defendants were guilty of the crime charged against them, then they found the defendants guilty. On the basis of this verdict, the trial judge ruled that the defendants were guilty of murdering Roger Whetmore. The judge then sentenced them to be hanged, the law of our Commonwealth permitting him no discretion with respect to the penalty to be imposed. After the release of the jury, its members joined in a communication to the Chief Executive asking that the sentence be commuted to an imprisonment of six months. The trial judge addressed a similar communication to the Chief Executive. As yet no action with respect to these pleas has been taken, as the Chief Executive is apparently awaiting our disposition of this petition of error.

It seems to me that in dealing with this extraordinary case the jury and the trial judge followed a course that was not only fair and wise, but the only course that was open to them under the law. The language of our statute is well known: "Whoever shall willfully take the life of another shall be punished by death." N.C.S.A. (n.s.) § 12–A. This statute permits of no exception applicable to this case, however our sympathies may incline us to make allowance for the tragic situation in which these men found themselves.

In a case like this the principle of executive clemency seems admirably suited to mitigate the rigors of the law, and I propose to my colleagues that we follow the example of the jury and the trial judge by joining in the communications they have addressed to the Chief Executive. There is every reason to believe that these requests for clemency will be heeded, coming as they do from those who have studied the case and had an opportunity to become thoroughly acquainted with all its circumstances. It is highly improbable that the Chief Executive would deny these requests unless he were himself to hold hearings at least as extensive as those involved in the trial below, which lasted for three months. The holding of such hearings (which would virtually amount to a retrial of the case) would scarcely be compatible with the function of the Executive as it is usually conceived. I think we may therefore assume that some form of clemency will be extended to these defendants. If this is done, then justice will be accomplished without impairing either the letter or spirit of our statutes and without offering any encouragement for the disregard of law.

Foster, J. I am shocked that the Chief Justice, in an effort to escape the embarrassments of this tragic case, should have adopted, and should have proposed to his colleagues, an expedient at once so sordid and so obvious. I believe something more is on trial in this case than the fate of these unfortunate explorers; that is the law of our Commonwealth. If this Court declares that under our law these men have committed a crime, then our law is itself convicted in the tribunal of common sense, no matter what happens to the individuals involved in this petition of error. For us to assert that the law we uphold and expound compels us to a conclusion we are ashamed of, and from which we can only escape by appealing to a dispensation resting within the personal whim of the Executive, seems to me to amount to an admission that the law of this Commonwealth no longer pretends to incorporate justice.

For myself, I do not believe that our law compels the monstrous conclusion that these men are murderers. I believe, on the contrary, that it declares them to be innocent of any crime. I rest this conclusion on two independent grounds, either of which is of itself sufficient to justify the acquittal of these defendants.

The first of these grounds rests on a premise that may arouse opposition until it has been examined candidly. I take the view that the enacted or positive law of this Commonwealth, including all of its statutes and precedents, is inapplicable to this case, and that the case is governed instead by what ancient writers in Europe and America called "the law of nature."

This conclusion rests on the proposition that our positive law is predicated on the possibility of men's coexistence in society. When a situation arises in which the coexistence of men becomes impossible, then a condition that underlies all of our precedents and statutes has ceased to exist. When that condition disappears, then it is my opinion that the force of our positive law disappears with it. We are not accustomed to applying the maxim cessante ratione legis, cessat et ipsa lex to the whole of our enacted law, but I believe that this is a case where the maxim should be so applied.

The proposition that all positive law is based on the possibility of men's coexistence has a strange sound, not because the truth it contains is strange, but simply because it is a truth so obvious and pervasive that we seldom have occasion to give words to it. Like the air we breathe, it so pervades our environment that we forget that it exists until we are suddenly deprived of it. Whatever particular objects may be sought by the various branches of our law, it is apparent on reflection that all of them are directed toward facilitating and improving men's coexistence and regulating with fairness and equity the relations of their life in common. When the assumption that men may live together loses its truth, as it obviously did in this extraordinary situation where life only became possible by the taking of life, then the basic premises underlying our whole legal order have lost their meaning and force.

Had the tragic events of this case taken place a mile beyond the territorial limits of our Commonwealth, no one would pretend that our law was applicable to them. We recognize that jurisdiction rests on a territorial basis. The grounds of this principle are by no means obvious and are seldom examined. I take it that this principle is supported by an assumption that it is feasible to impose a single legal order upon a group of men only if they live together within the confines of a given area of the earth's surface. The premise that men shall coexist in a group underlies, then, the territorial principle, as it does all of law. Now I contend that a case may be removed morally from the force of a legal order, as well as geographically. If we look to the purposes of law and government, and to the premises underlying our positive law, these men when they made their fateful decision were as remote from our legal order as if they had been a thousand miles beyond our boundaries. Even in a physical sense, their underground prison was separated from our courts and writ-servers by a solid curtain of rock that could be removed only after the most extraordinary expenditures of time and effort.

I conclude, therefore, that at the time Roger Whetmore's life was ended by these defendants, they were, to use the quaint language of nineteenth-century writers, not in a "state of civil society" but in a "state of nature." This has the consequence that the law applicable to them is not the enacted and established law of this Commonwealth, but the law derived from those principles that were appropriate to their condition. I have no hesitancy in saying that under those principles they were guiltless of any crime.

What these men did was done in pursuance of an agreement accepted by all of them and first proposed by Whetmore himself. Since it was apparent that their extraordinary predicament made inapplicable the usual principles that regulate men's relations with one another, it was necessary for them to draw, as it were, a new charter of government appropriate to the situation in which they found themselves.

It has from antiquity been recognized that the most basic principle of law or government is to be found in the notion of contract or agreement. Ancient thinkers, especially during the period from 1600 to 1900, used to base government itself on a supposed original social compact. Skeptics pointed out that this theory contradicted the known facts of history, and that there was no scientific evidence to support the notion that any government was ever founded in the manner supposed by the theory. Moralists replied that, if the compact was a fiction from a historical point of view, the notion of compact or agreement furnished the only ethical justification on which the powers of government, which include that of taking life, could be rested. The powers of government can only be justified morally on the ground that these are powers that reasonable men would agree upon and accept if they were faced with the necessity of constructing anew some order to make their life in common possible.

Fortunately, our Commonwealth is not bothered by the perplexities that beset the ancients. We know as a matter of historical truth that our government was founded upon a contract or free accord of men. The archeological proof is conclusive that in the first period following the Great Spiral the survivors of that holocaust voluntarily came together and drew up a charter of government. Sophistical writers have raised questions as to the power of those remote contractors to bind future generations, but the fact remains that our government traces itself back in an unbroken line to that original charter.

If, therefore, our hangmen have the power to end men's lives, if our sheriffs have the power to put delinquent tenants in the street, if our police have the power to incarcerate the inebriated reveler, these powers find their moral justification in that original compact of our forefathers. If we can find no higher source for our legal order, what higher source should we expect these starving unfortunates to find for the order they adopted for themselves?

I believe that the line of argument I have just expounded permits of no rational answer. I realize that it will probably be received with a certain discomfort by many who read this opinion, who will be inclined to suspect that some hidden sophistry must underlie a demonstration that leads to so many unfamiliar conclusions. The source of this discomfort is, however, easy to identify. The usual conditions of human existence incline us to think of human life as an absolute value, not to be sacrificed under any circumstances. There is much that is fictitious about this conception even when it is applied to the ordinary relations of society. We have an illustration of this truth in the very case before us. Ten workmen were killed in the process of removing the rocks from the opening to the cave. Did not the engineers and government officials who directed the rescue effort know that the operations they were undertaking were dangerous and involved a serious risk to the lives of the workmen executing them? If it was proper that these ten lives should be sacrificed to save the lives of five imprisoned explorers, why then are we told it was wrong for these explorers to carry out an arrangement which would save four lives at the cost of one?

Every highway, every tunnel, every building we project involves a risk to human life. Taking these projects in the aggregate, we can calculate with some precision how many deaths the construction of them will require; statisticians can tell you the average cost in human lives of a thousand miles of a four-lane concrete highway. Yet we deliberately and knowingly incur and pay this cost on the assumption that the values obtained for those who survive outweigh the loss. If these things can be said of a society functioning above ground in a normal and ordinary manner, what shall we say of the supposed absolute value of a human life in the desperate situation in which these defendants and their companion Whetmore found themselves?

This concludes the exposition of the first ground of my decision. My second ground proceeds by rejecting hypothetically all the premises on which I have so far proceeded. I concede for purposes of argument that I am wrong in saying that the situation of these men removed them from the effect of our positive law, and I assume that the Consolidated Statutes have the power to penetrate five hundred feet of rock and to impose themselves upon these starving men huddled in their underground prison.

Now it is, of course, perfectly clear that these men did an act that violates the literal wording of the statute which declares that he who "shall willfully take the life of another" is a murderer. But one of the most ancient bits of legal wisdom is the saying that a man may break the letter of the law without breaking the law itself. Every proposition of positive law, whether contained in a statute or a judicial precedent, is to be interpreted reasonably, in the light of its evident purpose. This is a truth so elementary that it is hardly necessary to expatiate on it. Illustrations of its application are numberless and are to be found in every branch of the law. In Commonwealth v. Staymore the defendant was convicted under a statute making it a crime to leave one's car parked in certain areas for a period longer than two hours. The defendant had attempted to remove his car, but was prevented from doing so because the streets were obstructed by a political demonstration in which he took no part and which he had no reason to anticipate. His conviction was set aside by this Court, although his case fell squarely within the wording of the statute. Again, in Fehler v. Neegas there was before this Court for construction a statute in which the word "not" had plainly been transposed from its intended position in the final and most crucial section of the act. This transposition was contained in all the successive drafts of the act, where it was apparently overlooked by the draftsmen and sponsors of the legislation. No one was able to prove how the error came about, yet it was apparent that, taking account of the contents of the statute as a whole, an error had been made, since a literal reading of the final clause rendered it inconsistent with everything that had gone before and with the object of the enactment as stated in its preamble. This Court refused to accept a literal interpretation of the statute, and in effect rectified its language by reading the word "not" into the place where it was evidently intended to go.

The statute before us for interpretation has never been applied literally. Centuries ago it was established that a killing in self-defense is excused. There is nothing in the wording of the statute that suggests this exception. Various attempts have been made to reconcile the legal treatment of self-defense with the words of the statute, but in my opinion these are all merely ingenious sophistries. The truth is that the exception in favor of self-defense cannot be reconciled with the words of the statute, but only with its purpose.

The true reconciliation of the excuse of self-defense with the statute making it a crime to kill another is to be found in the following line of reasoning. One of the principal objects underlying any criminal legislation is that of deterring men from crime. Now it is apparent that if it were declared to be the law that a killing in self-defense is murder such a rule could not operate in a deterrent manner. A man whose life is threatened will repel his aggressor, whatever the law may say. Looking therefore to the broad purposes of criminal legislation, we may safely declare that this statute was not intended to apply to cases of self-defense.

When the rationale of the excuse of self-defense is thus explained, it becomes apparent that precisely the same reasoning is applicable to the case at bar. If in the future any group of men ever find themselves in the tragic predicament of these defendants, we may be sure that their decision whether to live or die will not be controlled by the contents of our criminal code. Accordingly, if we read this statute intelligently it is apparent that it does not apply to this case. The withdrawal of this situation from the effect of the statute is justified by precisely the same considerations that were applied by our predecessors in office centuries ago to the case of self-defense.

There are those who raise the cry of judicial usurpation whenever a court, after analyzing the purpose of a statute, gives to its words a meaning that is not at once apparent to the casual reader who has not studied the statute closely or examined the objectives it seeks to attain. Let me say emphatically that I accept without reservation the proposition that this Court is bound by the statutes of our Commonwealth and that it exercises its powers in subservience to the duly expressed will of the Chamber of Representatives. The line of reasoning I have applied above raises no question of fidelity to enacted law, though it may possibly raise a question of the distinction between intelligent and unintelligent fidelity. No superior wants a servant who lacks the capacity to read between the lines. The stupidest housemaid knows that when she is told "to peel the soup and skim the potatoes" her mistress does not mean what she says. She also knows that when her master tells her to "drop everything and come running" he has overlooked the possibility that she is at the moment in the act of rescuing the baby from the rain barrel. Surely we have a right to expect the same modicum of intelligence from the judiciary. The correction of obvious legislative errors or oversights is not to supplant the legislative will, but to make that will effective.

I therefore conclude that on any aspect under which this case may be viewed these defendants are innocent of the crime of murdering Roger Whetmore, and that the conviction should be set aside.

Tatting, J. In the discharge of my duties as a justice of this Court, I am usually able to dissociate the emotional and intellectual sides of my reactions, and to decide the case before me entirely on the basis of the latter. In passing on this tragic case I find that my usual resources fail me. On the emotional side I find myself torn between sympathy for these men and a feeling of abhorrence and disgust at the monstrous act they committed. I had hoped that I would be able to put these contradictory emotions to one side as irrelevant, and to decide the case on the basis of a convincing and logical demonstration of the result demanded by our law. Unfortunately, this deliverance has not been vouchsafed me.

As I analyze the opinion just rendered by my brother Foster, I find that it is shot through with contradictions and fallacies. Let us begin with his first proposition: these men were not subject to our law because they were not in a "state of civil society" but in a "state of nature." I am not clear why this is so, whether it is because of the thickness of the rock that imprisoned them, or because they were hungry, or because they had set up a "new charter of government" by which the usual rules of law were to be supplanted by a throw of the dice. Other difficulties intrude themselves. If these men passed from the jurisdiction of our law to that of "the law of nature," at what moment did this occur? Was it when the entrance to the cave was blocked, or when the threat of starvation reached a certain undefined degree of intensity, or when the agreement for the throwing of the dice was made? These uncertainties in the doctrine proposed by my brother are capable of producing real difficulties. Suppose, for example, one of these men had had his twenty-first birthday while he was imprisoned within the mountain. On what date would we have to consider that he had attained his majority—when he reached the age of twenty-one, at which time he was, by hypothesis, removed from the effects of our law, or only when he was released from the cave and became again subject to what my brother calls our "positive law" ? These difficulties may seem fanciful, yet they only serve to reveal the fanciful nature of the doctrine that is capable of giving rise to them.

But it is not necessary to explore these niceties further to demonstrate the absurdity of my brother's position. Mr. Justice Foster and I are the appointed judges of a court of the Commonwealth of Newgarth, sworn and empowered to administer the laws of that Commonwealth. By what authority do we resolve ourselves into a Court of Nature? If these men were indeed under the law of nature, whence comes our authority to expound and apply that law? Certainly we are not in a state of nature.

Let us look at the contents of this code of nature that my brother proposes we adopt as our own and apply to this case. What a topsy-turvy and odious code it is! It is a code in which the law of contracts is more fundamental than the law of murder. It is a code under which a man may make a valid agreement empowering his fellows to eat his own body. Under the provisions of this code, furthermore, such an agreement once made is irrevocable, and if one of the parties attempts to withdraw, the others may take the law into their own hands and enforce the contract by violence—for though my brother passes over in convenient silence the effect of Whetmore's withdrawal, this is the necessary implication of his argument.

The principles my brother expounds contain other implications that cannot be tolerated. He argues that when the defendants set upon Whetmore and killed him (we know not how, perhaps by pounding him with stones) they were only exercising the rights conferred upon them by their bargain. Suppose, however, that Whetmore had had concealed upon his person a revolver, and that when he saw the defendants about to slaughter him he had shot them to death in order to save his own life. My brother's reasoning applied to these facts would make Whetmore out to be a murderer, since the excuse of self-defense would have to be denied to him. If his assailants were acting rightfully in seeking to bring about his death, then of course he could no more plead the excuse that he was defending his own life than could a condemned prisoner who struck down the executioner lawfully attempting to place the noose about his neck.

All of these considerations make it impossible for me to accept the first part of my brother's argument. I can neither accept his notion that these men were under a code of nature which this Court was bound to apply to them, nor can I accept the odious and perverted rules that he would read into that code. I come now to the second part of my brother's opinion, in which he seeks to show that the defendants did not violate the provisions of N.C.S.A. (n.s.) § 12–A. Here the way, instead of being clear, becomes for me misty and ambiguous, though my brother seems unaware of the difficulties that inhere in his demonstrations.

The gist of my brother's argument may be stated in the following terms: No statute, whatever its language, should be applied in a way that contradicts its purpose. One of the purposes of any criminal statute is to deter. The application of the statute making it a crime to kill another to the peculiar facts of this case would contradict this purpose, for it is impossible to believe that the contents of the criminal code could operate in a deterrent manner on men faced with the alternative of life or death. The reasoning by which this exception is read into the statute is, my brother observes, the same as that which is applied in order to provide the excuse of self-defense.

On the face of things this demonstration seems very convincing indeed. My brother's interpretation of the rationale of the excuse of self-defense is in fact supported by a decision of this court, Commonwealth v. Parry, a precedent I happened to encounter in my research on this case. Though Commonwealth v. Parry seems generally to have been overlooked in the texts and subsequent decisions, it supports unambiguously the interpretation my brother has put upon the excuse of self-defense.

Now let me outline briefly, however, the perplexities that assail me when I examine my brother's demonstration more closely. It is true that a statute should be applied in the light of its purpose, and that one of the purposes of criminal legislation is recognized to be deterrence. The difficulty is that other purposes are also ascribed to the law of crimes. It has been said that one of its objects is to provide an orderly outlet for the instinctive human demand for retribution. Commonwealth v. Scape. It has also been said that its object is the rehabilitation of the wrongdoer. Commonwealth v. Makeover. Other theories have been propounded. Assuming that we must interpret a statute in the light of its purpose, what are we to do when it has many purposes or when its purposes are disputed?

A similar difficulty is presented by the fact that although there is authority for my brother's interpretation of the excuse of self-defense, there is other authority which assigns to that excuse a different rationale. Indeed, until I happened on Commonwealth v. Parry I had never heard of the explanation given by my brother. The taught doctrine of our law schools, memorized by generations of law students, runs in the following terms: The statute concerning murder requires a "willful" act. The man who acts to repel an aggressive threat to his own life does not act "willfully," but in response to an impulse deeply ingrained in human nature. I suspect that there is hardly a lawyer in this Commonwealth who is not familiar with this line of reasoning, especially since the point is a great favorite of the bar examiners.

Now the familiar explanation for the excuse of self-defense just expounded obviously cannot be applied by analogy to the facts of this case. These men acted not only "willfully" but with great deliberation and after hours of discussing what they should do. Again we encounter a forked path, with one line of reasoning leading us in one direction and another in a direction that is exactly the opposite. This perplexity is in this case compounded, as it were, for we have to set off one explanation, incorporated in a virtually unknown precedent of this Court, against another explanation, which forms a part of the taught legal tradition of our law schools, but which, so far as I know, has never been adopted in any judicial decision.

I recognize the relevance of the precedents cited by my brother concerning the displaced "not" and the defendant who parked overtime. But what are we to do with one of the landmarks of our jurisprudence, which again my brother passes over in silence? This is Commonwealth v. Valjean. Though the case is somewhat obscurely reported, it appears that the defendant was indicted for the larceny of a loaf of bread, and offered as a defense that he was in a condition approaching starvation. The court refused to accept this defense. If hunger cannot justify the theft of wholesome and natural food, how can it justify the killing and eating of a man? Again, if we look at the thing in terms of deterrence, is it likely that a man will starve to death to avoid a jail sentence for the theft of a loaf of bread? My brother's demonstrations would compel us to overrule Commonwealth v. Valjean, and many other precedents that have been built on that case.

Again, I have difficulty in saying that no deterrent effect whatever could be attributed to a decision that these men were guilty of murder. The stigma of the word "murderer" is such that it is quite likely, I believe, that if these men had known that their act was deemed by the law to be murder they would have waited for a few days at least before carrying out their plan. During that time some unexpected relief might have come. I realize that this observation only reduces the distinction to a matter of degree, and does not destroy it altogether. It is certainly true that the element of deterrence would be less in this case than is normally involved in the application of the criminal law.

There is still a further difficulty in my brother Foster's proposal to read an exception into the statute to favor this case, though again a difficulty not even intimated in his opinion. What shall be the scope of this exception? Here the men cast lots and the victim was himself originally a party to the agreement. What would we have to decide if Whetmore had refused from the beginning to participate in the plan? Would a majority be permitted to overrule him? Or, suppose that no plan were adopted at all and the others simply conspired to bring about Whetmore's death, justifying their act by saying that he was in the weakest condition. Or again, that a plan of selection was followed but one based on a different justification than the one adopted here, as if the others were atheists and insisted that Whetmore should die because he was the only one who believed in an afterlife. These illustrations could be multiplied, but enough have been suggested to reveal what a quagmire of hidden difficulties my brother's reasoning contains.

Of course I realize on reflection that I may be concerning myself with a problem that will never arise, since it is unlikely that any group of men will ever again be brought to commit the dread act that was involved here. Yet, on still further reflection, even if we are certain that no similar case will arise again, do not the illustrations I have given show the lack of any coherent and rational principle in the rule my brother proposes? Should not the soundness of a principle be tested by the conclusions it entails, without reference to the accidents of later litigational history? Still, if this is so, why is it that we of this Court so often discuss the question whether we are likely to have later occasion to apply a principle urged for the solution of the case before us? Is this a situation where a line of reasoning not originally proper has become sanctioned by precedent, so that we are permitted to apply it and may even be under an obligation to do so?

The more I examine this case and think about it, the more deeply I become involved. My mind becomes entangled in the meshes of the very nets I throw out for my own rescue. I find that almost every consideration that bears on the decision of the case is counterbalanced by an opposing consideration leading in the opposite direction. My brother Foster has not furnished to me, nor can I discover for myself, any formula capable of resolving the equivocations that beset me on all sides.

I have given this case the best thought of which I am capable. I have scarcely slept since it was argued before us. When I feel myself inclined to accept the view of my brother Foster, I am repelled by a feeling that his arguments are intellectually unsound and approach mere rationalization. On the other hand, when I incline toward upholding the conviction, I am struck by the absurdity of directing that these men be put to death when their lives have been saved at the cost of the lives of ten heroic workmen. It is to me a matter of regret that the Prosecutor saw fit to ask for an indictment for murder. If we had a provision in our statutes making it a crime to eat human flesh, that would have been a more appropriate charge. If no other charge suited to the facts of this case could be brought against the defendants, it would have been wiser, I think, not to have indicted them at all. Unfortunately, however, the men have been indicted and tried, and we have therefore been drawn into this unfortunate affair.

Since I have been wholly unable to resolve the doubts that beset me about the law of this case, I am with regret announcing a step that is, I believe, unprecedented in the history of this tribunal. I declare my withdrawal from the decision of this case.

Keen, J. I should like to begin by setting to one side two questions which are not before this Court.

The first of these is whether executive clemency should be extended to these defendants if the conviction is affirmed. Under our system of government, that is a question for the Chief Executive, not for us. I therefore disapprove of that passage in the opinion of the Chief Justice in which he in effect gives instructions to the Chief Executive as to what he should do in this case and suggests that some impropriety will attach if these instructions are not heeded. This is a confusion of governmental functions—a confusion of which the judiciary should be the last to be guilty. I wish to state that if I were the Chief Executive I would go farther in the direction of clemency than the pleas addressed to him propose. I would pardon these men altogether, since I believe that they have already suffered enough to pay for any offense they may have committed. I want it to be understood that this remark is made in my capacity as a private citizen who by the accident of his office happens to have acquired an intimate acquaintance with the facts of this case. In the discharge of my duties as judge, it is neither my function to address directions to the Chief Executive, nor to take into account what he may or may not do, in reaching my own decision, which must be controlled entirely by the law of this Commonwealth.

The second question that I wish to put to one side is that of deciding whether what these men did was "right" or "wrong," "wicked" or "good." That is also a question that is irrelevant to the discharge of my office as a judge sworn to apply, not my conceptions of morality, but the law of the land. In putting this question to one side I think I can also safely dismiss without comment the first and more poetic portion of my brother Foster's opinion. The element of fantasy contained in the arguments developed there has been sufficiently revealed in my brother Tatting's somewhat solemn attempt to take those arguments seriously.

The sole question before us for decision is whether these defendants did, within the meaning of N.C.S.A. (n.s.) § 12–A, willfully take the life of Roger Whetmore. The exact language of the statute is as follows: "Whoever shall willfully take the life of another shall be punished by death." Now I should suppose that any candid observer, content to extract from these words their natural meaning, would concede at once that these defendants did "willfully take the life" of Roger Whetmore.

Whence arise all the difficulties of the case, then, and the necessity for so many pages of discussion about what ought to be so obvious? The difficulties, in whatever tortured form they may present themselves, all trace back to a single source, and that is a failure to distinguish the legal from the moral aspects of this case. To put it bluntly, my brothers do not like the fact that the written law requires the conviction of these defendants. Neither do I, but unlike my brothers I respect the obligations of an office that requires me to put my personal predilections out of my mind when I come to interpret and apply the law of this Commonwealth.

Now, of course, my brother Foster does not admit that he is actuated by a personal dislike of the written law. Instead he develops a familiar line of argument according to which the court may disregard the express language of a statute when something not contained in the statute itself, called its "purpose," can be employed to justify the result the court considers proper. Because this is an old issue between myself and my colleague, I should like, before discussing his particular application of the argument to the facts of this case, to say something about the historical background of this issue and its implications for law and government generally.

There was a time in this Commonwealth when judges did in fact legislate very freely, and all of us know that during that period some of our statutes were rather thoroughly made over by the judiciary. That was a time when the accepted principles of political science did not designate with any certainty the rank and function of the various arms of the state. We all know the tragic issue of that uncertainty in the brief civil war that arose out of the conflict between the judiciary, on the one hand, and the executive and the legislature, on the other. There is no need to recount here the factors that contributed to that unseemly struggle for power, though they included the unrepresentative character of the Chamber, resulting from a division of the country into election districts that no longer accorded with the actual distribution of the population, and the forceful personality and wide popular following of the then Chief Justice. It is enough to observe that those days are behind us, and that in place of the uncertainty that then reigned we now have a clear-cut principle, which is the supremacy of the legislative branch of our government. From that principle flows the obligation of the judiciary to enforce faithfully the written law, and to interpret that law in accordance with its plain meaning without reference to our personal desires or our individual conceptions of justice. I am not concerned with the question whether the principle that forbids the judicial revision of statutes is right or wrong, desirable or undesirable; I observe merely that this principle has become a tacit premise underlying the whole of the legal and governmental order I am sworn to administer.

Yet though the principle of the supremacy of the legislature has been accepted in theory for centuries, such is the tenacity of professional tradition and the force of fixed habits of thought that many of the judiciary have still not accommodated themselves to the restricted role which the new order imposes on them. My brother Foster is one of that group; his way of dealing with statutes is exactly that of a judge living in the 3900's.

We are all familiar with the process by which the judicial reform of disfavored legislative enactments is accomplished. Anyone who has followed the written opinions of Mr. Justice Foster will have had an opportunity to see it at work in every branch of the law. I am personally so familiar with the process that in the event of my brother's incapacity I am sure I could write a satisfactory opinion for him without any prompting whatever, beyond being informed whether he liked the effect of the terms of the statute as applied to the case before him.

The process of judicial reform requires three steps. The first of these is to divine some single "purpose" which the statute serves. This is done although not one statute in a hundred has any such single purpose, and although the objectives of nearly every statute are differently interpreted by the different classes of its sponsors. The second step is to discover that a mythical being called "the legislator," in the pursuit of this imagined "purpose," overlooked something or left some gap or imperfection in his work. Then comes the final and most refreshing part of the task, which is, of course, to fill in the blank thus created. Quod erat faciendum.

My brother Foster's penchant for finding holes in statutes reminds one of the story told by an ancient author about the man who ate a pair of shoes. Asked how he liked them, he replied that the part he liked best was the holes. That is the way my brother feels about statutes; the more holes they have in them the better he likes them. In short, he doesn't like statutes.

One could not wish for a better case to illustrate the specious nature of this gap-filling process than the one before us. My brother thinks he knows exactly what was sought when men made murder a crime, and that was something he calls "deterrence." My brother Tatting has already shown how much is passed over in that interpretation. But I think the trouble goes deeper. I doubt very much whether our statute making murder a crime really has a "purpose" in any ordinary sense of the term. Primarily, such a statute reflects a deeply-felt human conviction that murder is wrong and that something should be done to the man who commits it. If we were forced to be more articulate about the matter, we would probably take refuge in the more sophisticated theories of the criminologists, which, of course, were certainly not in the minds of those who drafted our statute. We might also observe that men will do their own work more effectively and live happier lives if they are protected against the threat of violent assault. Bearing in mind that the victims of murders are often unpleasant people, we might add some suggestion that the matter of disposing of undesirables is not a function suited to private enterprise, but should be a state monopoly. All of which reminds me of the attorney who once argued before us that a statute licensing physicians was a good thing because it would lead to lower life insurance rates by lifting the level of general health. There is such a thing as overexplaining the obvious.

If we do not know the purpose of § 12–A, how can we possibly say there is a "gap" in it? How can we know what its draftsmen thought about the question of killing men in order to eat them? My brother Tatting has revealed an understandable, though perhaps slightly exaggerated revulsion to cannibalism. How do we know that his remote ancestors did not feel the same revulsion to an even higher degree? Anthropologists say that the dread felt for a forbidden act may be increased by the fact that the conditions of a tribe's life create special temptations toward it, as incest is most severely condemned among those whose village relations make it most likely to occur. Certainly the period following the Great Spiral was one that had implicit in it temptations to anthropophagy. Perhaps it was for that very reason that our ancestors expressed their prohibition in so broad and unqualified a form. All of this is conjecture, of course, but it remains abundantly clear that neither I nor my brother Foster knows what the "purpose" of § 12–A is.

Considerations similar to those I have just outlined are also applicable to the exception in favor of self-defense, which plays so large a role in the reasoning of my brothers Foster and Tatting. It is of course true that in Commonwealth v. Parry an obiter dictum justified this exception on the assumption that the purpose of criminal legislation is to deter. It may well also be true that generations of law students have been taught that the true explanation of the exception lies in the fact that a man who acts in self-defense does not act "willfully," and that the same students have passed their bar examinations by repeating what their professors told them. These last observations I could dismiss, of course, as irrelevant for the simple reason that professors and bar examiners have not as yet any commission to make our laws for us. But again the real trouble lies deeper. As in dealing with the statute, so in dealing with the exception, the question is not the conjectural purpose of the rule, but its scope. Now the scope of the exception in favor of self-defense as it has been applied by this Court is plain: it applies to cases of resisting an aggressive threat to the party's own life. It is therefore too clear for argument that this case does not fall within the scope of the exception, since it is plain that Whetmore made no threat against the lives of these defendants.

The essential shabbiness of my brother Foster's attempt to cloak his remaking of the written law with an air of legitimacy comes tragically to the surface in my brother Tatting's opinion. In that opinion Justice Tatting struggles manfully to combine his colleague's loose moralisms with his own sense of fidelity to the written law. The issue of this struggle could only be that which occurred, a complete default in the discharge of the judicial function. You simply cannot apply a statute as it is written and remake it to meet your own wishes at the same time.

Now I know that the line of reasoning I have developed in this opinion will not be acceptable to those who look only to the immediate effects of a decision and ignore the long-run implications of an assumption by the judiciary of a power of dispensation. A hard decision is never a popular decision. Judges have been celebrated in literature for their sly prowess in devising some quibble by which a litigant could be deprived of his rights where the public thought it was wrong for him to assert those rights. But I believe that judicial dispensation does more harm in the long run than hard decisions. Hard cases may even have a certain moral value by bringing home to the people their own responsibilities toward the law that is ultimately their creation, and by reminding them that there is no principle of personal grace that can relieve the mistakes of their representatives.

Indeed, I will go farther and say that not only are the principles I have been expounding those which are soundest for our present conditions, but that we would have inherited a better legal system from our forefathers if those principles had been observed from the beginning. For example, with respect to the excuse of self-defense, if our courts had stood steadfast on the language of the statute the result would undoubtedly have been a legislative revision of it. Such a revision would have drawn on the assistance of natural philosophers and psychologists, and the resulting regulation of the matter would have had an understandable and rational basis, instead of the hodgepodge of verbalisms and metaphysical distinctions that have emerged from the judicial and professorial treatment.

These concluding remarks are, of course, beyond any duties that I have to discharge with relation to this case, but I include them here because I feel deeply that my colleagues are insufficiently aware of the dangers implicit in the conceptions of the judicial office advocated by my brother Foster.

I conclude that the conviction should be affirmed.

Handy, J. I have listened with amazement to the tortured ratiocinations to which this simple case has given rise. I never cease to wonder at my colleagues' ability to throw an obscuring curtain of legalisms about every issue presented to them for decision. We have heard this afternoon learned disquisitions on the distinction between positive law and the law of nature, the language of the statute and the purpose of the statute, judicial functions and executive functions, judicial legislation and legislative legislation. My only disappointment was that someone did not raise the question of the legal nature of the bargain struck in the cave—whether it was unilateral or bilateral, and whether Whetmore could not be considered as having revoked an offer prior to action taken thereunder.

What have all these things to do with the case? The problem before us is what we, as officers of the government, ought to do with these defendants. That is a question of practical wisdom, to be exercised in a context, not of abstract theory, but of human realities. When the case is approached in this light, it becomes, I think, one of the easiest to decide that has ever been argued before this Court.

Before stating my own conclusions about the merits of the case, I should like to discuss briefly some of the more fundamental issues involved—issues on which my colleagues and I have been divided ever since I have been on the bench.

I have never been able to make my brothers see that government is a human affair, and that men are ruled, not by words on paper or by abstract theories, but by other men. They are ruled well when their rulers understand the feelings and conceptions of the masses. They are ruled badly when that understanding is lacking.

Of all branches of the government, the judiciary is the most likely to lose its contact with the common man. The reasons for this are, of course, fairly obvious. Where the masses react to a situation in terms of a few salient features, we pick into little pieces every situation presented to us. Lawyers are hired by both sides to analyze and dissect. Judges and attorneys vie with one another to see who can discover the greatest number of difficulties and distinctions in a single set of facts. Each side tries to find cases, real or imagined, that will embarrass the demonstrations of the other side. To escape this embarrassment, still further distinctions are invented and imported into the situation. When a set of facts has been subjected to this kind of treatment for a sufficient time, all the life and juice have gone out of it and we have left a handful of dust.

Now I realize that wherever you have rules and abstract principles lawyers are going to be able to make distinctions. To some extent the sort of thing I have been describing is a necessary evil attaching to any formal regulation of human affairs. But I think that the area which really stands in need of such regulation is greatly overestimated. There are, of course, a few fundamental rules of the game that must be accepted if the game is to go on at all. I would include among these the rules relating to the conduct of elections, the appointment of public officials, and the term during which an office is held. Here some restraint on discretion and dispensation, some adherence to form, some scruple for what does and what does not fall within the rule, is, I concede, essential. Perhaps the area of basic principle should be expanded to include certain other rules, such as those designed to preserve the free civilmoign system.

But outside of these fields I believe that all government officials, including judges, will do their jobs best if they treat forms and abstract concepts as instruments. We should take as our model, I think, the good administrator, who accommodates procedures and principles to the case at hand, selecting from among the available forms those most suited to reach the proper result.

The most obvious advantage of this method of government is that it permits us to go about our daily tasks with efficiency and common sense. My adherence to this philosophy has, however, deeper roots. I believe that it is only with the insight this philosophy gives that we can preserve the flexibility essential if we are to keep our actions in reasonable accord with the sentiments of those subject to our rule. More governments have been wrecked, and more human misery caused, by the lack of this accord between ruler and ruled than by any other factor that can be discerned in history. Once drive a sufficient wedge between the mass of people and those who direct their legal, political, and economic life, and our society is ruined. Then neither Foster's law of nature nor Keen's fidelity to written law will avail us anything.

Now when these conceptions are applied to the case before us, its decision becomes, as I have said, perfectly easy. In order to demonstrate this I shall have to introduce certain realities that my brothers in their coy decorum have seen fit to pass over in silence, although they are just as acutely aware of them as I am.

The first of these is that this case has aroused an enormous public interest, both here and abroad. Almost every newspaper and magazine has carried articles about it; columnists have shared with their readers confidential information as to the next governmental move; hundreds of letters-to-the-editor have been printed. One of the great newspaper chains made a poll of public opinion on the question, "What do you think the Supreme Court should do with the Speluncean explorers?" About ninety per cent expressed a belief that the defendants should be pardoned or let off with a kind of token punishment. It is perfectly clear, then, how the public feels about the case. We could have known this without the poll, of course, on the basis of common sense, or even by observing that on this Court there are apparently four-and-a-half men, or ninety per cent, who share the common opinion.

This makes it obvious, not only what we should do, but what we must do if we are to preserve between ourselves and public opinion a reasonable and decent accord. Declaring these men innocent need not involve us in any undignified quibble or trick. No principle of statutory construction is required that is not consistent with the past practices of this Court. Certainly no layman would think that in letting these men off we had stretched the statute any more than our ancestors did when they created the excuse of self-defense. If a more detailed demonstration of the method of reconciling our decision with the statute is required, I should be content to rest on the arguments developed in the second and less visionary part of my brother Foster's opinion.

Now I know that my brothers will be horrified by my suggestion that this Court should take account of public opinion. They will tell you that public opinion is emotional and capricious, that it is based on half-truths and listens to witnesses who are not subject to cross-examination.

They will tell you that the law surrounds the trial of a case like this with elaborate safeguards, designed to insure that the truth will be known and that every rational consideration bearing on the issues of the case has been taken into account. They will warn you that all of these safeguards go for naught if a mass opinion formed outside this framework is allowed to have any influence on our decision.

But let us look candidly at some of the realities of the administration of our criminal law. When a man is accused of crime, there are, speaking generally, four ways in which he may escape punishment. One of these is a determination by a judge that under the applicable law he has committed no crime. This is, of course, a determination that takes place in a rather formal and abstract atmosphere. But look at the other three ways in which he may escape punishment. These are: (1) a decision by the Prosecutor not to ask for an indictment; (2) an acquittal by the jury; (3) a pardon or commutation of sentence by the executive. Can anyone pretend that these decisions are held within a rigid and formal framework of rules that prevents factual error, excludes emotional and personal factors, and guarantees that all the forms of the law will be observed?

In the case of the jury we do, to be sure, attempt to cabin their deliberations within the area of the legally relevant, but there is no need to deceive ourselves into believing that this attempt is really successful. In the normal course of events the case now before us would have gone on all of its issues directly to the jury. Had this occurred we can be confident that there would have been an acquittal or at least a division that would have prevented a conviction. If the jury had been instructed that the men's hunger and their agreement were no defense to the charge of murder, their verdict would in all likelihood have ignored this instruction and would have involved a good deal more twisting of the letter of the law than any that is likely to tempt us. Of course the only reason that didn't occur in this case was the fortuitous circumstance that the foreman of the jury happened to be a lawyer. His learning enabled him to devise a form of words that would allow the jury to dodge its usual responsibilities.

My brother Tatting expresses annoyance that the Prosecutor did not, in effect, decide the case for him by not asking for an indictment. Strict as he is himself in complying with the demands of legal theory, he is quite content to have the fate of these men decided out of court by the Prosecutor on the basis of common sense. The Chief Justice, on the other hand, wants the application of common sense postponed to the very end, though like Tatting, he wants no personal part in it.

This brings me to the concluding portion of my remarks, which has to do with executive clemency. Before discussing that topic directly, I want to make a related observation about the poll of public opinion. As I have said, ninety per cent of the people wanted the Supreme Court to let the men off entirely or with a more or less nominal punishment. The ten per cent constituted a very oddly assorted group, with the most curious and divergent opinions. One of our university experts has made a study of this group and has found that its members fall into certain patterns. A substantial portion of them are subscribers to "crank" newspapers of limited circulation that gave their readers a distorted version of the facts of the case. Some thought that "Speluncean" means "cannibal" and that anthropophagy is a tenet of the Society. But the point I want to make, however, is this: although almost every conceivable variety and shade of opinion was represented in this group, there was, so far as I know, not one of them, nor a single member of the majority of ninety per cent, who said, "I think it would be a fine thing to have the courts sentence these men to be hanged, and then to have another branch of the government come along and pardon them." Yet this is a solution that has more or less dominated our discussions and which our Chief Justice proposes as a way by which we can avoid doing an injustice and at the same time preserve respect for law. He can be assured that if he is preserving anybody's morale, it is his own, and not the public's, which knows nothing of his distinctions. I mention this matter because I wish to emphasize once more the danger that we may get lost in the patterns of our own thought and forget that these patterns often cast not the slightest shadow on the outside world.

I come now to the most crucial fact in this case, a fact known to all of us on this Court, though one that my brothers have seen fit to keep under the cover of their judicial robes. This is the frightening likelihood that if the issue is left to him, the Chief Executive will refuse to pardon these men or commute their sentence. As we all know, our Chief Executive is a man now well advanced in years, of very stiff notions. Public clamor usually operates on him with the reverse of the effect intended. As I have told my brothers, it happens that my wife's niece is an intimate friend of his secretary. I have learned in this indirect, but, I think, wholly reliable way, that he is firmly determined not to commute the sentence if these men are found to have violated the law.

No one regrets more than I the necessity for relying in so important a matter on information that could be characterized as gossip. If I had my way this would not happen, for I would adopt the sensible course of sitting down with the Executive, going over the case with him, finding out what his views are, and perhaps working out with him a common program for handling the situation. But of course my brothers would never hear of such a thing.

Their scruple about acquiring accurate information directly does not prevent them from being very perturbed about what they have learned indirectly. Their acquaintance with the facts I have just related explains why the Chief Justice, ordinarily a model of decorum, saw fit in his opinion to flap his judicial robes in the face of the Executive and threaten him with excommunication if he failed to commute the sentence. It explains, I suspect, my brother Foster's feat of levitation by which a whole library of law books was lifted from the shoulders of these defendants. It explains also why even my legalistic brother Keen emulated Pooh–Bah in the ancient comedy by stepping to the other side of the stage to address a few remarks to the Executive "in my capacity as a private citizen.'' (I may remark, incidentally, that the advice of Private Citizen Keen will appear in the reports of this court printed at taxpayers' expense.)

I must confess that as I grow older I become more and more perplexed at men's refusal to apply their common sense to problems of law and government, and this truly tragic case has deepened my sense of discouragement and dismay. I only wish that I could convince my brothers of the wisdom of the principles I have applied to the judicial office since I first assumed it. As a matter of fact, by a kind of sad rounding of the circle, I encountered issues like those involved here in the very first case I tried as Judge of the Court of General Instances in Fanleigh County.

A religious sect had unfrocked a minister who, they said, had gone over to the views and practices of a rival sect. The minister circulated a handbill making charges against the authorities who had expelled him. Certain lay members of the church announced a public meeting at which they proposed to explain the position of the church. The minister attended this meeting. Some said he slipped in unobserved in a disguise; his own testimony was that he had walked in openly as a member of the public. At any rate, when the speeches began he interrupted with certain questions about the affairs of the church and made some statements in defense of his own views. He was set upon by members of the audience and given a pretty thorough pommeling, receiving among other injuries a broken jaw. He brought a suit for damages against the association that sponsored the meeting and against ten named individuals who he alleged were his assailants.

When we came to the trial, the case at first seemed very complicated to me. The attorneys raised a host of legal issues. There were nice questions on the admissibility of evidence, and, in connection with the suit against the association, some difficult problems turning on the question whether the minister was a trespasser or a licensee. As a novice on the bench I was eager to apply my law school learning and I began studying these question closely, reading all the authorities and preparing well-documented rulings. As I studied the case I became more and more involved in its legal intricacies and I began to get into a state approaching that of my brother Tatting in this case. Suddenly, however, it dawned on me that all these perplexing issues really had nothing to do with the case, and I began examining it in the light of common sense. The case at once gained a new perspective, and I saw that the only thing for me to do was to direct a verdict for the defendants for lack of evidence.

I was led to this conclusion by the following considerations. The melee in which the plaintiff was injured had been a very confused affair, with some people trying to get to the center of the disturbance, while others were trying to get away from it; some striking at the plaintiff, while others were apparently trying to protect him. It would have taken weeks to find out the truth of the matter. I decided that nobody's broken jaw was worth that much to the Commonwealth. (The minister's injuries, incidentally, had meanwhile healed without disfigurement and without any impairment of normal faculties.) Furthermore, I felt very strongly that the plaintiff had to a large extent brought the thing on himself. He knew how inflamed passions were about the affair, and could easily have found another forum for the expression of his views. My decision was widely approved by the press and public opinion, neither of which could tolerate the views and practices that the expelled minister was attempting to defend.

Now, thirty years later, thanks to an ambitious Prosecutor and a legalistic jury foreman, I am faced with a case that raises issues which are at bottom much like those involved in that case. The world does not seem to change much, except that this time it is not a question of a judgment for five or six hundred frelars, but of the life or death of four men who have already suffered more torment and humiliation than most of us would endure in a thousand years. I conclude that the defendants are innocent of the crime charged, and that the conviction and sentence should be set aside.

Tatting, J. I have been asked by the Chief Justice whether, after listening to the two opinions just rendered, I desire to reexamine the position previously taken by me. I wish to state that after hearing these opinions I am greatly strengthened in my conviction that I ought not to participate in the decision of this case.

The Supreme Court being evenly divided, the conviction and sentence of the Court of General Instances is affirmed. It is ordered that the execution of the sentence shall occur at 6 a.m., Friday, April 2, 4300, at which time the Public Executioner is directed to proceed with all convenient dispatch to hang each of the defendants by the neck until he is dead.

Postscript

Now that the court has spoken its judgment, the reader puzzled by the choice of date may wish to be reminded that the centuries which separate us from the year 4300 are roughly equal to those that have passed since the Age of Pericles. There is probably no need to observe that the Speluncean Case itself is intended neither as a work of satire nor as a prediction in any ordinary sense of the term. As for the judges who make up Chief Justice Truepenny's court, they are, of course, as mythical as the facts and precedents with which they deal. The reader who refuses to accept this view, and who seeks to trace out contemporary resemblances where none is intended or contemplated, should be warned that he is engaged in a frolic of his own, which may possibly lead him to miss whatever modest truths are contained in the opinions delivered by the Supreme Court of Newgarth. The case was constructed for the sole purpose of bringing into a common focus certain divergent philosophies of law and government. These philosophies presented men with live questions of choice in the days of Plato and Aristotle. Perhaps they will continue to do so when our era has had its say about them. If there is any element of prediction in the case, it does not go beyond a suggestion that the questions involved are among the permanent problems of the human race.

Index

ACTIONS
See Contracts; Forms of Action; Property;
    Real Actions; Torts; see also actions
    by their specific names.

ADJECTIVE LAW
Characteristics of, 12.

ADMINISTRATIVE ACTS
As instruments of executive power, 15–16.

ADMINISTRATIVE REGULATIONS
Characteristics of, 13.

ADVERSARY SYSTEM
In common law, 11.

AFRICAN COUNTRIES
Legal systems, 10–11.

ANALOGY
    See also Civil Law; Legal Reasoning.
In case law, 148–49, 164–65.
In statutory law, 169, 226–27.
Reasoning by, description of, 148–49.
Reasoning by, illustration of, 150–59.

ASSUMPSIT
See General Assumpsit; Special Assumpsit.

BATTLE
See Trial, Modes of.

**CANONS OF STATUTORY INTERPRETA-
TION**
See Statutory Interpretation.

CASE LAW
    See also Judicial Power; Retroactivity;
        Stare Decisis.
Characteristics of, 13, 79–81.
Compared to statutes, 79, 86–105, 166.
Creation of, 13, 16.
Distinguished from legislation, 13, 79–80,
    166.
Distinguishing cases, 80–81, 119–22.
In the civil law, 11.

CASE METHOD
Of legal instruction, 71–78.

CHANCERY
    See also Equity.

CHANCERY—Cont'd
Court of, 46, 48–51.
Royal executive department, 31–35.

CHINA, PEOPLE'S REPUBLIC OF
Legal system, 10.

CIVIL LAW
    See also Roman Law.
Analogy, use of, 169.
Distinguished from common law, 11.
Geographical scope, 9–11.
Interpretation of statutes in, 169, 226–27.

CLASSIFICATION
Significance in general, 5–7.
Specific legal classifications, 8–17.

CODE OF LAWS
    See also Legislation.
Characteristics of, 12.
Napoleonic Code, 10.

COMMON LAW
    See also Forms of Action; Trial, Modes
        of.
Distinguished from civil law, 11.
Geographical scope, 10–11.
Historical origins, 10, 13.
Merger with equity, 56–58.
Reception in United States, 10, 51–56.
Writ system, 31–35.

COMMON LAW COURTS (ENGLISH)
As instrumentalities of the Crown, 34.
Common Pleas, Court of, 27, 28.
Exchequer, Court of, 28.
Exchequer Chamber, Court of, 28–29.
House of Lords, 29.
King's Bench, Court of, 27–28, 51.
Local courts, 26–27.
Privy Council, Judicial Committee of, 59,
    60.
Relations with Court of Chancery, 50–51.

COMMON LAW JURISDICTIONS
Legal systems, 9–11.

CONGRESS OF THE UNITED STATES
Powers of, 14–17.

CONSTITUTION OF THE UNITED STATES
See also Congress of the United States; Equal Protection of Laws; Executive Power; President of the United States; State Constitutions; Supreme Court of the United States.
Binding on states, 9, 13–14, 60–62.
Separation of powers under, 14–17, 17–24, 60–61.

CONTRACTS
As a private law subject, 11.
Assumpsit, action of, 40–42.
Covenant, action of, 38.
Debt, action of, 38, 41–42.
Equitable relief, 48–50, 57.
Privity of, 124–26.
Specific performance of, 48–50, 57.

CONVERSION
See Trover.

COURTS
See also Chancery; Common Law Courts (English); Jurisdiction; Supreme Court of the United States.
American federal courts, 60–62, 65–70, 71–78.
American state courts, 62–65.
English courts (early), 26–30, 59.
English courts (modern), 58–60.

COVENANT
Characteristics of action, 38.

CRIMINAL LAW
Interpretation of statutes in, 204–13.

CUSTOMARY LAW
African, 10–11.
Characteristics of, 14.
Hindu, 10.

DEBT
Characteristics of action, 38
Drawbacks of action, 38, 41–42.

DEDUCTIVE REASONING
See Legal Reasoning; Logic, Formal; Syllogism.
Description of, 148.
Illustration of, 159–62.

DETINUE
Characteristics of action, 37.
Drawbacks of action, 40.

DIALECTICAL REASONING
See Legal Reasoning.
Description of, 149.
Illustration of, 162–65.

DICTA
Meaning of, 119.
Obiter dicta, 119.

DICTA—Cont'd
Relation to *ratio decidendi*, 119.

DISTINGUISHING CASES
See Case Law.

EJECTMENT
Characteristics of action, 42–43.
Fictions relating to action, 42–43.

EJUSDEM GENERIS RULE
See Statutory Interpretation.

ENGLISH COURTS
See Chancery; Common Law Courts (English); Courts; House of Lords; Privy Council, Judicial Committee of.

EQUAL PROTECTION OF LAWS
Meaning of, 6–7.

EQUITY
See also Chancery; Jurisdiction.
Concept of, 46–48.
Historical development of, 48–51.
Merger with common law, 56–58.
Procedure in Court of Chancery, 48–50.

EUROPE, CONTINENTAL
Legal systems, 9.

EX POST FACTO LAWS
Unconstitutionality of, 106.

EXECUTIVE ORDERS
Characteristics of, 13.

EXECUTIVE POWER
See also Separation of Powers.
Meaning of, 15–16.
President of the United States, scope of powers, 15–17.

EXPRESS MENTION, IMPLIED EXCLUSION RULE
See Statutory Interpretation.

FEDERAL COURTS
See Courts.

FEDERALISM
Nature of, 60–62.

FORMALISM
As an interpretive attitude, 166, 168.

FORMS OF ACTION
See also actions by their specific names.
Abolition of, 35–36.
Characteristics of, 35–36.
Relation to writ system, 31–35.
Summary of, 37–43.

FREEDOM
As a goal of legal ordering, 2.

GENERAL ASSUMPSIT
See also Special Assumpsit.

GENERAL ASSUMPSIT—Cont'd
Characteristics of, 41–42.
Varieties of, 41–42.

GOLDEN RULE
See Statutory Interpretation.

HOLDING
See Ratio Decidendi.

HOUSE OF LORDS
Description of, 29, 58–60.

INDIA
Legal system, 10.

INDUCTIVE REASONING
  See Legal Reasoning.
Description of, 148.
Illustration of, 124–39.

INJUNCTION
Issued by courts of equity, 48–51, 56–57.

INQUISITORY SYSTEM
In civil law systems, 11.

INTERNATIONAL LAW
  See also Sovereignty; Treaties.
Characteristics of, 8.
Distinguished from municipal law, 8–9.

ISLAMIC WORLD
Legal systems, 9.

JAPAN
Legal system, 9.

JUDICIAL POWER
  See also Case Law; Courts; Jurisdiction.
Meaning of, 16.
Distinguished from other governmental
  powers, 16–17.
Judicial lawmaking powers, controversy on,
  86–105, 106–08.

JURISDICTION
  See also Common Law Courts (English);
    Courts; House of Lords; Privy
    Council; Supreme Court of the
    United States.
American federal courts, 60–62, 65–70.
American state courts, 62–65.
Court of Chancery, 48–51.
English common law courts, 26–30.
English modern courts, 58–60.

JURISPRUDENCE
Defined, 1.

JURY TRIAL
  See also Trial, Modes of.
In Constitution of the United States, 57–58,
  71–78.
In state constitutions, 57–58.

JUSTICE
As a conceptual ingredient of law, 2–4.

JUSTICE—Cont'd
As an element in judicial decisionmaking,
  13, 82–85, 105–06.
Relation to equity, 46–48.
Relation to stare decisis, 82–84.
Sense of, 82–85.

LANDOWNERS' LIABILITY
See Torts.

LATIN AMERICA
Legal systems, 9.

LAW
  See also Justice.
Definitions of, 1–4.
Functions of, 1–4, 143–44, 146.
Growth of, 143–44.

LEGAL REALISM
As an approach to the judicial process,
  143–44, 145–48.

LEGAL REASONING
  See also Analogy; Deductive Reasoning;
    Dialectical Reasoning; Inductive
    Reasoning; Logic, Formal; Ratio
    Decidendi; Syllogism.
Analogical, 148–49, 164–65, 226–27.
Deductive, 141–43, 144–46, 148, 166.
Dialectical, 149.
Inductive, 148.

LEGISLATION
  See also Code of Laws; Congress of the
    United States; Legislative Histo-
    ry; Legislative Power; Statutory
    Interpretation.
Compared to cases, 13–14, 86–105.
Concept of, 12–14.
Constitutionality of, 6–7, 13–14, 79.
Distinguished from case law, 13–14, 79–81,
  166.
Open texture of, 167.
Prospective force of, 15, 19–24, 79, 86.

LEGISLATIVE HISTORY
  See also Legislation; Statutory Interpre-
    tation.
As evidence of legislative intent in England,
  188–89.
As evidence of legislative intent in the Unit-
  ed States, 171–79, 184–88, 189–204.

LEGISLATIVE INTENT
See Legislation; Legislative History; Statutory Interpretation.

LEGISLATIVE POWER
  See also Legislation; Separation of Pow-
    ers.
Meaning of, 15.
President of the United States, partic-
  ipation in, 16.

LOGIC, FORMAL
  See also Legal Reasoning; Syllogism.

LOGIC, FORMAL—Cont'd
Deductive reasoning, 141–43, 144–46, 148, 166.
Role in legal reasoning, 143–48.
Syllogistic logic, 141–43.

LOSS OF CONSORTIUM
See Torts.

LOSS OF SOCIETY AND COMPANION-SHIP
See Torts.

LOUISIANA
Legal system, 10.

MANUFACTURER'S LIABILITY
See Torts.

MERGER OF LAW AND EQUITY
Procedural merger, 56–57.
Right to jury trial, 57–58.
Substantive law, incomplete merger as to, 56–57.

MUNICIPAL LAW
Characteristics of, 8–9.
Distinguished from international law, 8–9.

NEGLIGENCE
See Torts.

NISI PRIUS SYSTEM
Described, 29–30.

OBITER DICTA
See Dicta.

ORDEAL
See Trial, Modes of.

OVERRULING
See Stare Decisis.

PLAIN MEANING RULE
See Statutory Interpretation.

POLICY
Role in legal reasoning, 143–44, 150–65, 166.

PRECEDENT
See Case Law; Stare Decisis.

PRESIDENT OF THE UNITED STATES
See Constitution of the United States; Executive Power; Treaties.

PRIVATE ACTS OF CONGRESS
Power to enact, 15, 20–21.

PRIVATE LAW
Characteristics of, 11.
Subjects included in, 11.

PRIVY COUNCIL, JUDICIAL COMMITTEE OF
Jurisdiction, 59, 60.

PRODUCTS LIABILITY
See Torts.

PROPERTY
As a private law subject, 11.
Detinue, action of, 37.
Ejectment, action of, 42–43.
Replevin, action of, 37.
Trespass, action of, 38–39.
Trover, action of, 40.

PROSPECTIVITY
See also Legislation.
Complete prospectivity of judicial decisions, 108–110.

PROVISIONS OF OXFORD (1258)
Contents of, 34.

PUBLIC LAW
Characteristics of, 11–12.
Subjects included in, 11–12.

PUERTO RICO
Legal system, 10.

PURPOSIVE APPROACH
See Statutory Interpretation.

QUASI CONTRACT
Meaning of, 41–42.

QUEBEC, PROVINCE OF
Legal system, 10.

RATIO DECIDENDI
See also Case Law; Stare Decisis.
Illustrative cases on, 124–39.
Meaning of, 81, 119–24.
Theories on, 119–24.

REAL ACTIONS
Characteristics of, 42–43.
Jurisdiction in Court of Common Pleas, 27.
Varieties of, 42–43.

REPLEVIN
Characteristics of action, 37.

RES JUDICATA
Meaning of, 81.

RETROACTIVITY
In civil litigation, 105–10, 114–15.
In criminal litigation, 106, 110–17.
Of overruling decision, 105–17.

RIGHTS
Creation and enforcement of, 12.
Protection by private law, 11.
Protection by public law, 11–12.

ROMAN LAW
See also Civil Law.

ROMAN LAW—Cont'd
Attitude toward statutory interpretation, 169.
Relation to civil law, 9.

RUSSIA
Legal system, 9.

SCANDINAVIAN COUNTRIES
Legal systems, 9.

SECURITY
As a goal of legal ordering, 2–4.

SEPARATION OF POWERS
See also Constitution of the United States; Executive Power; Judicial Power; Legislative Power; State Constitutions.
As defined in California Constitution, 14–15.
In the federal system, 15–17, 19–24.
Qualifications under the federal system, 16–17.

SOURCES OF LAW
See Case Law; Constitution of the United States; Customary Law; Legislation; State Constitutions; Treaties.

SOUTH AFRICA, UNION OF
Legal system, 9.

SOVEREIGNTY
Law as command of the sovereign, 2–4.
Of nations, 8–9.
Of states under Constitution of the United States, 9, 60.

SPECIAL ASSUMPSIT
See also General Assumpsit.
Characteristics of action, 40–41.
History of action, 40–41.

SPECIFIC PERFORMANCE
See Contracts; Chancery; Equity.

STARE DECISIS
See also Case Law; Ratio Decidendi.
Advantages of, 82–84.
Definition of, 81–82.
Departures from (overruling precedent), 13, 81–82, 85–86, 92–102, 224–26.
Drawbacks of, 84.
In American courts, 85–86.
In English courts, 84–85.

STATE CONSTITUTIONS
Relation to Constitution of the United States, 13–14.
Right to jury trial under, 57–58.
Separation of powers in, 14–15.

STATE COURTS
See Courts.

STATUTES
See Code of Laws; Legislation; Statutory Interpretation.

STATUTORY INTERPRETATION
Basic approaches to, 169–79.
Canons of, 167, 179–84, 204–13, 213–26.
Civil statutes, construction of, 213–26.
Criminal statutes, construction of, 204, 206–13.
Ejusdem generis rule, 182–83.
Equity of the statute doctrine, 169–70.
Express mention, implied exclusion rule, 179–81.
Golden rule, 170, 171.
Legislative history, 184–204.
Lenity, rule of, 204–13.
Literal rule, 170, 173–75.
Noscitur a sociis rule, 181–82.
Penal statutes, construction of, 204–13.
Plain meaning rule, 170, 173–75, 189–204.
Purposive approach, 170–71, 171–73, 175–79, 189–204.
Reasoning from statutes by analogy, 226–27.

SUBSTANTIVE LAW
Characteristics of, 12.

SUPREME COURT OF THE UNITED STATES
As interpreter of the federal Constitution, 13–14.
General information on, 67–68.
Jurisdiction of, 67–68.
Relation to state supreme courts, 13–14.

SYLLOGISM
See also Legal Reasoning; Logic, Formal.
Explained, 141–43.

TORTS
See also Trespass; Trespass on the Case; Trover.
As a private law subject, 11.
Fraud and deceit, 124–26.
Liability of landowners, 159–65.
Loss of consortium, 44–46, 86–105.
Loss of society and companionship, 150–59.
Manufacturer's liability, 124–39.
Negligence, 39, 124–39.
Products liability, 124–39.
Wrongful death and survival actions, 45–46, 213–26.

TREATIES
See also Constitution of the United States.
As a source of international law, 8.
Binding on states of Union, 9.
President's authority to make, 16.
Senate's participation in, 16.

TRESPASS
Characteristics of action, 38–39.
Distinguished from trespass on the case, 39.
To chattels, 39.

TRESPASS—Cont'd
To land, 39.
To person, 39.

TRESPASS ON THE CASE
Characteristics of action, 39.
Distinguished from trespass, 39.
Relation to special assumpsit, 40.
Relation to trover, 40.

TRIAL, MODES OF
Battle, 30–31.
Jury, 30–31, 39–43, 57–58, 71–78.
Ordeal, 30–31.
Wager of law, 30, 39, 41.

TROVER
Characteristics of action, 40.
History of action, 40.

TRUSTS
See Uses and Trusts.

UNITED NATIONS
Law developed by, 8.
Power to enforce decisions, 8.

UNJUST ENRICHMENT
See Quasi Contract.

USES AND TRUSTS
Jurisdiction in Chancery, 49.

WAGER OF LAW
See Trial, Modes of.

WESTMINSTER II, STATUTE OF
Provisions regarding writs, 34–35.

WRIT SYSTEM
Description of, 31–35.
Illustrative cases, 44–46.
Relation to forms of action, 35–37.
Summary of forms of action, 37–44.

WRONGFUL DEATH AND SURVIVAL ACTIONS
See Torts.

†